The Syntax and Semantics of the Perfect Active in Literary Koine Greek

Publications of the Philological Society, 47

WILEY
Blackwell

The Syntax and Semantics of the Perfect Active in Literary Koine Greek

Robert Samuel David Crellin

University of Cambridge

Publications of the Philological Society, 47

WILEY
Blackwell

This edition first published 2016

© 2016 The Philological Society

Blackwell Publishing was acquired by John Wiley & Sons in February 2007. Blackwell's publishing program has been merged with Wiley's global Scientific, Technical, and Medical business to form Wiley-Blackwell.

Registered Office

John Wiley & Sons Ltd, The Atrium, Southern Gate, Chichester, West Sussex, PO19 8SQ, United Kingdom

Editorial Offices

350 Main Street, Malden, MA 02148-5020, USA

9600 Garsington Road, Oxford, OX4 2DQ, UK

The Atrium, Southern Gate, Chichester, West Sussex, PO19 8SQ, UK

For details of our global editorial offices, for customer services, and for information about how to apply for permission to reuse the copyright material in this book please see our website at www.wiley.com/wiley-blackwell.

The right of Robert Samuel David Crellin to be identified as the author of this work has been asserted in accordance with the UK Copyright, Designs and Patents Act 1988.

Wiley also publishes its books in a variety of electronic formats. Some content that appears in print may not be available in electronic books.

Designations used by companies to distinguish their products are often claimed as trademarks. All brand names and product names used in this book are trade names, service marks, trademarks or registered trademarks of their respective owners. The publisher is not associated with any product or vendor mentioned in this book. This publication is designed to provide accurate and authoritative information in regard to the subject matter covered. It is sold on the understanding that the publisher is not engaged in rendering professional services. If professional advice or other expert assistance is required, the services of a competent professional should be sought.

Library of Congress Cataloging-in-Publication Data

Library of Congress Cataloging-in-Publication Data is available for this work.

ISBN 978-1-119-24354-0

A catalogue record for this book is available from the British Library.

Set in Times by SPS (P) Ltd., Chennai, India

1 2016

CONTENTS

ACKNOWLEDGEMENTS

This book is a development of the doctoral thesis which I completed from 2008 to 2011 at the Faculty of Classics, University of Cambridge, UK, and which was funded by the UK Arts and Humanities Research Council. I am hugely grateful to all those who have been involved and helped in many and various ways from that point until now, especially to my PhD supervisor Geoffrey Horrocks for his support and advice throughout that project and since, to my PhD examiners Rupert Thompson and Amalia Moser, to James Clackson for first inspiring me to look at the Greek perfect, and to Susan Fitzmaurice at the Philological Society and three anonymous Philological Society reviewers for their comments and encouragement throughout the process of writing the present monograph. I owe a debt of gratitude to Katherine McDonald, and Vivian and Cecil Crellin for proof reading the original thesis, to Troy Griffiths for teaching me to programme in Java without which the project would not have been possible, to the Fry family for their generous hospitality while I was writing a substantial proportion of the book, as well as to my friends and colleagues at the Greek Bible College in Athens, Tyndale House in Cambridge, and the Faculty of Classics, Cambridge. I am also very thankful for the love and support of my friends and family during the process, of David, Hilary, Julia, Eleanor and Vivian Crellin, Ali and Rachel Wright, John Shinkwin, Richard Olney and Andy Liggins, as well as of my church family at Apostelkirken, Copenhagen. I would like to dedicate the book to the memory of my late grandfather Cecil Crellin. SDG.

I

1. INTRODUCTION

1.1 Problem of the Greek perfect active

What may be said to be the underlying semantics of the Ancient Greek perfect and pluperfect active? Indeed, may these morphological categories (or category) be said to have any unifying semantics at all? The presenting difficulty may be simply stated: these forms, though bearing the label (plu)perfect active, cannot be relied on to correlate with a meaning which is regularly perfect, i.e. having reference to some completed past event, or active. Specifically, in all periods up to at least the second century AD, the perfect and pluperfect active appear able to denote either a state concurrent with the reference time of the clause, with little or no reference to any past event *or* the present consequences of a past event. On some occasions, indeed, it is hard to tell between these two interpretations. At the same time, the perfect and pluperfect may have either active and transitive, or intransitive and passive-like sense.

Let us consider first the 'temporal' problem of the Greek perfect. To illustrate the problem, compare the following examples:[1]

(1) déndra   perì   autôi   **péphuke**
     tree.N-NOM-PL   *around*   *it.N-DAT-SG*   ***grow.PERF-IND-ACT-3-SG***
     kaì   stêlai   kúklōi   líthou
     and   *slab.F-NOM-PL*   *circle.M-DAT-SG*   *stone.M-GEN-SG*
     leukoû   **pepégasin...**
     white.M-GEN-SG   ***fix.PERF-IND-ACT-3-PL***
     'Trees **grow** around [the temple to Artemis], and slabs of white stone **are fixed** in a circle...' (Plu. *Them.* 8.2)[2]

(2) hền   gàr   ho   tês
     REL-PRON.F-ACC-SG   *PTCL*   *ART.M-NOM-SG*   *ART.F-GEN-SG*
     Thēsēídos   poiētḕs   Amazónōn
     Theseid.F-GEN-SG   *author.M-NOM-SG*   *Amazon.F-GEN-PL*
     epanástasin   **gégraphe**
     uprising.F-ACC-SG   ***write.PERF-IND-ACT-3-SG***
     'For the author of the "Theseid" **has written / wrote** "The insurrection of the Amazons".' (Plu. *Thes.* 28.1)

---

[1] Texts were provided electronically by the Perseus Project (http://www.perseus.tufts.edu/hopper), by the Loeb online library (http://www.loebclassics.com/), or by the *Thesaurus Linguae Graecae* (TLG, http://stephanus.tlg.uci.edu/). Sources are given under 'Textual Sources' at the end of the monograph. For *Liddell Scott Jones* (LSJ), provided by TLG, see http://stephanus.tlg.uci.edu.

[2] The translations given throughout are as far as possible my own, unless otherwise stated. Some key translations consulted are given under 'Textual Sources' at the end of the monograph.

The perfects *péphuke* and *pepégasin* in the first example are concerned only with the narrative present: there is apparently no interest in any prior situation leading to the state being described, even if such a situation must have pertained at some point. By contrast, in the second example, the perfect *gégraphe*, 'he has written / wrote', clearly refers to a past event. The problem may be expressed diagrammatically using a Reichenbachian framework according to Figure 1.[3]

Figure 1: The temporal problem of the perfect indicative

Let S and E be points in time. S is the narrative present (or speaker time). E represents the point in time at which some event takes place, or event time. The problem of the Greek perfect, in these terms, is that sometimes it appears to imply reference to some event taking place prior to S, and at others there is no hint of this, and S is the only consideration. Thus in example (2) both E, the occasion of writing, and the narrative present S (at least insofar as 'The Insurrection of the Amazons' exists at S) are in view. By contrast in (1) only S is in view.

Outside of the perfect indicative the problem becomes more complex as a third time point comes into play. Consider the following participial example:

(3) hoi   dè   perì   tòn
    ART.M-NOM-PL   PTCL   *around*   ART.M-ACC-SG
    Khárēta…   kaíper   **katapeplēgótas**
    Khares.M-ACC-SG   *although* ***terrify*.PERF-PTPL-ACT-M-ACC-PL**
    toùs   hoplítas   táttousin…
    ART.M-ACC-PL   *soldiers.M-ACC-PL* *command.PRES-IND-ACT-3-PL*
    'But Chares'… band… commanded the soldiers, even though **they were terrified**…' (Jos. *BJ* 4.18)

The three time points relevant here are: the narrative present, S, an event taking place, E, in this case the frightening of the soldiers, and R, or reference time, the commanding of the frightened soldiers. By implication E has taken place prior to R, according to the following schema:

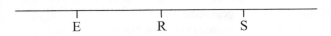

Figure 2: The problem of the perfect outside of the indicative

However, it is not always the case that all three time points are in view. Compare the following pluperfect examples:

---

[3] Reichenbach (1947).

(4) tês   dè   tetártēs   pleurâs...   eíkosi   mèn
ART.F-GEN-SG PTCL fourth.F-GEN-SG side.F-GEN-SG twenty   PTCL
pḗkheis   **aneṓgesan**   katà   púlas...
*cubit.M-NOM-PL **open.PLPF-IND-ACT-3-pl** for   gate.F-ACC-PL*
'Of the fourth side [of the enclosure] twenty cubits **were open** for gates...'
(Jos. *AJ* 3.111)

(5) tēlikoûton   gàr   **proenebeblḗkei**   katelpismòn
*so-much   PTCL **insert.PLPF-IND-ACT-3-SG** confidence.M-ACC-SG*
toîs   ókhlois   hóste   pleíous   eînai...
art.M-DAT-PL crowd.M-DAT-PL that   more.M-ACC-PL be.INF
toùs   ektòs   parepoménous...
art.M-ACC-PL outside   follow.PRES-PTPL-MIDPAS-M-ACC-PL
'For to such a degree **had he inspired** the crowd with confidence [lit. put confidence into the crowd] that those following outside were more numerous...'
(Plb. 3.82.8)

The first, involving the pluperfect *aneṓgesan* provides information on the circumstances of the enclosure. This is to say that only reference time R and the narrative present S are in view, but no event E prior to R. This is notably more static than *proenebeblḗkei* in the second example, which refers to a prior *action*, namely the inspiring of the men. This is to say that E, R and S are all in view.

Indeed, in a few instances no event can have taken place at all:

(6) hḗ   dè   Teúta...   polismátion...
art.F-NOM-SG PTCL Teuta.F-NOM-SG small-TOWN.N-NOM-SG
anakekhōrēkòs   mèn   apò   tês
***withdraw.PERF-PTPL-ACT-N-NOM-SG** PTCL from   art.F-GEN-SG*
thaláttēs...
sea.F-GEN-SG
'Teuta... a small town... **withdrawn** from the sea...' (Plb. 2.11.16)

It is clear that the subject, a small town, could have have undergone a withdrawing event.

Nor need E be entirely separate from S. Consider the following example, where the time period of E extends from the past up to and including S:

(7) epì   gàr   tḗn   proüpárkhousan
on   PTCL ART.F-ACC-SG exist-before.PRES-PTPL-ACT-F-ACC-SG
khíona kaì   **diamemenēkuîan**   **ek**
*snow.F-ACC-SG and **remain.PERF-PTPL-ACT-F-ACC-SG**   from*
toû   **próteron**   **kheimônos**   árti
***art.M-GEN-SG** **earlier** **winter.M-GEN-SG** recently*
tês   ep' étous   peptōkuías...
ART.F-GEN-SG present-year fall.PERF-PTPL-ACT-F-GEN-SG

'For on top of the snow which **had remained from the previous winter**, that from the present year had just fallen...' (Plb. 3.55.1)

The first, temporal, problem of the perfect and pluperfect may therefore be formulated as follows: under what circumstances, in the perfect indicative, does the perfect imply the existence of a time point E prior to S, or, outside of the perfect indicative, prior to R? In other words the Greek perfect appears able to denote:

1) Anterior, i.e. 'a past action with current relevance'.[4]
2) Resultant state[5], i.e. a state resulting from an event prior to reference time.
3) State concurrent with the reference time of the clause with no reference to any prior event.

The second problem of the perfect concerns transitivity. In each of the examples (2) and (5) the perfect is transitive and takes a direct object complement. By contrast in (1) and (4) both the perfects are intransitive, and in (3) *katapeplēgótas* has a distinctly 'passive' feel, despite the 'active' perfect morphology. This is particularly strange in view of the semantics of the present active, *pēgnumi*, *anoígnumi* and *kataplēssō* and respectively, which all have transitive active meaning. Indeed, this transitivity alternation can be seen in a single stem:

(8) heistḗkei   dè   katá   ti
    set-up.PLPF-IND-ACT-3-SG   *PTCL*   in   *INDEF-PRON.N-ACC-SG*
    prosbatòn   olígais   bathmîsi   khōríon
    accessible.N-ACC-SG   *few.F-DAT-PL*   *step.F-DAT-PL*   *space.N-ACC-SG*
    hupestalkòs   tôi   kat'
    hide.PERF-PTPL-ACT-N-ACC-SG   *ART.DAT-M-SG*   in
    autò   skótōi.
    it.N-SG-ACC   *darkness.M-DAT-SG*
'[Claudius] had stood in a space, accessible by a few paces, **taking cover** in the darkness there.' (Jos. *AJ* 19.216)

(9) ho   dè   Phílippos...   hupó
    ART.M-NOM-SG PTCL   *Philip.M-NOM-SG*   *under*
    tina   lóphon   **hupestálkei**
    INDEF-PRON.M-ACC-SG   *hill.M-ACC-SG*   **hide.PLPF-IND-ACT-3-SG**
    toùs   Illurioùs...
    ART.M-ACC-PL   *Illyrians.M-ACC-PL*
'But Philip... **had sent** the Illyrians behind a hill...' (Plb. 5.13.5)

Furthermore, the transitivity of a given perfect appears to be linked to its temporal denotation: where intransitive or passive senses are present, there is often little felt reference to any event taking place prior to reference time. Thus *pepḗgasin* in (1) and *aneōǵgesan* in (4) one wonders if any event of 'fixing' or 'opening' is being referred to. While *katapeplēgótas* in (3) implies that the men in question were frightened

---

[4] Bybee et al. (1994: 61).
[5] Here a narrow definition of the term state is adopted, equivalent to Parsons' Target state (see Parsons 1990).

prior to reference time, the focus is very much on the state of fear at reference time describes the state of the men when they were ordered. In contrast, both *gégraphe* in (2) and *proenebeblékei* in (5) have expressed direct objects, and either explicitly, by means of the adverb *pálai*, or implicitly, describe prior events which are in some way of relevance to the narrative present situation.[6]

From the foregoing analysis it is easy to see why it has been so hard to come up with a one-size-fits-all 'meaning' for the category 'perfect'. The problem in Greek is made harder still not only by the purely written nature of the corpus, but, setting it apart from other corpus languages, by the fact that the relevant forms occur relatively infrequently, and certainly much less so than their 'counterpart' forms in Latin. It is therefore not surprising that a wide variety of views have arisen.

Whatever the underlying 'meaning' of the perfect and pluperfect active, it must ideally be able regularly and predictably to produce a reference-time only reading in certain circumstances, and produce the implication of an event taking place prior to reference time in others. Furthermore, it should ideally be able to explain why some perfects function as transitive actives, and others as intransitive passives. Accordingly the investigation aims to consider:

1. The temporal problem: To establish under what circumstances the perfect and pluperfect imply the occurrence of an event prior to reference time, rather than focusing purely on the situation at reference time.
2. The transitivity problem: To establish under what circumstances perfect and pluperfect forms behave more like transitive actives, and which more like intransitive passives with respect to the semantics of the present active.
3. The underlying semantics that could regularly produce such outcomes.

Before embarking on this project, it will be helpful to survey the scholarship on the perfect and pluperfect.

1.2 *Existing frameworks for understanding the perfect*

Across languages, the perfect is associated with the following meanings:[7]

1. UNIVERSAL PERFECT, or perfect of 'persistent situation', denoting a state holding throughout an interval.

(10) Matilda has lived in Sydney for two years (and she still lives there).

2. EXISTENTIAL OR EXPERIENTIAL PERFECT, denoting an event occurring at least once in an interval starting in the past and continuing up to the present.

---

[6] It is true that in the Koine period so-called 'aoristic' uses of the perfect occur, as may be seen especially in the New Testament e.g. with *pépraken (sell.PERF-IND-ACT)* at *Matthew* 13.46 and *eilēphen (take.PERF-IND-ACT)* at *Revelation* 8.5. However, I could only find one clear example of this use within the corpus of literary Koine under investigation, namely *eilēphen* at Jos. *AJ* 16.254. Given the very marginal nature of this usage within literary Koine, I will not seek to account for this use of the perfect synchronically.

[7] For these categories see Ritz (2012: 883) and Comrie (1976: 56–61). Cf. also Bentein (2012: 175–181) who identifies each of these meanings in the Classical Greek perfect. Examples given above taken from Ritz (2012).

(11) Dean has been to Adelaide.

   3. PERFECT OF RESULT OR STATIVE PERFECT, denoting the result or consequences of a past event at speech time:

(12) Dean has arrived (and is here now).

   4. PERFECT OF RECENT PAST or "hot news" perfect.

(13) The Reserve Bank has just announced an increase in interest rates.

The perfect is, however, precluded from occurring in certain contexts. I will illustrate the two most important. The first is where the subject participant no longer exists, as in the following example:[8]

(14) *Einstein has visited Princeton.

The second is the perfect's compatibility with definite past time adverbials:[9]

(15) #John has arrived yesterday.

As a result of the wide range of meaning with which the perfect is associated, and the circumstances where it cannot be used, it has proven notoriously difficult to provide a convincing unified definition of the category perfect in semantic terms. Attempts to do so suffer from vagueness, and apparent conflating of the categories of semantics and pragmatics. This is particularly true of the definition of the perfect as denoting CURRENT RELEVANCE,[10] which Klein (1992: 531) describes as follows:

> There is a strong feeling that the present perfect, in contrast to the simple past, in a way participates both in the past and in the present. One way to capture this intuition is the notion of 'current relevance': The event, process or state, although as such situated in the past, has some ongoing relevance that prolongs it somehow in the present.

However, one is simultaneously left with an inability to define what this current relevance amounts to. Klein continues:

> ... it is not clear how to determine the 'relevance'. If no criterion is given, a current relevance analysis can hardly be falsified; it is always possible to find a reason why the event is still of some particular relevance to the present.

In consequence of this vagueness, Dahl & Hedin (2000: 391) reframe the notion of current relevance and suggest that the semantics of the perfect be seen in terms of 'continuance of result'. However, since this only properly accounts for situations with a result, that is to say change of state or telic events, e.g. 'the water froze', one

---

[8] From Chomsky (1970) quoted from Portner (2003: 464). For a more extensive list see Portner (2003: 461–6).

[9] Quoted from Portner (2003: 465).

[10] This is the name of a semantic definition of the perfect is given by McCoard's (1978), although he does not argue for it.

has to reckon with a 'relaxation of the requirements' that continuance of result might imply, a relaxation in turn connected with diachronic factors.

A similar approach is to identify a weaker kind of result that may obtain after all events, regardless of whether or not there is a designated target state. This is the approach adopted by Parsons (1990) who identifies such a state as the R-STATE, and contrasts it with the Target or T-STATE that eventuates after a change of state event. However, insofar as the perfect is able to denote two kinds of state, which must subsequently be disambiguated, this does not completely solve the problem of an underlying semantic for the perfect, if such exists. A variant on this approach might be consider that of Smith (1991, 1997). She (1991: 148) defines the semantics of perfect sentences as 'ascrib[ing] to their subjects a property that results from their participation in a prior situation. If at some time Henry has laughed, danced, built a sandcastle, the property of having done these things is asserted of Henry.'

Rather than conceptualise the perfect as denoting a kind of result, others take a strictly tense-based approach to the meaning of the perfect, whereby the perfect locates an event at some point prior to reference time. This is the essence of the so-called 'extended now' meaning of the perfect, first proposed by McCoard (1978), which Dowty (1979: 341) formulates as 'the view that the perfect serves to locate an event within a period of time that began in the past and extends up to the present moment.'[11] The difficulty here is distinguishing the perfect from the simple tenses, since all past tenses necessarily presuppose some time period beginning in the past and continuing to the present moment.[12]

Reichenbach's (1947) framework, given in Table 1 and already used in the previous section to elucidate the problem of the Greek perfect, provides a solution to this problem, however, by proposing that perfect tenses posit a reference time distinct from the present moment relative to which the occurrence of an event can be temporally located. Thus simple past and perfect are distinguished by means of the positing of this reference point: the simple past simply views an event as taking place prior to speaker time, while the perfect views the event as taking place with respect to its temporal location relative to a reference point.

Table 1. Reichenbachian framework (see Portner 2003: 478)

Present: e, r, s	Past: e, r < s
Present Perfect: e < r, s	Past perfect: e < r < s

Reichenbach's conception of the perfect as essentially denoting anteriority has been adopted by some as criterial of the perfect cross-linguistically. Thus Bybee et al. (1994: 55) in their cross-linguistic analysis use anteriority as the core notion defining the perfect.

---

[11] Quoted by Klein (1992: 532). For an analysis of the Ancient Greek perfect according to this model see Gerö & von Stechow (2003).

[12] For this criticism see Klein (1992: 532).

There is still a problem, however, with Reichenbach's framework for distinguishing between the perfect and the simple past. Positing a reference point is very helpful for explaining the distinctive temporal semantics of the past perfect in a sentence like, 'Someone had already done the washing up when I got home.' However, since in the present perfect R and S fall together, and in the simple past E and R fall together, both are still characterised by two time points, one being speaker time, and the other the event time. In order to understand the difference between the present perfect and the simple past under Reichenbach's analysis, we need to understand the distinctive contribution of the reference time, R.[13] There is, furthermore, a second problem with a Reichenbachian approach, namely that it cannot easily account for continuative readings of the perfect whereby the situation described continues to hold at reference time:[14]

(16) Mary has lived in London for five years (and continues to live there).

Klein (1992) provides a solution to the first problem by presenting a more formalised variation of Reichenbach's original scheme, comprising UTTERANCE TIME (TU), denoting the time at which the utterance is made, SITUATION TIME (TSit), the time at which the event or situation takes place, and TOPIC TIME (TT), occupying a position in the system equivalent to Reichenbach's 'reference time'. This latter Klein defines as 'the time span to which the claim made on a given occasion is constrained.'[15] In other words, topic time is 'the time we are talking about'.[16] By defining Reichenbach's reference time in this way, Klein is able to distinguish between the simple past and the present perfect. The simple past asserts that topic time is prior to utterance time, with topic time either including the end of situation time and the beginning of the time after situation time,[17] or including all of situation time[18]. By contrast, the present perfect asserts that topic time is included in utterance time, but that situation time is prior to topic time[19]

Cutrer's (1994: 204f.) framework, exploiting the framework of MENTAL SPACES THEORY, or MST (see Fauconnier 1985, 1997), provides another answer to the difference between the simple past and the perfect. This approach posits four 'discourse primitives': BASE, FOCUS, V-POINT, and EVENT, and the difference between different tense-aspect forms consists in different relations between these primitives.[20] Of particular relevance in understanding the difference between the perfect and the simple past space. Thus while for the simple past focus and event occupy the same mental space, with v-point occupying a different mental space, for the perfect v-point and FOCUS occupy the same mental space, with EVENT occupying a different mental

---

[13] For this point see Klein (1992: 534).
[14] For this point see Portner (2003: 467f.). Example from Portner (2003: 467).
[15] Klein (1992: 535).
[16] For which expression, see Harder (1996: 420).
[17] According to Klein (1992: 537).
[18] According to Klein (1994: 118).
[19] Klein's framework is important for the present study, and is discussed further at 2.1.5 below.
[20] Bentein (2012: 173).

space.[21] Note that anteriority is still criterial for the semantics of the perfect: '[t]he PERFECT specifies a temporal relationship between V-POINT and an EVENT space; that relationship is a "prior" one.'[22]

The second problem with Reichenbach's analysis, the continuity problem, is more difficult to solve. Klein attempts to do so by accounting for the continuative reading with reference to the delimiting adverbial expression 'for five years'.[23] However, as Portner (2003: 467) points out, this still does not account for cases where there is no such adverbial modification, as in the following:

(17) Mary has lived in London since 1966.

Cutrer's approach is more flexible in this regard, in that it is able to 'encode a past event, a series of past events, a habitual property, or an event or situation which belongs to both past and present temporal domains.'[24] However, there is still a problem in terms of identifying the precise circumstances under which continuity with reference time is maintained.

Portner (2003) overcomes the continuity problem in a different way. He accounts for the difference between continuative and non-continuitive readings with reference to lexical aspectual class, thus removing the question from the domain of the semantics of the perfect. Specificially, 'continuitive perfects may arise when the clause embedded by the perfect is stative' although he admits that '[t]he question of more precisely when they arise and when they don't is complex, and depends in part on the details of how the adverbials in the sentence are interpreted'.[25]

As can be seen from the preceding summary, much theoretical work on the perfect has been concentrated on the English perfect. However, the problems raised by the perfect in literary Koine Greek are similar but not entirely overlapping with those of the English perfect. The Greek perfect in the Koine period does share at least two problematic phenomena with the English perfect. First, the present perfect appears to resist definite time adverbial modification. It is therefore relatively easy to find definite time adverbials modifying the pluperfect and the participle, but much harder for the perfect indicative. The following gives an example of the perfect participle:[26]

(18)

Sēmâs	kaì	Iaphthâs	kaì	Khamâs	étesin
Shem	*and*	*Japheth*	*and*	*Ham*	*year.N-DAT-PL*
hékatòn		émprosthen	tês		epombrías
one-hundred		*before*	*ART.F-GEN-SG*		*flood.F-GEN-SG*

---

[21] Cutrer (1994: 180, 204).

[22] Cutrer (1994: 204).

[23] Portner (2003: 467).

[24] Cutrer (1994: 207).

[25] Portner (2003: 493).

[26] This restriction is not necessarily observed outside of the literary language. Thus we find a present perfect modified by a definite time adverbial in the New Testament at *1 Corinthians* 15.4: *egḗgertai (RAISE.PERF-IND-MIDPAS-3-SG) têi (ART.F-DAT-SG) hēmérāi (DAY.F-DAT-SG) têi (ART.F-DAT-SG) trítēi (third.F-DAT-SG)* 'he was raised on the third day'.

gegonótes…
become.PERF-PTPL-ACT-M-NOM-pl
'… Shem, Japheth and Ham, **having been born** one hundred years before the flood…' (Jos. *AJ* 1.109)

Secondly, the Greek perfect shares the possibility of continuitive readings:

(19) = (7)

epì	gàr	tền	proüpárkhousan
on	*PTCL*	*ART.F-ACC-SG*	*exist-before.PRES-PTPL-ACT-F-ACC-SG*
khíona kaì		**diamemenēkuîan**	**ek**
snow.F-ACC-SG and		*remain.PERF-PTPL-ACT-F-ACC-SG*	*from*
toû	**próteron**	**kheimônos**	árti
ART.M-GEN-SG	*earlier*	*winter.M-GEN-SG*	*recently*
tês	ep' étous	peptōkuías…	
ART.F-GEN-SG	*present-year*	*fall.PERF-PTPL-ACT-F-GEN-SG*	

'For on top of the snow which **had remained from the previous winter**, that from the present year had just fallen…' (Plb. 3.55.1)

Notably, however, there is no constraint, as there is on the English perfect, on the perfect describing a no longer existent entity:

(20)

koinòn	dé	pōs	autôn	kaì	tò
common.N-NOM-SG	*PTCL*	*PTCL*	*they.M-GEN-PL*	*PTCL*	*ART.N-NOM-SG*
atelès	**gégone**		tês		
incomplete	*become.PERF-IND-ACT-3-SG*		*ART.F-GEN.SG*		
stratēgías…					
military-career.F-GEN-SG					

'The incompleteness of their two military careers **had** in some way a common cause…' (Plu. *Cim.* 3.3)

At the time of writing Cimon was long dead and Lucullus had been dead for nearly one hundred years. In this sense, then, the Greek perfect of this period has even broader application than the English perfect.[27]

Indeed, we saw in the previous section that the Greek perfect also raises two distinctive problems of its own. First is the temporal problem, which, to put it in Klein's terms, is that TSit is not always prior to TT, but can include TT, a kind of behaviour that is not systematically observed with the English perfect.[28] In Cutrer's terms, the problem is that in these cases no event may be referenced at all. The transitivity problem has no analogue in English at all, and there is consequently no existing framework

---

[27] Hence the infelicity of the sentence, 'Einstein has lived in Princeton,' when Einstein is dead (see (14) above and Haug 2004: 396), cf. Smith (1997: 108).

[28] There are lexicalised exceptions to this in English, notably the present perfect of 'get', 'I've got', which behaves similarly to the stative Greek perfect in not making direct reference to any event prior to topic time. Thus 'I've got a car' does not reference any event of acquiring a car in the way that 'I've made a car' makes reference to an event of making. For a parallel in Greek see (152) below.

for dealing with it. In the light of these facts about the Greek perfect, it is clear that no existing framework will be adequate as is for describing the semantics of the Greek perfect. We need, therefore, to develop an approach that is able to take account of all the observed phenomena. Before setting out how this is to be done, however, it is important to review the existing approaches to the problem of the Greek perfect.

1.3 *Existing frameworks for understanding the Greek perfect*

Various tense-aspectual and diathetical phenomena have been associated with the Greek perfect, including stativity, anteriority, resultativity and intransitivity. Attempts to encapsulate the meaning of the Greek perfect have typically focused on generalising one or another of these phenomena, and explaining away or deriving the other phenomena from this. However, these approaches have not yielded satisfactory explanations.[29]

Research into the Greek perfect and pluperfect has been conducted in at least four fields: Greek philology, Indo-European linguistics, historical and synchronic typology, and Biblical Studies. A variety of views are held in each. Even though this study is primarily synchronic in nature, focusing on the semantics of the perfect in the literary Koine, since the state of affairs earlier in the history of Greek has frequently been brought to bear on the situation in the Koine, it is relevant to survey views on the perfect across the history of the language. In this section I provide an overview of the various viewpoints.

Historical linguists interested in languages other than Greek were originally drawn to the Greek perfect primarily for its value for the study of Indo-European.[30] Although the form certainly goes back to the period of Proto-Indo-European unity, it is commonly held that only Homeric Greek and Vedic Sanskrit preserve it in anything like its original form and use.[31] Interest in the perfect has grown since the discovery of Hittite and the recognition of some kind of relationship between the PIE perfect, the PIE middle, and the –*hi* conjugation in that language. More recently historical linguists with more cross-linguistic interests have entered the discussion, attracted by the great time-depth provided by the Greek data.[32]

---

[29] Previous studies tackling the Classical Greek perfect include Sicking & Stork (1996), Gerö & von Stechow (2003), Haug (2004), Haug (2008), and Orriens (2009). For recent work on the periphrastic perfect, see Bentein (2012). For work on the diachronic development of the Greek perfect see e.g. Wackernagel (1904), Chantraine (1927), Haspelmath (1992), Haug (2008). The post-Classical Greek perfect has principally been studied in the context of the New Testament, separately e.g. McKay (1981), and within the frame of the verb system as a whole, e.g. Porter (1989), Fanning (1990), Evans (2001) and most recently Campbell (2007). McKay (1980; 1965) concern the perfect outside the New Testament.

[30] Diachronic studies include Malden (1865), Wackernagel (1904), Chantraine (1927), McKay (1965), Moser (1988, 2008), Haspelmath (1992), Duhoux (2000), Gerö & von Stechow (2003), Haug (2004, 2008), Horrocks (2010).

[31] Wackernagel (1904: 5). In all other IE languages it has either merged with the preterite paradigm, or completely disappeared (see Clackson 2007: 122).

[32] Haspelmath (1992), Gerö & von Stechow (2003: 251); cf. also Malden (1865: 168).

Most historical linguists agree that the Greek perfect active of most verbs goes back to a form which in the proto-language was stative and intransitive.[33] This, it is said, accounts for the semantics of the majority of perfects in Homer.[34] Here scholarly consensus has held, and continues to hold, that the perfect and pluperfect essentially denote the state of the syntactic subject.[35] This state, especially in dynamic (as opposed to state) verbs is often said to be that resulting from some past event.[36] This view is supported by Mycenaean examples such as *a-ra-ru-wo-a*[37] 'fitted', corresponding to *arērós*; this does not have the transitive semantics associated with the perfect active endings in later periods. Exceptions to the resultant state function of the perfect in Homer are generally seen as presaging developments in a later stage of the language. Transitive examples, non resultant state perfects, are acknowledged to exist in Homer, but these, if accounted for, are generally seen as simple forerunners of the later situation.[38] However, the presence of the group of 'intensive' perfects does not accord well with a hypothesised original stative function for the perfect endings (see p. 13 below).[39]

The traditional view among scholars of Classical Greek[40] has been that the perfect stem denotes an action finished at the point where the present would denote the action as ongoing (i.e. reference time).[41] Two uses are recognised to fall within this definition: perfect stems denoting a prior event, and those referring only to a situation at hand.[42] However, starting in the mid-nineteenth century, and continuing through the first half of the twentieth, certain scholars began to see the key function of the Classical Greek perfect as denoting the state or condition of the subject.[43] Here a key motivation was the perceived similarity in many instances between the semantics of the perfect in Homer and the Classical period. Yet it was also recognised that new to the Classical period was an increased presence of perfects carrying reference to an event prior to

[33] e.g. Sihler (1995: 564–79), Kulikov (1999: 31) and George (2005: 80). The other parts of the perfect paradigm- the perfect middle and pluperfect- are usually said to have arisen during the history of Greek e.g. Haug (2008: 296).

[34] Kohlmann (1881: 23), quoted by Haspelmath (1992: 193); Chantraine (1927: 16); Haspelmath (1992: 191). Wackernagel (1904: 4) and Perel'muter (1988: 279–282) see the stative function as one of several performed by the Homeric perfect. The perfect is said to be in origin intransitive, despite *oîda*, probably the most archaic perfect, being transitive as far back as one can reconstruct (see Haug 2004: 396).

[35] e.g. Perel'muter (1988). For diachronic studies, see n. 30. For a study of the perfect in Mycenaean see Chantraine (1967).

[36] Kohlmann (1881: 23), quoted by Haspelmath (1992: 193); Chantraine (1927: 16); Perel'muter (1988), Haspelmath (1992: 191).

[37] KN Ra 1541, cited in George (2005: 82).

[38] Chantraine (1927: 11–16), Willi (2003: 129), Moser (2008: 10), Gerö & von Stechow (2003: 253 n. 4), Haspelmath (1992: 209f.).

[39] e.g. Haug (2004: 398, 404), Gerö & von Stechow (2003: 267).

[40] Studies include Donaldson (1859), Kühner & Gerth (1898), Gildersleeve (1900), Stahl (1907), Humbert (1945), Ruipérez (1982), Moorhouse (1982), Vásquez (1993), Sicking & Stork (1996), Willi (2003), Orriens (2009). For diachronic studies, see n. 30.

[41] So Goodwin (1894: 1273). See also Jannaris (1897: 1862), Kühner-Gerth (1898: 146f.) and Stahl (1907: 152).

[42] Stahl (1907: 152) distinguishes between present-only intensive perfects and extensive perfects with a preterital component.

[43] e.g. Wackernagel (1904: 4).

reference time, and a connection was seen between this behaviour and the form's transitivity.[44] The term 'resultative perfect' was coined, to describe the perfect of verbs such as *dídōmi* 'give' and *títhēmi* 'place' which could not be interpreted to denote a state or condition of the subject.[45] The perfect of these verbs was seen as denoting a past action whose effect continues to last in or for the object.[46] This was taken a stage further, with the assertion that these perfects came to denote the state of the object.[47]

In the mid-twentieth century others, responding to the concept of the resultative perfect, though not denying that the perfect can imply that the object is in a certain state, argued that the *essential* function of the Classical Greek perfect was to denote the state of the syntactic subject.[48] More recent exponents of this view have identified two types of state according to the semantic role played by the subject. Where the subject plays a patient role, the state denoted is that of the participant who has undergone the action denoted by the verb. By contrast, where the subject plays an agent role, the state denoted is that of a completed action.[49] Implicit here is a distinction between two different kinds of resultant state.[50]

However, the suggestion that the perfect in essence denotes the state of the subject was attacked on several grounds. First, it cannot explain perfects which appear not to denote a state, but rather an action as an ongoing process, as notably with the group of so-called 'intensive' perfects.[51] These supposedly denote 'durative' events, differing from the present in the intensity with which the event is presented,[52] although others have doubted the existence of this intensity.[53] Verbs denoting the production of sound appear particularly to behave in this way, e.g. *mémuka* 'I moo' and *tétriga* 'I squeal'. A related problem is that the perfect of certain state verbs, such as *espoúdaka*, from *spoudázō*, 'to be busy, eager', while denoting a state, does not appear to imply any event of which it might be considered to be the result. There are also many verbs, such as *títhēmi* 'place' and *dídōmi* 'give', whose perfect active forms hardly describe

---

[44] The connection between past reference and transitivity is implicit in Malden (1865), but is made explicit by Wackernagel (1904) and especially Chantraine (1927: 19).

[45] The term appears to be used first by Wackernagel (1904). Malden (1865) describes the concept but does not name it.

[46] Wackernagel (1904: 4).

[47] Chantraine (1927: 165) followed by Humbert (1945: 127).

[48] McKay (1965: 9), Sicking & Stork (1996: 136f., 146).

[49] Rijksbaron (2002: 35–6) implicitly distinguishes between two different kinds of state according to the semantic role played by the subject, i.e. whether agent or patient. Haug makes this more explicit giving different terms to the two kinds of state, drawing on work on the English perfect by Parsons (1990). For the history of the use of the term 'state' in describing the essential semantics of the perfect see n. 84.

[50] For critique of this see 1.4 below.

[51] Ruipérez (1954: 49).

[52] e.g. Gildersleeve (1900: 229).

[53] Chantraine (1927: 17), Sicking & Stork (1996: 125f.), Haug (2004: 394); Ruipérez (1954: 51) also expresses doubts, but reinstates the intensive reading as one realisation of the semantics of the perfect form (1954: 64).

events with lasting consequences for the subject, as is implied should be the case if the perfect always denotes a state.[54]

Various attempts have been made to provide a framework to take account of these difficulties. Some have applied models developed in the context of the English perfect. Thus according to the 'extended now' view,[55] the Greek perfect 'stretches the reference time into an indefinite past'.[56] Others have analysed the Greek perfect as denoting current relevance.[57] Another approach involves dividing verbs into semantic types and observing how the meaning of the perfect differs accordingly.[58] According to one version, verbs can be divided into groups, e.g. transformative and non-transformative. Perfects denoting an event or situation which cannot be said to be a resultant state, including the so-called 'intensive' perfects, all belong to this second group.[59] In these terms the semantics of the perfect can be said to be the consideration of the verbal idea after its terminal point.[60] Where the event denoted by the verb has no set final point, this terminal point is deemed to be the event's onset.[61] This has been followed by the suggestion that the perfect shares with the present the aspect feature of [+duration].[62]

There is widely acknowledged to have been an important change in the meaning and distribution of the perfect, and the perfect active in particular. In Homer the perfect appears to be heavily restricted lexically. By the later Classical period, however, the number of lexical items able to accept perfect active morphology increases markedly.[63] The causes of this change are, however, not so widely agreed upon. Chantraine suggested that the heart of the change was from the conveying of the state of the subject to conveying the state of the object.[64] More recently the change has been seen in terms of grammaticalisation parallel to the development of 'perfects' in many languages.[65]

Whatever view is taken on the nature of the underlying (change in) meaning of the perfect, the form is said to become available to more and more verbs, and towards the later Classical and into the post-Classical periods, starts to compete with the aorist.[66] Although there is disagreement on the identification of individual cases of 'aoristic'

---

[54] Orriens (2009: 223f.).

[55] See Gerö & von Stechow (2003).

[56] Gerö & von Stechow (2003: 280). Gerö & von Stechow (2003: 274): 'In terms of an XN-analysis [i.e. extended now], the speech time can be seen as a final subinterval of an interval which reaches into a contextually or lexically determined past...'

[57] Thus Comrie (1976: 52) for the perfect in general, and Orriens (2009: 222) and Horrocks (2010: 176) for Greek.

[58] Ruipérez (1954), Sicking & Stork (1996) and Rijksbaron (2002).

[59] Ruipérez (1954: 55).

[60] Ruipérez (1954: 65): la 'consideración del contenido verbal después de su término.'

[61] Ruipérez (1954: 62). Haug (2004: 394) explicitly starts from the aorist stem of these verbs, which carry inceptive sense, an approach that goes back to the nineteenth century; Kühner & Gerth (1898: 149 n. 2) express misgivings.

[62] Vásquez (1993: 93).

[63] Wackernagel (1904: 9–15, 22).

[64] Chantraine (1927: 6, 12).

[65] Haspelmath (1992), Haug (2008).

[66] e.g. Horrocks (2010: 177).

perfects, there is general agreement that these become more common.[67] The effective loss of the form in the medieval language, apart from a few relics, is generally assumed to be due to the perfect having become indistinguishable semantically from the aorist.[68]

Synchronic research[69] into the post-Classical and Koine perfect has, because of the specialised interest in the Bible and the papyri, tended to be conducted at one remove from that into the Classical and Homeric perfect. Nevertheless, it is possible to identify broadly the same range of views on the perfect in this later stage of the language as one can observe for the Classical, and the deficiencies of each position apply in much the same way. Many scholars of Koine Greek, particularly in the first half of the twentieth century, can be found adopting the traditional view that the perfect denotes an event finished at reference time.[70] The notion of the 'resultative' perfect is often invoked additionally as a framework for understanding perfects whose role does not denote the state of the subject.[71] Such analyses tend to see present-only perfects as an aberration and a vestige of a former state of affairs.[72]

Following the publication of work by McKay,[73] the present state understanding of the Koine perfect has been enthusiastically adopted and developed by many working on the Koine. Present-only perfects are brought forward as primary representatives and any past reference is seen purely as a function of lexical semantics.[74] This has been followed by the suggestion that the supposed stative aspect of the perfect should be analysed as a type of imperfective,[75] even able to denote progressive aspect.[76] Others, however, have sought to limit the present-only interpretation to stative verbs,[77] while still others have it that the perfect has no unified semantics in this period.[78]

The apparently medio-passive-like behaviour of some perfects has received little in the way of synchronic explanation for any period of the language. Explanations have either been given in diachronic or synchronic terms. A case of the former is the theory that the perfect and middle endings in Proto-Indo-European are derivable from the same (not necessarily stative) source.[79] Synchronic approaches have seen

---

[67] Evans (2001: 151).

[68] For a brief outline of how this process might have occurred, see Gerö & von Stechow (2003: 253).

[69] Robertson (1919) (albeit with a great deal of historical information), Mayser (1926), Turner (1963), de Foucault (1972), Mandilaras (1973), McKay (1980), McKay (1981), Porter (1989), Fanning (1990), Olsen (1997), Evans (2001), Decker (2001), Campell (2007), Campbell (2008), Good (2010), Porter (2011) and Crellin (2014). For diachronic studies see n. 30.

[70] Robertson (1919: 357, 892–910), Mayser (1926: 176–183), Turner (1963: 81).

[71] e.g. Turner (1963: 83), de Foucault (1972: 134).

[72] Robertson (1919: 892f.), Turner (1963: 81–5), Evans (2001: 42).

[73] i.e. McKay (1980; 1965, 1981).

[74] Porter (1989: 259), who, however, does not specify how this past reference is determined on a lexical level.

[75] Evans (2001: 30).

[76] Campbell (2007: 194) translates *tòn kalòn agôna ēgōnismai* (1 *Tim.* 4.7) 'I am fighting the good fight'. For criticism see e.g. Porter (2011) and Crellin (2012a).

[77] In Olsen's terms (1997: 232), 'unspecified for the privative [+dynamic] feature'.

[78] Haug (2008: 302).

[79] See Jasanoff (2003: 55–63), Clackson (2007: 149).

a connection between the semantics of certain verbs and the middle-like behaviour of the perfect active.[80]

1.4 Critical assessment of existing studies

Existing studies are lacking both methodologically and in the conclusions they reach. One problem is that, where the analysis has been diachronic, there has been a tendency to start from the supposedly well understood 'original' situation as exemplified in the Homeric poems, bolstered by other comparative, principally Vedic Sanskrit, data, and chart the development from there. While at first glance this seems a perfectly logical approach to adopt, it is in fact problematic because of the nature and paucity of the earliest evidence.[81] Specifically, Homeric Greek consists of multiple fragments of the Greek language at different points in its development before the seventh century BC, spliced together into two hexameter poems, totalling less than 200,000 words. Crucially, dating the different elements becomes essentially a matter of conjecture.[82] Arguing, therefore, for a particular development of the language as seen in the Homeric poems, while not impossible, runs the risk of circularity. A related difficulty is that some scholars conducting synchronic studies have been tempted to use data from earlier stages of Greek to substantiate their case.[83] Such an approach, adopted without reference to the potential development of the perfect over time, is deeply problematic.

In terms of their conclusions, existing analyses of the Greek perfect tend to fail at one of two key points. The first concerns the notion of state, specifically the capacity of the perfect to denote that a given participant is in a given state. As the foregoing analysis has shown, it has been popular in analyses of all stages of ancient Greek to assert that the function of the perfect is to denote the (resultant) state of the subject. However, such a view is fundamentally deficient when it comes to accounting for instances of the perfect where the subject does not enter into a state, at least in terms described by the predicate, as in the following cases:

(21) hṓs   tís   te   léōn   katà
     just-as   *INDEF-PRON.MF-NOM-SG*   *PTCL*   *lion.M-NOM-SG*   *ASP*
     taûron   **edēdṓs**.
     bull.M-ACC-SG   **eat.PERF-PTPL-ACT-M-NOM-SG**
     '... just as a lion which has **devoured** a bull.' (*Il.* 17.542)

---

[80] Sicking & Stork (1996: 130–7) see the perfect and middle sharing the feature of control. Donaldson (1859: 347) links the state meaning of the perfect to a cross-linguistic tendency for the perfect active of certain verbs to be used passively, although he does not specify what semantic elements must be present for the perfect active of a given verb to behave in this way.

[81] cf. Ruipérez' complaint (1954: 51f.).

[82] As tacitly accepted by Haug (2008: 288).

[83] In one instance Porter (1989: 260) uses a combination of Classical and post-Classical examples without any mention of the diachronic spread of these sources. Cf. also Porter (2011: 120f.) where he cites Clackson (2007: 121) without acknowledging that Clackson's discussion is in the context of Proto-Indo-European reconstruction.

(22) basileùs...   Kûron   **apéktone...**
     king.M-NOM-SG   *Cyrus.M-ACC-SG*   ***KILL.PERF-IND-ACT-3-SG***
     'The king... **had killed** Cyrus.' (Xenophon *Anabasis* 2.1.8)

(23) hoi   dè   ánthrōpoi   tò   kréas
     ART.M-NOM-PL   *PTCL*   *human.M-NOM-PL*   *ART.N-ACC-SG*   *meat.N-ACC-SG*
     esthíousin,   tà   d'   ostâ
     eat.PRES-IND-ACT-3-SG   *ART.N-ACC-PL*   *PTCL*   *bone.N-ACC-PL*
     hríptousin,   hóper   ánthrōpos
     throw.PRES-IND-ACT-3-PL   *REL-PRON.N-ACC-AG*   *human.M-NOM-SG*
     ồn   kagồ   **nûn**
     be.PRES-PTPL-M-NOM-SG   *and-I.NOM-SG*   ***now***
     pepoíēka.
     do.PERF-IND-ACT-1-SG
     'Men, however, eat the meat, but throw away the bones, which is exactly
     what I, who am also a man, **have now done.**' (Jos. *AJ* 12.213)

In each of these examples, one from each of Homer, Classical Greek and the post-Classical language, it is the object participant who may be said to be in a state, not the subject. Describing the subject in these examples as being in some state as a result of the action of the verb stretches the meaning of the term 'state' to breaking point. Indeed, far from denoting the present state of the subject, or indeed of the object, such perfects appear to have more to do with a past event and its relevance, in some way, at reference time.[84]

The second, related, difficulty, concerns the relationship between the transitivity of the perfect active form and its capacity to denote resultant state. Haspelmath (2001: 201) suggests that a form whose function is to denote resultant state of the subject should present the state of the affected participant, and therefore be capable of behaving in a passive-like fashion. However, this fails to account for why perfect actives such as *éorga* in Homer are always semantically active and transitive.[85] Indeed, there are many perfect active forms, including those given in the examples above, which never behave in a passive-like fashion.

Chantraine's view, that the perfect, at least of certain verbs after Homer, denotes the state of the object, is more promising, since at least in these cases it acknowledges that it is the object participant that changes state. However, this view too is problematic, since, as McKay (1965: 9ff.) has observed, the fact that the object enters a state does not necessarily mean that this it is the function of the perfect to denote this.

---

[84] McKay (1965) is the first to assert that the perfect denotes the state of the subject in all situations, even where it is an experience that is being described. Prior to this, e.g. Wackernagel (1904), Chantraine (1927), the term 'state' was reserved for the description of a situation holding at reference time in which the subject is found, i.e. excluding the experience of the subject.

[85] Haspelmath (1992: 210) distinguishes between effected versus affected objects and argues that *éorga* is therefore not a truly transitive perfect. However, this has the feel of special pleading. Sicking & Stork (1996: 130–7), who explain in terms of the semantic feature of control, give no framework for distinguishing different behaviour in different verbs.

Indeed, McKay produces convincing evidence to show that it is indeed unlikely that the function of these perfects is to denote the state of the object. Nor indeed would such an explanation suffice for the meaning of the perfect as a whole, since there are plainly many examples where the perfect does indeed denote the state of the subject. It seems, therefore, that the suggestions that the function of the perfect is to denote either the state of the subject or of the object are flawed.

What then of the traditional view that the perfect denotes an action or event finished at reference time? This is able to account both for those perfects denoting the state of the subject and those where the subject does not enter into a new state, but has rather participated in some event in the past. There are, however, three problems. The first is that such a definition still does not account for the passive-like behaviour of certain perfect actives: why should a form denoting that an action is finished behave as a passive in certain cases? A second problem is that, insofar as the perfect is seen as denoting current relevance, it falls victim to the objections which have been raised regarding the current relevance theory of the English perfect, in particular in regard to the apparent confusion within the theory of semantic and pragmatic considerations.[86] Thirdly, it fails to account for the use of the perfect with certain state and change of state verbs, as, for instance, at (4) and (6) above, where it is very unclear what action is presented as having finished.

The lexical semantic approach adopted by Ruipérez (1982; 1954) for Greek, and by Portner (2003) more generally, provides a framework for resolving this third problem, since it deliberately encompasses both verbs with terminal points and those without.[87] However, the approach is lacking in that it leaves the transitivity question to one side, drawing no distinction between perfects whose subjects enter a state and those whose objects do. Accordingly, no reason is given for why in certain verbs the perfect active should behave in a passive-like manner. What is needed, therefore, is an approach which combines the lexical semantic framework with one that can adequately explain the transitivity alternations seen in the perfect active.

1.5 *Aims and approach*

Existing frameworks for explaining the perfect across languages are not adequate to encapsulate the attested behaviour of the Greek perfect, at least in the literary Koine, which is the focus of the present study. The difficulty, in a nutshell, is that the Greek perfect active combines within a single morphological entity behaviour usually associated with categories having distinctive and separate morphology, including not only tense (both past and present) and aspect (stative, resultative and perfective), but also, crucially, diathesis (both active and passive). Accordingly, whatever framework is chosen to explain the phenomena associated with the Greek perfect, it cannot use

---

[86] See Fanning (1990: 111) who outlines concerns raised by McCoard (1978).

[87] The current relevance problem is, of course, not a relevant concern for this approach.

the categories of tense and aspect in isolation, but must also incorporate argument structure, an element which has too often been ignored.

Much work has been done in recent years on the relationship between event and argument structure. In fact, this relationship is an important part of the broader question of the relationship between syntax and semantics, an area of research known as 'linking'. The basic premise of such research is that arguments should not be conceived of as contracting certain grammatical relations, but that they in themselves have aspectual properties, which in turn affect the aspectual properties of the predicates and sentences in which they occur.[88]

The present study, therefore, adopts an approach which goes beyond lexical aspect to consider the temporal and aspectual properties of predicate. In turn this allows argument structure to be brought into consideration in a natural way, thus providing a unifying framework for understanding all the phenomena associated with the Greek perfect.

1.6 *Corpus*

The present investigation analyses the semantics of the perfect active stem in literary Koine Greek. The core of the data used for the study comes from that used for Crellin (2012b). As such, the greater part of the evidence comes from historians, namely Polybius (henceforth Plb., c. 200 – 118 BC),[89] Plutarch (henceforth Plu., b. before AD 50, d. after AD 120), Appian (henceforth App., b. end of C1st AD, d. after AD 160), and Flavius Josephus (henceforth Jos., b. AD 37/8). The precise works included for that investigation are:

Table 2. Corpus

Authors	Abbreviation	Works and Abbreviations	Dates	Word count
Polybius	Plb.	*Histories (books 1-5 only)*[3]	C2nd BC	128 000
Josephus	Jos.	*Antiquities (AJ), Jewish War (BJ), Life (Vit.)*	AD C1st	447 000
Plutarch	Plu.	*Alcibiades (Alc.), Aristides (Arist.), Cimon (Cim.), Lysander (Lys.), Nicias (Nic.), Pericles (Per.), Solon (Sol.), Themistocles (Them.), Theseus (Thes.)*	AD C1st – C2nd	73 000
Appian	App.	*Civil War (BC), Foreign Wars: Wars in Spain (Hisp.), Hannibalic War (Hann.), Punic War (Pun.), Illyrian Wars (Ill.), Syrian Wars (Syr.), Mithridatic Wars (Mith.)*	AD C2nd	210 000
TOTAL				858 000

---

[88] For an overview of linking, see Tenny (1994: 1–2).

[89] Author dates compiled from data from relevant articles in Hornblower, Spawforth & Eidinow (eds.) *Oxford Classical Dictionary* (2012) (OCD).

For the purposes of the present study, however, this is supplemented with material from the rest of Plutarch's works, as well as other literary Koine authors of the same period,[90] including Menander (C4th – C3rd BC), Dionysius Thrax (C2nd – 1st BC), Philodemus (C2nd – 1st BC), Diodorus Siculus (henceforth Diod. Sic., C1st BC), Dionysius of Halicarnassus (henceforth Dion. Hal., C1st BC – AD C1st), Strabo (C1st BC), Philo of Alexandria (C1st BC – AD C1st), Aristonicus of Alexandria (C1st BC – AD C1st), Babrius (not later than AD C2nd), Pausanias (AD C2nd), Phrynichus (AD C2nd), Aelius Herodianus (AD C2nd), Cassius Dio (AD C2nd – 3rd) and Galen (AD C2nd – 3rd).

The investigation is essentially synchronic in nature, focusing on the literary writers of the Hellenistic and Roman periods, for the following reasons. First, before a diachronic picture can be plausibly and accurately drawn, the synchronic situation in its various stages must be understood as well as possible.[91] The kind of large-scale study proposed here has yet to be carried out for the later period, whereas at least one study of this kind exists for the Classical language.[92] Related to this is the desirability in any investigation for as many variables as possible, apart from that being measured, to be kept constant. Register is acknowledged throughout the history of Greek to play a significant role in determining the kind of language written. This should therefore, as far as possible, remain constant, and an analysis based purely on the literary language of this period meets this requirement. Furthermore, an analysis of the literary writers should shed interesting new light on Koine Greek of the same period, especially the biblical texts and the papyri where the debate regarding the perfect has been particularly fierce.

1.7 *Outline*

The present monograph sets out to demonstrate that none of the observed phenomena are *per se* intrinsic to the perfect, but are rather evidence, on the one hand, of a lower level interaction in the domain of syntax and semantics between event and argument structure and, on the other hand, a higher level semantic of the perfect itself, yielding the observed results in both tense-aspect and diathesis. Accordingly the monograph not only seeks to provide a solution to the problem of the semantics of the Greek perfect, but through this also to provide evidence more generally for the ways in which event-argument structure and tense-aspectual semantics may be related.

The monograph is laid out in six chapters, as well as an introduction and conclusion. Chapter 2 looks at the interaction of lexical aspectual semantics and argument structure. A lexical aspectual framework is established and, for each lexical aspectual type identified, the temporal and aspectual semantics of the perfect is investigated. While lexical aspect is shown to play an important role in determining the temporal

---

[90] These are the authors from whom excerpts are given in the main text. Other authors and works are referred to in the footnotes. For the New Testament, the text of NA28 is used.

[91] cf. Sicking & Stork (1996: 121f.), Campbell (2007: 23f.).

[92] Sicking & Stork (1996). Evans (2001) is quantitative in its approach with regard to the LXX Pentateuch, but this is translational material.

and aspectual semantics of the perfect, it is concluded that it is not fully explicable with reference only to the lexical aspectual content of the verb concerned.

Chapter 3 therefore sets out the syntactic-semantic frameworks that will be employed during the course of the rest of the study. Chapter 4 then examines the causative alternations associated with the Greek perfect active and assesses the extent to which this may be seen as a product of the perfect *per se*. Chapter 5 goes on to bring aspectual questions to the fore, assessing the temporal semantics of the perfect according to predicate type. Adopting and developing Tenny's (1992, 1994) Aspectual Interface Hypothesis for a theory of temporal relations in a neo-Davidsonian and Government-Binding (GB) theory framework, the behaviour of the perfect is examined according to predicate types distinguished according to their temporal and aspectual properties. It is found that the semantics of the perfect are predictable according to the temporal and aspectual properties of the predicates which they head, suggesting that the perfect derives a state from its predicate. However, change of state predicates are shown to behave in an idiosyncratic way in perfect predicates. Furthermore, the semantic definition provided in this chapter is inadequate for explaining predicates that describe no (post)state.

Chapters 6 and 7 address these issues in turn, and refinements to the semantic definition of the perfect are thereby proposed. Since neither the diathetical nor the tense-aspect features associated with the perfect are found to be intrinsic to the perfect itself, a semantic must be found that correctly produces the required results in these terms. It is argued that the Greek perfect is a stativising function, returning a homogeneous atelic eventuality as a function of the predicate with all its arguments, which is then asserted to include reference time. Furthermore, the perfect is found to be able to suppress the internal argument, accounting for some of its idiosyncratic aspectual behaviour. Past time reference, including the related phenomena of resultativity, anteriority and continued state, is a derived product of the interaction of this semantic with the aspectual properties of lexical verbs and their arguments.

II

2 THE PERFECT AND LEXICAL ASPECT

2.1 Introduction

2.1.1 Events and the Greek perfect

The aim of our enquiry is to establish the semantic contribution of perfect morphology. In order to do this, we need to disentangle the contribution of three elements: the lexical semantics of the item to which the perfect is formed, perfect morphology itself, and the surrounding context.[93] Since verbs primarily describe events or situations, we will start in by assessing the fundamental properties of situations and how they relate to their linguistic representations. From there we will move on to discuss the notion which is central to our purpose, namely aspect, showing how it relates to our enquiry at a syntactic, morphological and lexical level.

2.1.2 The true domain of events

It appears self-evident that an event is 'something that happens'. Yet at what point does it become an event? Is it an event as soon as it happens, or as soon as it is perceived to have happened? This is to ask whether an event may be considered to be something taking place 'in the real world',[94] or as an interpretation of happenings in the world which takes place in the mind.[95]

For the purposes of this investigation I take an event to be a cognitive phenomenon. This is first because, while some happenings, such as the Earth's orbit of the Sun, are governed entirely by natural laws, the term 'event' can also be used of happenings which only make sense in the context of an observer with the capacity for understanding. Take, for example, the event 'dance a waltz'. This is an event which has an entirely human definition; there is no physical law which determines what a waltz is. In order for the event 'dance a waltz' to occur, an observer must be present

---

[93] In attempting to solve the problem of past reference in the Greek perfect it has frequently been suggested that diverse behaviour of the perfect is predictable at the lexical level. Thus Porter (1989: 259) states: 'While there may be reference to a previous act that results in a state or condition, this is a matter of lexis in context. The aspect [of the perfect] itself merely represents the state or condition of the grammatical subject, as conceptualized by the speaker or writer.' However, Porter leaves unexplained what 'lexis in context' actually means. In particular the formulation 'lexis in context' does not specify where the role of lexis ends and context starts.

[94] This view seems to be assumed rather than argued for in e.g. Bach (1986). According to Rothstein (2004: 2), Kamp (1979a, 1979b) argues for this position.

[95] This is the view taken by Partee (1999: 98), Rappaport Hovav, Doron, & Sichel (2010: 1ff.) and Rothstein (2004: 2f.).

who both knows what a waltz is, and who can identify that the event 'dance a waltz' is taking place.

A second consideration is the imperfective paradox: how is it possible to describe an event using the progressive, when the event need never come to an end for the statement in the progressive to hold. Consider the following sentences:[96]

(24) John was crossing the street, when he was hit by a bus.

(25) John crossed the street.

(24) denies that (25) ever happened, and yet the imperfective 'John was crossing the street' is perfectly felicitous. The most natural way to interpret this is that events are cognitive phenomena. (24) conceives of an event, 'John being hit by a bus', which takes place in the course of a hypothesised 'John crossing the street' event.

Of what may the cognitive phenomenon of an event be said to consist? I take an event, or EVENTUALITY, to use Bach's more generic term,[97] to be an extralinguistic cognitive unit[98] whereby the diverse happenings in the world may be separated into distinct units which may be described by linguistic means.[99] I take events to be extralinguistic first on the basis of the very widespread, albeit not universal, encoding of aspectual distinctions in the worlds languages, as well as evidence from language acquisition: aspectual distinctions are gained easily by children without specific teaching.[100]

2.1.3 Aspect: semantic, pragmatic or morphological?

The term 'aspect' can be used in two different senses. First, it can refer to a set of semantic distinctions regarding the temporal constitution of an eventuality. Secondly, it can be used to describe a formal opposition in a particular language (or group of languages) predicated on the semantic distinctions.[101] Finally, pragmatic categories are also wont to be identified with the 'meaning' of aspectual distinctions.[102]

---

[96] Examples modified from Bach (1986: 12).

[97] Bach (1981) coined the term 'eventuality' to cover both states and events, since these are often opposed to one another. However, other work continues to use the term 'event' to cover both (see Tenny & Pustejovsky 2000: 5). In what follows, I follow Bach in using the term 'eventuality' for the general concept, and 'event' to describe non-stative eventualities.

[98] A unit implies bounds. Yet for the purposes of identifying events these bounds are purely to enable reference to the eventuality; it says nothing about the 'boundedness' of the eventuality, a property which properly concerns aspect (see next sub-sections). Thus I take the unbounded state in e.g. 'the ice is frozen', i.e. the ice is in a frozen state, to be an eventuality in the same way that 'the car crashed' is an eventuality.

[99] cf. Rappaport Hovav, Doron, & Sichel's definition (2010: 1). Smith (1997: xiv) distinguishes between events and states, and gives the general term 'situation' to the category which contains both terms. I have not followed her in this because of the widespread use of the term 'event structure', which is a term as applicable to states as it is activities or any other kind of event.

[100] See Smith (1997: xv) and references ad loc.

[101] cf. Comrie (1976: 6).

[102] Campbell (2007: 24) states, summarising the literature in New Testament studies, that 'Aktionsart is regarded as a pragmatic category.' Comrie (1976: 52) seems to invoke a pragmatic distinction in describing the meaning of the perfect as indicating 'the continuing present relevance of a past situation'.

First, it is essential to distinguish semantic from pragmatic levels of interpretation, separating entailments from implicatures.[103] An entailment may not be cancelled by a further assertion made in the same context, and still remain true. By contrast, an implicature may imply that something is true, but this implication may be cancelled. Consider the following example from Russian:[104]

(26) #On   posidel   v   parke,   i   ešče   tam
     he   *sit.PFV-PAST* *in*   *park*   *and*   *still*   *there*
     sidit.
     sit.IMPFV-PRES
     'He sat for a while in the park, and is still sitting there.'

On the intended reading, namely that both verbs refer to the same event, this sentence does not make sense: the statement on posidel *v parke* (= 'he sat for a while in the park') excludes the possibility that *ešče* tam sidit (= 'he is still sitting there').[105] The difference between these two statements is on the level of an entailment, since they cannot be put together and coerced to make sense.

Contrast this with the following examples in English:

(27) Peter was building a castle.
(28) Peter was building a castle but he never completed it.
(29) Peter was building a castle and now it's finished.

All three of these examples make sense. On its own one might take (27) to indicate that Peter did not finish the castle. However, as (28) and (29) demonstrate, it is compatible both with assertions that the castle was completed, and that it was not. It may be taken from this that the sentence 'Peter was building a castle' carries no entailment regarding the completion of the action; any implication in this regard falls in the domain of implicature.

Since different languages mark aspect formally in different ways,[106] the term 'aspect' will be reserved here for the semantic distinction. Other terms will be used to label the specific means used by Greek and other languages to realise these semantic distinctions. For the purposes of the present investigation, therefore, I adopt Smith's definition of aspect:[107]

> Aspect is the semantic domain of the temporal structure of [events] and their presentation.

---

[103] Implicatures can be further distinguished between conventional and conversational, a distinction first made by Grice (1975), who was primarily interested in the latter. For a concise definition of the latter see Potts (2005: 11).

[104] Example from Smith & Rappaport (1997: 231). My thanks to Julia Crellin for her help in interpreting the Russian examples.

[105] Smith & Rappaport (1997: 231).

[106] Indeed, many languages, e.g. modern German, do not formally mark aspect at all.

[107] Smith (1997: 1).

2.1.4 *Viewpoint aspect, situation aspect and telicity*

Two kinds of aspect are generally recognised in the world's languages: viewpoint aspect and the aspect of a situation,[108] also known as AKTIONSART. Smith outlines the difference between these two as follows:[109]

> Viewpoint aspect gives temporal perspective to a sentence. More subtly, [situation] aspect also involves a point of view... [situation] aspect presents a situation as belonging to a certain category of event or state.

Across languages two viewpoint aspects are generally distinguished, PERFECTIVE and IMPERFECTIVE. Smith defines the semantic difference in general between the two as follows:[110]

> The main semantic difference among aspectual viewpoints is in how much of a situation they make visible. Perfective viewpoints focus a situation in its entirety, including endpoints; Imperfective viewpoints focus an interval that excludes endpoints...

Consider the following Russian examples:[111]

(30) On   napisal   pis'mo.
     he   write.PFV-PAST   letter
     'He wrote a letter.'

(31) On   pisal   pis'mo.
     he   write.IMPFV-PAST   letter
     'He was writing a letter.'

(32) On   posidel   v   parke.
     he   sit.PFV-PAST   in   park
     'He sat for a while in the park.'

(33) On   sidit   v   parke.
     he   sit.IMPFV-PRES   in   park
     'He is sitting in the park.'

The first two examples concern an event of 'writing a letter'. The second two, by contrast, concern an event of 'sitting in the park'. These two events differ in at least one critical respect: 'writing a letter' has a set termination point, the point when the letter is complete, while 'sitting in the park' has no set terminal point. The subject most likely will not continue sitting in the park forever, but there is no preset time

---

[108] Smith (1997) calls the latter 'situation aspect'.

[109] Smith (1997: 1).

[110] Smith (1997: 62). For a summary of the recent literature on imperfective and perfective viewpoint aspect, see Gvozdanović (2012).

[111] Examples adapted from Smith & Rappaport (1997: 230–2).

at which this event must terminate. An event with a set terminal point is said to be TELIC, while an event without a set terminal point is said to be ATELIC. The presence, or lack, of an endpoint, in an event, its TELICITY, is an aspectual property, and belongs to the event, or situation, as a whole.

Notice that both events, 'sitting in the park' and 'writing a letter' are compatible with both perfective and imperfective aspect marking, as demonstrated by the felicity of all four sentences. In (30) the telic event 'Him writing a letter' is presented as completed with perfective aspect. In (31), however, the imperfective is used, and a subinterval of the same telic event is presented. The same distinction holds between (32) and (33): in the former the atelic 'He sitting in the park' event is presented as completed, whereas in the latter a subinterval of that event is given.

It is clear from these examples that viewpoint aspect may, in principle, apply both to telic and atelic sentences, and that therefore the two categories of situation and viewpoint aspect should be distinguished. Situation aspect refers to the temporal properties a given event can possibly have, while viewpoint aspect selects which of those properties is in view in a given utterance.[112] It may be said, therefore, that '[t]he aspectual meaning of a sentence is a composite of the information from the components of viewpoint and situation type'.[113] In the case of telic events, therefore, the perfective asserts that the endpoint inherent to the event is reached. In the case of atelic events, by contrast, a perfective will, depending on the language, either impose an arbitrary endpoint on the event, or simply mark the start point.

A common test for telicity, which we will use frequently in what follows, is the felicity of adding a 'for α time' expression versus an 'in α time' expression. The former is in general felicitous with atelic sentences, since it provides an artificial bound, while the latter is felicitous with telic sentences, since it asserts the time frame in which the already telic event takes place. Consider the following examples:

(34) My brother built houses (for years / #in ten years).
(35) My sister built a house (in a day / #for a day).

The first example, 'My brother built houses,' is atelic, as shown by the felicity of combination with a 'for' adverbial expression, and infelicity of an 'in' adverbial expression. That the second example, 'My sister built a house,' is telic is shown by the felicity of the 'in' adverbial, and the infelicity of the 'for' adverbial.

2.1.5 *Tense and aspect in terms of Utterance Time and Topic Time*

Since at least Reichenbach (1947) it has been common to talk of tense as being a relationship to a 'reference time'. However, it has not always been clear how this 'reference time' is determined. In an attempt to provide greater precision, Klein (see Klein 1992, 1994) introduced a development of Reichenbach's framework where

---

[112] Smith (1997: 61): 'Aspectual viewpoints function like the lens of a camera, making objects visible to the receiver. [Eventualities] are like the objects on which the viewpoint lenses are trained.'
[113] Smith (1997: 1)

tense and aspect are defined in terms of UTTERANCE TIME (TU), TOPIC TIME (TT), and SITUATION TIME (TSit). These times are all sets of times, rather than single points,[114] which may either be identical, overlapping, or not overlapping.

Topic time is defined to be 'the span of time to which the claim made on a given occasion is constrained',[115] while utterance time and situation time are the time at which the utterance is made, and the time of the eventuality being described, respectively. Tense then concerns the relationship of topic time to utterance time,[116] so that the past tense asserts that topic time precedes utterance time, the future that utterance time precedes situation time and the present tense that situation time includes utterance time. Aspect, by contrast, relates topic time to situation time, so that in the imperfective situation time includes topic time,[117] while in the perfective situation time is included in topic time.[118]

Consider the following example:

(36) I was mowing the lawn at eleven o'clock.

This sentence contains the predicate 'mowing the lawn'. Topic time, eleven o'clock then bears a relationship of priority with respect to utterance time. This is a relationship of tense. Here the tense is 'past', because topic time precedes utterance time.

Aspect concerns the relationship that the predicate 'mowing the lawn' holds to topic time, which is eleven o'clock. Specifically, topic time, eleven o'clock, is located within the time during the event 'washing up the dishes'. In other terms it may be said that situation time properly includes topic time.[119] This is an aspectual relationship, and the predicate 'mowing the lawn' in (36) is imperfective.

2.1.6 *Viewpoint aspect in Greek*

Klein uses the term situation time (TSit) to refer to the time over which an eventuality takes place. I, however, adopt Krifka's TEMPORAL TRACE FUNCTION $\tau(e)$, which returns a set of times from an eventuality, to describe this.[120] Thus $\tau(e)$ returns the set of times of an event 'e'. We are interested in whether the set of times of an eventuality 'e':

1. Precedes the set of times comprising TT (henceforth t_{TT}), $\tau(e) < t_{TT}$, that is, is anterior.

---

[114] Krifka (1989, 1992) and Klein (1992, 1994).

[115] Klein (1992: 535).

[116] Klein (1992: 536).

[117] Klein (1992: 537). Bary (2009: 78) expresses imperfective in these terms as TT being a non-final subset of TSit.

[118] Bary (2009: 78), and Klein (1994). By contrast, Klein (1992: 537) offers the following definition: 'TT including end of TSit and beginning of time after TSit'.

[119] Set A is said to include set B properly if B is a subset of A, but A is not also a subset of B (see Enderton 1977: 85).

[120] This offers an easy way to incorporate non-temporal predicates into our framework, addressed in chapter 6.

2. Properly includes the set of times comprising TT, $\tau(e) \supset t_{TT}$, that is, is continuative.
3. Includes t_{TT}, $\tau(e) \supseteq t_{TT}$, that is, refers to TT only.[121]

Apart from the perfect, Greek distinguishes two viewpoint aspects: imperfective and perfective. Imperfective aspect is denoted by PRESENT (pres.) and IMPERFECT (impf.) morphology, while perfective aspect is denoted by AORIST (aor.) morphology. For the purpose of the present investigation, we follow Bary (2009: 171) in taking the semantic contribution of the aorist stem to be that:

... the eventuality takes place within the time about which we speak: its runtime is included in the topic time.

This entails that the endpoints of the predicate headed by the perfective are included in topic time. By contrast, the imperfective presents a situation without reference to endpoints, i.e. the runtime includes reference time.[122]

Where a bounded predicate is found with its verb in the aorist stem, it may be interpreted only as having start and end points included in topic time. By contrast, an unbounded predicate with verb in the aorist stem is capable either of complexive, interpretation, i.e. where an endpoint is posited bounding the event on the right, or ingressive, where the eventuality being talked about is assumed to be the start of the event only.[123]

2.1.7 Lexical aspectual categories: Aristotle, Kenny and Vendler

Telicity is only part of the picture of distinguishing situations in terms of aspect. The modern distinctions of situation aspectual types go back to Vendler (1957) and Kenny (1963), both of whose work relies on distinctions made by Aristotle.[124] While Aristotle is clearly concerned with ontological distinctions rather than lexical ones,[125] Vendler and Kenny distinguish between different kinds of verbs, the implication being that this is where the distinction, at least at the linguistic level, is primarily made. In his analysis Kenny first distinguishes STATES and EVENTS. Events may then be subdivided into ACTIVITIES and PERFORMANCES. His scheme is given in Table 3.[126]

---

[121] In addition, for situations where $\tau(e)$ does not include t_{TT}, or partially includes t_{TT}, we need to know whether, for an initial moment of $\tau(e)$, i.e. $\exists t_i \in \tau(e)$, is after the final moment of t_{TT} ($t_i > t_{TT}$) or before the first moment of t_{TT} ($t_i < t_{TTi}$). In practice, since we are not dealing with future eventualities, we will concern ourselves only with $t_i < t_{TTi}$.

[122] This is not to say that the imperfective *always* performs this function, notably in the case of the historic present. See McKay (1965: 5-6).

[123] For a full analysis and discussion of how the ambiguity between these interpretations is resolved, see Bary (2009). For examples see 2.1.9 below.

[124] Haug (2004: 387). Aristotle distinguishes at Metaphysics 1048b between *kinéseis*, and *enérgeiai*.

[125] Haug (2004: 389).

[126] This table is based on Haug's summary of Kenny's position in Haug (2004: 389–91).

Table 3. Kenny's semantic distinctions

	Kenny's distinctions	Examples		
States			[-change]	
Events	Activities	'run'	[+change]	[-endpoint]
	Performances	'build'	[+change]	[+endpoint]

Following Aristotle, Kenny introduces a test to establish the class to which a given verb may be said to belong, involving the perfect tense.

(37) I am running.
(38) I have run.
(39) I am building a house.
(40) I have built a house.

Sentence (37) may be said to entail (38). However, sentence (39) cannot be said to entail (40). That is to say that the present progressive of the verb 'run' entails the perfect tense of the same verb, while the same cannot be said for the verb 'build': if I am building a house, I cannot be said simultaneously to have built it, where one and the same building event is being described. Verbs which behave like 'run', where the present progressive entails the perfect, Kenny terms 'activities', while verbs like 'build', where there is no such entailment, he categorises as 'performances'. The fundamental semantic point distinguishing activities and performances is that the latter have a fixed endpoint in view with respect to which the completion of the event can be measured. In the case of the former, however, no such endpoint is in view. Consequently, any minimal amount of running may be said to fulfil the condition of 'having run'.

Vendler makes essentially the same distinctions as Kenny. However, he further divides performances into ACCOMPLISHMENTS and ACHIEVEMENTS, for which see Table 4.[127] In this table the feature [± stages] refers to whether or not the event described is a process or not. The feature [+ stages] is shared by activities and accomplishments, and is generally indicated by felicity with the progressive in English:

(41) Are you running? (activity)
(42) Are you building a house? (accomplishment)

By contrast, states and achievements are [-stages]:

(43) ?Are you loving this music?[128] (state)
(44) #Are you recognising this piece of work? (achievement)

The feature [+endpoint] is shared by achievements and accomplishments. Thus the following sentences are infelicitous, because they simultaneously assert that the envisaged endpoint has been reached and that it has not:

---

[127] Vendler (1957). The table is that given by Rothstein (2004: 12).
[128] In some colloquial varieties of English such a sentence is acceptable.

Table 4. Feature analysis of Vendlerian categories

	Kenny	Vendler	[± stages]	[± endpoint]
States	States	States	-	-
Events	Activities	Activities	+	-
	Performances	Accomplishments	+	+
		Achievements	-	+

(45) #I have run the 800 metres and I'm still running the 800 metres.

(46) #I have recognised you and I am recognising you.

By contrast the following sentences, involving activites and states respectively, are felicitous, showing that they are [- endpoint]:

(47) I have run and I'm still running.

(48) I have loved you and I still love you.

Vendler (1957: 149) summarises the differences as follows:

> ... the concept of activities calls for periods of time that are not unique or definite. Accomplishments, on the other hand, imply the notion of unique and definite time periods. In an analogous way, while achievements involve unique and definite time instants, states involve time instants in an indefinite and non-unique sense.

From a linguistic perspective, there is, however, a problem with Kenny's activity/performance and Vendler's activity/accomplishment distinctions. Compare (37) and (38) above with (49) and (50) below.

(49) I am running a marathon.

(50) I have run a marathon.

In (37) and (38) the verb 'run' was shown to denote an activity: there the present progressive entails the perfect. In (49) and (50) the predicate 'run' is expanded with an expression giving the path of the running event, in this case 'a marathon'. Now the present progressive may not be said to entail the perfect: it is not simultaneously the case that someone be running a marathon and having run a marathon, where the same event of running a marathon is being described. By the addition of a path, therefore, an activity verb may be seen to behave in the same way as an accomplishment verb. It seems then that the different types identified by Kenny and Vendler are really properties of predicates or sentences, rather than of verbs.[129]

---

[129] For this point see Haug (2004: 391–2).

2.1.8 *The domain of situation aspect: syntax or lexis?*

In the previous section we saw that the identification of Kenny and Vendler's aspectual classes at the lexical level was problematic. Specifically, the verbal head is not sufficient for determining the telicity of the sentence in which it sits, and that the presence of certain arguments and modifiers is also important.[130] Telicity should therefore be regarded as a property of predicates.[131]

Yet it is not clear, just because the verbal head cannot always finally determine the telicity of its predicate, that it has no role in determining the telicity of a sentence. This latter position has recently been argued by Rothstein.[132] For her '[t]he question to ask at the V level is not whether verbs are telic or not, but how different heads can be classified according to the contribution they make towards determining telicity'.[133]

That the verbal head can be the key factor in determining the aspectual properties of a sentence may be seen in state and achievement verbs. Thus while the predicates 'run' and 'run a marathon' have different properties according to Kenny's test, this is not the case for predicates headed by state verbs or achievement verbs.[134] Consider first the following instances involving the state verb 'to love':

(51) Fred loved his car (#in/for a year).
(52) Fred loved cars (#in/for a year).
(53) Fred loved cake (#in/for a year).

From these examples it is clear that predicates headed by a state verb are always atelic regardless of the properties of the arguments with which the verbal head is construed. The same may be said for achievement verbs. Consider the following examples involving the achievement verb 'to explode':

(54) The bomb exploded.
(55) The bombs exploded.

An event of exploding occurs in an instant. Consequently, whether there is only one bomb, or many bombs, it is of no consequence to the duration of the event described.[135]

This evidence suggests that the verbal head does play a role in determining the telicity of a sentence. Specifically, it may be said that:[136]

> ... a VP is telic when we can identify an atomic set[137] which makes counting events in the denotation of the VP possible... Achievements are naturally atomic, and thus telic.

---

[130] Verkuyl (1972), Dowty (1979). See also Krifka (1998: 207).
[131] See Rothstein (2008: 2–3) and Horrocks & Stavrou (2007: 290 n. 8).
[132] Rothstein (2008)
[133] Rothstein (2008: 2)
[134] Tenny (1992: 13)
[135] Assuming, of course, that the bombs go off simultaneously.
[136] Rothstein (2004: 174)
[137] i.e. a set of sub-events which may be counted.

States, as in (51)-(53), are not atomic, since they are composed of an arbitrary number of infinitesimally small instants. They are therefore inherently atelic.

The real issue, then, concerns activity and accomplishment sentences, where factors other than the verbal head certainly do play a role in determining telicity. Consider the following:

(56) Fred built houses (#in/for a year).

(57) Fred built his own house (#for/in a year).

Accomplishment sentences may be either telic or atelic. The atelicity of (56) comes from the fact that the number of houses is not specified (i.e. predetermined). Consequently, it is not possible, in Rothstein's terms, to count the number of building events. By contrast, in (57) the number of houses is specified. Therefore the number of building events is countable and the event is telic.

Now compare the following examples:

(58) Fred played the piano (#in/for ten seconds).

(59) Fred played the sonata (#for/in ten seconds).

The atelicity of (58) comes from the fact that the theme does not provide a criterion for counting events: you can in principle keep playing the piano for ever. By contrast, (59) does give these criteria, because a sonata has a predetermined extent.

In chapter 5 we shall consider the specific role(s) played by the arguments of a verb in determining the aspectual evaluation of a sentence. For the purposes of this chapter, however, it is important to identify what aspectual distinctions can be made between verbs at the purely lexical level.

2.1.9 Developing a lexical aspectual framework for Greek

2.1.9.1 Introduction

The foregoing section has shown that while the aspectual characteristics of a sentence are not finally determined in the verbal head, the verbal head nevertheless contributes important elements to the meaning of the sentence which have a crucial role in determining the aspectual characteristics of a sentence.[138] Since the perfect is formed to verbs, it makes sense to begin our analysis at the lexical level and consider how the perfect interacts semantically with verbs of different lexical aspectual types. This is the goal of the present chapter, before we move out and consider the perfect's semantic interactions with the entire predicate in the next

---

[138] Ramchand (1997: 126f.) presents the following analysis: 'The verbal lexical item comes specified for some basic temporal architecture, i.e. whether it determines a time structure that is non-atomic (States), atomic time structure with indeterminately many conceptual moments (Activities and Accomplishments), or atomic time structure with only two discrete conceptual moments (Achievements)... The classification in terms of the number of time atoms in the time interval described by the event represents a grouping that is not aspectual per se in the sense of the traditional Vendlerian classification. Rather it is a lower-level property which can be determined at the level of the verb itself, and in the absence of further information about the presence and type of objects and adjuncts.'

chapters. In order to do this, however, we need to identify the important lexical aspectual features of Greek verbs.

For the purposes of the present investigation we characterise the lexical aspectual semantics of Greek verbs on the basis of three semantic features: DURATIVITY, TERMI-NATIVITY and HOMOGENEITY.[139] The preceding analysis has already identified three key groups of verbs established on the basis of terminativity: state verbs, which describe atelic events, achievement verbs, whose sentences are always telic, and verbs introducing activity and accomplishment sentences, whose sentences may be either telic or atelic according to the properties of their direct arguments.

2.1.9.1.1 *Terminativity*

We follow Horrocks & Stavrou (2007) in identifying the feature of terminativity as a specifically lexical aspectual property. Terminative verbs either presuppose a goal or destination as obligatory complements or encode an obligatory endpoint as part of the event structure of the event described. Verbs in the terminative category include change of state verbs, e.g. 'to freeze' (including change of location verbs, e.g. 'to arrive'), achievement verbs, e.g. 'to frighten' and, in Greek, a special class of terminative state verbs. Terminativity is distinct from telicity, by which an event is delimited at the level of the predicate, and which has been discussed earlier in this introduction. Importantly, in this study the term 'telic' does not imply the presence of a goal state (although this may be present), but rather asserts that the predicate for which this property holds has a set endpoint.

Note that the feature of terminativity, insofar as it denotes the imposition of an endpoint by the lexical verb, is not EQUIPOLLENT. This is to say that achievement verbs impose a telic reading, and this cannot be cancelled,[140] while non-terminative verbs, i.e. state verbs and activity/accomplishment verbs can have their non-terminative readings cancelled by the addition of a bound, as we have seen earlier in this introduction.

2.1.9.1.2 *Homogeneity*

While activity/accomplishment verbs can introduce predicates with telic readings according to the arguments with which they are construed, they are like state verbs,

---

[139] There are parallels between this tripartite analysis and that of Olsen (1997) who distinguishes lexical aspectual types on the basis of dynamicity, durativity and telicity, where telicity is to be identified with terminativity in the terms I am using. I differ from Olsen principally in the use of homogeneity instead of dynamicity. Olsen identifies dynamicity with change (1997: 35). However, citing Comrie (1976: 49), Dowty (1979), Bach (1986) and Levin & Rappaport Hovav (1995), Olsen points out (1997: 38) that certain stative verbs may also be presented as dynamic, especially where statives may be expressed with a progressive in English, e.g. 'I am standing on the roof'. However, it seems that, at least for explaining the Greek verb system, homogeneity is a more relevant concept for us, since it is a broader category than states, and, as will be seen, allows us to explain present-only interpretation in the perfect in non-state verbs.

[140] At least as far as simultaneous events are concerned. It is of course possible for achievement verbs to introduce atelic predicates where this is not the case, as for example with the sentence, 'The bombs exploded for hours.'

in that the verbs themselves do not delimit the reading of the events they describe. However, they differ from state verbs in that it is only down to a certain granularity that they can only be subdivided into subevents which may also be regarded as instances of the same event (see Ramchand 1997: 123, Taylor 1977). Thus, an event of 'running' can be subdivided into subevents of running only down to a certain minimal level, i.e. a certain number of cycles of the legs in a particular pattern, below which, say one or two cycles of the legs in a particular pattern, the subevent cannot be said to be an event of running. Similarly, an event of 'building' may not be divided into an infinite number of subevents which may also be regarded as events of building. One might divide it into smaller events, e.g. cutting wood etc., but these are not in and of themselves also building events. What differentiates activity/accomplishment verbs from states, then, is their subdividability, a feature I will term 'homogeneity':[141] state verbs describe homogeneous eventualities, while activity/accomplishment verbs introduce non-homogeneous eventualities.[142]

This difference between activities and states has important consequences for the semantics of the perfect, and in particular for the semantics of the continuative perfect, both in English and in Greek. Consider the following English examples:

(60) Mary has lived in London since 1966, and she still lives there.
(61) ?I have walked in the park since four o'clock, and I'm still walking.
(62) I have been walking in the park since four o'clock, and I'm still walking.

While in the first example the continuative reading is unproblematic, in the case of non-homogeneous events (in the strong sense that we are using) such as 'to walk', the continuative reading is only truly felicitous in the perfect continuous.

Unlike the feature of terminativity, homogeneity is equipollent: an event described by a verb with homogeneous semantics cannot have the homogeneity cancelled, nor can a non-homogeneous event have its homogeneity cancelled.

2.1.9.1.3 Durativity

The final feature we will use is durativity. Durativity is a semantic feature corresponding to whether or not an eventuality is specified to have duration: durative

---

[141] As a feature homogeneity was first recognised for nouns with a view to accounting for mass/count noun distinction, for which see e.g. Quine (1960) and Tenny & Pustejovsky (2000). In view of the parallels as well as related phenomena between events and objects, it was carried over to eventualities e.g. Mourelatos (1978).

[142] Specifically, following Rothstein (2004: 186), who in turn follows Dowty (1979), we hold that an activity is an event *e* which has minimal parts which are the smallest events for an instance of the event *e* to be said to occur. In these terms the difference between activities and states is that in the case of the former, *e* is finite, while in the latter *e* is infinitely small. Thus Ramchand (1997: 123–4) states: '... stative verbs... have completely homogeneous reference in the sense that one cannot distinguish any change, gradual or otherwise, occurring as a part of the eventuality. The difference [with activities]... is that the divisibility of "running" is limited by a certain level of granularity. At some point, if the divisions get small enough, a subevent of running can no longer be distinguished as 'running' per se, as opposed to "walking" or "jumping" or "moving the foot".'

eventualities must hold for a certain amount of time in order to be regarded as having taken place, while non-durative eventualities are not required to have any duration.

Durativity is defined in terms of CONCEPTUAL MOMENTS.[143] This is to say that durative events are defined as consisting of multiple conceptual moments, while non-durative events do not require multiple conceptual moments in order to be said to have taken place.

We noted at 2.1.5 above in our discussion of topic time and situation time that these are time spans, not single instants. If conceptual moments and instants are the same thing, then in principle one could imagine that a durative event could be contained within topic time. This is the case, for example, with non-durative situations, e.g. 'sitting in a chair':

(63) I am sitting in this chair now.
(64) I was sitting in this chair then.

Here topic time is potentially coextensive with the situation time of 'sitting in the chair': there is no necessary implication, in either case, that once the time span 'now' is completed the sitting in the chair will continue. Thus it is perfectly possible to continue with a sentence describing a situation whereby the state did indeed not continue:

(65) I'm sitting in this chair now, but soon I won't be when I get up.

(66) I was sitting in this chair then, but soon after I wasn't when I got up.

Contrast this with durative situations:

(67) I'm staying in this chair now.

Here the claim being made has implications beyond topic time, and it would be infelicitous to continue with a sentence describing how the state did not continue:

(68) I'm staying here in this chair now, #but in a minute I won't be when I get up.

The second part of this sentence does not make sense, because implied in the first part is the fact that the event extends beyond topic time.

This behaviour also characterises other non-stative duratve events, e.g.:

(69) I'm going home now.

It would be odd, to say the least, to continue this sentence with a sentence that implies that before the event might be expected to be completed, it will no longer hold:

(70) I'm going home now, but in a minute I won't be because I'll be going to the library.

---

[143] The 'conceptual moments' introduced here, which for Ramchand (1997: 115ff.) are the key to distinguishing lexical types, are explicable in terms of the 'temporal trace function', introduced by Krifka (1989: 97). This function 'maps an event to its temporal trace, or "run time"'. Accordingly, 'single' verbs introducing states, such as 'love', since they have no conceptual moments, do not have a temporal trace function. 'Dual' verbs, such as 'explode' have a temporal trace with two values, relating to the state of affairs before and after the event. By contrast 'plural' verbs, such as 'run' and 'build' have a temporal trace which is multivalued.

I take these examples as evidence that a temporal instant is different from a conceptual moment. In particular, although topic time may consist of multiple temporal instants, it cannot comprise more than one conceptual moment. A durative event is then defined as consisting of more than one conceptual moment.

Durativity is not necessarily equipollent: durative verbs must head durative predicates, while non-durative verbs may be compatible with durative interpretation.[144] Thus 'to die', a non-durative verb, is compatible with both durative and non-durative interpretations:

(71) He died slowly.
(72) He died suddenly.

Durative verbs, however, such as those heading accomplishment and activity predicates, do not share the same ambivalence:[145]

(73) He built the house slowly.
(74) He ran slowly.
(75) ?He built the house suddenly.
(76) ?He ran suddenly.

Non-durative events include achievements, whose events have no conceptual duration,[146] and certain states. Durative events comprise activities, accomplishments and a class of durative states.

One final point should be noted: while it might be thought that, insofar as achievements describe a change of some kind, they are not homogeneous. However, in the minimal case, where the achievement has no conceptual duration, its homogeneity may be said to be moot. This is particularly clear where achievements engender a change of state on the part of the subject. Consider again following example:

(77) He died suddenly.

Since dying in this case has no conceptual duration, it may simply be regarded as the onset of the state of death. In event structure terms one can say that the achievement event 'dying' can be joined homogeneously with the state 'being dead' to form a homogeneous whole. This is because the verb 'die', along with a large number of other achievement verbs, introduce change of state predicates.[147]

---

[144] For an analysis of lexical aspectual types in English along these lines, see Olsen (1997). Olsen, however, opposes durativity to punctiliarity, while observing (1997: 42) that '[p]unctiliarity is... a conversational implicature associated with a verb unmarked for durativity, which may be canceled by durative temporal adverbs, such as *during the same period, for days...*'.

[145] Examples (71) and (72) are slightly modified from Olsen (1997: 43).

[146] Note that some achievement verbs require non-durative interpretation in an equipollent way, at least with singular atomic complements, such as 'explode'. Thus it is non-felicitous to say, '#The bomb exploded for an hour.'

[147] For specific treatment of change of state predicates, see 5.5 and chapter 6 below. For their relationship to terminativity in Greek, see 2.1.9.4.2 below.

2.1.9.2 *Durativity in Greek*

Durativity is a feature of both event and state verbs in Greek, but is not criterial of them. Some scholars assume that states are inherently durative.[148] Others assume that state verbs, insofar as they describe eventualities that are not associated with change, are not associated with distinguishable conceptual moments, and are therefore not durative under the analysis given above.[149] Yet in Greek, at least, state verbs may be distinguished on the basis of durativity, a difference which can be seen by comparing a verb such as *agapáō* 'to love', with a state verb such as *ménō* 'to remain' and its compounds. The latter, in contrast to the former, require a certain amount of time to elapse before an instance of the event they describe may be said to have occurred.

The two types do not contrast in the imperfective, which in both cases simply denotes that the states in question hold at topic time:[150]

(78) érxato   légein,   hóti...
      begin.AOR-IND-MID-3-SG   *say.PRES-INF-ACT*   *that...*
      stérgei   kaì   **agapâi**
      love.PRES-IND-ACT-3-SG   *and*   **love.PRES-IND-ACT-3-SG**
      tền...   douleían...
      ART.F-ACC-SG   *service.F-ACC-SG*
      '... he began to say that... **he loved and adored serving under him.**'
      (Jos. *AJ* 8.4)

(79) autóthi   **ménōn**   metà   tôn
      there   **remain.PRES-PTPL-ACT-NOM-SG**   *with*   *ART.GEN-PL*
      heautoû   lokhitôn   hupostésesthai
      himself.M-GEN-SG   *comrade.M-GEN-PL*   *endure.FUT-INF-MID*
      Mardónion
      Mardonios.M-ACC-SG
      '... **remaining** there with his own comrades he would endure Mardonius.'
      (Plu. *Arist.* 17.2)

However, the two types do distinguish themselves in the perfective. Specifically, durative state verbs are distinguished by never occurring with ingressive readings in the perfective, while non-durative state verbs occur with both ingressive and complexive readings. As an example of the latter, consider the following minimal pair involving *agapáō:*

(80) eulogéseien   án   tis
      praise.AOR-OPT-ACT-3-SG   *PTCL*   *INDEF-PRON.MF-NOM-SG*

---

[148] Thus Smith (1999: 481) and Olsen (1997: 41).

[149] Thus Ramchand (1997: 123–7).

[150] Cf. *agapâi* (App. *BC* 3.8.62), *elpízō* (App. *Mith.* 8.55) and *spoudázōn* (Jos. *AJ* 12.12).

tòn	theòn	**agapḗsanta**	ténde
ART.M-ACC-SG	*God.M-ACC-SG*	*love.AOR-PTPL-ACT-ACC-SG*	*this.F-ACC-SG*
tḕn	khṓran...	houtōs,	hṓste	sè
ART.F-ACC-SG	*land.F-ACC-SG*	*so*	*that*	*you.ACC-SG*
poiêsai	basiléa.
make.AOR-INF-ACT	*king.M-ACC-SG*

'May one praise God who has **loved** this land so much that he made you king.' (Jos. *AJ* 8.173)

(81)

mîsos	enteûthen	érxato
hatred.N-NOM-SG	*from-there*	*begin.AOR-IND-MID-3-SG*
eis	tòn	Skipíōna	toû
towards	*ART.M-ACC-SG*	*Scipio.M-ACC-SG*	*ART.M-GEN-SG*
dḗmou...		hóti	autòn
people.M-GEN-SG		*because*	*he.M-ACC-SG*
agapḗsantes...		hupèr	tôn
love.AOR-PTPL-ACT-NOM-PL		*on-behalf*	*ART.M-GEN-PL*

Italiōtôn	antipeprakhóta	sphísin
Italian.M-GEN-PL	*act-against.PERF-PTPL-ACT-ACC-SG*	*them.DAT-PL*
heórōn.
see.IMPF-IND-ACT-3-PL

'... hatred began from that time towards Scipio on the part of the people, because **though they once loved him**... they saw him having acted against them on behalf of the Italians.' (App. *BC* 1.3.19)

In the first example God is posited as having started to love the land at some time prior to topic time, and to continue in that state at topic time.[151] By contrast, in the second example it is clear that the love which the people have for Scipio has been replaced at topic time by hate, and has therefore terminated.[152]

By contrast, ingressive readings are not found in the perfective of durative state verbs. This is because a minimal amount of time must elapse for the state to be said to hold, and therefore it does not make sense to say something like 'I have begun to remain...' Where unbounded examples are found, the event is presented as having started before topic time:

(82)

hē	dè	stephánē...	mía
ART.F-NOM-SG	*PTCL*	*crown.F-NOM-SG...*	*one.F-NOM-SG*
ên	kaì	**diémeinen**	ákhri
be.IMPF-IND-3-SG	*and*	*remain.AOR-IND-ACT-3-SG*	*until*
têsde	tês	hēméras...
this.F-GEN-SG	*ART.F-GEN-SG*	*day.F-GEN-SG...*

'The crown, on which Moses wrote, was one and **has remained** up to the present day.' (Jos. *AJ* 8.93)

---

[151] Parallels: *ebasíleusen* (Jos. *AJ* 9.260), *basileúsas* (Jos. *AJ* 6.322).

[152] Parallel: *basileúsantos* (Plb. 2.44.2).

In the first example, the period of the Israelites' obedience does not overlap with the period of their departure from their forefathers' ways. However, in the second it is clear that it remains 'up to the present day'. The pair of examples of *diaménō* differ from that of *agapáō* in that duration is inherent in the semantic contribution of the former, but not the latter. This is to say that in both the examples involving *agapáō* it is the fact of loving, or not, that is at issue. In the examples involving *diaménō*, by contrast, it is a non-cancellable part of the semantic contribution of the verb that the state of the subjects held for a discernable period of time.

Among event verbs, durativity is a feature of those describing activity/accomplishment events.[153] Criterial is their use in the imperfective, where they describe an event in process:

(83) ekeînoi...   pragmateuómenoi   toùs
those.M-NOM-PL...   labour.PRES-PTPL-MIDPAS-M-NOM-PL   ART.M-ACC-PL
polítas...   sunethísai   zên...
citizen.M-ACC-PL   accustom.AOR-INF-ACT   live.PRES-INF-ACT...
tền   khốran   **phuteúontas,**
ART.F-ACC-SG   land.F-ACC-SG   plant.PRES-PTPL-ACT-M-ACC-PL
tòn...   diédosan   lógon
ART.M-ACC-SG   tell.AOR-IND-ACT-3-PL   story.M-ACC-SG
'For they... while labouring to accustom the citizens to live... **by planting** the land, told the story...' (Plu. *Them.* 19.3)

(84) Kleódēmos   dé   phēsin...
Kleodemos.M-NOM-SG   PTCL   say.PRES-IND-ACT-3-SG
historôn   tà   perì   Ioudaíōn...
relate.PRES-PTPL-ACT-M-NOM-SG   ART.N-PL-ACC   about   Jewish.GEN-PL
hóti...
that
'Kleodemos... says... **while he is relating** the Jewish affairs... that...' (Jos. *AJ* 1.240)

In the first example, the field is presented as being in the process of being planted. The goal of the event is the complete planting of the field. In the second example, *historôn* describes an event which terminates when all the Jewish affairs have been related, and presents the particular act of 'saying' as a subinterval of that.

Change of state verbs are no different in this respect. Consider the following examples:

(85) oúte...   edúnanto...   toùs
nor...   be-able.IMPF-IND-MID-3-PL   ART.M-ACC-PL
prosbaínontas   kathorân
approach.PRES-PTPL-ACT-M-ACC-PL   see.PRES-INF-ACT
'Nor were they able... to see those who **were approaching**.' (Jos. *BJ* 4.77)

---

[153] Achievement events are, by contrast, non-durative. However, because their non-durativity is impossible to isolate from their terminativity, their behaviour is dealt with in the next section on terminativity.

(86) trapéntes　　　　　　　　　hoi　　　　　　　perì　　　tòn
turn.AOR-PTPL-ACT-NOM-SG　　*ART.M-NOM-PL*　　*around*　*ART.M-ACC-SG*
Nikólaon　　　　　　　　　**épheugon**　　　　　protropádēn
Nikolaos.M-NOM-SG　　**flee.IMPF-IND-ACT-3-PL**　*headlong*
hápantes
all.M-NOM-PL
'… Nicolaos' men all turned and **started fleeing** headlong.' (Plb. 5.69.9)

In both of these the change of location denoted by the imperfective can be seen to be in progress. In the first example the observers need to see those who are in the process of approaching: it is no good seeing them when they have already approached, since then it will be too late. In the second example, the goal of the 'fleeing' event is a position out of reach of those who are pursuing.

2.1.9.3 *Homogeneity in Greek*

Homogeneity enables us primarily to distinguish state verbs from activity/accomplishment and achievement verbs. Many homogeneous verbs in Greek can be distinguished from non-homogeneous verbs with reference to their behaviour in the perfective. Specifically, verbs describing homogeneous events have the capacity for their events to include topic time in a way that is not possible for non-homogeneous verbs. Accordingly, the perfective of non-homogeneous verbs, even where occurring in activity predicates, are always bounded:

(87) **dramṑn**　　　　　　　　　ephístatai
run.AOR-PTPL-ACT-M-NOM-SG　*stand-on.PRES-IND-MIDPAS-3-SG*
tôi　　　　　　　polemíōi…
ART.M-DAT-SG　*enemy.M-DAT-SG*
'[David] **ran** and stood on his enemy…' (Jos. *AJ* 6.190)

By contrast, homogeneous verbs allow readings where the state continues up to and includes topic time:

(88) = (80)
eulogḗseien　　　　　　　án　　　tis
praise.AOR-OPT-ACT-3-SG　*PTCL*　*INDEF-PRON.MF-NOM-SG*
tòn　　　　　　theòn　　　　**agapḗsanta**　　　　　tḗnde
ART.M-ACC-SG　*God.M-ACC-SG*　**love.AOR-PTPL-ACT-ACC-SG**　*this.F-ACC-SG*
tèn　　　　　　khṓran…　　　houtōs,　hṓste　sè
ART.F-ACC-SG　*land.F-ACC-SG*　*so*　　*that*　*you.ACC-SG*
poiêsai　　　　　basiléa.
make.AOR-INF-ACT　*king.M-ACC-SG*
'May one praise God **who has loved this land** so much that he made you king.' (Jos. *AJ* 8.173)

(89) = (82)
hē　　　　　　　dè　　　stephánē…　　　　mía
ART.F-NOM-SG　*PTCL*　*crown.F-NOM-SG…*　*one.F-NOM-SG*

ên		kaì	**diémeinen**	ákhri
be.IMPF-IND-3-SG		*and*	**remain.AOR-IND-ACT-3-SG**	*until*
têsde	tês	hēméras...		
this.F-GEN-SG	*ART.F-GEN-SG*	*day.F-GEN-SG...*		

'The crown, on which Moses wrote, was one and **has remained** up to the present day.' (Jos. *AJ* 8.93)

Although activities are durative, they cannot be broken down into infinite sub-events which are also instances of the same original event and so the perfective bounds them on the right.[154]

As well as state verbs, I also class among homogeneous verbs those describing eventualities that might not be classically identified as states, yet describe eventualities that are homogeneous in internal temporal constitution. This is the case for two verbs that would normally be classed as activity verbs: *emblépō* 'to look', *kháskō* 'to yawn, to gape' and *epimeidiáō* 'to smile':

(90)
toîs	dakrúousin	atenès
ART.M-DAT-PL	*weep.PRES-PTPL-M-DAT-PL*	*directly*
emblépsas...	**eîpen...**	
look-at.AOR-PTPL-ACT-M-SG	**say.AOR-IND-ACT-3-SG...**	

'... **looking** directly at those who were weeping **he said**...' (Jos. *BJ* 7.341)

(91)
kaì	**khanoúsēs**	**exéblusen**
and	**gape.AOR-PTPL-ACT-F-GEN-SG**	**gush-out.AOR-IND-ACT-3-SG**
húdōr	polù	
water.N-NOM-SG	*much.N-NOM-SG*	

'... **when** [the rock] **opened**, a large quantity of... water **gushed out**.' (Jos. *AJ* 3.37)

(92)
kaì	ho	Grâtos
and	*ART.M-NOM-SG*	*Gratos.M-NOM-SG*
meidiásas		**epispâtai**
smile.AOR-PTPL-ACT-M-NOM-SG		**grasp.PRES-IND-MIDPAS-3-SG**
tês	dexiâs...	
ART.F-GEN-SG	*hand.F-GEN-SG*	

'And Gratus **smiled, took** [Claudius] by the (right) hand...' (Jos. *AJ* 19.219)

In all three examples, the activity described in the perfective overlaps with the second event described. Furtheremore, in all three, while the verb does not describe a state as such, the activity concerned does not have phases or stages in the way that an event of running does. Their homogeneity, therefore, is closer to that of states than to that of canonical activities.

---

[154] Of course, where an activity or accomplishment verb describes a change of state on the part of the subject, it is perfectly possible for the poststate to include topic time. What concerns us here is the prestate subevent.

An interesting case of a non-state homogeneous verb is *diateléō* 'to continue', which describes an eventuality which is both durative and homogeneous. It therefore demonstrates behaviour parallel to that of *diaménō* 'to remain'. In the perfective it describes an unbounded durative state which can include topic time:

(93) hoi   mèn   egkhórioi   polloîs
     ART.M-NOM-PL *PTCL* *inhabitant.M-NOM-PL* *many.N-DAT-PL*
     anathḗmasin   arguroîs   kaì   khrusoîs
     offering.N-DAT-PL *silver.N-DAT-PL* *and* *gold.N-DAT-PL*
     dietélesan   timôntes   ákhri
     continue.AOR-IND-ACT-3-PL *honour.PRES-PTPL-ACT-M-NOM-PL* *until*
     tônde   tôn   historiôn
     these.F-GEN-PL *ART.F-GEN-PL* *history.F-GEN-PL*
     graphoménōn
     write.PRES-PTPL-MIDPAS-F-GEN-PL

'The inhabitants have **continued** to honour [the goddesses] with many offerings of silver and gold up to the time of writing of this history.' (Diod. Sic. 4.80.4)

The perfective homogeneity test only works for non-terminative verbs. Terminative verbs always describe telic events in the perfective because of the set terminal point of the lexical semantics of the verb. However, this is only an issue for terminative state verbs, since the homogeneity of achievement verbs, by virtue of their non-durativity and terminativity, is not relevant. Indeed, as will become clear in the ensuing investigation, the behaviour of terminative state verbs in the perfect is entirely governed by their terminativity and durativity, so that their homogeneity is in effect irrelevant.

2.1.9.4 *Terminativity in Greek*

Three kinds of terminative verbs can be distinguished: achievement verbs, change of state verbs and terminative state verbs. In the perfective these verbs are always presented in terms of their event's terminal point.

2.1.9.4.1 *Achievement verbs*

Achievement verbs are by their nature terminative, in that they describe events which initialise and terminate without requiring any conceptual duration:

(94) taútēn   mèn   oûn   **ekphobḗsas**
     this.F-ACC-SG *PTCL* *PTCL* **frighten.AOR-PTPL-ACT-M-NOM-SG**
     tòn   Sisimíthrēn   **élaben**.
     ART.M-ACC-SG *Sisimithres.M-ACC-SG* **take.AOR-IND-ACT-3-SG**

'So **having frightened** Sisimithres **he took** this [citadel].' (Plu. *Alexander* 58.3)

Since achievement verbs describe events with no perceptible duration, their use in the imperfective could be regarded as problematic: an event without perceptible duration cannot very easily be presented without reference to endpoints. Where instances do occur, they tend to denote iterative events:

(95) hopóte   gàr   apokteînaí   tina

whenever   *PTCL*   *kill.AOR-INF-ACT*   *INDEF-PRON.MF-ACC-SG*

ethelḗseian,   **exephóboun**   autòn.

want.AOR-OPT-ACT-3-PL   **terrify.*IMPF-IND-ACT-3-PL*   *him*

'For whenever they wanted to kill someone, **they would terrify him.**' (Cassius Dio 60.14.1)

Where a change of state event is described (see 2.1.9.4.2) the sense often merges with the assertion of a result state. Consider the following examples:[155]

(96) drân   ti   katà   tês

do.PRES-INF-ACT   *INDEF-PRON.N-ACC-SG*   *against*   *ART.F-GEN-SG*

gunaikòs   **apethárrei...**

woman.F-GEN-SG   **lack-courage.*IMPF-IND-ACT-3-SG*

'**he lacked the courage** to do anything against his wife' (Jos. *AJ* 15.214)

(97) khórion   Phalēroî   phēsi

estate.M-ACC-SG   *Phaleron.N-LOC-SG*   *say.PRES-IND-ACT-3-SG*

ginṓskein   Aristeídou

**perceive.*PRES-INF-ACT*   *Aristeides.M-GEN-SG*

genómenon...

become.AOR-PTPL-MID-N-ACC-SG

'[Demetrius of Phalerum] says **he knows** an estate at Phalerum which once belonged to Aristeides...' (Plu. *Arist.* 1.2)

(98) hékontes   **pisteúomen**   humâs

willing.M-NOM-PL   **believe.*PRES-IND-ACT-1-PL*   *you.ACC-PL*

katà   anágkēn   táde   pepoiēkénai

by   *necessity.F-ACC-SG*   *this.N-ACC-PL*   *do.PERF-INF-ACT*

'... you deserved punishment, since **we** willingly **believe** that you did these things out of necessity...' (App. *BC* 5.1.5)

In the first case this is probably because it is a negative statement, and therefore a negative assertion of an event also entails a negative assertion of the result state 'having courage'. The second case one could regard as meaning 'to perceive with the mind', i.e. referring to an event of recall. In the third case, the event of believing entails the state.

This is not to say that an event cannot be in view, as in the following example involving *ginṓskō* 'to perceive, know': [156]

(99) dúo...   êsan   hoi   pólemoi...

two...   *be.IMPF-IND-3-PL*   *ART.M-NOM-PL*   *battle.M-NOM-PL*

---

[155] Parallels: Plb. 3.64.3, App. *BC* 2.12.85.

[156] *ginóskō* has two senses: 1) 'to perceive', i.e. 'to come to know', or 2) 'to decide', both describing change of state. The latter, however, can involve a process element. Consequently the imperfective can describe the process of deciding, without indicating a particular result, as at App. *BC* 3.8.58.

têi	diódōi	eirgómenoi
ART.F-DAT-SG	passage.F-DAT-SG	prevent.pres-ptpl-midpas-m-nom-pl
mè **ginóskein**	tà	allélōn
NEG **perceive.PRES-INF-ACT**	ART.N-ACC-PL	each-other.GEN-PL

'There were two battles over the two marshes which were there, each prevented from **perceiving** the other by the passage.' (App. *BC* 3.9.67)

2.1.9.4.2 *Change of state (COS) verbs*

The biggest class of terminative verbs are those describing changes of state on the part of the subject, so-called UNACCUSATIVES, to which we will generally refer as COS verbs. These include both verbs describing changes of nature, e.g. 'to freeze' and those describing changes of location, e.g. 'to arrive'. They differ from verbs describing both homogeneous and non-homogeneous eventualities, in that they are a hybrid of the two, describing complex events consisting of a non-homogeneous pre-state subevent and a homogeneous poststate. This is most clearly seen in the perfective, where an event is asserted to have taken place and terminated, resulting in the poststate, which then holds at least until the next event described in the narrative sequence. The following example involves the change of location verb *anabaínō* 'go up':[157]

(100) ... **anabàs**   epì   tòn   toû
      go-up.AOR-PTPL-ACT-M-NOM-SG upon   *ART.M-ACC-SG*   *ART.M-GEN-SG*
      kérukos   líthon   en   óidêi
      herald.M-GEN-SG   *stone.M-ACC-SG*   *in*   *ode.F-DAT-SG*
      diexêlthe   tèn   elegeían...
      go-through.AOR-IND-ACT-3-SG   *ART.F-ACC-SG*   *elegy.F-ACC-SG*
      '... **having climbed** onto the stone of the herald, **he performed** the elegy with a song...' (Plu. *Sol.* 8.2)

In the first example Solon goes up on to the platform, and his new state is assumed to continue to hold for the next event, denoted by diexêlthe.

Change of nature verbs show the same characteristics:

(101) hē   mèn   oûn...   philía...   éti
      ART.F-NOM-SG   *PTCL*   *PTCL*   *friendship.F-NOM-SG*   *still*
      mâllon   **ēúxēse**   kaì   diaménein
      more   **grow.AOR-IND-ACT-3-SG**   *and*   *remain.PRES-INF-ACT*
      ómosan   eis   hápan.
      swear.AOR-IND-ACT-3-PL   *for*   *all.N-ACC-SG*
      'So the friendship [between Hiram and Solomon] **grew** even more from this, and **they swore** that it would remain forever...' (Jos. *AJ* 8.58)

---

[157] cf. the relationship between *anekhórēse* (*withdraw.AOR-IND-ACT-3-SG*) and *epeítheto* (*obey.AOR-IND-MID-3-SG*) at App. *BC* 5.3.23.

It is clear that the newly strengthened friendship between Solomon and Hiram is the context for the swearing of allegiance.

Notice that the kind of behaviour seen here is not unique to intransitive COS verbs. Transitive COS verbs may also behave in this way, provided the subject changes state during the course of the event:

(102) tòn   kháraka
    ART.M-ACC-SG   *camp.M-ACC-SG*
    peristephanōsantes...   hóplōn
    ***surround**.AOR-PTPL-ACT-M-NOM-PL*   *armour.N-GEN-PL*
    ktúpon   epoíoun
    loud-noise.M-ACC-SG   *make.IMPF-IND*   *-ACT-3-PL*
    athróoi...
    together.M-NOM-PL

'... **having surrounded the camp**... they proceeded all together **to make** a loud noise with their weapons...' (Dion. Hal. *Ant. Rom.* 8.66.2)

Here the subject participants change state, specifically location, in that they surround the camp, and, in their new location of being around the camp begin making a noise with their weapons.

2.1.9.4.3 *Terminative state verbs*

State verbs are not all the same regarding the expectation of an endpoint. Specifically, there exists in Greek a group of state verbs that describe states with a natural expiry point. This group is primarily composed on verbs describing offices of state, such as *stratēgéō* 'to serve as general', *hupateúō* 'to serve as consul' and *dēmarkhéō* 'to serve as tribune'. Unlike being a king, for example, once a general, one is not always a general.[158] I call these TERMINATIVE STATE verbs. These are identified as distinct from other state verbs on the basis of their behaviour in the perfective: the states they describe are never presented as including topic time.[159] The following example of *stratēgéō* is typical:[160]

---

[158] However, although these verbs have a natural expiry which is a function of time, the precise expiry point is not pre-determined. For this reason they are compatible with 'for α time' expressions, for which see below in this section.

[159] As with all other state verbs, the imperfective simply asserts that the state holds, e.g. *hupateúousin* (*be-consul.PRES-PTPL-ACT-DAT-PL*, App. *Hisp.* 14.84).

[160] In total there are 7 non-negativised indicatives or participial aorist forms of this verb attested in the original corpus, and in all cases the state clearly terminated at a point prior to topic time. The examples are App. *Pun.* 11.74, where the Carthaginian Hasdrubal, general in the war against Massanassus (*stratēgḗsanti, be-general.AOR-PTPL-ACT-DAT-SG*) is put to death for his failure, App. *Mith.* 17.118 and 121, where Pompey described from the perspective of the writer Appian as *tòn stratēgḗsanta* (*be-general.AOR-PTPL-ACT-ACC-SG*) during the Mithridatic War, Plu. *Lys.* 16.1, where Lysander sends back the wealth he had obtained in Athens via Gylippus, who is described as *toû stratēgḗsantos* (*be-general.AOR-PTPL-ACT-GEN-SG*) at Sicily: the context is clear that he is no longer serving as general in Sicily; Plu. *Nic.* 8.1, where Cleon is described as having brought home as

(103) ho   dè   **estratḗgēse**   tôi
ART.M-NOM-SG PTCL   be-general.AOR-IND-ACT-3-SG   ART.M-DAT-SG
Broútōi   Bithunías   kaì Broútou
Brutus.M-DAT-SG Bithunia.F-GEN-SG   and Brutus.M-GEN-SG
pesóntos   Antōníōi   paradoùs
fall.M-GEN-SG   Antonius.M-DAT-SG   hand-over.AOR-PTPL-ACT-M-NOM-SG
Bithunían   **katékhthē**
Bithunia.F-ACC-SG   bring-back.AOR-IND-ACT-3-SG
'... the other **served as general** for Brutus over Bithynia, and when Brutus
fell, having handed the province over to Antony, **was brought back.**'
(App. *BC* 4.6.46)

Here Brutus is described as taking command of Bithynia, and then as surrendering it to Antony. Here there are two aorist indicatives, related in a non-overlapping
way as follows:

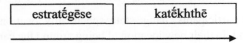

katékhthē is in turn related to two events described by the two perfective participles
pesóntos and paradoús as follows:

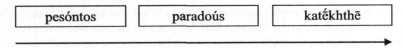

Note that, since serving as consul and/or general are events with a natural expiry,
they are not only terminative but also durative. This is explicit in the following example
where the expiry of Timoxenos' office is specifically referred to:

(104) ho   mèn   oûn Timóxenos   ho   tót'
ART.M-NOM-SG PTCL   PTCL Timóxenos.M-NOM-SG ART.M-NOM-SG then
éth'   **hupárkhōn**   **stratēgós**,
still   exist.PRES-PTPL-ACT-M-NOM-SG   general.M-NOM-SG
hóson   oúpō   lēgoúsēs   tês
for-as-long-as   not-yet   cease.PRES-PTPL-ACT-F-GEN-SG   ART.F-GEN-SG
arkhês...
beginning.F-GEN-SG
'So Timoxenus who **was** still **general** at that time, for as long as his office
did not cease...' (Plb. 4.7.6)

---

prisoners of war having served admirably as general alongside Demosthenes (*stratēgḗsas, be-
general.AOR-PTPL-ACT-NOM-SG*). At *Nic.* 16.3 and *Nic.* 17.1 *stratēgéō* is used in a different sense,
namely 'to show generalship'. Jos. *AJ* 7.197 uses *stratēgéō* in another sense, specifically, 'to plot
so as to achieve'.

However, they do occur with 'for *a* time' expressions showing that they are compatible with the interpretation of multiple conceptual moments:[161]

(105) Timoléōn...   eteleútēse,
       *Timoleon.*M-NOM-SG   *die.*AOR-IND-ACT-3-SG
       stratēgḗsas   étē   oktṓ
       be-general.AOR-PTPL-ACT-M-NOM-SG *year.*N-ACC-PL **eight**
       'Timoleon... died, **having been general for eight years**.' (Diod. Sic. 16.90)

2.1.9.5 *Conclusion*

Lexical aspectual classes in Greek may be differentiated in terms of three features of the events they describe:

1. Durativity: plurality of conceptual moments;
2. Terminativity: terminal point for the event set by the lexical verb;
3. Homogeneity: homogeneous internal temporal constitution.

The feature of durativity captures the difference between eventualities that have multiple conceptual moments and those that do not, i.e. plural vs. single events in Ramchand's terms. Thus accomplishments and activities, as well as terminative and durative states, are durative eventualities, since the denotation of multiple conceptual moments is intrinsic to the semantics of the eventualities described by the verb. By contrast, non-durative states, single eventualities in Ramchand's terms, do not carry the denotation of multiple conceptual moments. Thus while 'serving as general' entails a state lasting a certain length of time, 'being eager' may last only a moment. This is to say that there is no requirement that a non-durative state hold for any length of time.

The feature of terminativity captures the fact that certain verbs denote inherently delimited events, while others do not. A terminative state verb, such as *stratēgéō*, 'serve as general', describes an event with a set expiry, while *ékhō* 'have', does not. Similarly, the non-homogeneous durative eventuality *epanérkhomai*, 'return', has a terminal point set by the verb itself, while the similarly non-homogeneous durative eventuality *trékhō*, 'run', does not.

Finally, the feature of homogeneity captures in most cases the essential difference between states and events: since states may be analysed into an infinite number of sub-events that in themselves may be regarded as states in their own right, they are homogeneous. By contrast, accomplishments and activities cannot be infinitely sub-divided in this way, and are therefore non-homogeneous. However, we did identify some events that also demonstrate the property of homogeneity.

Within this framework achievement verbs, such as *ekphobéō*, 'frighten', and *anatharréō*, 'be encouraged', are treated as non-durative non-homogeneous termina-

---

[161] This does not in itself show that these verbs are durative, since, as we argued at 2.1.9.1, durativity is not in most cases equipollent. However, common sense allows us to say that 'being a general' is not an achievement, since it cannot be accomplished without conceptual duration.

tive verbs. This is to say that, insofar as the eventualities these verbs describe have no conceptual duration, they are tied to a single conceptual moment. However, they are non-homogeneous in that they cannot be subdivided, as can states, into an infinite number of sub-events of the same denotation. Finally, they are terminative since they have a set expiry, namely the completion of the event.[162]

Table 5 summarises the framework with which we will be working as we analyse the behaviour of the Greek perfect, while Table 6 gives examples of Greek verbs included in each category.

2.2 Homogeneous verbs

2.2.1 Introduction

All state verbs, as well as some others, are characterised by homogeneity. However, as we have argued in the introduction to this chapter, state verbs in Greek differ as to their denotion of durativity and terminativity. We argued that three types of state verbs are distinguishable. By far the biggest class is that of non-durative state verbs, which are not associated with any particular minimal duration or expiry. Among others this class consists of all mental state verbs, e.g. *agapáō* 'I love', *miséō* 'I hate', and verbs denoting physical properties, e.g. *ēreméō* 'to be quiet', *sigáō* 'to be silent'. Durative state verbs, by contrast, consisting largely if not solely of *ménō* 'I remain' and its compounds, denote a situation that must hold for a discernable amount of time before the state may be said to hold. As with non-durative state verbs, these verbs describe events not associated with a particular expiry. Finally, terminative state verbs are distinguished by denoting both durativity and terminativity. This group consists of verbs denoting the holding of public office, such as *stratēgéō* 'to be general/praetor', *hupateúō* 'to be consul'.[163]

Table 5: Lexical aspectual types

	Homogeneous	Durative	Terminative
Non-durative homogeneous	+	-	-
Durative state	+	+	-
Terminative state	+	+	+
Achievement	-	-	+
Activity/Accomplishment	-	+	-
Terminative durative COS	-	+	+

---

[162] This differs from Ramchand's analysis of achievement verbs as 'dual', i.e. with two conceptual moments. For her, an achievement event makes reference to two states, a 'before' and an 'after', and thereby two conceptual moments are in view. However, it seems to me that while achievement verbs inevitably make reference to two conceptual moments, this should be seen as an implication of the key event semantics of the verb, describing a single happening, which brings about a new state.

[163] *dēmarkhéō* 'be a tribune' also belongs in this group.

Table 6. Examples of lexical aspectual types

Non-durative homogeneous	*agapáō* 'I love', *miséō* 'I hate', *ēreméō* 'to be quiet', *sigáō* 'to be silent', *basileúō* 'to rule'
Durative homogeneous	*ménō* 'to remain' and compounds; *diateléō* 'to continue'
Terminative homogeneous	*stratēgéō* 'to be general', *hupateúō* 'to be consul', *dēmarkhéō* 'to be tribune'
Achievement	*ekphobéō* 'to frighten', *nikáō* 'to defeat', *apothnḗiskō* 'to die'
Activity/Accomplishment	*poiéō* 'to act, do', *trékhō* 'to run'
Terminative durative COS	*érkhomai* 'to come', *-baínō* 'to go'

2.2.2 Non-durative state verbs

The perfect of non-durative state verbs can be found denoting each of pure state, continued state and anterior state. Pure state readings are particular prevalent among mental state verbs:[164]

(106) ô   Mōüsê,   xrô   nómois
      PTCL   *Moses.M-NOM-SG*   *use.PRES-IND-MIDPAS-2-SG*   *law.M-DAT-PL*
      hoîs   autòs   **espoúdakas...**
      REL-PRON.M-DAT-PL   *self.M-NOM-SG*   **be-eager.PERF-IND-ACT-2-SG**
      'Moses, you are using laws, for which **you** yourself **are zealous**...' (Jos. *AJ* 4.145)

(107) ... metatheînai   toùs   **ēgnoēkótas**
      change.AOR-INF-ACT   *ART.M-ACC-PL*   **not-know.PERF-PTPL-ACT-M-ACC-PL**
      holoskherōs   astokhoûsin...
      completely   *fail.PRES-IND-ACT-3-PL*
      '... [the Carthaginians] completely fail... to change **those who are ignorant**.' (Plb. 1.67.5)

In the first example Moses is said to administer laws for which he is zealous. This statement only makes sense if he is still zealous at the time when he is administering the laws. In the second example, the people who fail to be corrected by the Carthaginians must be ignorant at topic time.

Pure state readings of the perfect are, however, not limited to mental state verbs. In the following example an inanimate fixed object, namely a corridor, is said to 'be quiet':

(108) trépetai   dè   katà   stenōpòn
      turn.PRES-IND-MIDPAS-3-SG   PTCL   *down*   *corridor.M-ACC-SG*

---

[164] Parallels: *espoúdake* (*be-eager.PERF-IND-ACT*, Jos. *AJ* 8.202), *espoudákesan* (*be-eager.PLPF-IND-ACT*, App. *Hisp.* 15.94), *espoudákei* (*be-eager.PLPF-IND-ACT*, Jos. *AJ* 1.265); *lelussēkósin* (*be-mad. PERF-PTPL-ACT*, Jos. *BJ* 4.371), *lelussēkótōn* (*be-mad.PERF-PTPL-ACT*, Jos. *BJ* 2.213); *memēnénai* (*be-mad.PERF-INF-ACT*, Plu. *Alc.* 17.4), *memēnósin* (*be-mad.PERF-PTPL-ACT*, App. *BC* 1.3.24), *memēnóta* (*be-mad.PERF-PTPL-ACT*, Jos. *AJ* 10.119), *memēnótas* (*be-mad.PERF-PTPL-ACT*, Jos. *AJ* 1.116), *memēnótes* (*be-mad.PERF-PTPL-ACT*, Jos. *BJ* 1.352, *AJ* 14.480), *memēnóti* (*be-mad.PERF-PTPL-ACT*, App. *BC* 1.7.61) etc.; *tetharrēkóti* (*have-courage.PERF-PTPL-ACT*, Jos. *AJ* 18.334).

ēremēkóta...
be-quiet.PERF-PTPL-ACT-M-ACC-SG
'Instead he turned down a **quiet** narrow corridor...' (Jos. *AJ* 19.104)

That past reference is not required of the perfect of non-durative state verbs is demonstrated by their capacity to occur as complements to control verbs or in contexts where past reference is impossible:

(109) ho   mèn   gàr   Hurkanòs...
      ART.M-NOM-SG PTCL   PTCL *Hyrcanus.M-NOM-SG*
      sugkhōrôn   têi   túxēi
      consent.PRES-PTPL-ACT-M-NOM-SG *ART.F-DAT-SG* *FATE.F-DAT-SG*
      pân   tò   di'   ekeínēs
      all.N-ACC-SG *ART.n-acc-sg* *through* *that.F-GEN-SG*
      ginómenon   **ēgapēkénai.**
      become.PRES-PTPL-MIDPAS-N-ACC-SG *be-content.PERF-INF-ACT*
      'For Hyrcanus... **consenting** with fate **to be content**[165] with everything that would happen through her.' (Jos. *AJ* 15.165)

(110) Hēródēs...   tēreîn   ēxíou
      Herod.M-NOM-SG   *watch.PRES-INF-ACT*   *ask.IMPF-IND-ACT-3-SG*
      parà   tò   deîpnon,   pôs   tà
      at   *ART.N-ACC-SG* *dinner.N-ACC-SG*   *how*   *ART.N-NOM-PL*
      pròs   allélous   **eskhḗkasin**
      between   *one-another.M-ACC-PL*   *hold.PERF-IND-ACT-3-SG*
      'Herod... asked [Pheroras] to watch at dinner, how matters **hold** between them.' (Jos. *AJ* 16.223)

In the second example it is clear that *eskhḗkasin* does not carry any past reference, since at topic time Pheroras cannot have carried out the task.

Lack of any prior event may also be made explicit with the collocation of adverbs such as *euthús* 'immediately', denoting onset of the state at topic time:

(111) kaì   tò   mèn   phármakon   **euthùs**
      and   *ART.N-ACC-SG* *PTCL* *poison.N-ACC-SG* *immediately*
      espoudakóti   zēteîn   oukh
      be-eager.PERF-PTPL-ACT-M-DAT-SG   *look-for.PRES-INF-ACT* *NEG*
      heuréthē.
      find.AOR-IND-PAS-3-SG
      'And though he **immediately set about eagerly** to look for a poison, none was found.' (Jos. *AJ* 16.254)

---

[165] For this meaning of *agapáō* see LSJ *ad loc.* III.

While pure state readings are certainly common among non-durative state verbs, they are not the only readings. Both continued state and anterior state may be found. Consider the following continued state example:[166]

(112) sunébaine...   Dēmétrion
    happen.IMPF-IND-ACT-3-SG   *Demetrius.M-ACC-SG*
    katapephronēkóta   dè   **próteron...**
    despise.PERF-PTPL-ACT-M-ACC-SG   *PTCL*   *previously*
    Rōmaíous...   portheîn...   tàs...   poleis
    Romans.M-ACC-PL *sack.PRES-INF-ACT* *ART.F-ACC-PL* *city.F-ACC-PL*
    hupò   Rōmaíous   tattoménas...
    under   *Romans.M-ACC-PL* *rule.PRES-PTPL-MIDPAS-M-ACC-PL*
    'For it happened... that Demetrius... **having previously despised** Romans... began sacking... the cities... which were under Roman rule.' (Plb. 3.16.2f.)

Demetrios starts despising the Romans prior to topic time, but this despising continues up to topic time, since it results in the sacking of Roman cities.

Some examples are ambiguous between pure state and continued state:

(113) gameîn   tàs
    marry.PRES-INF-ACT *ART.F-ACC-PL*
    hētairēkuías   ekóluse...
    be-prostitute.PERF-PTPL-ACT-F-ACC-PL *forbid.AOR-IND-ACT-3-SG*
    '[Moses] forbade [them] from marrying **(those who are or were?) prostitutes...**' (Jos. *AJ* 3.276)

The point seems to be that once one has been a prostitute, and therefore disqualified from marriage with a priest. Whether or not one actually is a prostitute at topic time may therefore not be relevant.

The flexibility in time reference terms of the perfect of non-durative state verbs is demonstrated by the behaviour of *bebasíleuka*. The examples below give pure state and anterior state respectively.

(114) Antíokhos...   héktos...   Asías...
    Antiochus.M-NOM-SG *sixth.M-NOM-SG* *Asia.F-GEN-SG*
    bebasileukótos...   Hellēspontíous
    rule.PERF-PTPL-ACT-GEN-SG *Hellespontine.M-ACC-PL*
    epéiei...
    invade.IMPF-IND-ACT-3-SG
    'Antiochus... the sixth **to rule** Asia... **invaded** the Hellespontines...' (App. *Syr.* 1.1)

(115) all'   éphthē   prìn   hupsôsai
    but   *be-previous.AOR-IND-MIDPAS-3-SG* *before* *raise.AOR-INF-ACT*

---

[166] That the perfect of this verb may be used in contexts where it is not clear that temporal depth is implied may be seen at Dinarchus *In Demosthenem* 104.

tò érgon teleutḗsas
ART.N-ACC-SG *work.N-ACC-SG* *die.AOR-PTPL-ACT-M-NOM-SG*
en Kaisareíāi **bebasileukṑs** mèn
in *Caesarea.F-DAT-SG* **reign.PERF-PTPL-ACT-M-NOM-SG** *PTCL*
étē tría
year.N-ACC-PL *three.N-ACC-PL*
'But [Agrippa] **died** in Caesarea before he could raise [the wall] **having reigned** for three years...' (Jos. *BJ* 2.219)

Temporal bounding of an event, such as by means of a 'for α time' expression, is not limited to such adjuncts if other elements in the context make it clear that the event must be bounded. In the next example the perfect participle clearly describes a series of rulers of Syria who cannot all be ruling at the same time:

(116) tosáde mèn dè kaì perì
  so-much.N-ACC-PL *PTCL* *PTCL* *PTCL* *about*
  Makedónōn **tôn** Surías
  Macedonian.M-GEN-PL *ART.M-GEN-PL* *Syria.F-GEN-SG*
  bebasileukótōn eîkhon
  rule.PERF-PTPL-ACT-M-GEN-PL *have.IMPF-IND-ACT-3-PL*
  eipeîn...
  say.AOR-INF-ACT
  'I had as much to say about the situation regarding the Macedonians **who had ruled Syria**...' (App. *Syr.* 11.70)

Indeed, one perfect, *éskhēka* from *ékhō* 'have', can be found denoting all three of pure state, durative state and anterior state:

(117) hḗ te Mariámmē...
  ART.F-NOM-SG *PTCL* *Mariam.F-NOM-SG*
  ḗkhtheto...   tôi mḗd' ei
  be-annoyed.IMPF-IND-MIDPAS-3-SG *ART.M-DAT-SG* *NEG* *if*
  páskhoi ti deinòn
  suffer.PRES-OPT-ACT-3-SG *INDEF-PRON.N-ACC-SG* *terrible.N-ACC-SG*
  ekeînos elpída toû
  that.M-NOM-SG *hope.F-ACC-SG* *ART.M-GEN-SG*
  biōsesthai di' autòn **eskhēkénai**...
  live.FUT-INF-MID *through* *he.M-ACC-SG* **have.PERF-INF-ACT**
  'Mariam... was annoyed by the fact that she did not **have the hope** of living through [the king] if something should happen to him...' (Jos. *AJ* 15.204)

(118) thaumáseie d' án tis
  wonder.AOR-OPT-ACT-3-SG *PTCL* *PTCL* *INDEF-PRON.MF-NOM-SG*
  tôn anthrṓpōn tḕn pròs
  ART.M-GEN-PL *person.M-GEN-PL* *ART.F-ACC-SG* *to*
  hēmâs apékhtheian, hḕn...
  we.ACC-PL *hostility.F-ACC-SG* *REL-PRON.F-ACC-SG*

diatetelékasin   **eskhēkótes.**
continue.PERF-IND-ACT-3-PL   *have.PERF-PTPL-ACT-M-NOM-PL*
'Someone might wonder at the hostility people show us, which... **they have continued to hold.**' (Jos. *AJ* 3.179)

(119) phronḗsei   kaì   ploútōi
     wisdom.F-DAT-SG   *and*   *wealth.M-DAT-SG*
     dienegkṑn   tôn   prò   autoû
     surpass.AOR-PTPL-ACT-M-NOM-SG   *ART.M-GEN-PL*   *before*   *he.GEN-SG*
     tḕn   Hebraíōn   arkhḕn
     ART.F-ACC-SG   *Hebrews.M-GEN-PL*   *rule.F-ACC-SG*
     eskhēkótōn   ouk   epémeine
     have.PERF-PTPL-ACT-M-GEN-PL   *NEG*   *remain-in.AOR-IND-ACT-3-SG*
     toútois   ákhri   teleutês...
     this.M-DAT-PL   *until*   *end.F-GEN-SG*
'... though he surpassed those who **had held** the throne of the Hebrews before him in wisdom and wealth, he did not remain in these until the end...' (Jos. *AJ* 8.190)

Since the perfect of a non-durative state verb may or may not carry past reference, it is clear that past reference is in principle independent of lexical semantics in state verbs. However, this observation does not permit us to generalise and say that any state verb may carry pure, continued or anterior state semantics. This is because there are two semantic categories of state verb which are obliged to carry past reference, whether continued or anterior state, namely durative and terminative state verbs. It is to these that I now turn.

2.2.3 *Durative state verbs*

Durative state verbs are distinguished from other state verbs by asserting not only that the time structure of the event described is homogeneous, but also that a minimal discernable passage of time must elapse in order for the situation to be said to hold. Perfects of this state verb class may denote either continued or anterior state. Prototypical of the durative state verb class is *ménō*, 'to remain', and compounds. In the following examples this semantic characteristic is highlighted by the external adverbial expressions *ek toû próteron kheimônos* 'from the previous winter' and *eis nûn* 'until now' respectively.

(120) = (7) (19)
     epì   gàr   tḕn   proüpárkhousan
     on   *PTCL*   *ART.F-ACC-SG*   *exist-before.PRES-PTPL-ACT-F-ACC-SG*
     khíona kaì   **diamemenēkuîan**   **ek**
     snow.F-ACC-SG and   **remain.PERF-PTPL-ACT-F-ACC-SG**   **from**
     toû   **próteron**   **kheimônos**   árti
     ART.GEN-SG   **earlier**   **winter.GEN-SG**   *recently*
     tês   ep' étous   peptōkuías...
     ART.F-GEN-SG present-year   *fall.PERF-PTPL-ACT-F-GEN-SG*
'For on top of the snow which **had remained from the previous winter**, that from the present year had just fallen...' (Plb. 3.55.1)

(121) oud'   àn   autoì   parabaíēmen
NEG   PTCL   self.M-NOM-PL   transgress.AOR-OPT-ACT-1-PL
toû   nómou   tèn   proagóreusin
ART.M-GEN-SG   law.M-GEN-SG   ART.F-ACC-SG   proclamation.F-ACC-SG
theoû...   **eis   nûn**   aparábatoi
*God.M-GEN-SG   **to   now**   untransgressing.M-NOM-PL*
memenēkótes
remain.PERF-PTPL-ACT-M-NOM-PL

'... nor would we transgress the proclamation of the law of God, since... we **have remained to this moment** guiltless of transgressing it...' (Jos. *AJ* 18.266)

The state described by the perfect of a durative state verb may have terminated prior to topic time:

(122) pâsin   ex   ísou   toîs
all.M-DAT-PL   from   equal.N-GEN-SG   ART.M-DAT-PL
sustrateusaménois   merízesthai
share-in-expedition.AOR-PTPL-MID-M-DAT-PL   share.PRES-INF-MIDPAS
tèn   ōphéleian,   kaì   taût'   epì
ART.F-ACC-SG   due.F-ACC-SG   and   this.N-NOM-PL   for
phulakêi   tôn   skeuôn
guarding.F-DAT-SG   ART.N-GEN-PL   baggage.N-GEN-PL
memenēkótōn...
stay.PERF-PTPL-ACT-GEN-PL

'[David said that they should]... distribute the dues to all those who had shared in the expedition, because the rest **had stayed behind** to protect their baggage...' (Jos. *AJ* 6.366)

This is may or may not be accompanied by bounding on the right by means of a 'for α time' expression.[167]

(123) heîlon   dè   kaì   tò
take.AOR-IND-ACT-3-PL   PTCL   PTCL   ART.N-ACC-SG
Muttístraton,   **polloùs   khrónous**
Myttistratus.m-acc-sg   many.m-acc-pl   year.m-acc-pl
hupomemenēkòs   tèn   poliorkían...
withstand.PERF-PTPL-ACT-N-ACC-SG   ART.F-ACC-SG   siege.F-ACC-SG

'And they took Myttistratus, **which had withstood** the siege **for many years...**' (Plb. 1.24.11)

As such these examples are to be interpreted as anteriors, as the following diagrammatic representation of the second example shows:

hupomemenēkòs	heîlon

---

[167] It should be noted that mental state verbs are not attested in the corpus with a 'for α time' expression bounding the event at its terminal point. Whether this is purely due to chance is hard to tell.

The perfects of durative state verbs, while always carrying past time reference, are in themselves indeterminate between continued and anterior state readings. The perfects of terminative state verbs, by contrast, covered in the next subsection, always denote anterior states.

2.2.4 Terminative state verbs

While states may be externally bounded by a 'for α time' expression, states may also be delimited by the semantics of the lexical verb. Such bounding is associated with states with a set expiry, i.e. states that have a natural expiration and cannot be assumed *ceteris paribus* to hold indefinitely. In the corpus examined two such verbs were found: *stratēgéō* 'serve as consul/general' and *hupateúō* 'serve as consul'.

Predicates headed by a terminative state verb in the perfect always describe a situation that terminated prior to topic time. The clearest case is the following:

(124) Thouránios   dè   ou
     Thouranius.m-nom-sg PTCL   NEG
     stratēgôn   mèn   éti,   all'
     be-general.PRES-PTPL-ACT-M-NOM-SG PTCL *still* *but*
     estratēgēkṓs...
     be-general.PERF-PTPL-ACT-M-NOM-SG
     'Thourianios, who was no longer praetor, but **had formerly served as such...**' (App. *BC* 4.4.18)

Here there is an explicit equation between the present stem and the perfect whereby *estratēgēkṓs* = not *stratēgôn*. This is to say that there is an explicit contrast between the imperfective and the perfect. The verb demonstrates the same behaviour in the pluperfect:

(125) ho   dè   huiòs   tōi
     ART.M-NOM-SG PTCL *son.M-NOM-SG*   *ART.M-DAT-SG*
     Kaísari   sunestrateúeto   kaì
     Caesar.M-DAT-SG *campaign-together.IMPF-IND-MIDPAS-3-SG* *and*
     estratēgékei   kaì   hóde   perì
     be-general.PLPF-IND-ACT-3-SG *and* *this.M-NOM-SG* *at*
     tò   Áktion.
     ART.N-ACC-SG *Actium.N-ACC-SG*
     'but the son [of Metellus] served under Caesar (i.e. Octavian), and **had been a general** too at Actium.' (App. *BC* 4.6.42)

The topic time of the pluperfect indicative *estratēgékei* is set by the events which immediately precede in the narrative, namely the capture of the younger Metellus' father after the battle (*heálō*, i.e. aorist indicative active).[168] At this point the younger Metellus was still a soldier (*sunestrateúeto*) but he was not

---

[168] The present sentence in turn sets the context for what follows, namely where the younger Metellus intercedes to Octavian on his father's behalf.

general at Actium (*estratēgékei perì tò Áktion*) because the battle of Actium is over at topic time. The adverbial phrase *perì tò Áktion* should therefore be seen as defining the event time, i.e. when he was general, not the topic time. The perfect stem of *stratēgéō* therefore describes in this example a state which is terminated at topic time.[169]

The same kind of behaviour may be seen in the case of the one example of the perfect active stem of *hupateúō*:

(126) tóte   dè   Soulpíkion...   kaì...   Márion,
then   PTCL   *Soulpikius.M-ACC-SG*   *and*   *Marius.M-ACC-SG*
hexákis   **hupateukóta...**
six-times   **be-consul.PERF-PTPL-ACT-M-ACC-SG**
polemíous   Rōmaíōn   epsēphisto ...
enemy.M-ACC-PL   *Roman.M-GEN-PL*   *vote.PERF-IND-MIDPAS-3-SG*
eînai   kaì   tòn   entukhónta   nēpoineì
be.INF   *and*   *ART.M-ACC-SG*   *meet.AOR-PTPL-ACT-M-ACC-SG*   *with-impunity*
kteínein   è   anágein   epì   toùs
kill.PRES-INF-ACT   *or*   *lead-up.PRES-INF-ACT*   *to*   *ART.M-ACC-PL*
hupátous...
consuls.M-ACC-PL...

'It was voted that Sulpicius... and... Marius, **who had been six times a consul**... were enemies of the Romans and that anyone that met them could kill them with impunity or take them before the consuls...' (App. *BC* 1.7.60)

Here not only does the perfect active participle *hupateukóta* collocate with the adverb *hexákis*, which implies that the state has terminated at least five times prior to topic time, but it is also clear that Marius is not consul at topic time, since it is decided that he should be brought to the consuls (*anágein eis toùs hupátous*), thereby implying that he is not consul at topic time.

---

[169] Parallel: App. *BC* 1.14.121 (where it is clear that the state does not hold at topic time because the verb is collocated with a *katá* + acc. phrase denoting the period of time during which the state did indeed hold). Although it remains to conduct an exhaustive search, the following instances of *hupáteuka* were found using TLG, in all of which the state is terminated prior to topic time: *dìs hupateukótos* (Diod. Sic. 34/35.5.1), *pollákis hupateukótos* (Diod. Sic. 38/39.15.1), *dothênai tèn hupáteian andrásin ek tôn hupateukótōn* (Dion. Hal. *Ant. Rom.* 8.87.1), *Mánios... Akúllios ho hupateukòs* (Posidonius *Frag.* [Theiler] 247; Manius Aquillius was consul in 101 BC, whereas the events being recounted here took place in 88 BC), *anèr tôn hupateukótōn* (Herodian *Ab excessu divi Marci* 2.6.8), *Mágnos... ên tôn... hupateukótōn* (Herodian *Ab excessu divi Marci* 7.1.5), *ándras te hupateukótas exépempsen* (Herodian *Ab excessu divi Marci* 8.5.5), *háte triton hupateukòs* (Cassius Dio 40.44.2; of Pompey: from the context it is clear that the events described take place under the following consulship), *hupateukòs* (52.22.5), *hupateukòs* (59.30.2), *oukh hupateukòs* (60.20.5), *hupateukòs gérōn* (75.8.2), *hupateukótōn* (36.23.4, 52.22.2, 52.33.3, 53.13.5, 53.13.8, 53.14.1), *katà tôn hupateukótōn* (52.32.3), *hustátōi tôn hupateukótōn* (54.15.5), *tôn d' hupateukótōn* (54.15.6); *hupáteuka* (Epictetus *Dissertationes* 4.1.8).

2.2.5 *Non-state homogeneous verbs*

In the introduction (2.1.9.3) we pointed out that homogeneity is not restricted to state verbs *per se*. We noted that *dateléō* 'to continue' demonstrates behaviour parallel to durative state verbs in the perfective, by describing a situation that can include topic time. This parallel behaviour extends to the perfect, where it can similarly be found describing a situation starting prior to topic time and including it:

(127) = (118)

thaumáseie	d'	án	tis
wonder.AOR-OPT-ACT-3-SG	*PTCL*	*PTCL*	*INDEF-PRON.MF-NOM-SG*
tôn	anthrṓpōn	tḕn	pròs
ART.M-GEN-PL	*person.M-GEN-PL*	*ART.F-ACC-SG*	*to*
hēmâs	apékhtheian,	hḕn...	
we.ACC-PL	*hostility.F-ACC-SG*	*REL-PRON.F-ACC-SG*	
diatetelékasin		**eskhēkótes.**	
continue.PERF-IND-ACT-3-PL		*have.PERF-PTPL-ACT-M-NOM-PL*	

'Someone might wonder at the hostility people show us, which... **they have continued to hold**.' (Jos. *AJ* 3.179)

The time structure that this verb displays in the perfect is therefore the same as that of durative state verbs.

2.2.6 *Conclusion*

Verbs with homogeneous time structure can be found denoting pure state, continued state and anterior state in the perfect. Past reference is not, therefore, guaranteed by a verb's homogeneous time structure. The temporal semantics of state verbs do, however, have a bearing on past reference, specifically the semantic features terminativity and durativity. Table 7 summarises the findings.

The finding that past reference is obligatory in state verbs carrying the semantic features of durativity and terminativity, while it is optional in others leads in turn to the inference that, while homogeneous time structure does not in itself lead to past time reference, the semantic features of durativity and terminativity do guarantee this for the perfect, in the denotation of continued state and anteriority respectively.

Table 7. State verbs and past time reference

	Pure state	Continued state	Anterior state
Non-durative	+	+	+
Durative	-	+	+
Terminative	-	-	+

2.3 Non-durative terminative verbs (describing achievements)

Achievement verbs describe eventualities without obligatory denotation of conceptual duration (durativity) but which are terminative. Minimally, events described by achievement verbs can have no conceptual duration at all.

For these verbs whether or not their perfects carry past time reference is dependent on where the event is located relative to topic time. The means of location is either contextual or by means of an adverbial expression. If the event is located at topic time, the event can be construed as taking place instantly at topic time:

(128) **hiketeúō,**   páter,   éphē,
beseech.PRES-IND-ACT-1-SG   *father.M-VOC-SG*   *say.PAST-IND-ACT-3-SG*
mēdén   mou   **prokategnōkénai...**
in-no-way   *I.GEN-SG*   **prejudge.*PERF-INF-ACT***
"'**I beseech** you, father," he said, "in no way **to prejudge** me..."' (Jos. *BJ* 1.621)

In behaviour parallel to that of non-durative state verbs, an achievement eventuality can be explicitly asserted to occur at topic time by means of the adverbial *euthús* 'immediately', as in the following example:[170]

(129) ho   dè   Nikías   **euthùs**   autòs
ART.M-NOM-SG   *PTCL*   *Nikías.M-NOM-SG*   **immediately**   *self.M-NOM-SG*
kaì   parà   phúsin   hupò   tês
and   *beyond*   *nature.F-ACC-SG*   *by*   *ART.F-GEN-SG*
en   tôi   parónti   hrṓmēs   kaì
in   *ART.F-DAT-SG*   *present.M-DAT-SG*   *strength.F-GEN-SG*   *and*
túkhēs   **anatetharrēkṓs...**
fortune.F-GEN-SG   **regain-courage.*PERF-PTPL-ACT-M-NOM-SG***
'But Nicias himself, immediately and unnaturally **encouraged** by his strength and good fortune in the present situation...' (Plu. *Nic.* 18.6)

An event described by the perfect of an achievement verb cannot overlap with another bounded eventuality:

(130) **nenikēkòs**   toùs   polemíous
defeat.PERF-PTPL-ACT-M-NOM-SG   *ART.M-ACC-PL*   *enemy.M-ACC-PL*
oíkade   pròs   hautòn
homeward   *towards*   *himself.M-ACC-SG*
hupéstrepse...
return.AOR-IND-ACT-3-SG
'[Saul] **having defeated** his enemies, returned home...' (Jos. *AJ* 6.141)

---

[170] While *tharréō* functions as a state verb, meaning 'be of good courage', *anatharréō* functions as a change-of-state verb, meaning 'regain courage'. Parallels: *egegónei* (*become.PLPF-IND-ACT*) with *euthús* (Jos. *AJ* 15.150, given below at (446); 15.198 and 16.358). Cf. also *héstēken* (*set-up.PERF-IND-ACT*) with *euthús* (Dio Chrysostom *Orations* 31.9).

Achievement verbs in the perfect are not limited to topic-time-only denotation. This is explicitly the case when the perfect is accompanied by adverbials with this denotation:

(131) hē   dè   boulḕ   **pálai**

ART.F-NOM-SG   *PTCL*   *Senate.F-NOM-SG*   **long-ago**

diegnōkuîa   polemêsai...   hôde

decide.*PERF-PTPL-ACT-F-NOM-SG*   *go-to-war.AOR-INF-ACT*   thus

apekrínato...

reply.AOR-IND-ACT-3-SG

'... the Senate, **having decided long ago** to go to war... replied thus...' (App. *Pun.* 11.74)

(132) tḕn   aitían   puthoménous   di'

ART.F-ACC-SG   *reason.F-ACC-SG*   *ask.AOR-PTPL-MID-M-ACC-PL*   *for*

hḕn   ep'   ándras   elēlúthasin,

rel-pron.F-ACC-SG   *for*   *man.M-ACC-PL*   *come.PERF-IND-ACT-3-PL*

hoì   **mikròn émprosthen**   timês

rel-pron.M-NOM-PL   **a-little**   **before**   *honour.F-GEN-SG*

kaì   xenías   **tetukhḗkasin**   autôn...

and   *hospitality.F-GEN-SG*   **obtain.*PERF-IND-ACT-3-PL***   *they.M-GEN-PL*

kakístous   apekáloun...

bad.SUPERL-M-ACC-PL   *call.IMPF-IND-ACT-3-PL*

'... when [Joseph's brothers] asked the reason why they had come for men, who a little earlier **had obtained** their honour and hospitality... they disparaged the them...' (Jos. *AJ* 2.128)

Even without adverbials this can be implied:

(133) hôn   heîs   mèn   ên

REL-PRON.M-GEN-PL   *one.M-NOM-SG*   *PTCL*   *be.PAST-IND-3-SG*

Gáios   Lutátios   ho

Gaius.M-NOM-SG   *Lutatius.M-NOM-SG*   *ART.M-NOM-SG*

tḕn   húpaton   arkhḕn

ART.F-ACC-SG   *consul.M-ACC-SG*   *command.F-ACC-SG*

eilēphṓs...

take.*PERF-PTPL-ACT-M-NOM-SG*

'Of these one was C. Lutatius, **who had [previously] held** the consulship, the other two the praetorship.' (Plb. 3.40.9)

According to Shuckburgh (1889), the consuls in this year were Publius Cornelius Scipio and Tiberius Sempronius Longus. From the context, therefore, the reader is obliged to understand that C. Lutatius could not have been consul at topic time.[171]

---

[171] C. Lutatius Catulus was consul in 242 BC, while his son C. Lutatius Catulus was consul in 220 BC with L. Veturius Philo.

Notice, finally, that an event of taking up the consulship is not specifically in view: the point that is being made is that C. Lutatius had been in the state of holding the consulship. This is a phenomenon that we will see again in the case of durative COS verbs.

In conclusion, we can see that neither past reference nor anteriority are obligatory in the perfect of achievement verbs. This shows that terminativity is not in and of itself a guarantee of anteriority. Putting this evidence together with that from verbs with homogeneous time structure, we may infer that in terminative state verbs it is the combination of durativity and terminativity that guarantees anterior readings of these perfects.

2.4 Non-homogeneous durative verbs (describing activities and accomplishments)

2.4.1 Introduction

In describing the behaviour of the perfects of state (homogeneous) and achievement (non-homogeneous non-durative) verbs, we saw that obligatory past reference arises from the semantic feature of durativity, and that obligatory anteriority arises from the combination of durativity with terminativity, both features being encoded at the lexical level. In the present section we consider verbs with non-homogeneous durative time structure, i.e. those heading activity and accomplishment predicates. Since these verbs describe durative events, given the behaviour of the perfect with durative state verbs, we expect their perfects to carry past reference obligatorily. We will see that this indeed is the case, provided that the subject cannot be construed as changing state. Where the subject can be construed as changing state neither past reference nor anteriority are obligatory. Furthermore, we find that anteriority is not dependent on the presence of the semantic feature of terminativity, since where the subject is not a patient the perfect bounds the predicate even where the latter is atelic.

We start by considering non-COS verbs, before moving on to describe the behaviour of the perfect with COS verbs. Finally, we consider verbs with specialised COS and non-COS perfect active stems.

2.4.2 Non-COS verbs

Prototypical of non-COS non-homogeneous verbs are those describing creation/ consumption type events, where the subject enacts some kind of progressive change directed towards a goal on a direct object complement. Perfects of these verbs always carry anterior denotation:

(134) = (2)

hèn	gàr	ho		tês
REL-PRON.F-ACC-SG	*PTCL*	*ART.M-NOM-SG*		*ART.F-GEN-SG*
Thēseḯdos		poiētḕs		Amazónōn
Theseid.F-GEN-SG		*author.M-NOM-SG*		*Amazon.F-GEN-PL*
epanástasin		**gégraphe**		
uprising.F-ACC-SG		**write.*PERF-IND-ACT-3-SG***		

'For the author of the Theseid wrote "The insurrection of the Amazons".'
(Plu. *Thes.* 28.1)

(135) = (23)

hoi	dè	ánthrōpoi	tò	kréas
ART.M-NOM-PL	*PTCL*	*human.M-NOM-PL*	*ART.N-ACC-SG*	*meat.N-ACC-SG*
esthíousin,		tà	d'	ostâ
eat.PRES-IND-ACT-3-SG		*ART.N-ACC-PL*	*PTCL*	*bone.N-ACC-PL*
hríptousin,		hóper		ánthrōpos
throw.PRES-IND-ACT-3-PL		*REL-PRON.N-ACC-AG*		*human.M-NOM-SG*
ồn		kagồ	**nûn**	
be.PRES-PTPL-M-NOM-SG		*and-I.NOM-SG*	***now***	
pepoíēka.				
do.PERF-IND-ACT-1-SG				

'Men, however, eat the meat, but throw away the bones, which is exactly what I, who am also a man, **have now done**.' (Jos. *AJ* 12.213)

Strikingly, however, the perfect carries anterior dentation in non-homogeneous non-COS verbs even where the same verbs are used to describe an activity, i.e. without subcategorisation for a direct object patient:[172]

(136)

ho	d'	ouk	**orthôs**	autòn
ART.M-NOM-SG	*PTCL*	*NEG*	***properly***	*he.ACC-SG*
éphē		**pepoiēkénai...**		
say.PAST-IND-ACT-3-SG		***act.PERF-INF-ACT***		

'But he said that he had not **acted properly**...' (Jos. *AJ* 6.102)

In this way these verbs behave like unergatives, which never subcategorise for a patient direct object, and which similarly denote anteriority in the perfect. The following example gives the perfect of the unergative verb *erízō* 'to quarrel':

(137)

theoús	ge	mèn	mália	perì
god.M-ACC-PL	*PTCL*	*PTCL*	*very*	*about*
toútōn	eikồs		**ērikénai**	
this.N-GEN-PL	*reasonable.M-NOM-SG*		***quarrel.PERF-INF-ACT***	

'It is very reasonable that the gods **should have quarrelled** about these things...' (Plb. 3.91.7)

The verbs given so far have been only those sub-categorising for an agent subject. However, this is not a requirement for anterior interpretation. The key factor is the time structure of the event described, specifically whether or not it is homogeneous. This is shown by non-homogeneous verbs subcategorising for a patient subject, such as *páskhō* 'I suffer', which similarly carries anterior denotation:

(138)

tí	tēlikoûton,	ô	tlēmonestátē
what.N-ACC-SG	*so-great.N-ACC-SG*	*PTCL*	*wretched.F-NOM-SG*

---

[172] Parallel: *pepoiēkénai* (*act.PERF-INF-ACT*) (Jos. *Vit.* 297).

pólis,	**péponthas**	hupò
city.F-NOM-SG	***suffer.PERF-IND-ACT-2-SG***	*at-the-hands-of*
Hrōmaíōn…		
Roman.M-GEN-PL		

'O most wretched city, what great [calamity] **you have suffered** at the hands of the Romans.' (Jos. *BJ* 5.19)

From this evidence, then, it seems that the perfect of a durative non-homogeneous verb necessarily carries anterior denotation, a fact which supports the notion that durativity is the key semantic feature responsible for past reference. However, the evidence from unergative uses of these verbs suggests that their anteriority is not dependent on the presence of the feature of terminativity, as it was in the case of achievement and terminative state verbs. Rather, it suggests that, at least in the case of non-homogeneous verbs, the critical factor is the non-homogeneity of the events being described.

There is, however, an exception to the rule that non-COS activity/accomplishment verbs always denote anteriority in the perfect: anteriority is not guaranteed if the subject can be construed as changing state. Indeed, anterior and resultative/pure state readings can stand side by side in a single lexeme if the lexeme may itself be read as denoting change of state or not. The following examples give a striking minimal pair involving *kámnō*:

(139) kataphroneîte   dè   hōs… pollà
despise.PRES-IND-ACT-2-PL   *PTCL*   *as*   *much.N-ACC-PL*
kekmēkótōn   akmêtes   ándres…
toil.PERF-PTPL-ACT-M-GEN-PL *fresh.M-NOM-PL*   *man.M-NOM-PL*
'…despise them as… fresh men treat **those who have been through much toil**…' (App. *BC* 2.11.72)

(140) autòs   dé,   **ekekmḗkei**   gár…   perì
self.M-NOM-SG   *PTCL*   ***toil.PLPF-IND-ACT-3-SG***   *PTCL*   *about*
loutròn   ên.
bath.N-ACC-SG   *be.PAST-IND-3-SG*
'He, on the other hand, as **he was tired**… set about having a bath.' (Jos. *AJ* 14.462)

In the first example *kámnō* is read as an unergative with meaning 'toil'. The perfect is consequently read as anterior. In the second example, it is read as a COS verb with meaning 'become tired'. Here the perfect simply denotes the state of tiredness of the king, without even any reference to him having done anything particular to make him tired. Indeed, when it comes to unambiguously change-of-state verbs, we find that both past reference and anteriority are not obligatory.

2.4.3 *COS verbs*

Here we consider the case of non-homogeneous durative verbs describing a change of state on the part of the subject. These verbs have two chracteristics which distinguish them from their non-COS counterparts in the perfect:

1. They may denote resultative readings, i.e. where the subject exists in a state as a result of a past event. This follows directly from their denotation of a change-of-state on the part of the subject.

2. They are not *obliged* to carry anteriority or past reference, although they may do so.

The following change of location examples are resultative: [173]

(141) ou   tharrḗsas   dè   toûto
      NEG *have-courage.AOR-PTPL-ACT-M-NOM-SG* PTCL *this.N-ACC-SG*
      poieîn   **anakekhōrēkṑs**
      do.PRES-INF-ACT **withdraw.PERF-PTPL-ACT-M-NOM-SG**
      estratopédeue   tês   Zakánthēs   en
      encamp.IMPF-IND-ACT-3-SG ART.F-GEN-SG   *Zakanthe.F-GEN-SG*   in
      toîs   pròs   thálattan   méresin.
      ART.N-DAT-PL *towards* *sea.F-ACC-SG*   *part.N-DAT-PL*
      'Not having the courage to do this, **having withdrawn** [Bostar] encamped in the parts of Zakanthe that are near the sea.' (Plb. 3.98.5)

(142) ho   de   Pompêios...   nûn...
      ART.M-NOM-SG   PTCL   *Pompey.M-NOM-SG*   *now*
      epibébēke   tês   paralíou
      set-foot-on.PERF-IND-ACT-3-SG ART.F-GEN-SG   *shore.F-GEN-SG*
      'And Pompey, while not having done so previously, has now, encouraged by Antony, **set foot** on the shore.' (App. *BC* 5.7.62) [174]

Resultative readings are paralleled in verbs denoting a change of nature:

(143) kaì   gàr   tà   tês   orgês   hupò
      and PTCL ART.N-NOM-PL   ART.F-GEN-SG   *anger.F-GEN-SG*   *with*
      toû   khrónou   **lelṓphēkei**
      ART.M-GEN-SG   *time.M-GEN-SG* **subside.PLPF-IND-ACT-3-SG**
      'For his anger **had subsided** with time...' (Jos. *AJ* 7.181)

Interestingly resultativity is also implied in perfects which are traditionally seen as archaisms with stative-only semantics:[175]

(144) nûn   dè...   lampróteron   ekkópsai   kaì
      now PTCL *noble.COMP-N-NOM-SG*   *fell.AOR-INF-ACT*   *and*
      aneleîn   sunestôsan   édē
      kill.AOR-INF-ACT *establish.PERF-PTPL-ACT-F-ACC-SG*   *already*
      kaì   **pephukuîan**
      and **grow.PERF-PTPL-ACT-F-ACC-SG**

---

[173] Example (142) is in direct speech.

[174] Parallels: App. *Pun.* 14.100, *BC* 2.15.102, 5.8.71, Jos. *BJ* 6.69, *AJ* 2.235 and 18.320.

[175] Parallel: *diephthoròs* (*destroy.PERF-PTPL-ACT*) with *édē* 'already', Jos. *AJ* 5.207, see (325)=(433).

'[he uttered the saying that]... in the present situation it was... a more noble task to fell and kill [the tyranny] now it was already established and was **full-grown**.' (Plu. *Sol.* 30.5)

Perhaps the most striking feature of the perfect of these verbs is that past reference is not obligatory. In the next example a town's location is given using the perfect of the change of location verb *anakhōréō* 'withdraw'. The town itself can clearly never have 'withdrawn'; the perfect must rather refer to the state of the town at topic time, i.e. 'at some distance from the sea'.

(145) = (6)

hē	dè	Teúta...	polismátion...
ART.F-NOM-SG	*PTCL*	*Teuta.F-NOM-SG*	*small-town.N-NOM-SG*

anakekhōrēkòs	mèn	apò	tês
withdraw.*PERF-PTPL-ACT-N-NOM-SG*	*PTCL*	*from*	*ART.F-GEN-SG*

thaláttēs...
sea.F-GEN-SG

'Teuta... a small town... **withdrawn** from the sea...' (Plb. 2.11.16)

The next example is similar. Here, an inanimate substance, asphalt, is described using the perfect of *phúō* 'to grow', *péphuka*. Since asphalt is incapable of 'growing', the perfect in this sentence must be interpreted as referring to a state, that of 'being by nature'.

(146)

tôi	gàr	húdati	tḕn...
ART.N-DAT-SG	*PTCL*	*water.N-DAT-SG*	*ART.F-ACC-SG*

apophráttein	eísodon	hē
prevent.PRES-INF-ACT	*entry.F-ACC-SG*	*ART.F-NOM-SG*

ásphaltos	**péphuken**...
asphalt.F-NOM-SG	**grow.***PERF-IND-ACT-3-SG*

'For asphalt **is by nature** able to prevent water entering through the wickerwork...' (Jos. *AJ* 2.221)

More frequent are cases where a COS event must, logically, have terminated at some point prior to topic time, but the context shows no interest in this. This use of the perfect is frequent in descriptions of locations:[176]

(147)

en	dè	Delphoîs	Palládion
in	*PTCL*	*Delphi.M-DAT-PL*	*Palladium.N-NOM-SG*

héstēke	khrusoûn	epì
set-up.PERF-IND-ACT-3-SG	*golden.N-NOM-SG*	*on*

phoínikos	khalkoû
date-palm.M-GEN-SG	*bronze.M-GEN-SG*

---

[176] Cf. *pepēgós* at Plu. *Thes.* 1.1 (431), where the perfect is used to describe a sea on a map. Parallel is the example at Plu. *Them.* 8.2, given at (1).

bebēkós...
go.PERF-PTPL-ACT-N-NOM-SG
'And in Delphi there **stands** a statue of Pallas, **mounted** on a bronze date palm.' (Plu. *Nic.* 13.3)

(148) brokhōtêra éxei... katà
opening.M-ACC-SG *have.PRES-IND-ACT-3-SG* by
mêkos **errōgóta...**
length.N-ACC-SG **break.PERF-PTPL-ACT-M-ACC-SG**
'[The tunic...] has an opening [for the neck] **separated** length-wise' (Jos. *AJ* 3.161)

In the first example, although in principle such an event must have taken place at some point in order for the Palladium to be where it is, the point of the passage is to describe the situation as it is found at topic time. The second example describes the making of a tunic: *errōgóta* does not refer to an event of breaking or tearing, but the point is rather that wherever you find this garment, it has been made so as to be open.

However, this kind of lack of reference to the culmination of a COS event is not limited to descriptions of fixed situations. It may also occur in descriptions of individuals or mobile entities:

(149) kaì... hē thálassa... toîs... hósoi
and *ART.F-NOM-SG* *sea.F-NOM-SG* *ART.M-DAT-PL* *as-many-as.M-NOM-PL*
tôn neôn **epebebḗkesan**
ART.F-GEN-PL *ship.F-GEN-PL* **board.PLPF-IND-ACT-3-PL**
éti... ên aporōtéra
still *be.PAST-IND-3-SG* *impassable.N-NOM-SG*
'And... the sea... was impassible... for those **who were still on board** the ships...' (App. *BC* 5.10.90)

In this example the perfect of *epibaínō* 'to board' collocates with *éti* 'still', suggesting that the focus the description of the event is entirely on the resultant state, and not on the event which led to it.[177]

Interestingly, the transitivity of the verb per se is not a factor, if the subject can still be viewed as changing state. Thus verbs which describe a change of state on the part of both the subject and the object, such as *peristephanóō* 'surround' and *hupozṓnnumi*, 'undergird', can denote pure states in the perfect:[178]

---

[177] Note the infelicity of the equivalent sentence in English with a perfect: '#Those who had still gone on board the ships.' Parallels with COS perfects collocating with *éti* 'still' are: *aphestēkós* (*rebel.PERF-PTPL-ACT*) at Jos. *BJ* 7.252; *pephukṓs* (*grow.PERF-PTPL-ACT*) at App. *BC* 4.14.109; *katepeplḗgesan* (*frighten.PLPF-IND-ACT*) at App. *BC* 5.6.58; *periestótas* (*encircle.PERF-PTPL-ACT*) at App. *Hann.* 8.51; *sunest-* (*establish.PERF-ACT*) at App. *BC* 2.1.6, 3.9.69, 4.16.129, Plu. *Nic.* 28.4, Jos. *BJ* 5.426.

[178] Parallels: *peplērōkóta* (*fill.PERF-PTPL-ACT*) describing *egképhalon* 'brain' (Plu. *Per.* 6.2), *apoléloipen* (*leave.PERF-IND-ACT*) describing 'the nature of the land of the Canaanites' (Jos. *AJ* 5.77f.).

(150) tò   dè   prò   autôn
ART.N-NOM-SG   *PTCL*   *in-front*   *they.GEN-PL*
apóbasis...   kúklōi
landing.F-NOM-SG   *circle.M-DAT-SG*
periestaphánōken   tòn   pánta
surround.PERF-IND-ACT-3-SG *ART.M-ACC-SG*   *all.M-ACC-SG*
liména...
harbour.M-ACC-SG
'In front of them a... landing area **surrounds** the entire harbour round in a circle...' (Jos. *AJ* 15.337)

(151) toútōn   mía   d'   egkarsía
this.F-GEN-PL   *one.F-NOM-SG*   *PTCL*   *oblique.F-NOM-SG*
pásas   **hupézōken**
all.F-ACC-PL   **undergird.PERF-IND-ACT-3-SG**
'Of these [passages]... one **undergirds** all of them running obliquely...' (Jos. *AJ* 15.340)

Possessive COS verbs in the perfect can behave in the same way, since the subject is affected by obtaining the object. The following example involves *lambánō* 'take, obtain':[179]

(152) kálliston   ōiéthēsan   tòn
good.SUPERL-M-ACC-SG   *think.AOR-IND-ACT-3-PL*   *ART.M-ACC-SG*
kairòn   toû   pròs   ekeínēn
opportunity.M-ACC-SG   *ART.N-GEN-SG*   *towards*   *that.F-ACC-SG*
mísous   **eilēphénai**
hatred.N-GEN-SG   **take.PERF-INF-ACT**
'[Perceiving that Herod was so disposed towards Mariamne his sister and mother] considered they **had the best opportunity** [to realise] their hatred towards her...' (Jos. *AJ* 15.213)

2.4.4 *Verbs with two perfect active stems*

A striking feature of the Greek perfect is that a number of verbs have more than one stem in the perfect active. Thus *héstēka*, from *hístēmi* 'to set up', is opposed to *héstaka*, *pépēkha*, from *pḗgnumi*, 'to fix', to *pépēga* etc. These stems demonstrate different temporal denotation according to which stem is used. Thus causative COS stems, such as *hestak-*, parallel the behaviour of non-COS perfects, while non-causative COS stems parallel perfects of COS verbs. Thus in the case of the former, anterior readings are the norm, while resultative and pure state readings are

---

[179] Parallels: *eilēphénai* (*take.PERF-INF-ACT*) at Jos. *BJ* 5.545 and *tetukhēkóta* (*obtain.PERF-PTPL-ACT*) at Jos. *AJ* 1.232. This behaviour is strikingly similar to the behaviour of 'got(ten)' in English, in e.g. 'I've got(ten) a house', for which see also n. 28.

the norm in the case of the latter. Consider the following pair of examples involving the perfects of *histēmi*:

(153) parêsan   pròs   autòn   eis   Siloûnta
      be-present.PAST-IND-ACT-3-PL *to*   *he.ACC-SG* *to*   *Shiloh.ACC-SG*
      pólin,   éntha   tèn   skēnèn
      city.F-ACC-SG *where* *ART.F-ACC-SG* *tabernacle.F-ACC-SG*
      hestákesan
      set-up.PLPF-IND-ACT-3-PL
      '[The men...] returned to him at the city of Shiloh, where **they had set up** the tabernacle.' (Jos. *AJ* 5.79)

(154) ekéleue   toùs   hippéas...
      order.IMPF-IND-ACT-3-SG *ART.M-ACC-PL* *cavalry.M-ACC-PL*
      hestánai
      stand.PERF-INF-ACT
      'He ordered the cavalry... **to stand**...' (App. *Hisp.* 14.88)

In the first example, involving the stem *hestak-*, the subject does not change state and the pluperfect is read as an anterior. In the second example, involving the stem *hest-/hestēk-*, a pure state reading follows.

This contrast is neatly illustrated in example (155), which gives a minimal pair of the transitive and intransitive uses of *histēmi*, the latter being used in a parallel wish expression, but the former anterior:

(155) nûn   oûn   ei   mèn   phtháneis
      now *PTCL* *if* *PTCL* *be-previously.PRES-IND-ACT-2-SG*
      tòn   andriánta   **hestakṓs,**
      ART.M-ACC-SG *statue.M-ACC-SG* *set-up.PERF-PTPL-ACT-M-NOM-SG*
      hestátō.
      stand.PERF-IMP-ACT-3-SG
      'So now, if you **have** already **set up** the statue, **let it stand**.' (Jos. *AJ* 18.301)

The same contrast can be seen in the following resultative/anterior pair involving the two stems of the perfect of *pḗgnumi*:

(156) **pepēgósi**   mónon   hupò   brakheías
      fix.PERF-PTPL-ACT-M-DAT-PL *only* *under* *gentle.F-GEN-SG*
      thermótētos   toîs   ap'   autôn
      heat.F-GEN-SG *ART.M-DAT-PL* *from* *they.GEN-PL*
      ártois   dietréphonto...
      bread.M-DAT-PL *nourish.IMPF-IND-MIDPAS-3-PL*
      '... they were nourished with this bread from them, bread which **had been cooked** only under a gentle heat...' (Jos. *AJ* 2.316)

(157) ou   dúnatai   dè   takhéōs
      NEG *be-able.PRES-IND-MIDPAS-3-SG* *PTCL* *quickly*

elēluthénai		epì	tḕn	Hródon
come.PERF-INF-ACT		*to*	*ART.F-ACC-SG*	*Rhodes.F-ACC-SG*
ho		próteron	mèn	naûs
ART.M-NOM-SG		*previously*	*PTCL*	*ship.F-ACC-PL*
pepēkhṓs				
fix.PERF-PTPL-ACT-M-NOM-SG				

'The one who **had** previously **moored his ships** cannot have come quickly to Rhodes.' (Aristonicus *De signis Iliadis, Il.* 2.664)

2.4.5 Verbs alternating between COS and non-COS readings without specialised stems

Finally, there exist verbs, such as *hupostéllō*, which do not have specialised causative and non-causative COS stems in the perfect. In these cases whether or not the subject changes state is determined purely at the syntactic level, according to the arguments supplied in the sentence. The following minimal pair involves *hupostéllō*, where the first, anticausative, instance is resultative, while the second, causative, instance is anterior:

(158) = (8)

heistḗkei		dè	katá	ti
set-up.PLPF-IND-ACT-3-SG		*PTCL*	*in*	*INDEF-PRON.N-ACC-SG*
prosbatòn		olígais	bathmîsi	khōríon
accessible.N-ACC-SG		*few.F-DAT-PL*	*step.F-DAT-PL*	*space.N-ACC-SG*
hupestalkṑs			tôi	kat'
hide.PERF-PTPL-ACT-N-ACC-SG			*ART.DAT-M-SG*	*in*
autò		skótōi.		
it.N-SG-ACC		*darkness.M-DAT-SG*		

'[Claudius] had stood in a space, accessible by a few paces, **taking cover** in the darkness there.' (Jos. *AJ* 19.216)

(159) = (9)

ho	dè	Phílippos...	hupó
ART.M-NOM-SG	*PTCL*	*Philip.M-NOM-SG*	*under*
tina		lóphon	**hupestálkei**
INDEF-PRON.MF-ACC-SG		*hill.M-ACC-SG*	*hide.PLPF-IND-ACT-3-SG*
toùs		Illurioùs...	
ART.M-ACC-PL		*Illyrians.M-ACC-PL*	

'But Philip... **had sent** the Illyrians behind a hill...' (Plb. 5.13.5)

If two arguments are supplied, a subject and a direct object, the perfect is taken to describe a non-homogeneous non-COS event. By contrast, if only a subject argument is supplied, a non-homogeneous COS event is taken to be described. The example of *hupostéllō* demonstrates that, while factors at the lexical level play an important role in determining the past reference of the perfect, past reference is only finally determined at the syntactic level, taking into account the verbal head and its arguments and adjuncts. It is to this task that we shall turn in the next chapter.

2.4.6 Conclusion

To conclude, we have seen first that the perfects of non-homogeneous durative verbs carry anterior denotation provided that the subject is not construed as changing state. Secondly, we have seen that this anteriority is not dependent on the presence of the lexical semantic feature of terminativity, as it was in the case of achievement and terminative state verbs. Rather non-homogeneity appears to lead to obligatory anterior readings in these verbs. The major exception to this pattern was that of COS verbs, where we saw that neither past reference nor anteriority are guaranteed. Indeed, anteriority is rare. In COS verbs the denotation is usually either resultative or pure state.

2.5 Noise verbs

Noise verbs make up a large part of the problematic group of so-called 'intensive' perfects.[180] While these appear to have closest affinities to activity verbs, in that they are non-terminative and appear to describe non-static situations, their perfects do not behave as those of other activity verbs, in that they only describe situations ongoing at topic time. Consider the following example involving *trízō* 'to shriek':[181]

(160) hai   gunaîkes   apantôsai
ART.F-NOM-PL   *woman.F-NOM-PL*   *meet.PRES-PTPL-ACT-F-NOM-PL*
metà   xiphôn   kaì   pelékeōn
with   *sword.N-GEN-PL*   *and*   *axe.M-GEN-PL*
deinòn   **tetriguîai**
terribly   **shriek.PERF-PTPL-ACT-F-NOM-PL**
ēmúnonto   toùs
drive-back.IMPF-IND-MIDPAS-3-PL   *ART.M-ACC-PL*
pheúgontas
flee.PRES-PTPL-IND-M-ACC-PL
'... the women met [them], holding swords and axes, and **shrieking** terribly tried to drive back those who were fleeing...' (Plu. *Gaius Marius* 19.7)

The in-process reading of the perfect is especially clear in the second example, where it must be inferred that *ekhoménas* and *tetriguías* refer to coextensive events. *krázō* 'to shout' is attested in a very similar usage:

(161) all'   **ekekrágei**   kaì   **ekḗrusse**
but   **shout.PLPF-IND-ACT-3-SG**   *and*   **shout.IMPF-IND-ACT-3-SG**
parainôn   tôi   pléthei
urge.PRES-PTPL-ACT-M-NOM-SG   *ART.N-DAT-SG*   *people.N-DAT-SG*
déxasthai   tòn   Babulṓnion...
accept.AOR-INF-MIDPAS   *ART.M-ACC-SG*   *Babylonian.M-ACC-SG*

---

[180] See 1.3.

[181] Parallel: *tetriguías* (shriek.PERF-PTPL-ACT) at Plu. *De sera numinis vindicta* 567e.

'...but [Jeremiah] **shouted** and **preached**, urging the people to accept the Babylonian...' (Jos. *AJ* 10.117)

(162) sunépratte   d'   autôi   kaì
      assist.IMPF-IND-ACT-3-SG   *PTCL*   *he.M-DAT-SG*   *and*
      Thrasúboulos   ho   Steirieùs
      Thrasyboulos.M-NOM-SG   *ART.M-NOM-SG*   *Steirieus.M-NOM-SG*
      háma   parṑn   kaì
      simultaneously   *be-present.PRES-PTPL-ACT-M-NOM-SG*   *and*
      kekragós...
      shout.PERF-PTPL-ACT-M-NOM-SG

'Thrasyboulus of Steiris assisted [Alcibiades] too, **by accompanying him** and **shouting**...' (Plu. *Alc.* 26.6)

Both *ekekrágei* and *kekragós* are coordinate with the imperfectives *ekḗrusse* and *parṑn* respectively.[182]

In terms of temporal relations, the perfect of noise verbs comes closest to matching the behaviour of the perfect of non-durative state verbs: both describe a situation ongoing at topic time without past reference. This seems to imply that, to the Ancient Greek mind at least, noise verbs are, or at least can be, closer to state verbs than to activity verbs in terms of event structure. This is reasonable, since noise events, unlike the majority of activities, but like those non-state homogeneous verbs discussed at 2.1.9.3 and 2.2.5 above, such as 'yawning', 'smiling' and 'looking', may be homogeneous if they are monotonous and constant. This is to say that a noise event is not necessarily associated with phases.

Durativity is another issue: one might think that, insofar as a noise must endure for some minimal amount of time in order to be recognised as a noise, noise verbs would carry the feature of durativity. However, the semantics of their perfects is not like that of other durative homogeneous verbs, such as *ménō* or *diateléō*, in that there is no continuity from a past situation as denoted in these other verbs. The key point is that, noise events are not required to last for multiple conceptual moments (see 2.1.9.1.3 above). One might argue, therefore, following with the principle we have been eliciting in this chapter, that the lack of obligatory past reference in the perfect of noise verbs can be tied to the lack of the semantic feature of durativity. The issue of noise verbs, or rather noise predicates, is taken up at 7.9.

2.6 *Conclusion*

This chapter has considered the question of past time reference in the Greek perfect in terms of lexical semantics. In the analysis we identified three lexical aspectual semantic features distinguishing Greek verbs: durativity, terminativity, and homogeneity. Durative verbs were identified as those describing eventualities associated

---

[182] A striking usage may be found at App. *Hisp.* 5.27, where *kekragós* introduces direct speech.

with an obligatory conceptual duration for the eventualities to be said to occur. These comprised activity/accomplishment verbs, such as *poiéō* 'to act, do', as well as homogeneous verbs such as *ménō* 'to remain' and *diateléō* 'to continue'. Terminative verbs were identified as those denoting an eventuality with a set endpoint or expiry. These comprised achievement verbs describing both COS events, such as *ginōskō* 'to come to know', and non-COS (i.e. where the subject does not change state) events, such as *ekphobéō* 'to frighten', state verbs describing offices of state, such as *stratēgéō* 'to be general', as well as COS accomplishment verbs such as *érkhomai* 'to come'.

The presence of durativity on its own led to obligatory continued state readings, but not anterior ones, as in durative state verbs. Anteriority was found to be guaranteed where the semantic features of terminativity and durativity were combined, as in terminative state verbs, or where the features of durativity and non-homogeneity were combined, as in the case of activity/accomplishment verbs. In homogeneous verbs, if both terminativity and durativity were lacking, past reference was found not to be obligatory. COS verbs constituted an exception to these findings: despite encoding both durativity and terminativity in their lexical semantics, past reference was found not to be obligatory.

Finally we considered the perfect of noise verbs. This is problematic because, while one might expect it to behave like the perfects of activity verbs, in fact the temporal presentation of the events they describe is without reference to any situation prior to topic time. We suggested accounting for this with reference to a non-durative and homogeneous semantic analysis of their event structure.

To conclude, lexical semantics play an important role in determining the temporal denotation of the perfect. However, in this chapter we have also seen that past reference is not finally determined at the lexical level. This was shown chiefly in the following ways:

1. The temporal properties of perfects of certain verbs, notably *hupostéllō*, 'to hide', was found to be dependent on the orientation and number of arguments supplied.
2. Regardless of the durativity or terminativity of a verb's lexical semantics, COS perfects were found only optionally to express past reference, in terms of anteriority or resultativity.

It remains to be determined, however, precisely what factors at the syntactic level are significant in determining whether anteriority, resultativity or pure state semantics are denoted in those cases where the subject is construed as changing state. This is the goal of the next chapter.

III

3 SYNTACTIC THEORETICAL FRAMEWORKS

3.1 *Introduction*

The present chapter sets out the two syntactic-semantic frameworks that will be used in combination for the remainder of this study for the purposes of elucidating and clarifying the exegesis of particular examples. These are neo-Davidsonian event semantics, and Government Binding (GB) theory. These two are used in combination so as to harness the benefits of both. As will become clear, the insights of both are necessary to get a complete grasp on the function of the perfect. We will start with neo-Davidsonian event semantics.

3.2 *Neo-Davidsonian tradition*

3.2.1 *Event semantics in the Davidsonian tradition*

In traditional predicate logic, arguments fill slots according to the valency of the verb. Consider the following sentence:[183]

> (163) Jones buttered the toast.

Here the verb 'butter' has two argument slots, for a subject and a direct object, and the arguments 'Jones' and 'the toast' fill those slots. However, Davidson (1967a), followed by Higginbotham (1985) and Parsons (1990), additionally posits an event variable. Davidson is trying to explain examples such as the following:

> (164) Jones did it slowly, deliberately, in the bathroom, with a knife, at midnight.

In this example 'it' does not refer to an entity, but an event, specifically, Jones buttering a piece of toast. In order to provide the logical form of such sentences, Davidson posits that the 'it' refers to an event e of the form:

> (165) $\exists e(\text{Buttered}(\text{Jones, toast, e}))$

On this account, the 'it' in 'Jones did it' of (164) is 'e'.

3.2.2 *Argument projection in a neo-Davidsonian framework*

Any account of transitivity in event semantics must be able to account for argument projection. The issue of the correct analysis of argument projection has been controversial over the last three decades. There are two possibilities:[184]

---

[183] Example from Davidson (1967a).

[184] For discussion, particularly in the context of the aspectual nature of the problem, see Levin & Rappaport Hovav (2005).

1. The lexical semantics of the verb determine the number and nature of the arguments in a sentence.
2. The arguments are freely projected onto syntax and are not determined by the verb.

There are two issues here:

1. How do you decide the number of arguments of the verb?
2. How do you assign particular semantic roles to the arguments that are projected?

In what follows we will outline the framework we use in the present study that accounts for these phenomena. However, before embarking, it is important to distinguish clearly between semantic roles and grammatical relations.

3.2.3 *Semantic roles and grammatical relations*

Semantic roles are 'semantic categories into which arguments may be classified according to the kind of role they play in the situations described by their predicates'.[185] Table 8 gives common semantic roles identified cross-linguistically.

Grammatical relations, by contrast, are non-semantic grammatical categories into which arguments may be classed. These often identified as including:

1. Subject
2. Object
3. Oblique

There are two types of grammatical relation into which arguments may be classified: direct and oblique arguments.[186] Direct arguments comprise subjects and objects, while obique arguments comprise other kinds of arguments. Direct arguments have a more intimate relationship with their verb than other arguments. This is reflected in English by the fact that oblique arguments are often marked by prepositions, while direct arguments tend not to be.[187]

The particular grammatical relations specified by a given verb are its SUBCAT-EGORISATION.[188] Thus the verb 'donate' in English subcategorises for a subject (the donor), an object (the thing donated) and an indirect object (the recipient of the thing donated). Its direct arguments are the subject and object. Its oblique argument is the indirect object. By contrast, the verb 'arrive' subcategorises for a subject only, a direct argument.

Identification of the grammatical relation of an argument differs from language to language, and is based on syntactic as well as morphological criteria. In

---

[185] Kroeger (2005: 54).

[186] For this distinction see Kroeger (2005: 57f.).

[187] Kroeger (2005: 57f.). The indirect object in English has the option of being marked by means of a preposition. Compare, 'He gave me the book' with, 'He gave the book to me'.

[188] Kroeger (2005: 67ff.).

Table 8. Semantic roles (see Kroeger 2005: 54f.)

AGENT	Causer or initiator of events
EXPERIENCER	Animate entity which perceives a stimulus or registers a particular mental or emotional process or state.
RECIPIENT	Animate entity which receives or acquires something.
BENEFICIARY	Entity (usually animate) for whose benefit an action is performed.
INSTRUMENT	Inanimate entity used by an agent to perform some action.
THEME	Entity which undergoes a change of location or possession, or whose location is being specified.
PATIENT	Entity which is acted upon, affected, or created; or of which a state or change of state is predicated.
STIMULUS	Object of perception, cognition, or emotion; entity which is seen, heard, known, remembered, loved, hated, etc.
LOCATION	Spatial reference point of the event (the SOURCE, GOAL, and PATH roles are often considered to be sub-types of LOCATION).
SOURCE	The origin or beginning point of a motion.
GOAL	The destination or end-point of a motion.
PATH	The trajectory or pathway of a motion.
ACCOMPANIMENT (or COMITATIVE)	Entity which accompanies or is associated with the performance of an action.

English the following are some of the criteria which have been used to identify the subject:[189]

1. Word order: the subject comes before the verb in a simple declarative sentence.
2. Number agreement with verb: the subject of the sentence will agree in number with the verb, where a distinction of form is made.
3. Pronoun forms: The pronoun has a special form which is directly related to it being a subject.

In languages with freer word order than English, such as Greek, the first criterion is not applicable. The second two, however, are very useful. Indeed, the case system is much more extended in Greek than it is in English, and therefore of great use in distinguishing grammatical relations.[190]

3.2.4 *Determining the number of arguments*

The semantics of the verbal head can certainly be decisive in determining the number of arguments. Consider the following examples:

(166) #Mary made.
(167) #Made cake.
(168) Mary made cake.

---

[189] Criteria from Kroeger (2005: 56), in turn from Bickford (1998: 43).

[190] Case is not, however, always a failsafe guide for determining grammatical relations. As Kroeger (2004: 259) observes, case in some languages, e.g. Icelandic, very often marks the semantic role played by an argument.

These sentences all involve the verb 'make'. Yet only one of them is well formed, namely that which has specified argument positions for both subject and direct object. It seems that the verb 'make' requires the specification of both a subject and an object participant in order for its sentence to be well formed.

It is also the case that, while in some verbs there is a fixed minimum number of arguments, there need not be a maximum. This is the polyadicity problem raised by Kenny (1963: 106ff.). Consider the following sentence:

(169) Brutus killed Caesar.

This may be modified with a potentially unlimited number of arguments, e.g.:

(170) Brutus killed Caesar with a knife in the Senate after he had entered into the room etc.

As Kenny (1963: 112) observes:

> If we cast our net widely enough, we can make 'Brutus killed Caesar' into a sentence which describes, with a certain lack of specification, the whole history of the world.

We need, then, to distinguish between the true arguments of a verb and optional adjunct arguments. Davidson deals with this by distinguishing between direct arguments, which are treated as necessary positions in relation to the verb, and optional adjuncts on the other, which are treated as adverbs. Thus the sentence, 'I flew a spaceship to the Morning Star' may be expressed as:[191]

(171) $\exists e(Flew(I, spaceship, e) \land To(the\ Morning\ Star, e))$

The main benefits of a Davidsonian approach for the semantic decomposition of predicates is the straightforward account of adverbial modification which is yielded by it,[192] and the ease of deducing entailments from such predicates. Thus in this example we can trivially infer that 'I flew my spaceship'.[193]

3.2.5 *Formally representing semantic roles in a neo-Davidsonian framework*

Various scholars, including Castañeda (1967), Krifka (1989) and Parsons (1990), have adopted and developed Davidson's framework by treating direct arguments of the verb in the same way as adverbial modifiers, i.e. as two place relations between an event and an entity or set of entities, although this approach was rejected by Davidson himself (see Davidson 1967b). In the case of arguments the entity or entities are related to the event by means of a thematic relation, such as Agent or Patient. On this principle (171) comes out as:

---

[191] Example sentence from Davidson (1967a).
[192] For this point see Maienborn (2008: 107).
[193] Davidson (1967a: 48).

(172) $\exists e(Fly(e) \wedge Agent(I, e) \wedge To(the\ Morning\ Star, e))$

Generalising 'I' to an entity 'x', and 'the Morning Star' to an entity 'y', this becomes:

(173) $\exists e(Fly(e) \wedge Agent(x, e) \wedge To(y, e))$

Although there are clear advantages to this approach, the main disadvantage is that the distinction between true arguments and optional adjuncts is lost. Ideally we would have access to a system of representation which captures the advantages of both. Accordingly, once we have introduced Government-Binding (GB) theory at 3.3 below, we will introduce a combination of GB and Davidsonian semantics, which will enable much clearer representations of the semantic and syntactic structure of sentences.

3.2.6 *Are states predicates of eventualities?*

While Davidsonian situation or event variables have been productively applied to action predicates, there has been some doubt in the literature concerning whether it is right to posit such a variable for state predicates.[194] This is an important question for an investigation that is concerned with the Greek perfect, a form that is very often associated with the denotation of state.

Many, notably Higginbotham (1985, 2000) and Chierchia (1995) have simply assumed that an eventuality variable is present in all verbal predicates.[195] However, since the Davidsonian eventuality variable was first introduced in order to provide an account of adverbial modification, a major argument against positing a Davidsonian eventuality variable for stative predicates is the difficulty of adverb collocation with stative predicates. For this reason, Katz (2000, 2003) prefers to analyse stative predicates as predicates of individuals rather than as predicates of eventualities.

Yet there are certainly cases where manner adverbial modification is possible, and given the ease of anaphoric reference, the presence of an eventuality variable seems clear:[196]

(174) The shoes were gleaming brightly. It was an incredible sight!

Even in cases where modification by a manner adverbial is not possible, anaphoric reference is:

(175) The shoes were (*strikingly) on the top of the lamp post. It was a strange sight!

Furthermore, as Maienborn (2008: 114) points out, modification by temporal adverbials is still possible even where modification by manner adverbials is not.

Nevertheless, a distinction between different kinds of states should still be made, since different kinds of states exhibit different kinds of linguistic behaviour. Consider the following modern German examples modified from Maienborn (2007: 110):

---

[194] For some of the discussion see Maienborn (2008), Katz (2003), Katz (2000) and Parsons (2000).
[195] See Maienborn (2008).
[196] Example modified from German example in Maienborn (2008).

(176) Die   Schuhe   glänzen.
ART.NOM-PL   *shoe.NOM-PL*   *gleam.PRES-IND-ACT-3-PL*
'The shoes are gleaming.'

(177) Das   Buch ist   auf dem   Tisch.
ART.N-NOM-SG *book be.PRES-IND-ACT-3-SG*   *on* *ART.M-DAT-SG* *table*
'The book is on the table.'

At first, and especially if one only considers the evidence from German, one might suppose that both the predicates 'gleam' and 'be on the table' should be regarded as equally stative. However, Maienborn observes that the first may occur as an infinitival complement to a perception verb, while the second may not:[197]

(178) Ich   sah   die   Schuhe
I.NOM-SG   *see.IMPF-IND-ACT-1-SG* *ART.ACC-PL* *shoe.ACC-PL*
glänzen.
gleam.INF
'I saw the shoes gleam.'

(179) #Ich   sah   das   Buch auf
I.NOM-SG *see.IMPF-IND-ACT-1-SG* *ART.N-ACC-SG* *book* *on*
dem   Tisch   sein.
ART.M-DAT-SG *table* *be.INF*
'#I saw the book be on the table.'

To account for this she posits two different kinds of states, namely Davidsonian states, which are capable, *inter alia*, of modification by manner adverbials, and Kimian states, which are 'ontologically poorer', but still introduce arguments which may be modified and referred to in certain circumstances.[198]

In studying the question of states in relation to the Greek perfect specifically there are some additional reasons for positing an eventuality variable. First, adverbial modification is possible with stative perfects, suggesting that for at least some states described by Greek perfects, modification of some kind of eventuality variable is possible:

(180) = (111)
kaì   tò   mèn   phármakon   **euthùs**
and *ART.N-ACC-SG*   *PTCL*   *poison.N-ACC-SG*   ***immediately***
espoudakóti   zēteîn   oukh
be-eager.PERF-PTPL-ACT-M-DAT-SG *look-for.PRES-INF-ACT*   *NEG*
heuréthē.
find.AOR-IND-PAS-3-SG
'And though he **immediately set about eagerly** to look for a poison, none was found.' (Jos. *AJ* 16.254)

---

[197] Examples from Maienborn (2008).

[198] For the time travel argument for the existence of a Davidsonian eventuality variable in stative predicates, see Parsons (2000) and Maienborn (2008: 123–26).

Secondly, positing the existence of a class of eventualities that has an entirely homogeneous situation structure allows us to account economically for the intuitive similarity between the different kinds of states we have examined in the previous chapter, namely non-durative, durative and terminative, by avoiding the need for different ontologies. This is to say that it is able to capture the similarity of internal temporal constitution between *ékhō* 'I have', *ménō* 'I remain' and *stratēgéō* 'I serve as general'.

In this study, therefore, we will represent all eventualities, including events as well as Davidsonian and Kimian states, by means of an eventuality variable 'e'. The different properties of these eventualities will be attributed to the eventuality variable in the same way in which arguments are shown to modify the event variable. For our purposes the key distinctions will be the aspectual categories identified in the previous chapter at 2.1.9, i.e. homogeneity of internal temporal constitution, durativity, and terminativity. Since, however, we are now concerned with whole sentences rather than lexical verbal semantics, and since terminativity is properly a lexical semantic property, we will concern ourselves with the equivalent property at the sentence level, namely telicity. Equally, insofar as both Kimian and Davidsonian states may be said to be homogeneous non-durative and atelic in terms of internal temporal constitution, the distinction between Kimian and Davidsonian variables will not concern us.

3.2.7 *Theme hierarchies and thematic proto-roles*

So far we have accounted for the different semantic roles that can be present in a given sentence. However, this is only half of the story. At 3.2.3 we introduced the distinction between semantic roles and grammatical relations. We defined the former as 'semantic categories into which arguments may be classified according to the kind of role they play in the situations described by their predicates'.[199] These, as we saw in the last section, can be seen as projections of the verbal head. In the most straightforward case, as in the verb 'make', a verb projects both an agent and patient argument. We can posit the following analysis of the lexical semantics of the verb 'make':[200]

(181) $\exists e \exists x \exists y [\text{Make}\{\text{make}(e) \land \text{agent}(x,e) \land \text{patient}(y,e)\}]$

The sentence 'Mary made cake' can therefore be represented as follows:

(182) $\exists e \exists x \exists y [\text{Mary}\{x\} \land \text{Make}\{\text{make}(e) \land \text{agent}(x, e) \land \text{patient}(y, e)\} \land \text{Cake}\{y\}]$

According to this analysis Mary is identified with the agent participant, while the cake is identified with the patient participant.

By contrast, grammatical relations are non-semantic grammatical categories such as subjects, objects and indirect objects. It seems natural that in the example given above, the subject should be identified with the agent, while the object be identified

---

[199] Following Kroeger (2005: 54).

[200] Curly brackets are used in my notation purely to make distinguishing of groups clearer, and has no further signification.

with the patient. Some verbs, however, project different sets of arguments entirely. Consider the verb 'fear', as in:[201]

(183) The toddler feared the lion.

Here the verb 'fear' involves an experiencer subject and a stimulus object, with the toddler playing the experiencer role and the lion that of stimulus:

(184) $\exists e \exists x \exists y$[The-toddler$\{x\} \wedge$ Fear$\{$fear$(e) \wedge$ experiencer$(x, e) \wedge$ stimulus$(y, e)\}$ $\wedge$ The-lion$\{y\}$]

This does not seem nearly so intuitive as the first case. On what basis is the assignment carried out? One could imagine that there exists in the minds of speakers a kind of table by which they align case and semantic roles. Table 9 gives a list of correspondences between grammatical relations and semantic roles in English in the active voice.

Is there anything motivating these alignments? For many, the concept of a hierarchy of thematic roles has been an attractive solution. A number of different theme hierarchies have been suggested. The following is a summary of various positions:

1. $Agent > \begin{Bmatrix} Benefactive \\ Goal \end{Bmatrix} > Theme > Location$[202]

2. $Agent > \begin{Bmatrix} Goal \\ Experiencer \\ Location \end{Bmatrix} > Theme$[203]

3. $Agent > Theme > \begin{Bmatrix} Goal \\ Benefactive \\ Location \end{Bmatrix}$[204]

4. $Agent > \begin{Bmatrix} Instrument \\ Experiencer \end{Bmatrix} > Patient > \begin{Bmatrix} Source \\ Goal \end{Bmatrix}$[205]

From this summary it is clear that there are at least two problems:

1. There is little agreement about what semantic roles exist / should be included on the thematic hierarchy.

---

[201] For this example, see Levin & Rappaport Hovav (2005: 159).

[202] Baker (1996: 7f.) citing Kiparsky (1987) and Machobane (1989).

[203] Baker (1996: 7f.) citing Jackendoff (1972), Grimshaw (1990), Li (1990) and Foley & Van Valin (1984).

[204] Baker (1996: 7f.) citing Carrier-Duncan (1985), Larson (1988) and Baker (1989).

[205] Dowty (1991: 578).

Table 9. Alignments of grammatical relations and semantic roles in English in the active

Verb	Subject	Object	Transitivity
'give', 'make'	Agent	Patient	Transitive
'run', 'crawl'	Agent	-	Intransitive
'see', 'hear', 'suffer'	Experiencer	Stimulus	Transitive

    2. There is little agreement about the relative placing of the different semantic roles on the thematic hierarchy.

The first problem comes about because of the difficulty of identifying distinct semantic roles in the first place: they seem to shade into each other and be difficult to distinguish easily in many cases.[206] The latter problem is brought about in part by conflicting evidence across languages from so-called 'dative shift' alternations, whereby verbs with three arguments may optionally encode the third argument either as a prepositional phrase or as a second object, e.g.:

    (185) They gave a present to me.
    (186) They gave me a present.

The issue is that in (185) the theme has precedence over the goal, whereas the situation appears to be reversed in (186).[207] Furthermore, some languages do not have constructions like (185), while others do not have those like (186),[208] while still others, like English, appear to have both.

    It is not within the scope of the present investigation to resolve these questions. One feature which all proposed analyses share, however, is the placing of the theme/ patient lower than the agent.[209] This has led to the suggestion of macro- or proto-roles of agent and theme/patient respectively (see Dowty 1991, Marantz 1981: 58ff., Van Valin 2004). These proto-roles can provide a template according to which other less prototypical roles can be compared. Dowty (1991: 572) identifies their contributing properties as follows:

    1. Agent proto-role properties:
      a Volitional movement
      b Sentience (and/or perception)
      c Causing an event or change of state in another participant
      d Movement (relative to the position of another participant)
      e Exists independently of the event named by the verb

---

[206] cf. Dowty (1991: 548, 553ff.), Van Valin (2004: 63).

[207] For this point, although with different examples, see Baker (1996: 8) citing Larson (1988).

[208] Baker (1996: 8).

[209] In some of the literature a distinction is maintained between a 'theme' and a 'patient'. As Levin (1983: 33 n. 25) explains, the former term was introduced by Gruber (1965) to refer to an entity undergoing motion, while 'patient' is restricted to entities changing state or being affected by an action.

2. Contributing properties for the Patient proto-role:
   a Undergoes change of state
   b Incremental theme
   c Causally affected by another participant
   d Stationary relative to movement of another participant
   e Does not exist independently of the event, or not at all

Dowty (1991: 576) then posits an argument selection principle:

> In predicates with grammatical subject and object, the argument for which the predicate entails the greatest number of Proto-Agent properties will be lexicalized as the subject of the predicate; the argument having the greatest number of Proto-Patient entailments will be lexicalised as the direct object.

He also states that:

> If two arguments of a relation have (approximately) equal numbers of entailed Proto-Agent and Proto-Patient properties, then either or both may be lexicalized as the subject (and similarly for objects).

However, he is careful to state that:

> Although I am using the traditional term 'argument selection', I do not mean by 'selection' a step that occurs during the derivation of a sentence (as in early Case Grammar), or the linking-up of two different levels of representation, the syntactic level and the 'thematic level'... Rather, I mean a constraint on what kind of lexical predicates may exist in a natural language, out of many imaginable ones.

Dowty's approach seems to capture the intuitive nature of subjecthood and object-hood in active constructions. Furthermore, since semantic roles, as we have seen, easily shade into one another, Dowty's framework could, by modifying the properties of the prototypical agent and patient, allow different languages to connect different semantic roles with subject and object.

In order to implement Dowty's approach, one needs an account of nominal semantics. I propose that the lexical entries of nominals specify the maximum level of agency with which they can be associated. Let us consider the sentence 'Mary made a cake'. Here Mary, as a human, can be associated with prototypical agenthood. The cake, however, as an inanimate object can only be associated with prototypical patienthood. Accordingly, Mary is naturally assigned subject position, while the cake is assigned object position.

At first sight, however, this approach runs into difficulty in the case of verbs like 'fly', with examples like the following:

(187) I flew a spaceship.
(188) The spaceship flew.

In the first case the spaceship is in object position, and is presented, in some sense, as the patient of the action of flying. However, the same participant, namely the spaceship, is a subject in the second position. Yet the event in which it participates, namely flying is the same. The only difference is that in the second case it is not specified who is actually doing the flying. 'Fly' is not the only verb to behave like this. Consider the following examples involving the verb 'freeze':

(189) I froze the water.
(190) The water froze.

Here the verb 'freeze' appears to take both an agent and a patient argument in the first example. Yet in the second example the water, which undergoes the same process as the object in the first example, has been promoted to subject position. This alternation between subject and object in sentences of this kind is known as the CAUSATIVE ALTERNATION. Verbs participating in the causative alternation may be said to be LABILE. Participation in the causative alternation may be termed LABILE TRANSITIVITY.[210]

It is clear, however, that this kind of freedom does not extend to all verbs:

(191) Mary made a cake.
(192) #A cake made.
(193) #A cake made Mary.

In the case of sentences involving the verb 'make', it seems that there is a selectional restriction whereby the subject is an agent, and a patient participant must be specified as object. It is important, then, to take account of the selectional restrictions placed by the verb on the kinds of arguments that can be projected. In order to do this, we must provide an outline of another framework that has become very influential in analysing verbal syntax, Government-Binding (GB) theory.

3.3 Government-Binding (GB) theory

3.3.1 Introduction

GB theory arose in the eighties within the broader project, led by Noam Chomsky, of formulating rules for a Universal Grammar (UG) of human language, and constitutes a development of Chomsky's earlier ideas.[211] Chomsky (1977: 207), quoted in Chomsky (1993: 2), summarises the project as follows [his]:

> The pure study of language, based solely on evidence of the sort reviewed here, can carry us only to the understanding of abstract conditions on grammatical systems. No particular realization of these conditions has any privileged status. From a more abstract point of view, if it can be attained, we may see in retrospect that we moved towards the understanding of the abstract general conditions on linguistic structures by the detailed investigation of one or another 'concrete' realization: for example, transformational grammar, a

---

[210] For the use of the term 'labile' in this sense, see e.g. Kulikov (2003) and Labidas (2009: 113).

[211] Chomsky introduces the term Government-Binding theory in Chomsky (1981: 1).

particular instance of a system with these general properties. The abstract conditions may relate to transformational grammar rather in the way that modern algebra relates to the number system.

We should be concerned to abstract from successful grammars and successful theories those more general properties that account for their success, and to develop [universal grammar] as a theory of these abstract properties, which might be realized in a variety of different ways. To choose among such realizations, it will be necessary to move to a much broader domain of evidence. What linguists should try to provide is an abstract characterization of particular and universal grammar that will serve as a guide and framework for this more general inquiry.

A key claim of GB theory, in common with Chomsky's earlier proposals, is that human language consists of multiple levels of representation. In his earlier work, Chomsky presents the idea as follows (see Chomsky 1965: 16f., *his*, [mine]):

> ... the syntactic component of a grammar must specify, for each sentence, a *deep structure* that determines its semantic representation and a *surface structure* that determines its phonetic interpretation... The central idea of transformational grammar is that [surface and deep structures] are distinct and that the surface structure is determined by repeated application of certain formal operations called "grammatical transformations" to objects of a more elementary sort.

In GB theory deep and surface structure representations are replaced with a slightly more elaborate system, comprising the following components:[212]

(i) lexicon
(ii) syntax
(ii) PHONETIC FORM (PF)-component
(iii) LOGICAL FORM (LF)-component

Within this framework, lexicon and syntax combine to generate D-STRUCTURES, while D-structures map to the S-STRUCTURES PF and LF via the operation Move-α, whereby elements are moved from underlying positions at D-structure to new positions at S-structure. The two elements comprising S-structure, namely PF and LF, correspond to form and meaning respectively.[213]

Since in the present study we are concerned with the relationship between syntax and semantics in relation to the Greek perfect, it is the LF, rather than PF, component of S-structure with which we will be referring to as S-structure. Accordingly, this study is not concerned with Greek word order per se, but rather in how semantics interacts with syntax in Greek to generate particular results in terms of logical form.

---

[212] Slightly simplified from Chomsky (1993: 5).
[213] Carnie (2013: 397).

3.3.2 *Unaccusativity hypothesis and (causative) change of state*

GB theory provides us with the tools we need to account for the behaviour of verbs like 'fly' and 'freeze', whereby the entity undergoing the action described by the verb may occur either in subject or object position. This is otherwise known as the causative alternation. One influential way of accounting for this phenomenon is with reference to the unaccusativity hypothesis. This hypothesis, first introduced by Perlmutter (1978), proposes that 'there are two classes of intransitive verbs, the unaccusative verbs and the unergative verbs, each associated with a different underlying syntactic configuration' (see Levin & Rappaport Hovav 1995: 3).

Interpreting this within a GB framework, the unaccusative hypothesis proposes that unaccusative verbs have only an object argument at D-structure, while unergative verbs have only a subject argument at D-structure. In the case of unaccuatives, the D-structure object is then realised as a subject at S-structure. Some evidence for this comes from resultatives in English (see Levin & Rappaport Hovav 1995: 11). Consider the following examples:

(194) They are making cake.
(195) Cake is being made.
(196) Cake is made.

These examples involve the transitive verb 'make'. Example (195) is a present passive progressive construction, which may be treated as a transformation from a sentence like (194). Both describe the ongoing process of cake making. These examples can also be transformed into a resultative describing the result state of the process, as at (196). This kind of transformation is not expected with intransitive verbs where there is no direct object, as in the following examples involving the verb 'run':

(197) They are running.
(198) #They are run.

The syntactic issue that appears *a priori* to account for the infelicity of (198) is that 'they' in (198) does not bear the same relationship to 'they' in (197) as 'cake' in (196) does to 'cake' in (194): in both (198) and (197) 'they' is a subject, while in (194) 'cake' is an object, but a subject in (196). On the basis of these examples, one might well feel justified to posit a rule that the resultative transforms the object of an active construction into a subject, much like the passive construction. (198) is an infelicitous transformation of (197) because 'they' in the active construction in (197) is not an object.

Now, however, consider the following examples:

(199) I am going.
(200) I am gone.

These examples involve the intransitive verb 'go'. The present progressive in (199) describes an event of 'going' in progress, and is structurally parallel to 'They are running' in (197). However, unlike with the verb 'run', the resultative construction is acceptable, as demonstrated by the felicity of (200). It seems, then, that the resultative construction, at some level of representation, treats the subject of the verb 'go' as an object.

Unaccusative verbs may be said to be verbs whose subjects show some characteristics both of prototypical subjects, and prototypical objects. Furthermore, the verbs concerned have been observed to share certain semantic characteristics. This has led some to go further and posit a semantic basis for their behaviour, in particular in terms of the kinds of arguments that these verbs project. This is on the basis of a semantic alignment between D-structure subjects and agent arguments, on the one hand, and D-structure objects and patient arguments on the other.[214]

We can now frame the problem we presented at the end of 3.2.7 in terms of the unaccusativity hypothesis: on what basis can the active voice realise a D-structure object as an S-structure subject, when the D-structure object position is aligned with theme/patient arguments, which should, if they really are patients, be realised as objects? We can see that this is not only a problem for verbs with a causative alternation like 'fly' and 'freeze', but also for straight unaccusatives like 'go'. There are, of course, languages that do realise the D-structure objects of unaccusatives as S-structure objects, namely ergative languages. However, accusative languages tend not to do this, but realise them as S-structure subjects instead. We therefore need a principled basis for treating the D-structure objects of unaccusatives differently from the D-structure objects of transitive verbs.

Let us compare the following examples:

(201) I froze the water.
(202) I made a cake.

On the most basic analysis, 'water' and 'cake' occupy the same D-structure argument position, namely that of patient, and are, according to their D-structure syntax, objects. However, the relationship of the agent to the patient in the two cases is not identical. In the case of 'freeze', the role of the agent is not to freeze the water directly, but rather to put the water in a position where it will itself freeze (for example, in a freezer). By contrast, there is no natural or intermediate process by which a cake can make itself: the subject of the active construction must be involved at all stages of the operation. This is to say that the water itself plays some role in bringing the event of freezing about, in a way that a cake does not.

The distinction in the semantics between kinds of D-structure object corresponds to the distinction between unaccusative and accusative verbs.[215] Thus unaccusatives can be said to have D-structure objects that play some causal role in bringing about the change described by the verb. This is the concept of internal causation, introduced by Levin & Rappaport Hovav (1995: 90ff.). The interesting thing about the role of

---

[214] See Levin & Rappaport Hovav (1995: 4) and references there.

[215] Thus Levin (1983: 33) observes that '[v]erbs of motion are difficult to characterise. The single argument of these verbs seems to be both a patient (theme) and an agent.'

INTERNAL CAUSE is that it sits across the boundary between proto-typical agent- and patient-hood: on the one hand, as an entity that may itself move and/or change, an internal cause can be seen as a kind of agent, but, on the other, as an entity that undergoes a change, it may also be seen as an incremental theme and affected by another participant, characteristics of a prototypical patient. Accordingly, internal cause is an intermediate category.

It is possible to describe predicates headed by causative COS verbs in the same terms. In this case, however, we have two causes. This second cause Levin & Rappaport Hovav identify as the EXTERNAL CAUSE. Since the external cause has only an indirect relationship to the entity undergoing the change, whereas the internal cause actually undergoes the change, where present the external cause is readily identified as more 'agent-like' than Levin & Rappaport Hovav's internal cause. In these terms, then, unlike the internal cause, the external cause fully meets the requirements of proto-agency.

As will become clear later, certain COS verbs in Greek project a particular kind of cause argument that cannot fully participate in the causative alternation: these are cause arguments, but they are restricted to the internal argument position.[216] I therefore reserve the term INTERNAL CAUSE for these arguments. Since Levin & Rappaport Hovav's internal cause may move to subject position, in contrast to the external cause which must be in subject position, I will henceforth refer to Levin & Rappaport Hovav's internal cause role as UNDERLYING CAUSE, so as to capture this

Table 10. Thematic proto-roles

Proto-Agent	Proto-Patient
Agent	Patient
Experiencer	Source
External cause	Internal cause
Underlying cause	

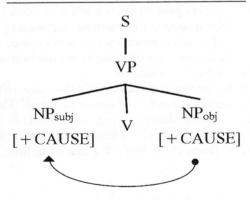

Figure 3. Ambiguity of the underlying cause argument

---

[216] For internal and external argument positions, see 3.3.4 below.

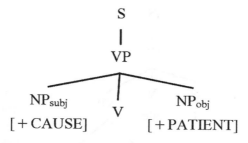

Figure 4: Distinct argument positions for cause and patient roles

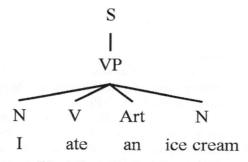

Figure 5: 'I ate an ice cream' (flat structure)

ambiguity. Where an opposition to EXTERNAL CAUSE is not in view, this role may simply be referred to as CAUSE.

Argument roles and their relationship to the proto-roles of agent and patient may be represented according Table 10. The ambiguity of interpretation of the underlying argument projected by causative COS verbs can account, therefore, for its capacity to move to subject position, as illustrated in Figure 3. By contrast, where the object is a patient, no such ambiguity, and hence movement, is possible, as illustrated in Figure 4.

3.3.3 X-bar theory

X-bar theory was developed to take account of the fact that not all elements in a sentence have the same status.[217] Consider the following sentences:

(203) I ate an ice cream.
(204) I ate that.
(205) I ate a strawberry ice cream with chocolate sprinkles, not a chocolate one.
      For (203) we can draw the (flat) structure given in Figure 5.

---

[217] See Carnie (2013: 165ff.) for further details and references on the principles outlined in this section.

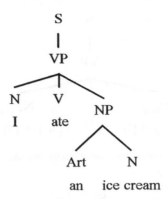

Figure 6: 'I ate an ice cream' (hierarchical structure)

In (204), however, we can take 'that' to refer to two elements of the first sentence, namely the article 'an' and 'ice cream'. This suggests that 'an' and 'ice cream' form a closer bond with one another than with other elements of the sentence, and can together be said to constitute a noun phrase (NP).[218]

Further levels of hierarchy can appear. In (205), 'one' in the second part occupies the same structural position as 'ice cream with chocolate sprinkles' in the first part, and chocolate in the second occupies the same structural position as 'strawberry' in the first. This suggests that 'ice cream' and 'with chocolate sprinkles' belong hierarchically to a higher element allowing for the replacement by 'one'. This higher order element is termed N' (or N-bar), and is termed a PROJECTION of N.

Indeed, it turns out that there is a further hierarchical level within this structure. Consider the following sentence:

(206) I ate this strawberry ice cream with chocolate sprinkles, not that one.

In this case, 'one' replaces not just 'ice cream with chocolate sprinkles', but 'strawberry ice cream with chocolate sprinkles'. Accordingly, we need another N' to account for this, as illustrated in Figure 8.

X-bar theory gives a way of generalising the phrase structure of any element of a language. In these terms, sentences may be composed of specifiers, heads, complements and adjuncts. Figure 9 gives a general structure for the XP.

Notice that within a given XP, there is only one specifier, head and complement, but there may be more than one adjunct. In this way, X-bar theory offers another way of accounting for the polyadicity of adjuncts addressed within a neo-Davidsonian framework at 3.2.4 above. X' projections can be multiplied indefinitely. Only the maximal projection, X, cannot be repeated. In turn this means that Adjuncts, ZP, may be repeated indefinitely, while complements, WP, may not. This difference between

---

[218] For various reasons this is now generally referred to in the literature as the determiner phrase (DP), see Carnie (2013: 208-9).

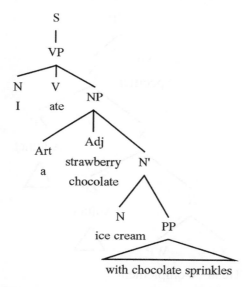

Figure 7: 'I ate a strawberry/chocolate ice cream with chocolate sprinkles' (hierarchical structure with N' for N and PP)

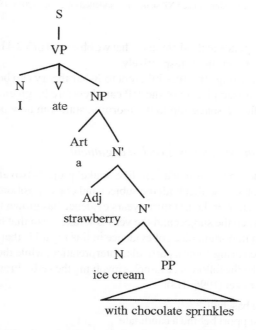

Figure 8: 'I ate a strawberry ice cream with chocolate sprinkles' (hierarchical structure with N' for Adj, N and PP)

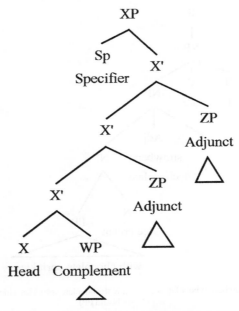

Figure 9: Generalised XP structure, modelled on Carnie (2013: 181)

ZP and WP corresponds to the difference that we observed in 3.2.4 between optional adjuncts and direct arguments respectively.

The binary branching structure inherent to X-bar theory can be applied to verb phrases. A generalised picture of the VP can therefore be given as in Figure 10. The sentence 'I flew a spaceship to the morning star,' can now be analysed as in Figure 11.

3.3.4 *Status of the subject as a verbal argument*

It may seem a priori obvious that a verb like 'make' projects two arguments, a subject and a direct object, so that both the subject and object positions are projections of the VP. However, over the last thirty years evidence has grown that the semantic relationship between the subject and the verb is weaker than that between the verb and its object. An important piece of evidence in this regard is that the direct object of a verb may often bring about a particular interpretation, while the subject rarely if ever does. Consider the following examples involving the verb 'throw', from Marantz (1984) cited by Kratzer (1996: 113):

    (207) Throw a baseball
    (208) Throw support behind a candidate
    (209) Throw a boxing match
    (210) Throw a party
    (211) Throw a fit

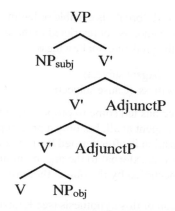

Figure 10: Generalised VP structure

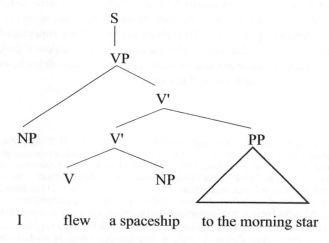

Figure 11: 'I flew a spaceship to the morning star.'

By contrast, the subject seems capable, at least for some verbs, of accepting a wide range of semantic roles. Consider the following examples from Alexiadou & Schäfer (2006: 40):[219]

(212) John broke the window. (Agent subject)
(213) The hammer broke the window. (Instrument subject)
(214) The storm broke the window. (Cause subject)

---

[219] See also Ramchand (1997: 178).

In these examples, the verb 'break' is capable of having subjects in a variety of semantic roles. This phenomenon is not restricted to the verb 'break'. Consider the following examples with the predicate 'make a mess':

(215) John made a mess. (Agent subject)
(216) The storm made a mess. (Cause subject)

This and other evidence has led some to propose that the verb does not actually project a prototypical agent at all, but only a prototypical theme/patient. For this reason the subject position is often termed the EXTERNAL ARGUMENT, or, using theta notation, θ_{ext}, since it is external to the argument projection of the verb.[220] The argument position occupied by the object therefore becomes the INTERNAL ARGUMENT, or θ_{int}.

According to one version of this hypothesis (see Kratzer 1996), it is voice that actually assigns the subject position. According to this view, the active voice that assigns an abstract causer/initiator role to the external argument. The sentence 'I flew a spaceship to the morning star' could therefore be represented according to Figure 12.

There are, however, problems with such an analysis. Most important from our point of view is the issue of accounting for the causative alternation: if the subject is completely external to the argument structure of the verb, the infelcicity of (218) in the following pair of examples is hard to explain:[221]

---

[220] This concept was first introduced in Williams (1981) (see Tenny 1994: 9). Tenny (1994: 9) defines the external argument as 'the noun phrase (NP) argument of the verb which is projected in the phrase structure outside the maximal projection of the verb, and which receives a thematic role from the verb phrase via predication. This argument always becomes the syntactic subject... the verb's direct internal argument is that NP argument which is governed by the verb at D-structure and which receives its thematic role directly from the verb... Indirect internal NP arguments are governed by a preposition (as in English) or by a case marker other than nominative or accusative in some languages.'

[221] In languages which allow for labile transitivity, exactly which verbs are regarded as describing causative versus spontaneous changes of state is language-dependent. In modern Greek many motion verbs, e.g. *páo* 'go', are labile, while in English they may not, e.g. 'go'. Also language-dependent is the allocation of transitive verbs to causative COS and non-COS types. Furthermore, in a given language verbs with very similar semantics may behave differently in regards to labile transitivity. Thus, although *bállō* 'throw' in ancient Greek may be labile, the semantically very similar verb *hríptō* 'throw' is not attested as valency reducing (see LSJ *ad loc.*). Similarly in English 'build' may be labile, while a verb with similar semantics, such as 'construct' does not:

i) I built a house.
ii) I constructed a house.
iii) A picture is building of his final movements.
iv) A picture *is contructing of his final movements.

Compare Levin & Rappaport Hovav (2005: 19): '... certain happenings can be construed as events by languages in more than one way. Verbs used to describe such a happening will not have precisely the same meaning if they lexicalize distinct, though largely overlapping, sets of properties... When alternate construals are possible and involve different grammatically relevant aspects of meaning, the result can be pairs of near-synonyms within or across languages showing different argument realization options.'

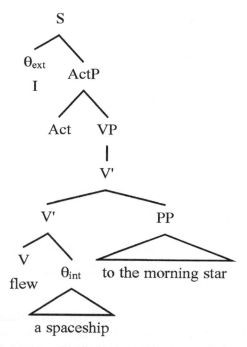

Figure 12: 'I flew a spaceship to the morning star' with internal and external argument positions

(217) I went home.
(218) #He went me home.

There should be no problem with (218) under an external argument analysis, since the structure is identical to that of 'I flew a spaceship to the morning star'. In order to generate the correct results, we need to say that, at some level at least, the subject, even of a causative COS verb, is an argument of it. One way to achieve this, while recognising that the selectional restrictions on the internal argument are tighter than those on the external argument, is to view the verb phrase in terms of a prototypical transitivity.[222] On this analysis, active voice would simply produce the default clause structure as prescribed by the VP. Other voices would then represent variations of this default pattern. We could then analyse causative change of state verbs as composite eventualies consisting of at least two subeventualities: a light, generic, verb (v), i.e. a cause event licencing the external argument followed by a posteventuality containing the lexical semantic information of the verb. Both eventualities would then together constitute the 'verb'. Under this analysis, the possibility of the anticausative construction emerges because the verb 'fly' projects a

---

[222] This concept was first introduced in Hopper & Thompson (1980). For this approach applied in the case of the Greek middle, see Allan (2002). See also Allan (2002: 4) for more references.

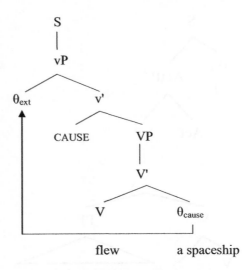

Figure 13: Anticausative phrase structure

cause role as opposed to a straight patient. Optionally, then, the internal argument 'a spaceship' can be interpreted as an external argument, since it may be analysed as a cause, and move to the external position in the absence of a dedicated external argument. In turn this external argument is expressed as the grammatical subject, as shown in Figure 13.

So far we have been assuming that the external argument is equivalent to the subject at S-structure. However, in order to account for voice alternations (for which see 3.5), as well as for aspectual reasons (for which see chapter 5) it is necessary to accord a subject position within the phrase structure distinct from that of the external argument. For the time being, therefore, we will place the assigning of subjecthood at the level of the sentence, with a view to revising this later. Accordingly, we will say that the external argument position moves to subject position, and the previous analysis given at Figure 13 can be modified so as to give the analysis in Figure 14.

3.3.5 *Subject of state sentences*

Since the semantics of the Greek perfect have been so closely linked to the question of stativity, an important question to ask is what semantic role is projected by a state verb. Stative verbs in the minimal case project only one argument:

(219) I stand at the red light.
(220) The monument stands at the crossroads.

This argument position has been variously analysed as that of experiencer, source or location (see Ramchand 1997: 188). In contrast to arguments projected by eventive verbs, however, the semantic properties of the argument appears to

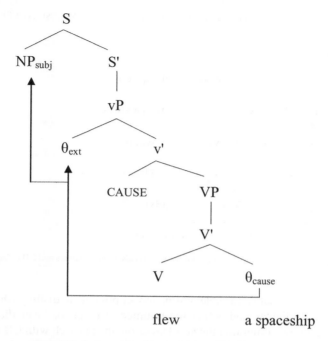

Figure 14: Anticausative phrase structure with subject position

have little effect on the interpretation of the sentence. Consequently, following Ramchand (1997: 187–8) it seems reasonable to accord the subject position of a state verb a very minimal semantic status of LOCATUM, corresponding essentially to a path with a single position (since states by definition describe situations which do not change). This Ramchand defines as simply 'a degenerate version of the Θ_{ext} role'. She goes on:

> The fact that LOCATUM is simply the degenerate case of path participation (i.e. where there is only one location on the path) represents what the stative and eventive subjects have in common (i.e. their externality).

We will refer to this role simply as an external argument, θ_{ext}, which is then realised as subject in active constructions.[223]

3.3.6 Combining Davidsonian semantics with GB theory

We noted at 3.2.5 above that one of the weaknesses of the neo-Davidsonian framework used by Parsons, Ramchand, and others is that, in treating arguments as modifi-

---

[223] For a list of aspectual arguments see Table 17, p. 160 below.

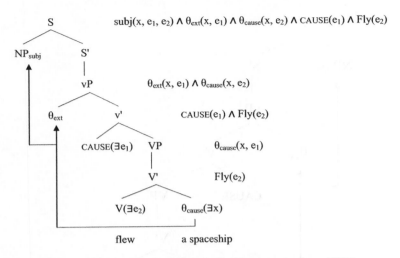

Figure 15: 'A spaceship flew' combining neo-Davidsonian semantics and GB theory

cations of the eventuality variable, it is no longer possible to distinguish between arguments and adjuncts, and as such the argument structure of the predicate is not clear. However, by combining the neo-Davidsonian approach with GB theory, it is possible to arrive at a solution which is able to represent clearly both argument structure and semantics. Specifically, each functional projection in the syntax tree can be said to contribute semantic attributes to the eventuality variable(s) modified by the predicate.[224]

The sentence 'A spaceship flew' is represented in Figure 15. It will be seen from this representation that the contributions are cumulative. Therefore, each new phrase projection adds entailments to the predicate until the highest level is reached, comprising all the entailments of the predicate. For the sake of clarity I have divided the semantic contributions of arguments and verbal elements to phrase-level and bar-level projections respectively.

3.4 Predicate types

3.4.1 Introduction

As noted in the introduction, one of the key problems to address in reference to the Greek perfect active is its transitivity alternations. Since these occur in change of state and causative change of state predicates, it is worth spending some time analysing the structure of change of state and causative change of state predicates in the terms we have been introducing.

---

[224] For similar approaches, albeit involving lambda calculus, see e.g. Doron (2005) and Sæbø (2001).

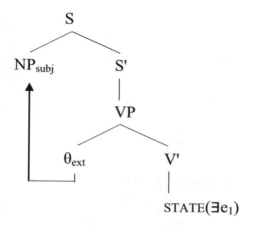

Figure 16: State sentence with one participant

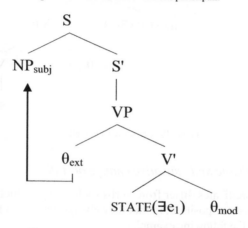

Figure 17: State sentence with two participants

3.4.2 *State predicates*

State predicates are in many ways the most basic kind of predicate. As discussed at 3.3.5, many states have only a single participant, the external argument. However, in others, e.g. 'love', the verb may project an object as well. Since state events do not describe progressive change, the role of this object has a different character from that of eventive predicates, in that it has a looser modificatory roll in relation to the notion of the state being described. As such it does not fit easily into the proto-patient category as outlined at 3.2.7 above. Following Ramchand (1997: 123ff.) I will refer to this role as θ_{mod}, for 'modifying'. The event structure of the former is given in Figure 16, and the latter in Figure 17.

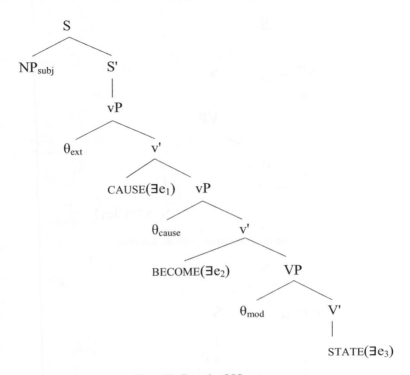

Figure 18: Causative COS sentence

3.4.3 *Change of state and causative change of state*

Change of state predicates differ from verbs such as 'fly', which only optionally describe a final state or position, in that they always describe a final state for the subject. Compare the following examples:

(221) The water froze.
(222) The plane flew.

In the first example, according to the semantics of the predicate, the final state of the water is being 'frozen'. By contrast, there is no final state for the plane in the second example. Accordingly, following Rappaport & Levin (1998) and Kiparsky (2002), I take changes of state to be complex eventualities comprising two events: a become subevent, projecting a cause internal argument, and a POSTSTATE, projecting a mod argument. Verbs participating in the causative alternation have in addition a cause subevent, projecting an external argument, according to the structure given in Figure 18.

In this analysis, the VP is a state predicate with prior become and cause events. Thus, the predicates 'I froze the water' and 'The water froze' may be represented respectively as in Figure 19 and Figure 20.

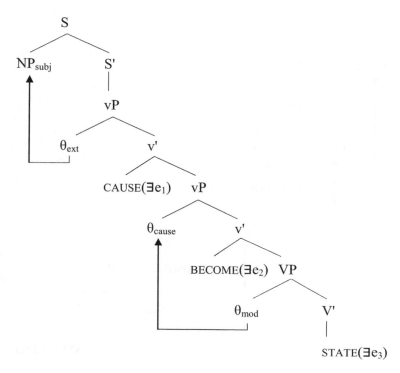

Figure 19: 'I froze the water.'

Notice that under this analysis, the argument is not a complement of V, but rather its specifier.[225] This is so in the first instance for the state subeventuality.[226] However, the become subevent also has a specifier position, the internal argument that undergoes the change. In both the causative and anticausative examples the subject of the state subeventuality moves to specifier position of the become subevent.

The causative and the anticausative cases differ, however, in that in the former an external argument is explicitly provided, while in the latter it is not. Furthermore, in the latter case, since the internal argument of these predicates is a cause argument, and therefore interpretable as an external argument, the former is free to move to external position where this is not otherwise given.

---

[225] The predicate structures used from this point on are substantially similar to those proposed by Larson (1988) and Hale & Keyser (1993). They differ in some details, however, notably in the projection of a state eventuality below the become eventuality. Another important difference is that Hale & Keyser do not take the external argument to be an argument of the verb.

[226] For this way of treating the subjects of result states of COS predicates see Butt & Ramchand (2005). The key point is that there are not the same selectional restrictions on the nominal argument of state verbs as exist for the internal argument of accusative verbs. Accordingly, the relationship is best seen as that of specifier-head than head-complement.

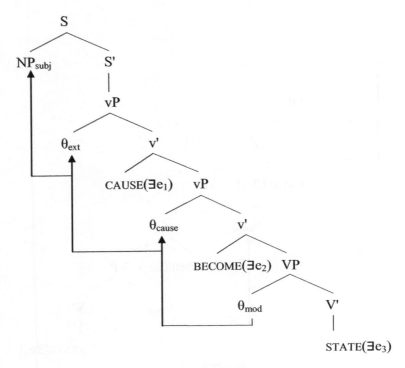

Figure 20: 'The water froze.'

3.4.4 *Change of state and change of location*

So far, verbs describing change of location (COL) events, e.g. 'move', 'come', 'go', have been treated as verbs describing COS events not entailing a change of location, e.g. 'freeze', 'stand', 'break'. These latter events I will term change-of-nature (CON) events. However, although parallels have often been drawn between these two sets of verbs,[227] there are reasons for thinking that they should not necessarily be treated together. That they behave differently in terms of argument realisation has been shown for English.[228] Specifically a CON verb, such as 'break', must have the entity which is broken as either its subject or object, and cannot have this participant as an adjunct. By contrast, verbs describing causative COL events in English show flexibility in argument realisation which is not seen in causative CON verbs. Consequently the distinction will be born in mind for the present analysis.

---

[227] See Rappaport Hovav & Levin (2005: 285) and references there.
[228] Rappaport Hovav & Levin (2005: 278).

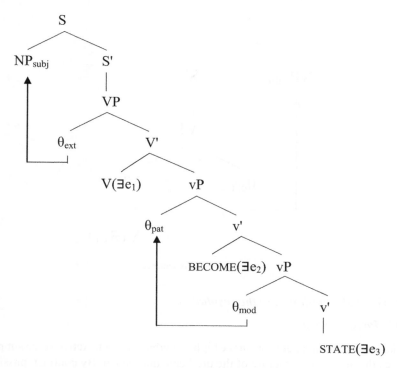

Figure 21: Accomplishment sentence

3.4.5 *Accomplishment predicates*

I take accomplishment predicates to have a similar structure to causative COS predicates, except that in their case the VP is the highest order verbal element, with two aspectual light verbs 'become' and 'state' below it. The eventuality described by V projects a θ_{ext} argument, in the same way as the cause eventuality in causative COS predicates. However, the become eventuality does not project a cause argument, but a patient, an argument which is incapable of interpretation as external, and requiring voice morphology in order to rise to external position. The result is that accomplishments, unlike COS predicates, cannot participate in the causative alternation, because the patient argument in internal position cannot be interpreted as an external argument and cannot move to subject position. The event structure is illustrated in Figure 21.

3.4.6 *Activity predicates*

Activity predicates have a much simpler structure, lacking as they do the subeventualities 'become' and 'state', and therefore having only a single, external, argument. The structure of an activity predicate is given in Figure 22.

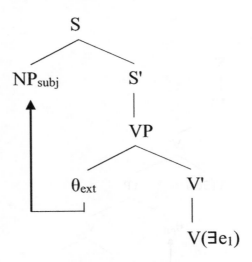

Figure 22: Activity sentence

3.5 *Voice alternations and the resultative*

3.5.1 *Passive voice*

I take voice to be an operation on the highest verbal element. Active voice simply leaves the argument structure of the predicate untouched. By contrast, passive voice suppresses the external argument, for predicates that have such, and explicitly allows the patient argument to move to subject position in the sentence. Figure 23 and Figure 24 give the passive of causative COS and accomplishment sentences respectively.

From a comparison of Figure 20 with Figure 23, it can be seen that the principal difference between the passive of a causative construction, on the one hand, and the anticausative, on the other, is that in the anticausative, but not the passive, the event takes place without the implication of an external cause, since the sole participant is interpreted as both the internal and external argument. By contrast, in the passive, the external cause is simply left unspecified, but is crucially not identified with the internal argument.

3.5.2 *Resultative*

The resultative differs from the passive in that it may (albeit marginally) operate on single argument verbs, unlike the passive:

(223) *He is being gone.
(224) He is gone.

If a verb like 'go' projects only a cause internal argument, the infelicity of the passive makes sense: there is no external argument to remove. However, the resultative

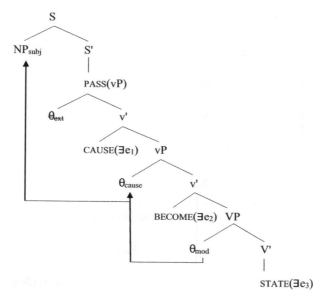

Figure 23: Passive of a causative COS sentence

is felicitous with at least some examples of this kind of verb. This, I propose, is because the resultative in English suppresses both the external argument (where present) and the internal argument, and allows the subject of the underlying state subeventuality to move to subject position, as represented in Figure 25 and Figure 26 for causative COS and accomplishment sentences respectively. In unaccusatives like 'go', since there is no cause eventuality, only the internal argument is suppressed, as represented in Figure 27.

It is true, however, that a number of unaccusatives in modern English are not felicitous with the resultative, where in earlier periods they were:

(225) ?He is come.

(226) #He is arrived.

The only way to express the result state in these verbs in modern English is to use the perfect:

(227) He has come.

(228) He has arrived.

If the analysis of the resultative given above is correct, it suggests that the argument structure of these verbs has changed in English, from projecting an internal argument, to projecting an external argument only. The passive is still infelicitous because there is no internal argument that can surface as subject. Accordingly, at least in respect of the resultative, these verbs now behave like unergative verbs:

(229) #He is danced.

A prototypical unergative sentence is represented in Figure 28.

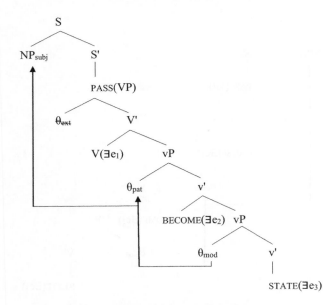

Figure 24: Passive of an accomplishment sentence

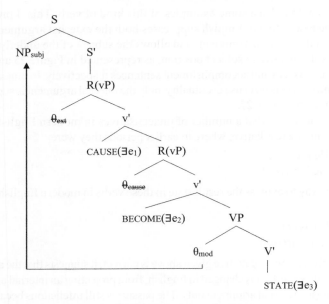

Figure 25: Resultative of a causative COS sentence

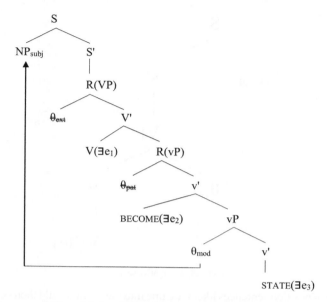

Figure 26: Resultative of an accomplishment sentence

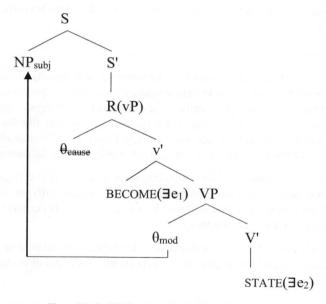

Figure 27: Resultative of an unaccusative COS sentence

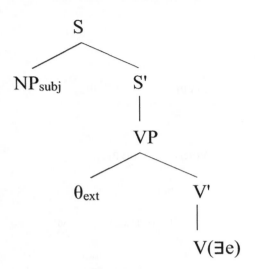

S

NP$_{subj}$　　　　S'

VP

θ$_{ext}$　　　　V'

V(∃e)

Figure 28: Unergative sentence

Change of position sentences like 'He came into the room' would then be analysed as cases of unaccusativisation of exactly the same kind as 'He danced into the room', whereby state and become events are not imposed by the verb, but rather derived from the predicate.

3.5.3 *The middle*

Across languages there are recognised to exist categories superficially similar in function to the passive in its capacity to reduce valency. One such category is the middle. Linguists differ widely as to the specific value of the middle both cross-linguistically and in particular languages.[229] It is generally recognised, however, that the middle is a semantic category, related to reduction in agency. Thus Manney summarises recent research into the Greek middle, both ancient and modern, in the following way:[230]

> ... the inflectional middle voice comprises a basic verbal category which is opposed, both morphosyntactically and semantically, to the active inflectional system, and that middle voice typically functions to encode reduced or absence of agency.

For this study I will take it that the middle encodes that the external argument θ$_{ext}$ may be interpreted as an underlying cause θ$_{cause}$. Importantly, it does not delete the external

---

[229] Recent cross-linguistic studies in include Kemmer (1993), Klaiman (1991), Andersen (1994). For lack of consensus on the middle see Stroik (2006). Faultlines in the scholarly debate include the relationship of the middle voice to other, at least superficially similar, categories such as reflexive and reciprocal, as well as what the middle asserts about the agentivity of the subject. See Manney (2000: 15–70) for a more detailed summary of different views.

[230] Manney (2000: 25).

argument, but instead renders its semantics to be compatible with prototypical patienthood. This may be seen as the reverse of the process by which cause arguments in internal position may optionally be interpreted in external position, yielding the causative alternation: in just the same way that underlying causes may be viewed as sharing sufficient semantic characteristics to participate in prototypical agency, so, going the other way, may θ_{cause} be viewed as sharing sufficient characteristics to share in prototypical patienthood.

The middle, defined in this way, differs from the passive in that while the passive is an operation on the arguments projected by the cause subeventuality by entirely removing the external argument and allowing subject status to arguments falling under prototypical patienthood, the middle merely demotes the agency of the external argument. Thus unlike a passive form, a middle form is able, optionally, to fill both subject and object positions, where both the subject and object are viewed as in some way affected by the event. Consider the following examples in English:

(230) They got the water frozen.
(231) The water got frozen.
(232) #They were frozen the water.
(233) The water was frozen.

Here while the English 'get' construction is able either to occur as transitive, (230), or as intransitive, (231), the English passive construction is obliged to occur as intransitive. Example (231) can be represented in as in Figure 29.

Notice that the entailments in terms of agency/causation of 'I got the water frozen', and 'I froze the water' are very similar, if not identical, namely that the subject caused the water to freeze. A verb like 'kill', however, differs from 'freeze' in that it

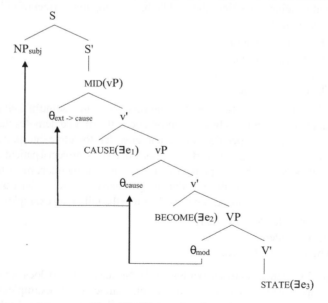

Figure 29: 'The water got frozen.'

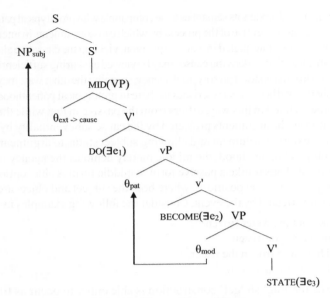

Figure 30: 'They got the man killed.'

specifies a patient argument, rather than a cause in internal position. 'Kill' projects a patient in internal position, rather than a cause. However, since the middle has demoted θ_{ext} to θ_{cause}, the patient can move to this position. Where prototypical agents are specified in subject position, the middle has the apparent effect of reducing the agency of the subject:

(234) They got the man killed.
(235) The man got killed.
(236) #They were killed the man.
(237) The man was killed.

The middle, passive and anticausative do, however, overlap in some of their functions. Notice that, under the analysis being proposed here, the middle demotes the external argument to a cause, not a specifically external cause. It is therefore interpretable either as an internal or external cause. In verbs, such as 'kill', which project a patient argument, the patient will optionally be interpretable as a cause, and can therefore move to external position. In this way a raising/valency-reducing operation will appear to have taken place, similar to the passive and anticausative, as shown in the following examples:

(238) He got killed (e.g. by a car).
(239) He was killed.
(240) The water got frozen.

Example (238) can be analysed per Figure 31. Notice that (238) does not imply any active participation on the part of the subject, cf. change of state examples where the same participant is interpreted as both internal and external cause. In the case of

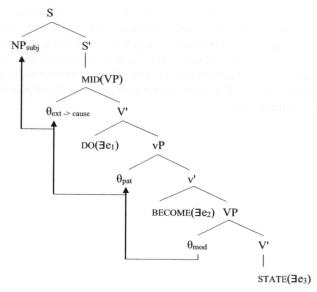

Figure 31: 'He got killed.'

Table 11. Theta roles and behaviour with different voice alternations

		Behaviour with active voice	Behaviour with middle	Behaviour with passive	Resultative
θ_{ext}		Always becomes subject if present	Converts to θ_{cause}	Suppressed	Suppressed
θ_{int}	θ_{cause}	Can become subject	Can become subject	Can become subject	Suppressed
	θ_{pat}	Cannot become subject	Can become subject	Can become subject	Suppressed
	θ_{mod}	Cannot become subject	Cannot become subject	Cannot become subject	Can become subject

'kill' this only comes about where both external and internal positions are explicitly filled, as in:

(241) He got himself killed.

3.6 *Conclusion*

The theta roles that we will be using for this investigation, and their behaviour with active, middle and passive are given in turn in Table 11.[231]

---

[231] We will have cause to expand this system slightly on investigation of the Greek verb system at 4.2.3.5 and Table 14, p. 129 below.

Having established the general syntactic-semantic framework(s) under which we will be working, we are now in a position to assess the function of the perfect at the syntactic level. Chapter 4 will first assess the detransitivisation associated with the perfect by looking at the manifestation of the causative alternation in the Greek verb system in general and in the perfect more specifically, passing over for the time being any aspectual phenomena. Then in chapter 5 we will assess the aspect function of the perfect by predicate type.

4 The causative alternation

4.1 Introduction

4.1.1 Transitivity in traditional Greek grammar

Traditionally Greek scholars have defined transitivity in terms of the ability of a verb to take a direct object. This is the approach taken, for example, by Goodwin (italics his):[232]

> 893. Verbs which can have a direct object are called *transitive*; those which cannot are called *intransitive*.

This formulation is in essence equivalent to the assertion that a transitive verb requires more than one participant role to be filled, and transitivity in these terms is a question of grammatical relations, not semantic roles.

However, the active ~ passive opposition is explained in terms which mix semantic roles and grammatical relations:[233]

> 1233. In the passive voice the subject is represented as acted upon; as *ho paîs hupò toû patròs phileîtai*, the child is loved by the father.

Thus in the passive, on the one hand, a valency-reducing operation is described as taking place, whereby the object of the active becomes the subject of the passive, an operation which concerns grammatical relations. On the other hand the role of the subject is expressed in terms of semantic roles: 'in the passive voice the subject is represented as acted upon', i.e. the subject is a patient.

The traditional account of the means of reintroducing the subject similarly mixes grammatical relations and semantic roles:

> 1234. The object of the active becomes the subject of the passive. The subject of the active, the personal agent, is generally expressed by *hupó* with the genitive in the passive construction.

Here the subject of the active is termed 'the personal agent'.

It is desirable, therefore, to provide a framework for analysing the Greek voice system in terms that clarify the role of grammatical relations and semantic roles.

---

[232] Goodwin (1894: 196), cf. Smyth (1920: 257).
[233] Goodwin (1894: 265).

4.1.2 *The function and development of the Greek middle and passive*

While Homeric Greek may in large part be said to inherit the PIE voice distinction of active and middle, Classical Greek developed a three-way morphological distinction between active, middle and passive. The distinction between middle and passive forms was, however, only present in the perfective and future. Furthermore, it does not appear to correspond to a strict semantic distinction. Thus already in the Classical language supposedly middle forms were used with passive denotation, while supposedly passive morphology is used with intransitive but not passive denotation. Accordingly, it can be more helpful to distinguish, in terms of the semantics of the voice system, between active and non-active, with two different sets of morphological realisations of the non-active in the perfective and future (see Table 12).[234]

Non-active morphology in Greek performs a wide range of functions, consistent with a semantic category middle denoting that the subject plays a role of diminished agency, including reflexive, benefactive, passive and anticausative.[235] For our purposes

Table 12. Non-active forms in post-Homeric Greek

	Imperfective	Perfective	Future
Non-active I	*-omai (pres.)*	*-s-ámēn / -ómēn*	*-s-omai*
	-ómēn (past)		
Non-active II	-	*-thē-n*	*-thḗ-s-omai*
		-ēn	

it is the latter that is of primary interest. Contrast the following:[236]

(242) kaì   tò   sôma,   hósonper
       and ART.N-NOM-SG *body.*N-NOM-SG REL-PRON.M-ACC-SG
       khrónon   kaì   hē   nósos
       *time.*M-ACC-SG PTCL ART.F-NOM-SG *disease.*M-NOM-SG
       akmázoi,   ouk
       *flourish.*PRES-OPT-ACT-3-SG   NEG
       emaraíneto…
       *wither.*IMPF-IND-NON-ACT-I-3-SG
       'And the body, for as long as the disease was at its peak, would not **waste away…**' (Thucydides 2.49.6)

(243) theósutón   te   nóson,
       *heaven-sent.*F-ACC-SG   PTCL   *illness.*F-ACC-SG

---

[234] For this points and examples Labidas (2009: 79f.). See also Andersen (1993: 198f.).

[235] The Classical Greek middle appears not to denote reciprocal in the light of examples such as Thucydides 3.12.1: *allélous hupedekhómetha (receive.*PRES-IND-MID*)*. Here the middle is used along with the reciprocal pronoun *allélous*. This can be paralleled for post-Classical Greek, e.g. Jos. *AJ* 1.236: *ēspázonto… allélous (greet.*PRES-IND-MID*)*.

[236] Quoted by Labidas (2009: 89).

THE CAUSATIVE ALTERNATION

ōnómasas	hà
name.AOR-IND-ACT-2-SG	*rel-pron.F-NOM-SG*
maraínei	me
cause-to-waste-away.PRES-IND-ACT-3-SG	*I.ACC-SG*
khríousa	kéntrois...
prick.PRES-PTPL-ACT-F-NOM-SG	*goad.N-DAT-PL*

'[Who are you]... who have named a heaven-sent illness that **causes** me **to waste away** by pricking me with... goads?' (Aeschylus *Prometheus Bound* 597)

By the end of the Classical period, however, the anticausative and reflexive functions begin to be lost from the non-active.[237] Already in the Classical language reflexive is denoted by means both of the middle voice and a reflexive pronoun, indicating that the middle was not viewed as denoting this category inherently:[238]

(244)
hoi	mén	phasi	basiléa
ART.M-NOM-P	*PTCL*	*speak.PRES-IND-ACT-3PL*	*king.M-ACC-SG*
keleûsaí	tina		epispháxai
order.AOR-INF-ACT	*indef-pron.M-ACC-SG*		*slaughter.AOR-INF-ACT*
autòn	Kúrōi,	hoi	d'
he.ACC-SG	*Cyrus.M-DAT-SG*	*ART.M-NOM-PL*	*PTCL*
heautòn		**epispháxasthai**	
refl-pron.M-ACC-SG		***slaughter.AOR-INF-NON-ACT-I***	

'... some say that the king bade someone despatch him upon Cyrus' [body], while others say that **he killed himself**...' (Xenophon *Anabasis* 1.8.29)

Anticausativity may be denoted by both active and non-active morphology in the Koine, as we can see in the following examples from the New Testament:

(245) **egeíresthe**   ágōmen;
rise.PRES-IND-NON-ACT-I-2-PL *leave.PRES-SUBJ-ACT-1-PL*
idoù   éggiken   ho
behold   draw-near.PERF-IND-ACT-3-SG   ART.M-NOM-SG
paradidoús   me
betray.PRES-PTPL-ACT-M-NOM-SG   me
'**Get up**, let us leave: for my betrayer is near.' (*Matthew* 26.46)

(246) **égeire**   kaì   peripátei
rise.PRES-IMP-ACT-2-SG   and   walk.PRES-IMP-ACT-2-SG
'**Get up** and walk!' (*Matthew* 9.5)

---

[237] Labidas asserts that benefactive is also lost. However, the examples given of active use in the Koine are sometimes unconvincing. Thus he gives *psēphízei (count.PRES-IND-ACT) dapánēn (cost.F-ACC-SG)* at *Luke 14.28* (see Labidas 2009: 108f.) as a case where active morphology is used where the subject participates in the action of the verb. However, it is unclear that this verb in the sense 'to count' was ever used in the middle (see LSJ *ad loc.*). At LXX *Exodus* 6.7 *lḗpsomai (take.FUT-IND-MID) emautôi (myself.DAT-SG)* 'I will take for myself' is given (see Labidas 2009: 111) as a case where the dative pronoun is supplied to strengthen the benefactive sense of the middle. Yet *emautôi* is likely a translation of the underlying Hebrew *l-i* 'for myself' at this point.

[238] Labidas (2009: 111).

The use of active forms for anticausative is particularly significant for the present investigation because this is precisely the kind of behaviour seen in some cases of the perfect active stem.[239] It could be therefore that this phenomenon is part of a broader picture of labile transitivity in the Greek active system. However, in order for the observed alternation to be describable in terms of the causative alternation, there needs to be evidence of the following:

(1) That the Greek perfect active of a given anticausative stem also behaves in a causative way.

(2) That the other, i.e. non-perfect, active forms of the verbs with anticausative perfect actives can also be observed to participate in the causative alternation.

It is these questions which the current chapter will seek to answer. First, however, it is necessary briefly to make some comments on voice and argument projection in Greek. This will be helpful in assessing the syntax of the perfect vis-à-vis the rest of the verb system.

4.1.3 Voice and argument projection in Greek

4.1.3.1 Perfective forms in -ēn and -thēn

It can be seen from Table 12 above that the perfective has two non-active II forms, in -thēn and -ēn. This is often treated synchronically as a morphological variant of the 'passive' in -thēn,[240] although their common origin is doubtful (see Sihler 1995: 498, 564). For Homeric Greek it is true that the variation is at least in part driven by phonological factors (see Allan 2002: 96ff.). However, there is also evidence in Homeric Greek for a semantic distinction, or at least a predilection for certain lexical semantic types. Allan (2002: 98) concludes (emphasis his): [241]

(1) 'Forms that denote a **spontaneous process** have -ē-;

(2) Forms that have a **passive meaning** or denote **body motion** have -thē-.'

Allan gives the distributions of the -ē- ~ -thē- distinction presented in Table 13, of cases where phonological issues are not determinative.

As is clear, verbs describing events that can occur spontaneously use the -ē- stem for the anticausative, while verbs projecting a straight patient argument tend to use the -thē- stem.[242]

---

[239] The situation is clearly still in a state of flux since there are examples in the Koine of anticausative being denoted by the middle. Thus the aorist middle infinitive *anoigesthai* is used for the anticausative at Plb. 8.25.10, quoted by Labidas (2009: 114).

[240] e.g. Allan (2002: 94).

[241] Sihler (1995: 564) also characterises forms in -thē- in Homer as passive.

[242] This is not to say that there are not exceptions (see Allan 2002: 99f.), for example the -ē- aorists with passive sense *eblábēn*, *etúpē*, and *plḗgē*. However, these are relatively few. Allan suggests that were in various ways modelled on equivalent forms in verbs denoting spontaneous processes. Sihler (1995: 562) notes that aorists in -ē- 'are in origin imperfects to present stems built with the stative suffix *-eH₁-... though in the later language these lost salient stative force.'

Table 13. Distribution of the -ē- ~ -thē- distinction (see Allan 2002: 99)

Spontaneous process	Passive	Body motion
eágē 'broke (intr.)'	phrakhtheís 'be fenced'	klínthē 'bent aside'
epágē 'got stuck'	etúkhthē 'be done'	tráphthē 'turned (intr.)'
-rágē 'broke (intr.)'	drúphthē 'be scratched'	
ekáē 'burnt (intr.)'	krínthē 'be chosen'	
hrúē 'flew'	krúphthē 'be hidden'	
sapéēi 'rotted'		
tráphē 'grew up'		
phánē 'appeared'		

While most -ē- stem formations are old, this is not universally the case. In the Koine period anoígnumi 'open' at least receives -ē- perfective forms to denote anticausative alongside the previously used -thē-.[243] However, this seems to be restricted to relatively low status sources.[244]

4.1.3.2 Adjunct expression of an agent or cause participant

As described in the previous chapter, the function of the passive and resultative is in principle to suppress arguments in various ways. However, these arguments can under certain circumstances be reintroduced obliquely. In Greek the principal means by which an agent participant may be expressed in Greek is through construal with a hupó + gen. phrase:[245]

(247) tôn   dè   loipôn   hoi   mèn
ART.GEN-PL   PTCL   rest.GEN-PL   ART.M-NOM-PL   PTCL

pleîstoi   perì   tòn   potamòn
most.M-NOM-PL   around   ART.M-ACC-SG   river.M-ACC-SG

ephthárēsan   hupó   te   tôn
destroy.AOR-IND-NON-ACT-II-3PL   by   both   ART.N-GEN-PL

thēríōn   kaì   tôn   hippéōn...
beast.N-GEN-PL   and   ART.M-GEN-PL   horsemen.M-GEN-PL

'Of the rest, most were killed around the river **by both the wild animals and the horsemen...**' (Plb. 3.74.7)

---

[243] For the alternation see New Testament, Acts of the Apostles 12.10 and Revelation 20.12, quoted below at (292) and n. 260.

[244] A TLG search for these forms attests the stem anoigē- occurring in the following sources up to the end of the second century: LXX, 2 Esdras (ed. Rahlfs) 23.19; Jos. AJ 2.337; Life of Adam and Eve 10, 11; New Testament, Acts of the Apostles 12.10; Gospel of Peter 37; Acts of Paul and Thecla 18, and the Shepherd of Hermas 1.4.

[245] cf. Labidas (2009: 106).

Notably, however, the *hupó* + gen. phrase is not limited to the expression of an agent participant, since it may also be used to introduce a non-agent participant which is viewed as a cause:

(248) = (156)

pepēgósi		mónon	**hupò**	**brakheías**
fix.PERF-PTPL-ACT-M-DAT-PL	*only*		**under**	**gentle.***F-GEN-SG*
thermótētos	toîs	ap'	autôn	
heat.*F-GEN-SG*	*ART.M-DAT-PL*	*from*	*they.GEN-PL*	
ártois	dietréphonto...			
bread.M-DAT-PL	*nourish.IMPF-IND-NON-ACT-I-3-PL*			

'... they were nourished with this bread from them, bread which **had been cooked** only **under a gentle heat**...' (Jos. *AJ* 2.316)

Other means by which a cause may be introduced obliquely include use of a dative, *diá* + gen. or acc. phrase, or *ek* + gen. phrase.[246] On occasion such constructions may appear to introduce an animate agent participant:

(249)	... tôn	**di'**	**autòn**
	... *ART.M-GEN-PL*	**on-account-of**	**he.***ACC-SG*
	apolōlótōn...		adelphôn.
	destroy.PERF-PTPL-ACT-M-GEN-PL		*brother.M-GEN-PL*

'... the brothers who had been killed **on his account**.' (Jos. *BJ* 1.560)

It is important to distinguish between the semantic role played in a particular instance by a given participant, and the role that it is capable of playing elsewhere. Thus, while Herod in this example is an animate human being, and is therefore clearly capable of agenthood, this does not require potential agents to be interpreted as agents wherever they occur. Consequently, at (249) Herod should be analysed as a cause, since it is not clear that he was necessarily the agent in the killing.

4.1.3.3 *Direct object argument not a patient*

Sometimes both subject and direct object positions of a predicate may be filled, but the direct object is a location, i.e. 'mod', rather than a patient:

(250)	háteros	dè	ho
	other.M-NOM-SG	*PTCL*	*ART.M-NOM-SG*
	kaloúmenos		Ákra	kaì
	call.PRES-PTPL-NON-ACT-I-NOM-SG		*Akra.F-NOM-SG*	*PTCL*
	tền	**kátō**	**pólin**
	ART.F-ACC-SG	*lower*	*city.F-ACC-SG*
	huphestòs		amphíkurtos.
	place-under.PERF-PTPL-ACT-M-NOM-SG		*on-each-side.M-NOM-SG*

'The other [hill], called Akra, **supports the lower city** [of Jerusalem] on each side.' (Jos. *BJ* 5.137)

---

[246] e.g. Plb. 3.105.8, given at (345), with *diá* + cause participant.

The hill Akra is asserted to support the lower city. Contrast this with transitive and causative usage in the aorist, where the direct object is a patient:[247]

(251) thaumásas   d'   ho
   wonder.AOR-PTPL-ACT-M-NOM-SG   *PTCL*   *ART.M-NOM-SG*
  basileùs   toû   phutoû
  king.M-NOM-SG   *ART.GEN-SG*   *plant.N-GEN-SG*
  tò   mégethos...
  ART.N-ACC-SG   *size.N-ACC-SG*
  kormòn   éreisma   têi   stégēi
  trunk.M-ACC-SG   *support.N-ACC-SG*   *ART.F-DAT-SG*   *roof.F-DAT-SG*
  hupéstēse.
  place-under.AOR-IND-ACT-3-SG
  'The king, in wonder at the size of the plant... **placed the trunk under the roof as a support.**' (Plu. *De Iside et Osiride* [= *On Isis and Osiris*] 357a)

Here the subject causes the object to be under the roof. In the previous example, however, involving *huphestôs*, the subject is under the city. Therefore, even though *huphestôs* has an object complement, its subject plays the role of the object in a non-reducing example. Therefore *huphestôs* should also be regarded as anticausative.

4.1.3.4 *Unergative / object drop*

Greek is an object-drop language. This is to say that transitive verbs may often supply the patient argument from previous context. In such circumstances, despite the lack of an overt object participant, the semantic role played by the subject participant does not change. Compare the following examples, where the object argument specified in the first example is not present in the second:

(252) ho   dè   basileùs
  ART.M-NOM-SG   *PTCL*   *king.M-NOM-SG*
  akoúsas...   tà
  hear.AOR-PTPL-ACT-M-NOM-SG   *ART.N-ACC-PL*
  gegonóta
  happen.PERF-PTPL-ACT-N-ACC-PL
  'But the king, **having heard what had happened**...' (Plb. 4.80.8)

(253) diò   kaì   nûn   éxíou...
  for-this-reason   *also*   *now*   *think-best.IMPF-IND-NON-ACT-I-3-SG*
  kaleîn   toùs   **akēkoótas...**
  call.PRES-INF-ACT   *ART.M-ACC-PL*   ***hear.PERF-PTPL-ACT-ACC-PL***
  'For this reason he thought it best... to summon **those who had heard**...' (Plb. 4.85.6)

---

[247] *hupéstēse (AOR-IND-ACT)* at Plb. 1.50.6 is an example of *huphístēmi* in a slightly different sense, namely 'to bring to a halt'. See LSJ *ad loc.* I.3.

Since in these cases the transitivity of the verb is not changed, this phenomenon will not concern us. Rather we will focus on establishing the conditions under which the internal argument can move to external position.

4.1.4 *Transitivity and the Greek perfect*

At 1.1 we noted that the perfect active stem can be either active and transitive, or intransitive and passive-like. This is to say that we expect the Greek perfect to describe the same relationship in terms of transitivity between the different participants that other active forms do. Thus in the case of the verb *poiéō* 'I do, make' we expect an agent subject and patient object, as in the following example:

(254) **akhreîon** en stenôi tò
useless.N-ACC-SG *in* *confined-area.N-DAT-SG* *ART.N-ACC-SG*
krátiston toû stratoû
best.N-ACC-SG *ART.M-GEN-SG* *army.M-GEN-SG*
pepoiēkótos...
make.PERF-PTPL-ACT-M-GEN-SG
'... **having rendered the best part** of the army **useless** [by putting it] in a confined area...' (App. *Syr.* 7.37)

The problem is that we frequently find perfects where the subject appears to play an affected role, which we would normally associate with the object of a transitive construction. This can be seen in the following examples involving *parabállō*. We might expect the subject and object to play agent and patient roles, respectively, as in the following example:

(255) **parabállontes**   **[lémbous]**
put-alongside.PRES-PTPL-ACT-M-NOM-PL *[ships.ACC-PL]*
plagíous   sunérgoun...
alongside.M-ACC-PL   *fasten-together.IMPF-IND-ACT-3-PL*
'[The Illyrians]... **putting their enemies' [ships]** alongside [their own], they fastened [the ships] together...' (Plb. 2.10.3)

In the perfect, however, we can find the following:

(256) hóste tinàs   epì dúo
that *INDEF-PRON.M-ACC-PL* *for* *two*
kaì treîs   geneás...   mè **parabeblēkénai**
and *three.F-ACC-PL* *generation.F-ACC-PL* *NEG* **put-by.PERF-INF-ACT**
eis halían.
into *court-room.F-ACC-SG*
'[For some of the Eleans so love life in the fields] that many have not... **set foot** in a court room for two or three generations...' (Plb. 4.73.7)

Here the subject plays a patient-like role, and no agent-like participant is specified. Given the framework outlined in 3.4 we can consider the issue within the broader context of the cross-linguistically attested causative alternation. This is to say that in the case of *poiéō*, the verb projects an external argument and a patient. The perfect active, then, as any other active form, requires the agent/external cause and the patient to be expressed separately. By contrast, in the case of *parabállō* the internal argument can be realised as subject, in behaviour familiar from the causative alternation.

It is the aim of the present chapter to establish the precise relationship of the Greek perfect to this phenomenon: is the detransitivisation seen in the Greek perfect purely a function of labile transitivity in the verb system as a whole, or does the perfect have a more direct role to play? I.e. does the perfect *qua* perfect suppress the optional agent/external cause role, or is the internal argument realised as subject by means of the causative alternation operating generally in the active system in Greek? In order to achieve our aim we must first explore the nature of the causative alternation in Greek as a whole. This task is undertaken in section 4.2. After this the relationship of the perfect to labile transitivity is considered in 4.3. Finally conclusions are drawn in 4.4.

4.2 Labile transitivity outside of the perfect

4.2.1 Introduction

The causative alternation is well attested outside of the perfect system in Greek. There are three basic kinds of verbs:

(1) Verbs that demonstrate the causative alternation in a single stem.
(2) Verbs that have specialised causative and anticausative stems.
(3) Verbs that do not participate in the causative alternation.

In the present subsection I will address each of these three kinds of behaviour in turn.

4.2.2 Verbs fully participating in the causative alternation

The active voice is capable of demonstrating true labile transitivity in a number of cases. However, this appears to be restricted to particular verbs. There is good evidence for it in compounds of *bállō* 'throw'. Thus *metabállō* 'change', an archetypal COS verb, can be used both as a causative and an anticausative:

(257) ho   dè   theòs...   eis   thálassan
ART.M-NOM-SG   *PTCL*   *god.M-NOM-SG*   *to*   *sea.F-ACC-SG*
tèn   **épeiron**   **metébale.**
ART.F-ACC-SG   **land.***F-ACC-SG*   **change.***AOR-IND-ACT-3-SG*
'But God... **changed the land** into sea.' (Jos. *AJ* 1.75)

(258) hē   dè   Lótou   gunè̀...   eis
ART.F-NOM-SG   *PTCL*   *Lot.M-GEN-SG*   *wife.F-NOM-SG*   *into*
stélēn   halôn   **metébalen**
pillar.F-ACC-SG   *salt.M-GEN-PL*   **change.***AOR-IND-ACT-3-SG*
'But Lot's wife... **turned** into a pillar of salt...' (Jos. *AJ* 1.203)

In the first example, Joseph describes how God transformed the land into sea by means of the flood.[248] By contrast, in the second example it is the subject, Lot's wife, who changes into a pillar of salt.[249] We can analyse these examples as follows:

(259) $\exists e_1 \exists e_2 \exists e_3 \exists x \exists y \exists z[\text{CAUSE}(e_1) \wedge \text{delim}(e_1) \wedge \theta_{\text{ext}}(y, e_1) \wedge \text{God}(y) \wedge \text{BECOME}(e_2) \wedge$ change$(e_2) \wedge \text{delim}(e_2) \wedge \theta_{\text{cause}}(y, e_2) \wedge \text{STATE}(e_3) \wedge \text{homog}(e_3) \wedge \theta_{\text{mod}}(x, e_3) \wedge$ land$(x) \wedge \text{into}\{\text{GOAL}(z, e_2, e_3)\} \wedge \text{sea}(z)]$

(260) $\exists e_1 \exists e_2 \exists e_3 \exists x \exists z[\text{CAUSE}(e_1) \wedge \text{delim}(e_1) \wedge \theta_{\text{ext}}(x, e_1) \wedge \text{BECOME}(e_2) \wedge \text{change}(e_2) \wedge$ delim$(e_2) \wedge \theta_{\text{cause}}(x, e_2) \wedge \text{STATE}(e_3) \wedge \text{homog}(e_3) \wedge \theta_{\text{mod}}(x, e_3) \wedge \text{Lot's\_wife}(x)$ $\wedge \text{into}\{\text{GOAL}(z, e_3, e_3)\} \wedge \text{a\_pillar\_of\_salt}(z)]$

This is to say that the verb *metabállō* 'change' allows the argument in internal position, optionally, to move to external position. In the first example both the external cause and underlying cause are specified, as *theós* 'God' and and *épeiros* 'land' respectively, and the external cause, *theós*, realised as the subject. By contrast, in the second example the external cause is not specified and the underlying cause participant, Lot's wife, is interpreted as external and realised as the subject.

Predicates involving the verb *prosbállō* 'approach', a change of location verb, demonstrate parallel behaviour:

(261) hoi peiratài...

ART.M-NOM-SG *pirates.M-NOM-PL*

prosbalóntes klímakas

***throw-against.**AOR-PTPL-ACT-M-NOM-PL* *ladder.F-ACC-PL*

'... the pirates... **throwing** scaling ladders [against the walls]...' (Plb. 4.4.1)

(262) ho dè koureùs...

ART.M-NOM-SG PTCL *barber.M-NOM-SG*

prosbalòn toîs árkhousin...

***approach.**AOR-PTPL-ACT-M-NOM-SG* *ART.M-DAT-PL* *archon.M-DAT-PL*

'The barber... **having approached** the archons...' (Plu. *Nic.* 30.1)

In the first example the movement of the ladders is externally caused by the pirates,[250] while in the second example only the underlying cause participant is presented, namely the barber bringing news of Nikias' defeat at Syracuse.[251]

It is interesting to note that it is not necessary for both external and underlying cause arguments to be specified overtly by the verb's own sentence in order to trigger a causative COS reading if the relevant arguments can be picked up from the previous

---

[248] cf. App. *Hisp.* 14.85: *autoùs es sōphrosúnēn metéballen* 'he turned them to moderation'.

[249] cf. App. *BC* 2.11.77: *hē mèn ekkaíousa kaì tuphloûsa pántas philotimía esbénnuto kaì metéballen* (change.IMPF-IND-ACT) *es (to) déos* (fear.N-ACC-SG) 'the jealousy which inflames and blinds all was extinguished and turned to fear'.

[250] Plb. 3.93.8 seems likely to be a parallel for this, as taken by Shuckburgh (1889).

[251] The anticausative is frequently used in the sense of 'attack', e.g. Jos. *AJ* 6.110, App. *Hann.* 7.43. Cf. also the use of *embállō* in the sense of 'invade', e.g. App. *Mith.* 15.101.

text. Consider the following example of *embállō*, where the subject plays an external cause role, but with no overt underlying cause:[252]

(263) ho   Opímios   sullabṑn
      ART.M-NOM-SG   *Opimius.M-NOM-SG*   *arrest.AOR-PTPL-ACT-M-NOM-SG*
      es   tḕn   phulakḕn   enébalé...
      into ART.F-ACC-SG prison.F-ACC-SG   throw.AOR-IND-ACT-3-SG
      'Opimius arrested [the conspirators] and **threw** [them] into the prison...'
      (App. *BC* 1.3.26)

However, it is by no means restricted to these verbs. Labile transitivity of this kind can also be seen in *hupostéllō* 'hide' and *sunaspízō* 'form a *testudo*'.[253] In the following passage *sunaspízō* is used transitively, taking a direct object complement of the men who would form the *testudo*. Here Vespasian finds himself isolated with a few men in the upper part of the town of Gamala:

(264) **sunaspízei**   mèn   toùs   ham'
      lock-shields.*PRES-IND-ACT-3-SG*   *PTCL ART.M-ACC-PL* *with*
      autôi...
      he.M-DAT-SG
      '[Vespasian] **formed** those around him **into the *testudo***...' (Jos. *BJ* 4.33)

In the next example, however, the external cause is not specified, and the underlying cause moves to external position:[254]

(265) en tôi   taútēn   te   meînai
      meanwhile   this.F-ACC-SG PTCL   remain.AOR-INF-ACT
      sunaspísasan
      form-into-a-testudo.AOR-PTPL-ACT-F-ACC-SG*
      'meanwhile the first company remained, **their shields locked together**...'
      (Plb. 4.64.7)

hupostéllō 'hide' also demonstrates the causative alternation, with the first of the following examples demonstrating causative and the second anticausative behaviour:

(266) toùs   dè   Baliareîs   kaì   logkhophórous...
      ART.M-ACC-PL   *PTCL* *Balearic.M-ACC-PL and*   *pikemen.M-ACC-PL*
      hupò   toùs   en   dexiâi   bounoùs......
      under ART.M-ACC-PL on   right.F-DAT-SG   *hill.M-ACC-PL*
      hupésteile
      send-under.AOR-IND-ACT-3-SG*

---

[252] cf. Plu. *Alc.* 20.3: *toùs mèn... **enéballon** (AOR-IND-ACT) akrítous eis tò desmōtḗrion* 'they threw some into prison'; App. *Mith.* 7.48: *Zēnóbion mèn es tò desmōtḗrion **embalóntes** (AOR-PTPL-ACT) ékteinan* 'Having thrown Zenobius into the prison they killed him.'

[253] On the *testudo* and for other texts discussing its use and formation see Knapp (1928). My translation in this case follows that of Shuckburgh (1889). Cf. Dio Cassius 49.29.2 where the verb is used in this sense.

[254] cf. Jos. *AJ 5.50*: *sunaspísantas (AOR-PTPL-ACT) autoîs (they.M-DAT-PL)* lit. 'having locked shields with them'; App. *BC 4.3.14*: *sunéspizon (IMPF-IND-ACT) allélois (each-other.DAT-PL)* lit. 'they locked shields with one another'.

'He **sent** the Balearic troops along with their pikemen… **under** the cover **of** the hills on the right hand side…' (Plb. 3.83.3)

(267) autoì   mèn   hupò   tền   parṓreian
they.NOM-PL *PTCL* *under* *ART.F-ACC-SG hill.F-ACC-SG*
huposteílantes   émenon
send-under.*AOR-PTPL-ACT-M-NOM-PL*   *remain.IMPF-IND-ACT-3-PL*
'[the Aetolian cavalry] **headed off for refuge** under the hill and stayed there…'
(Plb. 4.12.4)

This verb will turn out to be very important for the analysis of the role of the perfect in bringing about anticausativity.

In the light of the evidence presented here, it seems that predicates headed by these verbs behave very like verbs in English which participate in the causative alternation. I therefore propose an argument structure of the verb phrase on exactly the same lines as that proposed for English verbs participating in the causative alternation at Figure 19 and Figure 20 (see p. 99f.).

4.2.3 *Anticausative denoted by inflection*

4.2.3.1 *Anticausative through non-active morphology*

Many COS verbs do not participate in the causative alternation, but use voice morphology to distinguish between causative and anticausative uses. Verbs in this category include *anoígnumi* 'open', *apóllumi* 'destroy, kill', *diaphtheírō* 'destroy', *egeírō* 'raise', *histēmi* 'make stand', *peíthō* 'persuade', *pléssō* 'strike', *kataplḗssō* 'terrify, amaze' and *hrḗgnumi* 'break'.

In the imperfective of these verbs the causative is always expressed by active terminations, while the anticausative is expressed by non-active morphology. The imperfective stem in both cases is the same. The following are examples of *apóllumi*:

(268) paíōn   gár…   toùs
strike.PRES-PTPL-ACT-M-NOM-SG   *PTCL*   *ART.M-ACC-PL*
entugkhánontas   ho   Térmeros
meet.PRES-PTPL-ACT-ACC-PL   *ART.M-NOM-SG*   *Termerus.M-NOM-SG*
apṓlluen.
destroy.*IMPF-IND-ACT-3-SG*
'For by striking… those whom he met… Termerus **would kill** them.' (Plu. *Thes.* 11.2)[255]

(269) hoi   mèn   díkas   tinnúontes
ART.M-NOM-PL *PTCL*   *penalty.F-ACC-PL* *pay.PRES-PTPL-ACT-M-NOM-PL*
apṓllunto   kakoì   kakôs…
destroy.*IMPF-IND-NON-ACT-I-3-PL* *bad.m-nom-pl* *badly*
'… some poor souls paid the penalty and **met a terrible end**…' (Plu. *Brutus* 33)

The same alternation can be seen in the case of *hrḗgnumi* and *histēmi*:

---

[255] Parallel: Plu. *Timoleon* 28.

(270) polù   pûr,
much.N-NOM-SG   *fire.N-NOM-SG*
anaphthén,   eîta
kindle.AOR-PTPL-NON-ACT-II-N-NOM-SG then
hrēgnúmenon   eis   phlógas...
break.PRES-PTPL-NON-ACT-I-N-NOM-SG into   *flames.F-ACC-PL*
'... a great fire having started, then **started breaking** into flames...'
(Plu. *Alexander* 2)

(271) ... tôn   oïstôn...   hópla   te
... ART.M-GEN-PL   *arrow.M-GEN-PL*   *armour.N-ACC-PL*   PTCL
hrēgnúntōn
break.PRES-PTPL-ACT-GEN-PL
'... of the arrows which both **pierced** armour...' (Plu. *Crassus* 24)

(272) **hístē**   dè   prṓtous   mèn toùs
set-up.IMPF-IND-ACT-3-SG PTCL *first.M-ACC-PL* PTCL *ART.M-ACC-PL*
eléphantas...
elephant.M-ACC-PL
'**He put** the elephants first in line...' (App. *Pun.* 7.40)

(273) tóte gàr dè̀   tôn   te   hēgemónōn...
then PTCL PTCL ART.M-GEN-PL PTCL *leader.M-GEN-PL*
hékastos   **hístato**
each.M-NOM-SG   *set-up.IMPF-IND-NON-ACT-I-3-SG*
par'   autón
beside   *he.ACC-SG*
'Then each of the leaders... **stood** beside him...' (App. *BC* 2.104)

In the perfective, the situation is more complex. While the causative is given by a perfective stem in *-s-* with active endings, in the case of the anticausative there are three possibilities, varying by lexical item:

(1) Anticausative denoted by a non-active-I form in *-ómēn* (*peíthō, apóllumi*)
(2) Anticausative denoted by a non-active-II form in *-ēn* (*pléssō, katapléssō, anoígnumi, hrḗgnumi, diaphtheírō*)
(3) Anticausative denoted by a non-active-II form in *-thēn* (*anoígnumi, egeírō*)

We argued above (4.1.2) that it is better to regard non-active-I and non-active-II forms as allomorphs of a non-active voice, rather than trying to maintain a rigorous distinction between middle and passive. Accordingly, in each case we can say that anticausative readings are brought about by non-active inflection.

4.2.3.2 Anticausative perfective in –ómēn

Several verbs denote anticausative through non-active-I morphology. Thus *apóllumi* contrasts the non-active *apōlómēn* (anticausative) with *apólesa* (causative):

(274) hópou   kaì   Dorúlaos   ho   stratēgós...
where   PTCL   *Dorylaüs.M-NOM-SG*   ART.*M-NOM-SG*   *general.M-NOM-SG*
apóleto   dià   taútēn
destroy.AOR-IND-NON-ACT-I-3SG   *for*   *that.F-ACC-SG*
'... where Dorylaüs, the general, **died** for that...' (Plu. *Lucullus* 17)

(275) tòn   mèn   gàr   prôton...   en   toîs
ART.*M-ACC-SG*   PTCL   PTCL   *first*   *in*   ART.*M-DAT-PL*
emphulíois   polémois   pûr
inner-tribe.M-DAT-PL   *war.M-DAT-PL*   *fire.N-NOM-SG*
apólese...
destroy.AOR-IND-ACT-3-SG
'For fire **destroyed** the first [temple] in the civil wars.' (Plu. *Publicola* 15)

It is interesting to note that this verb has two distinct senses, one 'destroy', as exemplified above, the other 'lose'. The essential difference between the two is the nature of the arguments projected. Thus in the sense 'destroy' the verb projects an agent and patient, while the sense 'lose' it projects an experiencer and a source, as in the following examples, causative and anticausative respectively:

(276) tòn   stratēgòn   **apolésantes**
ART.*M-ACC-SG*   *general.M-ACC-SG*   *lose.AOR-PTPL-ACT-M-NOM-PL*
eis   phugèn   etrápēsan
to   *flight.F-ACC-SG*   *turn.AOR-IND-NON-ACT-II-3-PL*
'... since they **had lost** their general they turned to flight...' (Jos. *AJ* 12.410)

(277) kaì   **apólonto**   hai   ónoi
and   *lose.AOR-IND-NON-ACT-I-3-PL*   ART.*F-NOM-PL*   *donkey.F-NOM-PL*
Kis   patròs   Saoul...
Kish   *father.M-GEN-SG Saul*
'And the donkeys of Kish, Sauls' father, **were lost**...' (LXX (ed. Rahlfs), *1 Kingdoms [= 1 Samuel]* 9:3)

The distinction may well be an artefact of the English language, which has two separate verbs projecting different kinds of arguments. It may be better to analyse *apóllumi* as projecting a common set of arguments, which may then be variously interpreted as either agent or external cause etc. according to the sense of the context. This is to say that the common denominator shared by the two senses is that something is lost, either to the universe, or to a particular individual, and this event of losing is projected to have both an external and an underlying cause. This accords with the capacity of this verb to receive *pûr* 'fire', an external cause rather than an agent, as a subject above at (275).

4.2.3.3 *Anticausative perfective in –ēn*

A similar picture can be drawn for cases where the anticausative is denoted by non-active-II forms in -*ē*-. Thus for *kataplēssō*, the root form is used for the perfective anticausative, while the sigmatic form is used for the perfective causative:

(278) hoútō **kateplágēsan** hoi
so ***strike.****AOR-IND-NON-ACT-II-3-PL* *ART.M-NOM-PL*
Surakoúsioi pròs tò mégethos tês
Syracusan.M-NOM-PL at ART.N-ACC-SG size.N-ACC-SG ART.F-GEN-SG
dunámeōs
force.F-GEN-SG
'... the Syracusans **were** so **amazed** at the size of the force...' (Plu. *Timoleon* 25)

(279) hōs dè **katéplēxen,** es tò...
*when PTCL **strike.****AOR-IND-ACT-3-SG* *into ART.N-ACC-SG*
hieròn parêlthe.[256]
temple.N-ACC-SG enter.AOR-IND-ACT-3-SG.
'When he **had struck fear** [into them], he entered the temple...' (App. *BC* 1.8.64)

In the case of *pléssō* and *diaphtheírō* the -*ē*- suffix is used to denote passive rather than anticausative:

(280) Agúlaios, hōs **eplḗgē,**
*Agulaeus.M-NOM-SG when **strike.****AOR-IND-NON-ACT-II-3-SG*
pesṑn...
fall.AOR-PTPL-ACT-M-NOM-SG
'Agylaeus having fallen when **he was struck**...' (Plu. *Agis and Cleomenes* 8)

(281) tò anthoûn málista
ART.N-NOM-SG bloom.PRES-PTPL-ACT-N-NOM-SG especially
tês dunámeōs **diephthárē...**
*ART.F-GEN-SG force.F-GEN-SG **destroy.****AOR-IND-NON-ACT-II-3-SG*
'The flower of their force **was destroyed**.' (Plu. *Coriolanus* 39)

Nevertheless, at least in the case of *pléssō*, the stem in -*ē*- can also be used for the anticausative:

(282) **eplḗgē** mèn oûn kaì
strike.*AOR-IND-NON-ACT-II-3-SG* *PTCL PTCL CONJ*
élgēsen
suffer.AOR-IND-ACT-3-SG
'**He was struck** then with grief...' (Plu. *Agis and Cleomenes* 22)

The -*ē*- perfective of *hístēmi*, -*stē*-, also belongs here, as originally from *-*stH₂*-eH₁*- (see Sihler 1995: 562). This form alternates with the causative sigmatic aorist as follows:[257]

---

[256] cf. App. *BC* 2.16.116: *toùs (ART.M-ACC-PL) mèn hḗ te ópsis... katéplēsse (IMPF-IND-ACT);* App. *BC* 4.2.8: *tàs (ART.F-ACC-PL) dè katapléxantes (AOR-IND-ACT).*
[257] As previously, *hístēmi* is used to illustrate all its compounds.

(283) ... éstēsan   epì   tês
set-up.AOR-IND-ACT-3-PL   *upon*   *ART.F-GEN-SG*
agorâs   eikónas   khalkâs
market-place.F-GEN-SG   *statue.F-ACC-PL*   *bronze.F-ACC-PL*
dúo...
two
'... [the Romans] **set up** two bronze statues in the market place...' (Plu. *Numa* 8)

(284) epeì   d'   oûn   eisékhthē   pròs
when *PTCL* *PTCL* *bring-to.AOR-IND-NON-ACT-II-3-SG*   *to*
basiléa   kaì   proskunḗsas
king.M-ACC-SG   *and*   *bow.AOR-PTPL-ACT-M-NOM-SG*
éstē   siōpêi
**stand.*AOR-IND-NON-ACT-3-SG*   *silence.F-DAT-SG*
'So when [Themistocles] was led to the King, he bowed and **stood** in silence...' (Plu. *Them.* 28.1)

4.2.3.4 Anticausative perfective in –thēn

peithō is normally glossed 'persuade', and straightforwardly carries this sense in the active and non-active-II forms:

(285) ei   gàr   ou   dúnamai
if   *PTCL* *NEG*   *be-able.PRES-IND-NON-ACT-I-1-SG*
peîsai   tà   díkaia
**persuade.*AOR-INF-ACT*   *ART.N-ACC-PL*   *right.N-ACC-PL*
poieîn...   Kaísara...
do.PRES-INF-ACT   *Caesar.M-ACC-SG*
'For if I am not able **to persuade** Caesar to act with justice...' (App. *BC* 2.2.11)[258]

(286) hup'   Alkibiádou   kaì   tôn   állōn
by   *Alcibiades.M-GEN-SG*   *and*   *ART.M-GEN-PL*   *other.M-GEN-PL*
epeísthē   phílōn
**persuade.*AOR-IND-NON-ACT-II-3-SG*   *friend.M-GEN-PL*
proeltheîn
advance.AOR-INF-ACT
'[Pericles]... **was persuaded** by Alcibiades and his other friends to advance' (Plu. *Per.* 37)

The non-active-I forms often carry the sense of 'obey', as in the following example:

(287) ... tôn   ou   **peithoménōn**
ART.GEN-PL   *NEG*   **persuade.*PRES-PTPL-NON-ACT-I-GEN-PL*
tà   ónta   dēmeúsein
ART.N-NOM-PL   *property.NOM-ACC-PL*   *confiscate.FUT-INF-ACT*

---

[258] Parallels in the imperfective stem: App. *BC* 1.0.4 *and* Plu. *Thes.* 24.3.

'... [the Romans] would seize the property of those who did not **obey**.' (App. *Mith.* 13.90)

However, when the goal of obedience is divine, this turns into trust or confidence in that being:

(288) hupekríneto   pánta   poieîn
pretend.AOR-IND-NON-ACT-1-3-SG   *all.N-ACC-PL*   *do.PRES-INF-ACT*
peithómenos   theôi.
persuade.*PRES-PTPL-NON-ACT-1-M-NOM-SG*   *god.M-DAT-SG*
'[Scipio] pretended to do everything **by putting his faith in the divinity**...'
(App. *Hisp.* 12.74)

The middle can also carry the sense of 'be persuaded', i.e. of a fact:

(289) hôn   héneka   **peíthesthai**
REL-PRON.N-GEN-PL   *on-account*   **persuade.*PRES-INF-NON-ACT-1***
tà   pedía   potè   thálattan
ART.N-NOM-PL   *plain.N-NOM-PL*   *once*   *sea.F-ACC-SG*
genésthai
become.AOR-INF-NON-ACT-1
'and therefore [Eratosthenes] **was persuaded** that these plains had once been sea.' (Strabo 1.3.4, trans. after Jones)

However, this can easily shade into 'believing (a fact)':

(290) ... katháper   kaì   Hípparkhos   **peíthetai**
just-as   *also*   *Hipparchus*   **persuade.*PRES-IND-NON-ACT-1***
'... just as Hipparchus too **believes**...' (Strabo 2.4.3)

In the case of *anoígnumi* there is a three-way opposition between active, *-ē-* and *-thē-* forms, where the first denotes causative, the second anticausative and the third passive:

(291) kaì   tôn   **phulákōn**...
and   *ART.M-GEN-PL*   *guard.M-GEN-PL*
anoixántōn...
open.AOR-PTPL-ACT-M-GEN-PL
'And when the guards, as was their custom **had opened** [the gates]...' (App. *Hann.* 6.32)[259]

(292) púlēn...   hḗtis   automátē
gate.F-ACC-SG   *REL-PRON.F-NOM-SG*   *spontaneous.F-NOM-SG*
ēnoígē   autoîs
open.AOR-IND-NON-ACT-II-3-SG   *they.3-PL-DAT*
'a gate... which **opened** automatically for them.' (*Acts* 12.10)[260]

---

[259] cf. App. *BC* 2.19.138 *tís... ḗnoige (open.IMPF-IND-ACT) tà tamieîa?* 'who opened treasuries?'
[260] cf. also New Testament, *Revelation* 20.12: *állo biblíon ēnoíkhthē (open.AOR-NON-ACT-II)* 'another book was opened'.

(293) takhù   dè   tôn   pulôn
      quickly   *PTCL* *ART.M-GEN-PL* *gate.M-GEN-PL*
      anoikhtheisôn,   eiselthóntes
      open.*AOR-PTPL-NON-ACT-II-GEN-PL*   *enter.AOR-PTPL-ACT-M-NOM-PL*
      hoi   diskhílioi
      ART.M-NOM-PL   *two-thousand.M-NOM-PL*
      katelábonto   tền   toû
      occupy.AOR-IND-NON-ACT-I-3-PL   *ART.F-ACC-SG*   *ART.N-GEN-SG*
      theátrou   stephánēn
      theatre.N-GEN-SG   *periphery.F-ACC-SG*
      'When the gates had been **opened**, the two thousand went in and took over
      the area round the theatre.' (Plb. 7.18)

In the case of *egeírō* 'raise', the non-active-II forms may be used to express the
anticausative:

(294) **égeire**   parà   tôn   en
      collect.*AOR-IND-ACT-3-SG*   *from*   *ART.F-GEN-PL*   *in*
      Turrēníāi   póleōn
      Etruria.F-DAT-SG   *city.F-GEN-PL*
      'Scipio **collected** [money] from the cities in Etruria...'
      (Plu. *Fabius Maximus* 25)

(295) hōs   méntoi perì   órthron
      when   *PTCL*   *around*   *dawn.M-ACC-SG*
      egertheìs...
      raise.*AOR-PTPL-NON-ACT-II-M-NOM-SG*
      'However, when he **got up** around dawn...' (Plu. *Pompey* 36.4)

4.2.3.5 *Argument structure and semantics*

The verbs discussed in this section, 4.2.3, differ from those in 4.2.2 in that they require
voice morphology in order to generate the anticausative. According to the framework
developed in the previous chapter, this suggests that the argument projected by the
VP in such sentences is semantically different from that projected by verbs fully
participating in the causative alternation: the underlying cause argument projected
by the verb in these cases is not capable of being reinterpreted as an external cause
without modification of the semantics of the external argument by means of non-
active morphology.[261] This is to say that these verbs project a specifically internal
cause, θ_{cause_int}, rather than the more generic underlying cause argument, θ_{cause},
which may be interpreted either as an internal or external cause, projected by verbs
which fully participate in the causative alternation. We can therefore add this to list
of theta roles given earlier at Table 11, p. 109. Table 14 gives a list of theta roles includ-

---

[261] For the semantics of the middle see 3.5.3 above.

Table 14 – Theta roles including θ_{cause_int} and behaviour with active voice

θ		Behaviour with active voice
θ_{ext}		Always becomes subject if present
θ_{int}	θ_{cause}	Can become subject
	θ_{cause_int}	Cannot become subject
	θ_{pat}	Cannot become subject
	θ_{mod}	Cannot become subject

ing θ_{cause_int}, along with syntactic behaviour found with the active voice in Greek.[262] The significance of this for the semantics of the two sets of verbs concerned will be discussed below at 4.2.5.

4.2.4 Anticausative perfective with a root stem

Before moving on to the perfect, it is important to treat an important subgroup of (causative) COS verbs which only partly participate in the causative alternation. In the perfective, these verbs have specialised causative and anticausative active stems: a root stem which is anticausative, and a sigmatic stem which is causative. By contrast, in the imperfective the active denotes either causative or anticausative according to the specific verb. The two members of this group are *epibaínō* 'embark' and *phúō* 'grow' (plus compounds).

In the case of *epibaínō*, the root aorist provides the anticausative sense 'embark' while the sigmatic aorist provides the causative sense with the meaning 'put someone on something':[263]

(296) tḕn   stratiàn   es   tàs   naûs
      ART.F-ACC-SG   *army.F-ACC-SG*   *on*   *ART.F-ACC-SG*   *ship.F-ACC-PL*
      nuktòs   **epébēse**...
      night.F-GEN-SG   **embark.*AOR-IND-ACT-3-SG***
      'he **embarked** his army on ships during the night...' (App. *Mith.* 4.26)

(297) ho   dè   Pompḗios...   skáphous
      ART.M-NOM-SG   *PTCL*   *Pompey.M-NOM-SG*   *ship.N-GEN-SG*
      epébē   smikroû
      embark.*AOR-IND-ACT-3-SG*   *small.N-GEN-SG*
      'Pompey... **embarked** on a small ship...' (App. *BC* 2.12.83)

By contrast, the imperfective stem of *epibaínō* is always valency-reducing:

---

[262] The middle and passive are not included since that is beyond the scope of the present investigation. The resultative is closely associated with the perfect in Greek, and consequently the behaviour of different theta roles belongs under the analysis of the syntactic behaviour of the perfect in 4.3.

[263] Parallels: *epibḗsas (AOR-IND-ACT)* at Jos. *BJ* 4.439, 4.659, App. *BC* 2.9.59 and 5.10.92. Non-reducing uses such as those given here are only attested in the sigmatic aorist active stem. The present, however, is never attested as non-valency-reducing.

(298) épheugen   aûthis,
      flee.IMPF-IND-ACT-3-SG   *immediately*
      epibaínōn   skáphous
      **embark.*PRES-PTPL-ACT-M-NOM-SG*   *ship.N-GEN-SG*
      'he fled immediately, **getting on** a ship.' (App. *BC* 2.15.105)

phúō is also intransitive in the root aorist stem, but transitive in the sigmatic stem:

(299) memnēménous   tês   toû
      remember.PERF-PTPL-NON-ACT-I-M-ACC-PL   *ART.F-GEN-SG*   *ART.M-GEN-SG*
      phúsantos   humâs...   proairéseōs
      ***phúō.AOR-PTPL-ACT-M-GEN-SG*   *you.M-ACC-PL*   *plan.F-GEN-SG*
      'mindful of the plan of the one who **sired you**...' (Jos. *AJ* 12.280)[264]

(300) éphu   dè   kaì   tò
      ***phúō.AOR-IND-ACT-3-SG*   *PTCL*   *PTCL*   *ART.N-ACC-SG*
      sôma   mégas
      body.N-ACC-SG   *tall.M-NOM-SG*
      'His body **was** tall [lit. he was tall as to his body]...' (App. *Pun.* 16.106)

In the imperfective stem, however, the active is causative, while the non-active is used for the anticausative:[265]

(301) ei   zôia   **phúei**   kaì
      if   *living-being.N-ACC-PL*   ***phúō.PRES-IND-ACT-3-SG*   *and*
      tréphei   metékhonta
      nourish.PRES-IND-ACT-3-SG   *partake.PRES-PTPL-ACT-N-ACC-PL*
      kinēseōs   anapnoês   thermótētos
      motion.F-GEN-SG   *breath.F-GEN-SG*   *warmth.F-GEN-SG*
      '[The inhabitants of the moon would be amazed]... that [the earth] **causes** animate beings **to grow** and nourishes them, partaking as they do of movement, respiration, and heat.' (Plu. *Concerning the Face which appears in the Orb of the Moon* 940e)

(302) hóthen   autôi   kháris   te   kaì
      from-where   *he.3-SG-DAT*   *grace.F-NOM-SG*   *both*   *and*
      dóxa   agathè...   parà   toîs
      glory.F-NOM-SG   *good.F-NOM-SG*   *with*   *ART.M-DAT-PL*
      Alexandreûsin   **ephúeto**
      Alexandrian.M-DAT-PL   ***phúō.IMPF-IND-ACT-3-SG*
      'From where he **came to have** favour and esteem in the eyes of the Alexandrians' (App. *BC.* 2.13.89)

---

[264] For examples of the aorist active of compounds of *phúō* behaving likewise cf. Jos. *AJ* 12.75 (*ekphúsantes, AOR-PTPL-ACT*), and Jos. *AJ* 1.317 (*emphûsai, AOR-INF-ACT*). The imperfective stem occurs once at Jos. *BJ* 7.180 (*phúei, PRES-IND-ACT*), where it is transitive.

[265] Rarely the active imperfective of *phúō* can be used as an anticausative, meaning 'put forth shoots'. LSJ *ad loc.* A.II. cites Mosch. 3.101 and Theoc. 7.75.

Since *epibainō* does not have a causative in the imperfective, in this case at least it seems best to analyse the verb as a root intransitive, per Figure 32.

The causative aorist formation can then be accounted for by positing a further cause subevent, corresponding to the sigmatic aorist, per figure Figure 33 (cause subevent highlighted in bold). Note, however, that since this form is only used for the causative, the internal argument projected must be θ_{cause_int}.

For *phúō*, however, it seems best to suppose the verb is causative COS in the imperfective, per Figure 33, projecting a θ_{cause_int} argument such that it cannot participate in the causative alternation, and requires non-active inflectional morphology to derive the anticausative. The sigmatic aorist would simply be the aorist of this form. The root aorist stem, however, could be seen as projecting a simpler event structure, along the lines of Figure 32. However, at least from a synchronic perspective, it could also be seen as a detransitivising stem, suppressing the external argument and explicitly permitting the θ_{cause_int} argument to be expressed as subject. As we will see with the analysis of the perfect in 4.3, this appears to be the synchronic function of the perfect root stem.

4.2.5 *Semantic distinction determining participation in the causative alternation*

In sections 4.2.2 and 4.2.3 two types of verb were distinguished according to their participation in the causative alternation, namely those participating in it, and those requiring voice morphology to render the anticausative. It is worth establishing whether there is any systematic semantic distinction between the two types. Table 15 gives the breakdown of verbs according to whether or not they participate in the causative alternation. Four types of causative COS verb can be distinguished:

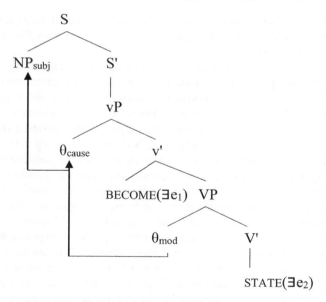

Figure 32: Analysis of event and argument structure of *epibainō*

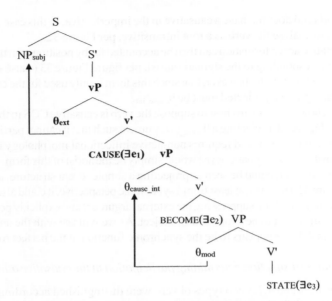

Figure 33: Analysis of event and argument structure of *epébēsa*

- Change of Location (COL) e.g. *prosbállō* 'approach';
- Change of Nature (CON) e.g. *pḗgnumi* 'freeze, cook, fix';
- Change of Orientation (COO) e.g. *hístēmi* 'make stand';
- Psych verbs e.g. *peíthō* 'persuade'.

Some verbs cross categories. Thus *anastréphō* can mean both 'turn upside down' (COO) and 'return' (COL). Similarly *plḗssō* can mean 'strike physically' (CON) and 'strike mentally' (Psych).

Table 15 shows that there is a strong correlation between expressing change of location and participation in the causative alternation. By contrast, no change of nature verbs participate in the causative alternation except *metabállō*, which is itself a compound of a COL verb, namely *bállō* 'throw'. Change of orientation verbs are also much more likely to be found not to participate in the causative alternation. Only psych verbs can be found roughly equally distributed among the two groups.

This distribution is suggestive that a semantic feature is responsible for the difference of syntactic behaviour. To help identify the feature in question, recall the deduction at 4.2.3.5 that the VP of verbs participating in the causative alternation projects a θ_{cause} participant capable of moving to external position, while the VP of non-labile verbs projects a θ_{cause_int} role, that is, a participant which is unable to move to external position. This suggests that the latter group of verbs in principle describe COS events which must have an external cause separate from the participant undergoing the change. If we look at the list of non-labile verbs, we see in general that this holds. Thus in the case of *anoígnumi* 'open', *apóllumi* and *diaphtheírō* 'destroy', (*kata-*)*plḗssō* 'strike', *peíthō* 'persuade' *hrḗgnumi* 'break' and *pḗgnumi* 'fix/cook/

Table 15. Participation in the causative alternation by semantic type

	Labile	Type of COS
anoígnumi 'open'	No	COO
apóllumi 'open'	No	CON
diaphtheírō 'destroy'	No	CON
egeírō 'raise'	No	COO
hístēmi 'set up'	No	COO
-hrḗgnumi 'break'	No	CON
kataplḗssō 'strike (in the mind)'	No	Psych
pḗgnumi 'fix'	No	CON
peíthō 'persuade'	No	Psych
plḗssō 'strike'	No	CON/Psych
pteróō 'give wings'	No	CON
anastrḗphō 'return; overturn'	Yes	COL/COO
embállō 'throw in; invade'	Yes	COL
epistrḗphō 'return'	Yes	COL
katalúō 'disband'	Yes	COL
metabállō 'change'	Yes	CON
pisteúō 'believe; entrust'	Yes	Psych
prosbállō 'put in / throw against'	Yes	COL
sunaspízō 'form a testudo'	Yes	COL
exagrióō 'make angry'	Yes	Psych
parembállō 'insert; encamp'	Yes	COL

freeze' it must be the case that an external cause is in part responsible for bringing the state about. By contrast, verbs describing changes of location, par excellence, do not describe events where this is the case: objects and especially animate beings may readily move of their own accord without a separate external causer needing to be present (although of course it may be). This can also be said to be the case for those labile verbs which do not describe changes of location. Thus events described by the psych verbs *exagrióō* '(cause to) become angry' and *pisteúō* 'believe, (en)trust', as well as the very generic *metabállō* 'change', may have, but do not require, a separate external cause argument.

The only verbs in the list whose syntax and semantics *a priori* do not submit to this analysis are *hístēmi* 'make to stand' and *egeírō* 'raise'. As demonstrated in example (295), *egeírō* may refer to events which need not have an external cause, namely 'waking up'. Yet it is not entirely the same as a change of location event: while waking up may happen spontaneously, generally speaking the undergoer does not have control over when they wake up. Nevertheless, while in literary Koine it seems that this verb does not participate in the causative alternation, there is some evidence that it does at least in lower level Greek, namely the Greek of the New Testament:[266]

---

[266] From the New Testament data, however, it seems that this is limited to the imperative.

(303) = (246)

    égeire   kaì   peripátei

    rise.PRES-IMP-ACT-2-SG   *and*   *walk.PRES-IMP-ACT-2-SG*

    '**Get up** and walk!' (Matt. 9.5)

hístēmi is different, however, since here, if the undergoer is animate, s/he may exercise a high degree of control over the event. One must suppose that, for whatever reason, this verb projects an underlying internal cause, despite what might seem to us to be an event with a more generic cause internal argument position.

Finally, it is worth considering the relationship of the semantic distinction laid out here to the two verbs with dedicated root aorist stems denoting the anticausative, namely *epibaínō* and *phúō*, discussed at 4.2.4. Both of these describe processes that may occur spontaneously without any external cause, namely 'embarking' and 'growing'. This is to say that these differ semantically from verbs which otherwise do not participate in the causative alternation. This in turn supports the view that the event and argument structures of these verbs should be analysed differently from non-labile causative COS verbs. It is striking, nonetheless, that despite describing potentially spontaneous processes, these verbs are not fully labile as in the case of other verbs of the same kind. In the case of *epibaínō* I suggest that this is because the verb is fundamentally non-causative, but irregularly has a causative stem in the perfective. In the case of *phúō* there may be a semantic reason for its different patterning: while growing is an entirely spontaneous process, it is not one, generally, over which the undergoer may have any control. In this respect it differs from verbs of motion, where if the subject is animate, it may exercise a high degree of control over the event.

4.2.6 *Conclusion*

This section has identified three classes of causative COS verb in Greek:

(1) Verbs fully participating in the causative alternation, describing processes which may occur entirely spontaneously. This class is largely composed of change of location verbs.

(2) Verbs where anticausative is denoted through voice, describing change in nature or orientation. These verbs describe processes which must have an external cause.

(3) Verbs where the perfective has dedicated causative/anticausative stem. These verbs describe spontenous processes, but apparently do not share the same syntax with other verbs of the same semantic type.

4.3 *Labile transitivity in the perfect*

4.3.1 *Introduction*

There are three kinds of COS verb where the perfect engages in the causative alternation:

(a) Verbs that have one, fully labile, perfect active stem.
(b) Verbs that have two perfect active stems, one of which is causative and the other anticausative.
(c) Verbs that have only one, anticausative, perfect active stem.

It is immediately apparent that the perfect active system of COS verbs shares a similar structure with that of the rest of the active system, in that some verbs have fully labile active forms, while others have specialised forms for causative and anticausative. There is also an important difference, however: in the perfect active system there are causative COS verbs whose perfect active stems are restricted to anticausative use, without the existence, apparently, of a causative counterpart. It is the existence of this group of perfects that has given the impression of the perfect active having a detransitivising function. However, as I will argue, the presence of fully labile perfect active stems demonstrates that this cannot be part of the semantic description of the perfect *per se*. Rather, we should attribute the apparent detransitivisation to a stem-level modification of the semantics of the lexical head. In what follows in the next section, I first treat perfects with a fully labile perfect active stem, before moving on to perfects with two active stems, ending with an analysis of verbs with an anticausative perfect active only. The implications of this for the semantics of the perfect are then discussed.

4.3.2 *Causative/anticausative distinctions in the perfect*

4.3.2.1 *Verbs fully participating in the causative alternation*

A number of perfect active stems of causative COS verbs demonstrate full labile transitivity. Furthermore, these verbs are in general the same verbs that were demonstrated to be fully labile in section 4.2.2. Thus, the verb *bállō* and its compounds attest one, kappatic, perfect active stem which is labile. Compare the following examples involving *metabállō* 'change':

(304) douloprepoûs   gàr...   psukhês tà
      slavish.F-GEN-SG   *PTCL*   *soul.F-GEN-SG*   *ART.N-ACC-PL*
      epitēdeúmata   **metabeblēkuías**
      habit.N-ACC-PL   **change.*PERF-PTPL-ACT-F-GEN-SG***
      eis   agriótēta
      to   *savagery.F-ACC-SG*
      '... for with a slavish... soul which **has changed** its ways to savagery...'
      (Philo *De virtutibus* [= *On Virtue*] 87)

(305) Hēródēs...   ēneíkheto
      Herod.M-NOM-SG   *bear.IMPF-IND-NON-ACT-I-3SG*
      metabeblēkuías   autôi   tês
      change.*PERF-PTPL-ACT-F-GEN-SG*   *he.3-SG-DAT*   *ART.F-GEN-SG*
      parrēsías.
      confidence.F-GEN-SG
      'Herod suffered, **his confidence having changed** [which he had had because of Caesar]...' (Jos. *AJ* 16.293)

Just as we saw before in the imperective and perfective, this alternation suggests that the verb projects an underlying cause argument which may optionally be interpreted as an external argument.

The use of *prosbállō* 'put, throw against' is parallel:

(306) taûta   gàr...   tandrì   **prosbébleke**...
this.N-NOM-PL   *PTCL*   *ART-man.M-DAT-SG*   **hurl-at.PERF-IND-ACT-3-SG**
'For these accusations **he has hurled** at the man...' (Plu. *Per.* 10.6)[267]

(307) tàs   ogdoékonta   Phoiníssas   triéreis...
ART.F-ACC-PL   *eighty*   *Phoenician.F-ACC-PL*   *trireme.F-ACC-PL*
Húdrōi   **prosbeblekénai**...
Hydros.DAT-SG   **put-in.PERF-INF-ACT**
'... [Cimon], having found out that the eighty Phoenician triremes, **had put in at Hydros**...' (Plu. *Cim.* 13.3)[268]

Similarly *hupostéllō* 'hide' and *kataлúō* 'disband' are fully labile in the perfect active stem:

(308) = (9), (159)
ho   dè   Phílippos...   hupó
ART.M-NOM-SG   *PTCL*   *Philip.M-NOM-SG*   *under*
tina   lóphon   **hupestálkei**
INDEF-PRON.MF-ACC-SG   *hill.M-ACC-SG*   **hide.PLPF-IND-ACT-3-SG**
toùs   Illurioùs...
ART.M-ACC-PL   *Illyrians.M-ACC-PL*
'But Philip... **had sent** the Illyrians behind a hill...'   (Plb. 5.13.5)

(309) = (8), (158)
heistékei   dè   katá   ti
set-up.PLPF-IND-ACT-3-SG   *PTCL*   *in*   *INDEF-PRON.N-ACC-SG*
prosbatòn   olígais   bathmîsi   khōríon
accessible.N-ACC-SG *few.F-DAT-PL*   *step.F-DAT-PL*   *space.N-ACC-SG*
hupestalkòs   tôi   kat'
hide.PERF-PTPL-ACT-N-ACC-SG   *ART.DAT-M-SG*   *in*
autò   skótōi.
it.N-SG-ACC   *darkness.M-DAT-SG*
'[Claudius] had stood in a space, accessible by a few paces, **taking cover** in the darkness there.' (Jos. *AJ* 19.216)

(310) ... Korínthioi   **katalelukótes**
Corinthians.M-NOM-PL   **dismantle.PERF-PTPL-ACT-M-NOM-PL**

---

[267] Parallels: Plu. *Cim.* 13.3 and Jos. *AJ* 12.338, the latter with *prosbállō* in the sense 'to attack'.

[268] The perfect of *embállō* is paralleled in an anticausative sense meaning 'invade' at a number of places including Plu. *Arist.* 23.5, Alc. 29.2; Jos. *BJ* 1.116, 5.295, 6.397, *AJ* 6.271, 9.8; Plb. 2.26.1 and 5.29.7.

tền	en	Surakoúsais	turannída...
ART.F-ACC-SG	*in*	*Syracusae.F-DAT-PL*	*tyranny.F-ACC-SG*

'... the Corinthians, **having dismantled the tyranny** in Syracusae...' (Plu. *Timoleon* 23)

(311) diskhílioi   mèn   tôn   huph'
two-thousand.M-NOM-PL   *PTCL*   *ART.M-GEN-PL*   *under*
Hērṓdēi   potè   strateusaménōn
Herod.M-DAT-SG   *once*   *serve-as-soldier.AOR-NON-ACT-I-M-GEN-PL*
kaì   ḗdē   **katalelukótes**
PTCL   *already*   **disband.PERF-PTPL-ACT-M-NOM-PL**

'... two thousand of those who had once served under Herod, and who **had** already **disbanded**...' (Jos. *AJ* 17.270)

It is interesting to note, however, that labile transitivity is not restricted to kappatic perfects, as the following causative and anticausative examples involving *anastréphō* 'overturn, return' demonstrate:

(312) **anéstrophan**   gàr   tền
turn-upside-down.PERF-IND-ACT-3-PL   *PTCL*   *ART.F-ACC-SG*
zóēn   hoûtoi.
life.F-ACC-SG us.GEN-PL   *hēmôn this.M-NOM-PL*

'... for **they have turned** our lives **upside down**.' (Cercidas, *Frag.* 17 col. 2, 30)

(313) tôn   idíōn   présbeōn   apò
ART.M-GEN-PL   *own.M-GEN-PL*   *ambassador.M-GEN-PL*   *from*
Hrṓmēs   **anestrophótōn**
Rome.F-GEN-SG   **return.PERF-PTPL-ACT-M-GEN-PL**

'... although... [the Carthaginians'] own ambassadors **had not yet come back** from Rome' (App. *Pun.* 6.34)

Finally, it is worth noting that verbs which are labile elsewhere in the system sometimes have perfects which are only attested as anticausatives, as in the case of *sunaspízō*:[269]

(314) ho   basileùs...   parḗggeile
ART.M-NOM-SG   *king.M-NOM-SG*   *order.AOR-IND-ACT-3-SG*
toîs   peltastaîs...   poieîsthai
ART.M-DAT-PL   *peltast.M-DAT-PL*   *do.PRES-INF-NON-ACT-I*
tền   ékbasin   hathróous
ART.F-ACC-SG   *movement-out.F-ACC-SG*   *together.M-ACC-PL*
katà   tagma
according-to   *formation.N-ACC-SG*

---

[269] Whether or not a *testudo* is implied here or not is not clear. Jos. *BJ* 3.271 could be parallel, where a *testudo* does seem to be implied.

sunēspikótas.
lock-shields.PERF-PTPL-ACT-M-ACC-PL
'[T]he king ordered the peltasts to come out of [the river] arranged in line
with their shields locked together.' (Plb. 4.64.6)

However, the verb itself is very rare in the perfect, being attested only nine times
up to the end of the period of our investigation.[270] Accordingly, given the lability of
the other stems, it is not unreasonable to expect that the perfect might exist in a labile
sense in an as yet unattested source.

4.3.2.2 *Verbs with specialised causative and anticausative perfect active stems*

Several verbs do not freely participate in the causative alternation, but instead have
specialised causative and anticausative perfect active stems. Verbs in this category
include *apóllumi, histēmi, diaphtheírō, egeírō, peíthō, pḗgnumi* and *plḗssō*. In these
verbs the root perfect functions as the anticausative, while a kappatic or aspirated
perfect functions as the causative. It is often supposed that the anticausative stem of
these verbs has a somewhat lexicalised meaning, and that therefore these instances
are in some sense not properly part of the verb system. While in a few stems this may
be the case, I wish to demonstrate that there is in general a closer connection with the
semantics of the lexical verb than is commonly believed to be the case.

Let us look first at examples of the causative perfects of these verbs:[271]

(315) Asdroúban   dè...   hoû   tòn
       Hasdroubal   PTCL   *REL-PRON.M-GEN-SG ART.M-ACC-SG*
       despótēn   ōmôs   **diephthárkei,**
       master.M-ACC-SG ruthlessly destroy.PLPF-IND-TR-ACT-3-SG
       'Hasdrubal, whose master he **had** ruthlessly **destroyed**...' (App. *Hisp.* 2.8)

(316) = (157)
       ou   dúnatai   dè   takhéōs
       NEG   be-able.PRES-IND-NON-ACT-I-3-SG PTCL quickly
       elēluthénai   epì   tèn   Hródon
       come.PERF-INF-ACT to   ART.F-ACC-SG Rhodes.F-ACC-SG
       ho   próteron   mèn   naûs
       ART.M-NOM-SG   previously   PTCL   ship.F-ACC-PL
       pepēkhṓs
       fix.PERF-PTPL-TR-ACT-M-NOM-SG
       'The one who **had** previously **moored his ships** cannot have come quickly
       to Rhodes.' (Aristonicus *De signis Iliadis, Il.* 2.664)

---

[270] According to a TLG search: Plb. 4.64, 12.21; Asclepiodotus *Tactics* 4.1, 4.4; Jos. *BJ.* 3.272,
6.139; Aelian *Tactics* C.48, 11.2, 11.6.
[271] Throughout the morphological tag TR will refer to the causative stems, while INTR will refer to
the anticausative.

(317) = (155)

nûn	oûn	ei	mèn	phtháneis
now	PTCL	*if*	PTCL	*be-previously.PRES-IND-ACT-2-SG*
tòn		andriánta		**hestakốs,**
ART.M-ACC-SG		*statue.M-ACC-SG*		**set-up.PERF-PTPL-TR-ACT-M-NOM-SG**
hestátō.				
stand.PERF-IMP-INTR-ACT-3-SG				

'So now, if you **have** already **set up** the statue, let it stand.' (Jos. *AJ* 18.301) [272]

(318)
kaì	tò		kerámion	**anéōikhas**
and	*art.N-ACC-SG*		*jar.N-ACC-SG*	**open.PERF-IND-TR-ACT-2-SG**

'And you **have opened** the jar; you smell, you temple-robber, very much of wine.' (Menander *Frag.* [Kock] 229.2) [273]

(319)
ekdikeísthō		tautòn
avenge.PRES-IMP-NON-ACT-I		*same-way*
pathóntos		toû
suffer.AOR-PTPL-ACT-M-GEN-SG		*ART.M-GEN-SG*
peplēkhótos		
strike.PERF-PTPL-TR-ACT-M-GEN-SG		

'retribution should fall on the one **who has done the striking** by suffering in the same way.' (Jos. *AJ* 4.277) [274]

(320)
horôn			dè	Tolmídēn	tòn
see.PRES-PTPL-ACT-M-NOM-SG			PTCL	*Tolmides.M-ACC-SG*	*ART.M-ACC-SG*
Tolmaíou...				**pepeikóta**	
Tolmaeus.M-GEN-SG				**persuade.PERF-IND-TR-ACT-M-ACC-SG**	
tôn		en	hēlikíāi		toùs
ART.M-GEN-PL		*in*	*prime-age.F-DAT-SG*		*ART.M-ACC-PL*
arístous...			ethelontì		strateúesthai...
best.M-ACC-PL			*willingly*		*serve-in-the-army.PRES-INF-NON-ACT-I*

'And seeing Tolmides the son of Tolmaeus... of those who were of the right age **having persuaded the best**... to voluntarily take part in the campaign...' (Plu. *Per.* 18.2) [275]

(321)
Matthían,		hòs
Matthias.M-ACC-SG		*REL-PRON.M-NOM-SG*

---

[272] Cf. parallel uses of *parestak-*: Jos. *BJ* 2.89, Jos. *AJ* 16.98 and Plb. 3.94.7, the last of which is given at (450).

[273] Causative perfects of this verb are rather hard to come by.

[274] The participant labelled *toû* (*ART.GEN-SG*) *peplēkhótos* (*PERF-PTPL-ACT*) is the participant that must suffer the same punishment as the one who has died. It only makes sense to take the subject of *plếssō* as playing an agent role, the same role played by the subject in the equivalent non-perfect active construction.

[275] Parallel in the pluperfect: App. *Pun.* 15.102.

egēgérkei	tền	stásin...
stir-up.PLPF-IND-TR-ACT-3-SG	*ART.F-ACC-SG*	*revolt.F-ACC-SG*

'Matthias, who **had stirred up** the revolt...' (Jos. *AJ* 17.167)

In each case, it is clear that the subject is at least an external causer, if not an outright agent.

The suggestion that the anticausative perfect stem in these verbs has a specialised meaning arises naturally from the fact that these are root stems, and therefore, for the most part very old. Furthermore, in many cases the perfect apparently carries little, if any, reference to a causing event or causer argument, and can have a specialised sense, as in the case of *egrḗgora*, from *egeírō* 'raise'. This anticausative perfect is apparently only used in the sense 'be awake', rather than 'being raised' or 'raising oneself' more generally. There is rarely any specific reference to an event of 'becoming awake':[276]

(322) ... nuktòs   **egrēgoróta...**
       night.F-GEN-SG   *raise.PERF-PTPL-INTR-ACT-M-ACC-SG*
       ópsin   ideîn...
       vision.F-ACC-SG   *see.AOR-INF-ACT*

'[They say that] as [Brutus]... **while awake** during the night... saw a vision...' (App. *BC* 4.17.134)

The pure stativity of this perfect is perhaps supported by the existence of the derived present *grēgoréō* meaning 'be or become awake'.

Other anticausative perfects appear to demonstrate similar characteristics, as frequently with *hístēmi*:

(323) = (147)

en	dè	Delphoîs	Palládion
in	*PTCL*	*Delphi.M-DAT-PL*	*Palladium.N-NOM-SG*
héstēke		khrusoûn	epì
set-up.PERF-IND-ACT-3-SG		*golden.N-NOM-SG*	*on*
phoínikos		khalkoû	
date-palm.M-GEN-SG		*bronze.M-GEN-SG*	
bebēkós...			
go.PERF-PTPL-ACT-N-NOM-SG			

'And in Delphi there **stands** a statue of Pallas, **mounted** on a bronze date palm.' (Plu. *Nic.* 13.3)

Indeed, on occasion there can never have been a causing prior event:

(324) ... spélaion   bathù   kaì   koîlon   eis
       cave.N-ACC-SG   *deep.N-ACC-SG* *and*   *hollow.N-ACC-SG* *to*
       polù   kaì   mêkos
       much.N-ACC-SG   *and*   *length.N-ACC-SG*

---

[276] I could not find any instances of the anticausative perfect of this verb which did not carry the sense 'be awake'.

aneōigòs   kaì   plátos...
open.PERF-PTPL-INTR-ACT-N-ACC-SG   and   width.n-acc-sg
'... [Saul saw] a cave, deep and hollow, **open** deep and wide a long way
back...' (Jos. *AJ* 6.283)[277]

The anticausative perfect of other verbs appears at first sight to behave in similarly idiosyncratic ways. Thus *diéphthora*, from *diaphtheírō* 'destroy' can be used in the sense 'go off', of food products:

(325)   ... potòn   aitḗsanti
        drink.M-ACC-SG   *ask.AOR-PTPL-ACT-M-DAT-SG*
        dídōsi   gala
        give.PRES-IND-ACT-3-SG   *milk.N-ACC-SG*
        diephthoròs   **ḗdē.**
        go-off.PERF-PTPL-ACT-N-ACC-SG   *already*
        '... he gave a drink to him when asked for it, milk **which had gone off already**...' (Jos. *AJ* 5.207)

Similarly, *péplēga*, from *plḗssō* 'strike', is used in the more metaphorical sense of 'being struck in the mind':

(326)   toû   Nikíou...   ákhei   kaì
        ART.M-GEN-SG   *Nikias.M-GEN-SG*   *distress.N-DAT-SG*   *and*
        thaúmati   **peplēgótos...**
        wonder.N-DAT-SG   **strike.PERF-PTPL-INTR-ACT-M-GEN-SG**
        'While they were astir, as it seems, and while Nicias was unable to speak, but was **struck** with distress and wonder...' (Plu. *Nic.* 10.6)

The anticausative perfect of *peíthō*, *pépoitha*, 'be persuaded', i.e. 'be sure, confident', as in the following example, could be regarded as a similar case:

(327)   **pepoithṑs**   apónōs
        persuade.PERF-PTPL-INTR-ACT-M-NOM-SG   *without-difficulty*
        anairḗsein
        kill.FUT-INF-ACT
        '[Goliath]... **sure** that he would kill [David]... without difficulty.' (Jos. *AJ* 6.188)[278]

However, these phenomena are in many cases explicable, I believe, within the framework of the causative alternation, and are directly derivable from the semantics of the lexical verb without necessarily appealing to a process of lexicalisation. Importantly, it is possible to find examples of the anticausative perfect which have a more transparent derivation from the lexical meaning of the verb. Thus while *diephthorós* at (325) refers to gone off milk, the next example is more straightforwardly related to the sense of destroy seen in (315):

---

[277] Parallel: Jos. *AJ* 3.111, see (4) above.
[278] cf. App. *BC* 2.9.58, for which see (335).

(328) **diephthorótōn**   tôn
destroy.PERF-PTPL-INTR-ACT-M-GEN-PL   *ART.M-GEN-PL*
anthrṓpōn
person.M-GEN-PL
'the people **having been killed**' (Jos. *AJ* 15.123)

Indeed, there are also causative uses of the verb which come closer to the use seen at (325):

(329) Alikibiádēs   **diéphtharke**
Alcibiades.M-NOM-SG   *destroy.PERF-IND-ACT-3-SG*
tà   prágmata
ART.N-ACC-PL   *affair.N-ACC-PL*
'[And he stirred up the people by saying that] Alcibiades had **brought** their affairs **to ruin**...' (Plu. *Alc.* 36.1)

anéōiga, the anticausative perfect of *anoígnumi* 'open', while obviously capable of referring only to states of 'being open', is also not prevented from referring to events of opening:

(330) prìn   **aneōigénai**   tò   stóma
before   **open**.*PERF-INF-INTR-ACT*   *ART.N-NOM-SG*   *mouth.N-ACC-SG*
tò   katà   Buzántion...
ART.N-NOM-SG   *at*   *Byzantium.N-ACC-SG*
'[... supposing the bed of the Euxine Sea was lower than that of the Propontis and of the sea next after the Propontis] before **the opening of** the outlet at Byzantium, [what was there to prevent the Euxine from being filled up by the rivers...?]' (Strabo 1.3.6, trans. Jones)

We noted above at 4.2.3.2 that *apóllumi* (at least from an English perspective) has two senses: 'destroy' and 'lose'. As one might expect, the causative perfect of the verb *apóllumi* is found in both senses 'destroy' and 'lose':

(331) ... tòn   kairòn...
ART.M-ACC-SG   *opportunity.M-ACC-SG*
apolōlekótes...
lose.PERF-PTPL-TR-ACT-M-NOM-PL
'[Gracchus and Flaccus]... **having lost the chance** [of doing what they had planned]...' (App. *BC* 1.3.25)

(332) andrós...   hòn   autòs
man.M-GEN-SG...   *REL-PRON.M-ACC-SG* *self.M-NOM-SG*
apolólekas.
destroy.PERF-IND-TR-ACT-2-SG
'[God said, "I am amazed that you are not able to say what happened concerning] a man whom you yourself **have killed**."' (Jos. *AJ* 1.58)

However, it is perhaps less to be expected that both senses should also be present in the anticausative perfect stem. The first of the following examples describes the destruction of the Amalekites while the second describes men being lost to Hannibal:

(333) pántes   àn   **apolóleisan...**
all.M-NOM-PL *PTCL* **destroy.PLPF-IND-INTR-ACT-3-PL**
'... and everyone **would have been destroyed** [if at nightfall they had not held back from the slaughter.]' (Jos. *AJ* 3.54)

(334) tóte   dè   **apolólótōn**   autôi
then *PTCL* **lose.PERF-PTPL-INTR-ACT-M-GEN-PL** *he.3-SG-DAT*
pollôn
many.M-GEN-PL
'... many **had been lost** to him [i.e. Hannibal]' (App. *Hann.* 3.16)

Note that in this second example, the experiencer participant, i.e. the person who loses something, is reintroduced by means of a dative complement expression, *autôi*, thus distinguishing it from the reading of 'destroy'.[279]

Additionally, if these uses of the perfect were genuinely lexicalised, one would not expect parallels elsewhere in the verb system. Yet many of these senses and uses can be paralleled in this way. Thus at (284) *éstē*, from *hístēmi*, focuses attention on the state in which the subject exists rather than in the process of causation that brought it about. At (282) *eplégē*, from *pléssō*, is used in the metaphorical mental sense, and not the physical one. We even saw at (295) that the aorist of *egeírō* in *-thē-* can be used in the sense of 'to get/wake up', and that therefore this sense was, to the mind of the ancient Greek, derivable from the lexical semantics of the verb.

The semantics of *pépoitha*, from *peíthō*, are explicable within the same terms. The lexical verb, as we saw earlier, means 'persuade', which is carried by the active and non-active-II endings. However, as shown at (288), (289) and (290), the non-active-I endings can be used in the sense 'believe', i.e. that something, or 'trust', i.e. in something. These senses are much closer to that of *pépoitha* that we find at (327). Indeed, we even find examples where the perfect stem used where there is apparent reference to entering the state of belief:

(335) hoútō mèn antì   logismôn   ho
so *PTCL* *instead-of* *calculation.M-GEN-PL* *ART.M-NOM-SG*
Kaîsar   **epepoíthei**
Caesar.M-NOM-SG **persuade.PLPF-IND-INTR-ACT-3-SG**
têi   túkhēi
ART.F-DAT-SG *chance.F-DAT-SG*
'In this way Caesar **put his faith** in chance instead of calculation.' (App. *BC* 2.9.58)

In almost all cases, then, it seems that there is a much tighter connection between the anticausative perfect stem with both the lexical semantics of the verb and the

---

[279] A parallel may be seen at App. *BC* 5.8.72 with *apolólei (destroy.PLPF-IND-ACT)*, with an experiencer argument *autoîs*.

interpretation of these semantics in anticausative uses elsewhere in the verb system. The only case where there does seem to be evidence for specialisation is that of *egeírō*, where it is difficult to find any anticausative instances of the intransitive perfect stem which do not have to do with being awake. The most economical view overall is therefore to see the anticausative stem as a fully integrated part of the verb system, while positing some specialisation in the case of *egeírō*.

However, it is clear that in accounting for the behaviour of these perfects semantically, we are dealing with a different situation from that seen in verbs with fully labile perfect active stems discussed in the previous section. There the lability is traceable directly to the lexical semantics of the verb. In this case, however, the lability must be licenced by a particular perfect stem. To this extent, then, the detransitivisation is attributable to the perfect.

4.3.2.3 *Verbs with an anticausative perfect active stem only*

A number of verbs are attested with only one, anticausative, perfect active stem. These include *epibaínō, phúō, hrḗgnumi, kataplḗssō* and *pteróō*. Consider the following examples:

(336) = (148)

brokhōtéra	éxei...	katà
opening.M-ACC-SG	have.PRES-IND-ACT-3-SG	by
mêkos	**errōgóta...**	
length.N-ACC-SG	**break.PERF-PTPL-ACT-M-ACC-SG**	

'[The tunic...] has an opening [for the neck] **separated** length-wise' (Jos. *AJ* 3.161)

(337)

pétran	ouk	olígēn	têi
rock.F-ACC-SG	NEG	small.F-ACC-SG	ART.F-DAT-SG
periódōi...		pantakhóthen	
circle.F-DAT-SG		from-all-sides	
perierrṓgasi		batheîai	
break-around.PERF-IND-ACT-3-PL	*deep.F-NOM-PL*		
pháragges...			
ravine.F-NOM-PL			

'Deep ravines **break** (lit. are broken) **around** a not insignificant high rock from all sides in a circle...' (Jos. *BJ* 7.280)

These perfect actives are intransitive and anticausative, and it is their existence which gives the impression that the perfect may be in some way inherently detransitivsing. Their behaviour, however, can be seen in very much the same light as the intransitive perfect active of verbs with two perfect active stems. Just as we saw there, the behaviour of the perfect is in line with anticausative forms elsewhere in the verb system, and there is no sign of semantic specialisation. The only difference is that these verbs happen not to be attested with a causative active stem.

Similarly *kataplếssō*, is not only restricted to the mental sense 'strike with terror/ awe', but is also restricted to having only one stem in the perfect:

(338) blépōn   dè   houtōs   ho
see.PRES-PTPL-ACT-M-NOM-SG PTCL   so   ART.M-NOM-SG
Iēsoûs   tḗn   te   stratiàn
Joshua.M-NOM-SG ART.F-ACC-SG   *PTCL   army.F-ACC-SG*
katapeplḗguîan
strike.PERF-PTPL-INTR-ACT-ACC-SG
'Joshua, seeing the army **frightened** in this way...' (Jos. *AJ* 5.38)

When the perfect active of this verb does take an object complement, this complement does not play the same semantic role as it would play in an equivalent transitive active construction. Consider the following example:

(339) ... toû   plḗthous...
      ART.N-GEN-SG   people.N-GEN-SG
      katapeplḗgótos
      strike.PERF-PTPL-INTR-ACT-M-GEN-SG
      autòn   kaì   tóte
      DEM.3-SG-ACC   even   then
      '... the people... **were awestruck by him** even then.' (App. *BC* 1.12.104)

Here the subject plays the role of experiencer, while the object complement plays the role of source.

The following examples involve *epibaínō* and *phúō,* verbs which, as we saw at 4.2.4, use root stems to form their anticausative forms in the perfective:

(340) = (142)
      ho   dè   Pompêios...   nûn...
      ART.m-nom-sg   PTCL   Pompey.M-NOM-SG   now
      epibébēke   tês   paralíou
      set-foot-on.PERF-IND-ACT-3-SG ART.F-GEN-SG   shore.F-GEN-SG
      'And Pompey, while not having done so previously, has now, encouraged by Antony, **set foot** on the shore.' (App. *BC* 5.7.62)

(341) tís   autôi   tôn   huiôn
      INTER-PRON.M-NOM-SG   he.3-SG-DAT ART.M-GEN-PL   son.M-GEN-PL
      pròs   aretèn   eû   **péphuken**
      in-respect-of   virtue.F-ACC-SG well phúō.PERF-IND-ACT-3-SG
      '[Joseph wanted to know] which of his sons **was well born** in respect of virtue...' (Jos. *AJ* 12.191) [280]

---

[280] For the examples of the perfect active of compounds of *phúō* behaving likewise cf. Jos. *AJ* 10.270 (*ekpephukóta,* PERF-PTPL-ACT), Jos. *AJ* 16.175 (*empephukuías,* PERF-PTPL-ACT) and Jos. *AJ* 15.84 (*empephukótes,* PERF-PTPL-ACT).

Of course, it is possible that a given verb might not be attested with a causative COS perfect simply by accident. This is to say that such forms existed, but it just so happens that they are not attested in the corpus of material that has come down to us. While less likely in very common verbs like *phúō* and *epibaínō*, this is not an implausible suggestion in very rare verbs such as *pteróō*. This verb originally means 'to furnish with feathers or wings', or, of a bird 'to be fledged'.[281] The perfect active is only attested three times in TLG, and only twice in antiquity, in Polybius and Galen. In Galen it is used of a bird's young and means 'fledged':

(342) spodôi   neossôn   khelidónos   mḗpō
     ashes.F-DAT-SG   *young.GEN-PL*   *swallow.F-GEN-SG not-yet*
     epterōkótōn
     furnish-with-wings.PERF-PTPL-ACT-M-GEN-PL
     diákhrie
     smear.PRES-IMP-ACT-2-SG
     '... smear with the ashes of the young of a swallow that are not yet **fledged**...'
     (Gal. *De compositione medicamentorum secundum locos* 12.978)

When used with reference to ships the verb means 'to make spread the oars', i.e. so as the ship 'has wings'.[282] This is the sense in which it is used in Polybius, where an anticausative perfect and causative aorist occur in quick succession. Both occur in the same context, namely the account of the Roman naval blockade of Lilybaeum, in which a certain Hannibal the Rhodian successfully runs the blockade. First the Roman ships ensuring the blockade are described in the following terms:

(343) hai   dè   nêes...   epeîkhon
     ART.F-NOM-PL   *PTCL*   *ship.F-NOM-PL*   *hold.IMPF-IND-ACT-3-PL*
     epterōkuîai
     furnish-with-wings.PERF-PTPL-ACT-F-NOM-PL
     'But the [Romans'] ships held [close by the mouth of the harbour on both sides, coming as close to the shallows as possible,] **oars out ready** [to attack and seize any ship that tried to sail out.]' (Plb. 1.46.9)

A couple of paragraphs later, however, Hannibal the Rhodian is described acting as follows:

(344) epéstē
     stand-still.AOR-IND-ACT-3-SG
     pterṓsas
     furnish-with-wings.AOR-PTPL-ACT-M-NOM-SG
     tḕn   naûn...
     ART.F-ACC-SG   *ship.F-ACC-SG*

---

[281] See LSJ *ad loc.* I.1.a.
[282] See LSJ *ad loc.* I.2 and references.

'[But Hannibal the Rhodian]… stood still, **putting the oars** of his ship **out**…'
(Plb. 1.46.11)

Given how rarely the perfect of this verb occurs, at least in this case it does not seem unreasonable to suppose that, given a greater corpus of Greek, one might find more, and potentially causative, instances of the perfect.

4.3.3 Re-expression of external cause argument by means of an adjunct phrase

Unlike the English resultative, where it is difficult if not impossible to reintroduce an external cause argument obliquely, various means can be used to reintroduce the external cause argument in detransitivising uses of the perfect. The following example is with a *diá* + gen. phrase:[283]

(345) toîs   mèn   oûn   par'   autòn
ART.M-DAT-PL   *PTCL*   *PTCL*   *at*   *itself.M-ACC-SG*
genoménois   tòn   kíndunon
become.AOR-PTPL-NON-ACT-I-DAT-PL   *ART.M-ACC-SG*   *danger.M-ACC-SG*
ên   enargès   hóti
be.PAST-IND-3-SG   *clear.N-NOM-SG*   *that*
dià   mèn   **tền**   **Márkou**
on-account-of   *PTCL*   **ART.F-ACC-SG**   **Marcus.M-GEN-SG**
tólman   **apólōle**
recklessness.F-ACC-SG   **lose.PERF-IND-INTR-ACT-3-SG**
tà   hóla…
ART.N-NOM-PL   *entire.N-NOM-PL*

'So to those who had been present in the danger itself it was clear that everything had been lost **on account of Marcus' recklessness**…' (Plb. 3.105.8)

Where *apóllumi* is used in the sense of 'lose', the external participant can also be reintroduced with a dative phrase, as seen at (334).

The external cause may also be reintroduced by *hupó*, as in the following examples:[284]

(346) = (156), (248)
pepēgósi   mónon
fix.PERF-PTPL-INTR-ACT-M-DAT-PL   *only*
hupò   brakheías   thermótētos
under   *gentle.F-GEN-SG*   *heat.F-GEN-SG*
toîs   ap'   autôn
ART.M-DAT-PL   *from*   *they.GEN-PL*

---

[283] See also (249) above. *apolōlóta* (Plb. 2.41.14, *destroy.PERF-PTPL-INTR-ACT*) is construed with a *diá* + gen. phrase with animate participant. *apōlólei* (App. *BC 5.8.72*, *destroy.PLPF-IND-INTR-ACT*) is construed with an *ek* + gen. phrase with inanimate participant.

[284] cf. *katapepēgóta* (Plb. 3.55.5, *stick-fast.PERF-PTPL-INTR-ACT*) where the particple is construed with a *diá* + acc. phrase giving the cause of the resultant state.

ártois   dietréphonto…
bread.M-DAT-PL   *nourish.IMPF-IND-NON-ACT-I-3-PL*

'… they were nourished with this bread from them, bread which **had been cooked** only under a gentle heat…' (Jos. *AJ* 2.316)

(347) toùs mèn oikeíous… hupò   tês
   ART.M-ACC-PL *PTCL* *people.M-ACC-PL* *by-means-of* *ART.F-GEN-SG*
   héttēs   **katapeplēgótas**
   loss.F-GEN-SG **strike.PERF-PTPL-INTR-ACT-M-ACC-PL**

'[Moses saw that] his people **had become fearful on account of their loss**…' (Jos. *AJ* 4.9)

It is possible also for *hupó* to introduce a human participant, as here:

(348) tò   khalkoûn   **anestánai**
   ART.N-ACC-SG *bronze.N-ACC-SG* **set-up.PERF-INF-INTR-ACT**
   trópaion **hupò** tôn **Ephesíōn…**
   trophy.N-ACC-SG *by* *ART.M-GEN-PL* **Ephesians.M-GEN-PL**

'[For it had happened that, not much earlier…] the bronze monument of defeat **had been set up by the Ephesians**…' (Plu. *Alc.* 29.1)

However, in the light of the fact that *hístēmi* is a causative COS verb, and the fact that *hupó* is not restricted to introducing agent participants, it is best to analyse this example not as denoting an agent~patient relationship between the participants, but rather of external~internal cause.

The fact that Greek is capable of doing this with perfects of this kind will turn out to have important implications for the aspectual evaluation of perfect sentences.

4.3.4 *Productivity of the specialised causative/anticausative perfect stems*

It is clear that for for fully labile verbs, discussed at section 4.3.2.1 above, participation in the causative alternation is a product of labile transitivity in the verb system as a whole, rather than being a feature specific to the perfect. However, in the case of verbs with dedicated causative~anticausative stems, it is clear that the perfect stem licences causative/anticausative readings. In order to assess the relevance of this for the semantics of the perfect in literary Koine Greek, it is important to ask what the place of these stems is in the verb system as a whole, and to what extent the existence of these specialised stems should be seen as a productive part of the verb system in the Koine period, or a relic from a former state of affairs.

It is tempting to see these forms as lexicalised archaisms. According to this view,[285] between Homer and Attic Greek the apparently detransitivising perfect active forms in Homeric Greek are gradually replaced by middle forms, so that the shape of the perfect system corresponds more closely to that seen elsewhere in the verb system, with active forms generally subcategorising for patient/theme objects and agent/

---

[285] See Haug (2008: 300ff.).

cause subjects, so that these describe not the resultant state of the subject, but rather a carry anterior semantics. However, the old resultative perfects retain their resultative force. The result of this is that the perfect cannot be said to have a unified semantic description in the post-Classical period.

In favour of this view is the fact that many of the stems concerned are old formations, and the behaviour of the detransitivising stem appears to be very similar in Homer and in the Koine period. Compare the following examples of the intransitive perfect active of *diaphtheírō* from Homer and Josephus:

(349) mainómene   phrénas
      be-mad.PRES-PTPL-NON-ACT-I-VOC-SG   *mind.F-ACC-PL*
      ēlè   **diéphthoras**
      crazed.M-VOC-SG   **destroy.PERF-IND-INTR-ACT-2-SG**
      'Madman! Crazed of mind, **you are doomed!**' (*Il.* 15.128)

(350) = (328)
      diephthorótōn   tôn
      destroy.PERF-PTPL-INTR-ACT-M-GEN-PL   *ART.M-GEN-PL*
      anthrṓpōn
      person.M-GEN-PL
      'the people **having been killed**' (Jos. *AJ* 15.123)

However, if the valency-reducing resultative stem had indeed become a lexicalised fossil one might also expect the following tendencies:

(1) No new perfects of this kind to be produced.

(2) This kind of form to become increasingly infrequent, surrendering to the morphologically 'regular' medio-passive.

(3) Where these forms exist, that they do so only in higher register documents written by the learned.

The problem with the lexicalisation/fossilisation thesis is exactly that the opposite of these phenomena is observed: new root perfect actives are produced in the post-Classical period, there is no indication that these forms are becoming less frequent, and where they exist they appear particularly in low register varieties.

It has been observed that certain root perfect actives become more common in the post-Classical period, and are possibly even created. Thus *pépoitha* is very frequent in the New Testament, in many respects a low-register set of documents, [286] and *anéōiga* is first only certainly attested in its anticausative sense in the Hippocratic corpus. [287]

---

[286] Haug (2008: 300) who notes that the fact that the 'irregular' perfect *pépoitha* becomes more frequent in later Greek is 'a sure sign that it was no longer linked to the verbal paradigm'. However, I am not sure that this evidence need necessarily point in this direction.

[287] e.g. Hippocrates *De corde [= On the Heart]* 7, according to a search of TLG. *anéōige* is attested twice in Homer (*Il.* 16.221 and 24.228), as well as once in the *Homeric Hymns* (4.247), but in all three cases it occurs in a narrative context, leading to the suspicion that this is not a perfect form.

Certainly, it seems that the grammarians regarded these forms as non-standard usage, and to be avoided:[288]

(351) **anéōigen**　　　　　　　hē
    open.PERF-IND -ACT-3-SG　*ART.F-NOM-SG*
    thúra:　　　　　soloikismós:
    door.F-NOM-SG　*solecism.M-NOM-SG*
    khrḕ　　　　gàr　légein
    it-is-necessary　*PTCL*　*say.PRES-INF-ACT*
    anéōiktai
    open.PERF-IND-NON-ACT-I-3-SG
    'The door **anéōigen**: solecism. For you should say, "The door **anéōiktai**."'
    (Phrynichus *Eclogae* 128)

Phrynichus makes similar comments on the intransitive use of *diéphthora*:[289]

(352) *diéphoren* [*destroy.PERF-IND-ACT-3-SG*]: This does not mean *diéphthartai* [*destroy.PERF-IND-NON-ACT-I-3-SG*]. Accordingly, those who say, 'The child [*ou*] *diéphoren*' are in error; they should say '*diéphthartai*'. *diéphthore* means *diéphtharke* [*destroy.PERF-IND-TR-ACT-3-SG*]. (Phrynichus *Praeparatio sophistica* 63)

(353) *diephthorós* [*destroy.PERF-PTPL-ACT-N-NOM-SG*] blood: some of the uneducated doctors say this, committing a solecsism; they should say *diephtharménon* [*destroy.PERF-PTPL-NON-ACT-I-N-NOM-SG*] blood. For *diéphthore* [*destroy.PERF-IND-ACT-3-SG*] is like *diéphtheire* [*destroy.AOR-IND-ACT-3-SG*]. (Phrynichus *Eclogae* 131)

If the grammarians, the 'guardians' of the language, did not like this kind of usage, it is a strong indication that it was not they who were promoting it. Instead, such a response on the part of the grammarians suggests that the colloquial variety of the language was driving this use of the perfect active. This fits with the widespread use of at least some of the forms in the New Testament.

Indeed, there is evidence of re-systematisation of the root perfects vis-à-vis kappatic perfects in the post-Classical period. Thus we saw at (349) and (350) that both in Homer and in post-Classical Greek, *diéphthora* is detransitivising. In the Classical period, by contrast, *diéphthora* is used transitively:

(354) … tàs　　　　　oúsas　　　　　　　té　　　mou
    ART.F-ACC-PL　*be.PRES-PTPL-ACC-PL*　*PTCL*　*I.GEN-SG*
    kaì　　tàs　　　　apoúsas　　　　　elpídas
    and　*ART.F-ACC-PL*　*be-absent.F-ACC-PL*　*hope.F-ACC-PL*
    diéphthoren
    destroy.PERF-IND-ACT-3-SG

---

[288] cf. Lucian *Soloecista* 8. *ou* is the negative operator.
[289] cf. Lucian *Soloecista* 3.

'... **he has destroyed** both the hopes I have and those that I do not.' (Sophocles *Electra* 305f.)

Similarly, *péplēga* from *plḗssō*, which is intransitive in post-Classical Greek, per example (326), is used transitively in both Homer and Classical Greek:

(355) ... Laertiádēn   Odusêa
        son-of-Laertes.M-ACC-SG   *Odysseus.M-ACC-SG*
        hrábdōi   **peplēguîa**
        rod.M-DAT-SG   ***strike.PERF-PTPL-ACT-F-NOM-SG***
        '... [Athena] **having struck** Odysseus, son of Laertes...' (*Od.* 16.455) [290]

(356) hòs   àn   **peplḗgēi**   tòn
        REL-PRON.M-NOM-SG PTCL   ***strike.PERF-SUBJ-ACT-3-SG***   *ART.M-ACC-SG*
        patéra   neottòs ón.
        father.M-ACC-SG   *chick.M-NOM-SG*   *be.PRES-PTPL-M-NOM-SG*
        '[we consider him courageous] **who has struck** his father though a chick.' (Aristophanes *Birds* 1349f.)

Indeed, there is in the Koine period at least one root perfect that participates in the causative alternation, something that one would not expect if lexicalisation were tied to old root formations:

(357) = (312)
        anéstrophan   gàr   tḕn
        turn-upside-down.PERF-IND-ACT-3-PL   *PTCL*   *ART.F-ACC-SG*
        zóēn   us.gen-pl   hoûtoi.
        life.F-ACC-SG   *hēmôn*   *this.M-NOM-PL*
        'for they have turned our lives upside down.' (Cercidas, *Frag.* 17 col. 2, 30)[291]

(358) = (313)
        tôn   idíōn   présbeōn   apò
        ART.M-GEN-PL   *own.M-GEN-PL*   *ambassador.M-GEN-PL*   *from*
        Hrṓmēs   **anestrophótōn**
        Rome.F-GEN-SG   ***return.PERF-PTPL-ACT-M-GEN-PL***
        'although... [the Carthaginians'] own ambassadors had not yet come back from Rome' (App. *Pun.* 6.34)

It seems then that, with the creation of kappatic and aspirated causative perfects, the root perfects are integrated into the system and are specialised in the denotation of the anticausative. Support for this view comes from the grammarians, who regard the root perfects of causative COS verbs as a 'passive' or 'middle':

(359) There are three diatheses: active, passive and middle; active is, for example, *túptō* [*strike.PRES-IND-ACT-1-SG*]; passive is, for example, *túptomai* [*strike.PRES-IND-NON-ACT-1-1-SG*]; middle sometimes gives active, and sometimes passive

---

[290] Parallel: *Il.* 5.762f.
[291] Parallel: Theognetus Fr. 1.8.

sense, as, for example, *pépēga* [*fix.PERF-IND-INTR-ACT-1-SG*], *diéphthora* [*destroy.*
PERF-IND-INTR-ACT-1-SG], *epoiēsámēn* [*make.AOR-IND-ACT-1-PL*] and *egrapsámēn*
[*write.AOR-IND-ACT-1-PL*]. (Dionysius Thrax *Ars Grammatica*, 1.1.48f.)

(360) So if then the *energētikós* [*active.M-NOM-SG*] and *mésos* [*middle.M-NOM-SG*]
perfect do not have a participle in *-nt-*, and if instead they have a participle
in *-s* with oxytone, like *tetuphṓs* [*strike.PERF-PTPL-TR-ACT-NOM-SG*] *tetuphótos*
[*strike.PERF-PTPL-TR-ACT-GEN-SG*], *tetupṓs* [*strike.PERF-PTPL-INTR-ACT-NOM-SG*]
tetupótos [*strike.PERF-PTPL-INTR-ACT-GEN-SG*], it is clear that it cannot have an
imperative in *-thi*. (Aelius Herodianus *Perì hrēmátōn* [= *On verbs*] 816.29)[292]

From the order of the designation *energētikós* and *mésos*, Aelius Herodianus identifies the former term with *tetuphṓs*, and the latter with *tetupṓs*.

These statements by the grammarians all point in the same direction, that the root
perfect active stem was understood to perform a 'middle' function, which could
function either in a causative or anticausative way.

In the light of this, as with non-perfects at 4.2.5 above, it is worth asking whether
there is any semantic criterion which systematically distinguishes between verbs that
fully participate in the causative alternation in the perfect, and those where dedicated
causative and anticausative stems are needed. Table 16 provides a breakdown of verbs
with dedicated causative~anticausative stems in the perfect and those without. Strikingly, there is a very strong correlation between verbs that are labile in the perfect,
and those that are labile elsewhere in the verb system.

At 4.2.5 we proposed that the semantic criterion determining whether or not a
given stem was fully labile was whether or not the event described by the predicate
could be regarded as arising entirely spontaneously. From the table it can be seen
that the same generalisation holds for the perfect. Indeed, it is striking that none of
the verbs with dedicated causative ~ anticausative stems describe change of location,
while verbs describing change of nature (e.g. *pḗgnumi, diaphtheírō*) or change of
orientation (e.g. *hístēmi, anoígnumi*) dominate among verbs with specialised stems.
These facts suggest that lexical semantic distinctions drive the semantic development and reanalysis of root perfect active stems, i.e. that verbs not participating in
the causative alternation but having specialised detransitivising stems can be said
to project θ_{cause_int} argument incapable of interpretation as external. By contrast,
verbs with labile perfect active stems project a θ_{cause} argument that is capable of
interpretation as external.

Furthermore, unlike in the perfective, where there are two sets of non-active
forms available, the perfect had only two sets of forms available, namely active
and non-active. Crucially, even though non-labile causative COS verbs project a
θ_{cause_int} argument, there is still a useful distinction to be made between events where
there is a specific independent external cause (albeit suppressed) and one where the
event comes about through a less specific process. Accordingly, the root perfect ~

---

[292] cf. *Perì hrēmátōn* Pages 795, 819, 821, 822; Theodosius *Canones isagogici de flexione verborum*
Page 79.

Table 16–Breakdown of verbs with specialised causative~anticausative stems in the perfect

Lemma	Gloss	Spontaneous	Labile perf.	Specialised perf. stems	Labile elsewhere
anastréphō	'turn over' or 'return'	Yes	Yes	No	Yes
hupostéllō	'hide'	Yes	Yes	No	Yes
katalúō	'disband'	Yes	Yes	No	Yes
metabállō	'change'	Yes	Yes	No	Yes
parabállō	'put alongside'	Yes	Yes	No	Yes
prosbállō	'put in / throw against'	Yes	Yes	No	Yes
synaspízō	'form a testudo'	Yes	Yes	No	Yes
epibaínō	'board'	Yes	No	No	No
exagrióō	'make angry'	Yes	No	No	Yes
-fúō	'grow'	Yes	No	No	No
-hrḗgnumi	'break'	No	No	No	No
kataplḗssō	'strike' i.e. mentally	No	No	No	No
anoígnumi	'open'	No	No	Yes	No
apóllumi	'destroy, lose'	No	No	Yes	No
diaphtheírō	'destroy, ruin'	No	No	Yes	No
egeírō	'raise'	Yes	No	Yes	No
-hístēmi	'make stand'	No	No	Yes	No
pḗgnumi	'freeze, fix, cook'	No	No	Yes	No
peíthō	'persuade'	No	No	Yes	No
-plḗssō	'strike'	No	No	Yes	No
epistréphō	'return'	Yes	No	No	Yes

non-active opposition could have been pressed into service to denote this distinction. Some evidence along these lines is provided by the following examples of the non-active perfect, where it seems clear that a specific independent external cause has been at work:

(361) toû   d'   hieroû   pantòs
     ART.N-GEN-SG   *PTCL*   *temple.N-GEN-SG*   all.gen-sg
     ên   en   kúklōi
     be.PAST-IND-3-SG   *in*   *circle.M-DAT-SG*
     pepēgména   skûla
     fix.PERF-PTPL-NON-ACT-N-NOM-PL   *spoils.N-NOM-PL*
     barbariká…
     barbarous.N-NOM-PL

'...the barbarian plunder **had been fixed** in a ring around the whole temple...'
(Jos. *AJ* 15.402)

(362)   tò   mégethos   tôn
   ART.N-ACC-SG   *size.N-ACC-SG*   *ART.N-GEN-PL*
  errēgménōn
  ***break**.PERF-PTPL-NON-ACT-N-GEN-PL*
  kataskeuasmátōn...   eis   mnémēn
  building.N-GEN-PL   *into*   *memory.F-ACC-SG*
  ballómenos...
  place.PRES-PTPL-NON-ACT-I-NOM-SG
  'and [Titus] bringing to mind the greatness of the **ruined** buildings...'
  (Jos. *BJ* 7.5.2)

(363)   áphnō   dè   hósper   hupó   tinos
   suddenly   *PTCL*   *as-if*   *by*   *INDEF-PRON.F-GEN-SG*
  plēgês   iskhurâs
  blow.F-GEN-SG   *strong.F-GEN-SG*
  peplēgménos   anesténaxe
  ***strike**.PERF-PTPL-NON-ACT-M-NOM-SG*   *groan.AOR-IND-ACT-3-SG*
  '[H]e suddenly let out a groan as if he has been **struck** by a hefty blow...'
  (Diod. Sic. 17.117.2)

(364)   autèn...   **diephtharménēn...**
   it.F-ACC-SG   ***destroy**.PERF-PTPL-NON-ACT-F-ACC-SG*
  heûron...
  find.AOR-IND-ACT-3-PL
  hupò   tôn   barbárōn...
  by   *ART.M-GEN-PL*   *barbarian.M-GEN-PL*
  '[T]hey found the [shrine of Ares] **destroyed** by the barbarians...'
  (Plu. *Camillus* 32.6)

Accordingly, we could take the root perfect active and morphologically non-active perfect to be semantically middle and passive respectively, as per Figure 29, p. 107 above, and Figure 23, p. 103 above, respectively.

However, if this analysis is correct, there are two problems to confront. First, it is conspicuous that, unlike other middle formations in Greek, which are capable, optionally, of filling both external and internal argument positions, with the root perfect actives it is only ever the internal position that is filled. Secondly, we have to presuppose a mismatch between the semantics and the morphology of the de-transitivising perfects: if these verbs project θ_{cause_int} arguments which cannot be taken to be external, why do their root perfects have active morphology and not middle morphology, as we saw outside the perfect system?

There is, however, another analysis of the root perfect active that avoids both of these difficulties. Rather than behaving as a classic middle, we can say that root

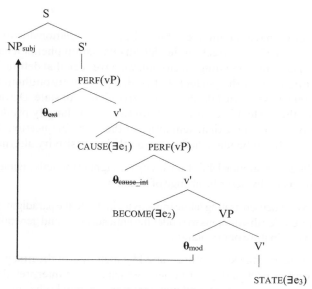

Figure 34: Specialised anticausative perfect active

perfect active stem, where it contrasts with a causative stem, suppresses both the internal and external arguments, as illustrated in Figure 34. In this way the perfect would allow the internal argument to be expressed as the subject just as a classic resultative.

We will have cause in chapter 6 to revise this view slightly, but for the time being this picture will help us understand the the role of the anticausative perfect active stem.

4.3.5 *Implications for the meaning of the perfect*

In general the findings presented here show that the perfect active is not in itself an intransitive or detransitivising category, and, indeed, that even in the same lexical item it may behave both as a causative and as an anticausative. Any formulation of the meaning of the perfect active cannot, therefore, be so rigid as to ascribe a particular diathetical role to the perfect, whether intransitive, active transitive, or detransitivsing, since it is attested in each of these. However, the formulation should provide parameters for predicting which of these will be carried in a given context. The core value of the perfect active should therefore be sought in terms that do not directly invoke transitivity, but which carry implications for transitivity. This is to say the perfect active means something, x, which permits both causative and anticausative readings. However, a formulation for x cannot be found until the aspectual data are analysed.

4.4 *Conclusion*

In this chapter we have sought to establish the precise relationship of the Greek perfect in literary Koine Greek to the detransitivisation phenomena often associated with it. In the foregoing discussion we have seen that detransitivisation is not a feature only of the perfect, but is also present throughout the active system in Greek in verbs that describe causative change of state. Detransitivsing behaviour in the perfect is connected with this and is largely productive and predictable based on the lexical semantics of the verbs in question. In general two types of verb can be identified based on their transitivity alternations:

(1) Verbs demonstrating labile transitivity throughout the active paradigm: these verbs generally describe change of location;

(2) Verbs not demonstrating labile transitivity in the active paradigm: these verbs require voice distinctions to render the anticausative, and generally describe change of nature or orientation.

In semantic terms, the key feature shared by members of the first group is that the lexical verb projects a θ_{cause} argument, which may be interpreted both as an internal and an external cause, and may therefore occupy both internal position and, if no explicit external cause is specified, external. By contrast, in the second group the verb projects a θ_{cause_int} argument which cannot be interpreted as an external argument. Accordingly, the function of the specifically detransitivising perfect active stem is to suppress the external and internal arguments, allowing the mod argument specifying the state eventuality to move directly to subject position. There is evidence both from the testimony of ancient grammarians and from oppositions in literary Koine texts to suggest that this is part of a three-way voice distinction with non-active morphology, although the precise relationship to the semantics of non-active morphology of this period will need to await a dedicated investigation.

V

5 THE INTERACTION OF THE PERFECT WITH DIFFERENT

PREDICATE TYPES

5.1 *Introduction: tense and aspect in a neo-Davidsonian framework*

5.1.1 *Approach*

So far in this study we have seen that the lexical semantic feature of durativity is key to establishing past reference in the perfect: perfects of durative state verbs, terminative state verbs, and non-COS activity/accomplishment verbs, all carry past reference routinely. By contrast, in achievement and non-durative state verbs past reference is optional. Furthermore, where the feature of homogeneity is absent, the past reference encoded is anterior. By contrast, where homogeneity is absent, as in the case of durative state verbs, anteriority is not guaranteed. Thus the perfects of terminative state verbs and non-COS durative verbs always denote anteriority, while the perfects of durative state verbs may either denote anteriority or continued state. Crucially, however, the presence of the lexical semantic feature of durativity does not guarantee past reference if the subject changes state according to the event described by the lexical verb. Accordingly perfects formed to verbs where the subject can change state were found to carry past reference optionally. Thus, the perfect of unaccusative verbs such as *anakhōréō* 'I withdraw' can occur with either resultative reading, 'I have withdrawn', or with a pure state reading 'I am distant'. These findings show that past reference in the Greek perfect is in many circumstances unpredictable on the basis of purely lexical semantic considerations. As such they suggest that the semantics of the perfect itself do not allow us to predict anterior, resultant state, pure state and continued state denotation. However, it remains to be established exactly what factors, beyond the lexical semantic ones already identified, finally determine the temporal and aspectual semantics of a Greek perfect in a particular instance.

Chapter 2 considered the temporal and aspectual denotation of the perfect purely from a lexical semantic point of view, while chapter 4 considered the interaction of the perfect with the causative alternation. The present chapter returns to the temporal and aspectual question and now considers the question from a syntactic standpoint. First, however, we must give an account of the relationship between syntax and aspect.

5.1.2 *Aspectual Interface Hypothesis (AIH)*

So far we have been considering the temporal constituency of events described by the perfect purely from the perspective of the semantics of the verbal head. However, we have seen that the temporal properties of the perfect are not fully explicable in terms of the semantics of the verbal head alone. To come to a fuller understanding, we need to take account of the sentence as a whole, and the aspectual properties that are encoded by it. In order to achieve this, we need first to understand how lexical semantic properties are systematically related to the syntax of a sentence.

At 2.1.7 above we saw that the verbs 'run' and 'build', classed by Kenny as an activity and performance respectively, can in certain circumstances demonstrate the same behaviour with respect to Kenny's perfect/progressive test: the activity verb 'run' was shown to have the same behaviour with respect to Kenny's test as the performance verb 'build' with the addition of a path argument. It is useful to consider what it is about the addition of this argument that brings about the change in behaviour with respect to Kenny's test.

We noted that the key distinction between activities and performances is that performances have a fixed endpoint in view for the event to be able to be said to have taken place, whereas this expectation is absent in the case of activities. When a path argument is added to the activity verb 'run', such as 'a marathon', according to Kenny's test the verb behaves in the same way as 'build a house'. However, it is not simply the addition of a path argument that is key: the path argument must have a set endpoint for it to have an effect on the result of Kenny's test. This can be seen from the following examples:

(365) Mark is pushing the trolley along the road.
(366) Mark has pushed the trolley along the road.
(367) Mark is pushing the trolley along the road to the shop.
(368) Mark has pushed the trolley along the road to the shop.

Examples (365) and (366) include a path argument, namely 'along the road' but no destination. By contrast (367) and (368) include a path argument with a destination, namely 'to the shop'. However, only in the first pair, namely that where a path is given but no endpoint, does the present progressive entail the perfect.

This insight, that the specification of a delimited path has aspectual implications for the sentence as a whole was developed by Tenny (1987, 1992, 1994) into a hypothesis that specifically links lexical semantics and syntax through what is known as the ASPECTUAL INTERFACE HYPOTHESIS (AIH). The hypothesis rests on the distinction between internal and external arguments introduced at 3.3.4 above. Tenny further divides internal arguments into direct internal arguments and indirect internal arguments, a distinction which corresponds to that between complements and adjuncts, respectively, introduced in chapter 2. In terms of realising the aspectual properties of a sentence, telicity is criterial. Thus, as we have seen, the verb 'to run' can head both an activity and an accomplishment predicate:

(369) I ran #in/for three hours.
(370) I ran a marathon in/#for three hours.

Similarly, the verb 'to build' can head both types of predicate:

(371) I built houses #in/for ten years.
(372) I built a house in/#for six months.

The only difference between the two sentences is the nature of the internal argument, and it is this that determines the telicity of each case. In the first example of each pair there is no quantisation by means of an internal argument, in the first pair because there is no internal argument, in the second pair because the internal argument is not quantised. By contrast, in the second example of each pair the predicates are delimited by means of a quantised internal argument. It is the quantisedness of this internal argument that determines a specific endpoint for the event described by the sentence, thereby delimiting it, and telic reading follows.

However, while the quantisedness of the internal argument is criterial for telicity for some verbs, this is not the only factor determining telicity. Terminative verbs always head telic predicates. Consider the following examples headed by the achievement verb 'explode':

(373) The bomb exploded.
(374) Bombs exploded all around them.

Achievement verbs, because of their telicity, head telic predicates because the lexical semantics of the verb imposes a bound on the event being described. Thus despite the fact that the internal argument in the first example, 'the bomb', is quantised, and the internal argument in the second, 'bombs', is not, both sentences are telic and read as achievements.[293]

Similarly, a predicate headed by a state verb will not be modified aspectually by adding a quantised argument. The following examples are quoted again from the previous chapter:

(375) Fred loved his car (#in/for a year).
(376) Fred loved cars (#in/for a year).
(377) Fred loved cake (#in/for a year).

Each of these sentences is atelic regardless of the quantisation of the direct argument.

Nevertheless, for activity/accomplishment verbs, the aspectual properties of the internal argument are critical for the telicity of the events their predicates describe. The key insight of the AIH for our purposes may be summarised as follows (see Tenny 1992: 3, 4):

> The internal argument of a simple verb is constrained so that it either undergoes no change or motion, or it undergoes change or motion which 'measures out the event' over time... The verb's internal argument may be thought of as being converted into a function of time at some level of semantic representation. This is an aspectual property, because aspect refers to the internal temporal organization of an event. The term 'measures out' is used here in an informal sense, as a convenient metaphor for uniform and consistent change, such as change along a scale...

---

[293] However, it should be noted that where the sentence in question does not describe an instantaneous event involving multiple entities, an iterative, and therefore atelic, interpretation will normally follow, i.e. of a series of telic events, e.g.: 'Bombs exploded all day.'

5.1.3 Situation aspect

Krifka (1989) and Parsons (1990) relate events to arguments by means of standard thematic relations such as Agent and Patient. However, while the semantic content of such relations is clear from such categorisation, their aspectual properties are not. We therefore need a way to designate the aspectual properties of such relations which makes clear how the aspectual properties of a sentence are determined by them. Ramchand (1997: 127ff.) formulates a set of theta roles that are explicitly tied to aspectual properties.

Table 17. Aspectual properties of patients (slightly modified from Ramchand (1997: 127))

Patient-Partition (pat=)	Cells of a partition of the object are mapped onto the temporal duration of the verb to construct the path (creation and consumption verbs)
Patient-Move (pat→)	The different physical locations of the Object are mapped onto the temporal structure of the verb to construct the path (motion verbs, change of location verbs)
Patient-Change (pat+/-)	The varying properties of the Object are mapped onto the temporal structure of the verb to construct the path (change of state verbs).
Mod	The meaning of the Object modifies and restricts the denotation of the verb (underspecified semantic relation).

The following examples illustrate each kind of internal argument:

(378) Mary ate an apple.
(379) Mary rolled a ball.
(380) Mary rolled the dice.

In these examples, the patients, namely 'an apple', 'a ball', and 'the dice', insofar as they are direct arguments construed with non-terminative activity/accomplishment verbs, determine the aspectual interpretation of their predicates. Specifically, in the first example, the quantised internal argument 'an apple' determines the endpoint of the event described by the predicate: the path of the event is constructed as the apple is progressively eaten. In Ramchand's terms, therefore, the apple is Patient-Partition (pat=).

In turn 'a ball' in the second example, insofar as it does not determine any final moment for the event, renders the predicate atelic. Here the roll of the internal argument is different: the path is constructed as the ball moves along its path. By contrast, with 'the dice', because of the non-circular nature of dice, rolling dice necessarily entails a telic event. This example is like the previous example, only that, because it is dice that are being rolled, there is a set expiry to the event. Both of these are, in Ramchand's terms, Patient-Move (pat→).

These cases are to be contrasted with the following examples:

(381) Mary ripened the banana.
(382) Mary loved cake.

In (381) the banana is an internal argument which provides a measure function of event 'ripen'. In this case, it is the property of ripeness of the banana that allows for the measuring out of the event. The endpoint is set at where the banana becomes ripe.[294] By contrast, in (382) 'cake' is, in Ramchand's terms, mod. This is because 'love' describes a state, and does not allow for the progressive measuring out of an event with respect to the internal argument.

We will adopt Ramchand's framework in respect of the different kinds of internal argument that can be projected, whether 'Patient-Move', 'Patient-Partition' or 'Patient-Change'. However, we will apply these to the theta roles that we introduced earlier at Table 11, p. 109 and Table 14, p. 129. θ_{cause} and θ_{cause_int} roles for the underlying cause (i.e. one that may be interpreted as external) and internal cause (i.e. one that may not be interpreted as external) roles respectively. Each of these can belong to the three subtypes identified by Ramchand for the patient role, i.e. partition ($=$), move ($\rightarrow$) and change ($+/-$). Thus $\theta_{cause\rightarrow}$ will read 'theta cause-move').

We noted in chapter 2 that two of the features discussed, telicity and durativity, are not equipollent: the assertion by the verbal head of telicity denied the possibility of atelic readings, but the converse was not true. Thus an achievement verb always heads a telic predicate, but an activity verb may or may not head a telic predicate. The same can be said for durativity: a predicate headed by a durative verb will always be durative, but a predicate headed by a non-durative verb may or may not be durative. Thus it is possible to die both 'in an instant' and 'over many days'. This lack of equipollence contrasts with homogeneity: a predicate headed by a non-homogeneous verb will always be non-homogeneous, and *vice versa*. In terms of the formal representation of aspectual semantic properties for this study, only the positive members of non-equipollent oppositions will be represented. By contrast, both members of equipollent oppositions will be represented. Thus (378) will be represented as follows:

(383) $\exists e \exists x \exists y [eat(e) \wedge \theta_{ext}(x, e) \wedge \theta_{pat+/-}(y, e) \wedge dur(e) \wedge delim(e) \wedge non\text{-}homog(e)]$
where x is 'Mary' and y is 'an apple'. By contrast, (379) will be represented:
(384) $\exists e \exists x \exists y [roll(e) \wedge \theta_{ext}(x, e) \wedge \theta_{pat\rightarrow}(y, e) \wedge dur(e) \wedge non\text{-}homog(e)]$
where x is 'Mary' and y is 'a ball'. Finally, (382) will be represented as follows:
(385) $\exists e \exists x \exists y [love(e) \wedge \theta_{ext}(x, e) \wedge \theta_{mod}(y, e) \wedge homog(e)]$

In developing and articulating the AIH, Tenny is primarily interested in establishing the conditions for a delimited (or telic) predicate. This is shown by her minimising the distinction between accomplishments and achievements (see Tenny 1994: 5):

> The distinction between achievements and accomplishments, which hinges on whether an event has significant duration or not, is of secondary importance in this theory. Seemingly instantaneous events are grouped together with events transpiring over a longer period of time, as delimited events having a definite terminus.

---

[294] However, because 'to ripen' is terminative, the nature of the event is in fact prescribed by the verbal head.

Our concern is different, however, since we are interested not primarily in establishing the conditions for telic predicates, but in explaining past reference when it occurs in the Greek perfect. In assessing the conditions under which past reference is denoted by the perfect, we found in chapter 2 that the presence of the semantic feature of durativity, not terminativity, led, except in cases where the subject changes state, to past reference being expressed. Accordingly, while an event's telicity will be important, whether or not an event takes conceptual time to elapse, i.e. durativity, will also be significant. As a result, unlike for Tenny, it will be important for us to maintain the difference between accomplishments and achievements, since, as we will see, very different behaviours in terms of past time reference can be seen in the two types of predicate.

Related to this is the fact that Tenny leaves states entirely out of her analysis. This is, of course, because a direct argument cannot delimit a state in the way that it can an activity. However, just because a direct argument cannot delimit an event, does not mean that it cannot affect the truth conditions of a sentence in terms of its temporal, as opposed to aspectual, constitution. Consider the following examples:

(386) I have hope.
(387) I have a smoking habit.

Both examples involve the state verb 'have'. Both predicates, moreover, are atelic. However, what they assert in temporal terms is different, on account of the temporal properties of the direct arguments. The first example is merely an assertion that a state of having hope holds at topic time. The second example, however, as well as asserting that a state holds at topic time, also asserts facts about the past. Specifically, in order to have a habit, the action which is associated with the habit, namely smoking, must have occurred at least once in the past, and probably several more times. Thus as well as asserting that the subject has something in the present, because that something also asserts things about the past, the predicate as a whole makes assertions about the time period before topic time. In this way it can be seen that the internal argument is in fact important not only for determining the telicity of an event, but more generally for determining the internal temporal constitution, with or without telicity, of states as well as other kinds of event. In this case, we may say that the direct argument 'habit' contributes the semantic feature of durativity to the predicate.

However, the way in which the internal argument in this case contributes durativity is not the same as 'an apple' does this in example (378) above, since there is no measure function. The argument 'a smoking habit' is therefore still 'mod' in these terms. Accordingly, we need to distinguish a special kind of 'mod' argument, 'mod-dur' that can carry durative semantics. The opposition between 'mod' and 'mod-dur' is not equipollent: 'having hope' does not preclude 'having hope for many years'. However, 'having a smoking habit' does preclude non-durative readings. Accordingly, the first sentence, 'I have hope', can be represented in neo-Davidsonian terms as follows:

(388) $\exists e \exists x \exists y [\text{have}(e) \land \theta_{ext}(x, e) \land \theta_{mod}(y, e)]$
       where x is 'I' and y is 'hope'. The second sentence, by contrast, can be represented as follows:

(389) $\exists e \exists x \exists y [\text{have}(e) \wedge \theta_{ext}(x, e) \wedge \theta_{mod\text{-}dur}(y, e) \wedge \text{dur}(e)]$
    where x is 'I' and y is 'a smoking habit'.

For reference purposes, Table 18 gives the full list of roles that will be available for use in the present study.

Table 18. Roles and aspectual properties

θ	Description	partitition (=)	change (+/-)	move (→)	mod
ext	external argument which may be agent or cause	$\theta_{ext=}$	$\theta_{ext+/-}$	$\theta_{pat\rightarrow}$	
cause	cause argument which may be interpreted as external as well as internal	$\theta_{cause=}$	$\theta_{cause+/-}$	$\theta_{pat\rightarrow}$	
cause_int	cause argument which can only be internal	$\theta_{cause\_int=}$	$\theta_{cause\_int+/-}$	$\theta_{pat\rightarrow}$	
pat	patient	$\theta_{pat=}$	$\theta_{pat+/-}$	$\theta_{pat\rightarrow}$	
mod	modifier (i.e. no measure function) argument				θ_{mod}
mod_dur	modifier (i.e. no measure function) argument carrying the feature of durativity				θ_{mod_dur}

5.1.4 *Tense and aspect in a Government-Binding (GB) and neo-Davidsonian framework*

In section 3.3 we introduced GB theory and employed it in chapter 4 to help explain the lability shown in the perfect. In chapter 2 we saw that the aspectual entailments of a perfect predicate in Greek are affected by whether the undergoer surfaces as subject or not and that for this reason an account of the aspectual semantics of the perfect cannot be restricted to the lexical level, but must be extended to the level of the sentence.

In seeking to provide a framework to do this in the present chapter we have so far used a neo-Davidsonian model to capture the aspectual contribution of a sentence's arguments and adjuncts. However, since the aspectual behaviour of perfect predicates is dependent not just on the nature of the arguments, but on their syntactic position, it will be helpful to incorporate GB theory in order for us to see clearly how this is the case. Since the issue is affected specifically by whether or not a given argument surfaces in subject position, we will start with the assignment of subjecthood.

Originally it was assumed that subjecthood was assigned by the highest order element of the sentence, which in Chomsky (1981) is Infl (for inflection), also responsible for assignment of finiteness to a sentence.[295] Pollock (1989) proposed that Infl be best separated into two projections Tense (TP) and Agr (AgrP). Chomsky (1991)

---

[295] For a brief summary of the history of Infl, TP and AgrP see Murasugi (1992: 10).

followed this up by proposing two Agr heads, one for subject and one for object, Agr-S and Agr-O respectively. Crucially for our purposes, Chomsky locates Agr-S above TP. Chomsky's primary interest in defining TP is in its finiteness, so as to explain null subject phenomena in dependent sentences.[296] However, if TP is taken as a functional head assigning tense features more generally, including viewpoint aspect information, the placing of Agr-S at a level higher than TP entails that the subject only receives tense and aspect information by predication. Since in Greek aspect is more significant than tense, with the latter only being marked in the indicative, we relabel TP as VAspP (for VIEWPOINT ASPECT PHRASE). In what follows we take the subject of a predicate to be in a specifier relationship with the VAspP.[297]

The VAspP is opposed to the SITUATION ASPECTUAL PHRASE (SAspP, previously vP), which carries situation aspectual information relating to durativity, telicity and homogeneity. Let us consider this in the context of (causative) COS predicates. It was stated above (3.4.3) that I follow Rappaport & Levin (1998) and Kiparsky (2002) in taking changes of state to be complex eventualities comprising two subevents: a 'become' subevent and a poststate containing the lexical semantic information in the verb. Causative COS predicates comprise both of these subeventualities as well as a cause subevent, located at a level higher than 'become'. COS predicates can be said to consist of the light verbs 'cause' and 'become', which are fundamentally aspectual in nature, and a VP containing the lexical semantic information of the verb. We take the light verbs 'cause' and 'become' to be projections of SAspPs. Following the key insight of the AIH that the essence of the link between syntax and semantics is aspectual,[298] we also take VP to be a kind of SAspP. However, since the functional head V also contains lexical semantic information unique to the verb in question, we retain the label VP. In this case, then, the 'verb', minus tense and aspect, may be said to be a composite of the two SAspPs and the VP. This may be generalised to say that the 'verb' of a predicate in these terms is the composite of all the SAspPs and the VP.

As we outlined at 3.4 above, each aspectual head is specified by a theta argument role, with 'cause' specified by the external argument, and 'become' specified by the internal argument. In aspectual terms we take the role of specifier to define the path of change, which is to say that the argument filling that position fully participates in the event described by the functional head from start to finish (if such is defined; see more below, 5.1.5).

In (causative) COS verbs, the V element is in fact a state, that is a homogeneous atelic eventuality. In such predicates the argument is in specifier position in relation to the verbal head, and is mod. The argument structure of a prototypical causative COS sentence is given in Figure 35.

---

[296] Thus in Chomsky (1991: 69) this phrase is labelled FP.
[297] For this see Murasugi (1992: 10f.), who in turn follows Chomsky (1991, 1992).
[298] Tenny (1994: 1–2).

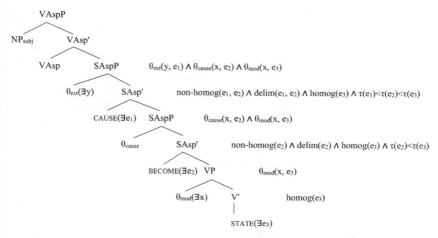

Figure 35: Causative COS sentence

As we saw at 3.4.5 above, accomplishment predicates have a very similar structure to causative COS predicates, except that in their case the VP is the highest order verbal element, with two aspectual light verbs 'become' and 'state' below it. However, there is also an important difference in aspectual terms, in that the eventuality described by V is always simultaneous with that described by 'become'. The event structure is illustrated in Figure 36.

Activity predicates are characterised by projecting an external argument only. Their structure is much simpler than that of accomplishments, since they lack the subeventualities 'become' and 'state'. The structure of a prototypical activity predicate is given in Figure 37.

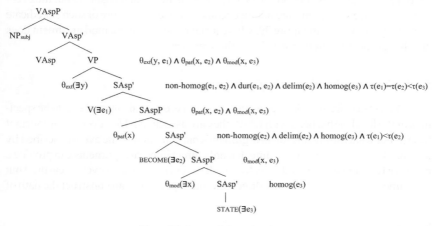

Figure 36: Accomplishment sentence

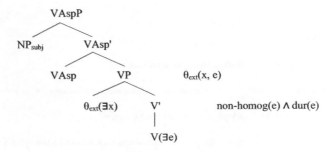

Figure 37: Activity sentence

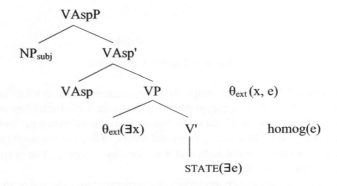

Figure 38: State sentence with a single participant

State predicates are similar, except that the verbal eventuality is homogeneous. The event structure of a state with a single participant is given in Figure 38.

As we have noted,[299] some state verbs, such as 'love' project two arguments, but the object of such constructions does not provide a means of measuring out the event over time, since state events are homogeneous. The event structure of such a predicate can be represented as in Figure 39, where it can be seen that the mod argument does not change the aspectual properties of the sentence.

5.1.5 *Constructing the path of an event*

In 5.1.4 we stated that we take argument positions, i.e. external, internal etc., to be specifiers of the local verbal head with which they are associated. However, it is important to spell out what this means for an argument's participation in the event described by its head. We follow Tenny in holding that only direct internal arguments can provide a measure function for the predicate, by which the event is progressively measured out over time. This is to say that only direct internal arguments can construct the path of

---

[299] 3.4.2 and 5.1.3 above.

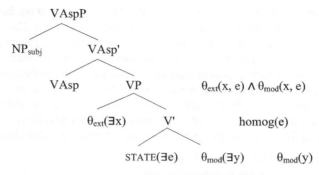

Figure 39: State sentence with two participants

a predicate. However, as we showed in 5.1.3, providing a measure function is not the only way in which an argument can add situation aspectual information to a predicate.

Minimally, the relationship of a verb phrase to its specifier is one of predication. This is to say that the verb phrase is asserted to hold of the specifier in some way. In terms of aspect, I take this to mean that the specifier *participates* in the eventuality described by the head. Conversely, where an argument does not form a specifier relationship to a particular head, the predicate lacks this assertion. This is not to say that the predicate denies participation. Rather, participation in the given eventuality is left to inference.

Where a given eventuality is non-homogeneous, its specifier is asserted to participate in the change described by the eventuality. This is to say that the specifier of an aspectual head is explicitly asserted to pass along the path described by that head. We will say that if an argument specifies or modifies an eventuality, then, minimally, that argument will be explicitly said to traverse the path of that event. However, an entity may also receive theta marking from its head.[300] Accordingly, for example, the subject of an unaccusative predicate, as given at Figure 27, p. 105, above can receive the θ_{cause} role from its head.

Where an argument is mod, i.e. without any aspectual implications, the argument makes no aspectual contribution to the predicate. However, insofar as the argument is a specifier, if the argument does carry additional aspectual entailments, the event is 'specified' accordingly. Thus durativity may be entailed where the argument position in question is mod, but the lexical semantics of the argument carry the feature of durativity, as in the case of 'habit' discussed at 5.1.3 above.

---

[300] Following Larson (1990: 599) citing Chomsky (1981: 36–38), theta marking may occur either directly or indirectly. An element x directly theta-marks y where y is an object of x, while x indirectly theta-marks y where y is a subject of x. As such an argument in specifier position with respect to its head may be said to be indirectly theta-marked by that head.

Related to the foregoing discussion is the question of whether or not the external argument should be regarded as aspectual. Tenny (1994: 9), quoted at n. 220 above, takes the view that the external argument is projected outside the maximal projection of the verb. Similarly, Ramchand (1997: 179–80) argues that the external argument is generated in specifier position to the aspectual head and is therefore external to the construction of the path. In contrast to both, I take all theta arguments, both external and internal, to be aspectual insofar as they specify the path of the events they describe. The difference between external and internal arguments is that they specify different kinds of events, or paths. Let us consider the following examples, which Ramchand also uses (see Ramchand 1997: 180f.):

(390) The ball rolled down the hill.
(391) John rolled the ball down the hill.

Ramchand points out that there is a difference between the first and the second example: in the first example, the ball must be involved in constructing the path, i.e. the ball must go all the way down the hill. By contrast, in the second example, John may or may be involved in constructing the path, or he may not if he simply pushes the ball at the top of the hill and watches it roll down. Ramchand sums up her position as follows (see Ramchand 1997: 178):

> The crucial thing about the external argument in this view, will be precisely that it is *external* to the construction of the path corresponding to the AspP. Under the simplest possible view, the external argument is simply associated directly with that path. I will argue that once the path is constructed, the external argument is mapped onto that path via some participancy function whose precise relation is filled in by context and the lexical nature of the actual path involved.

While I agree with Ramchand's readings of these examples, I account for them in a different way: the ambiguity in John's involvement in the event emerges from the ambiguity in the relationship between 'cause' and 'become', rather than in John's externality per se. Specifically, there are two ways for a cause event to take place: it may either be completely simultaneous with the become event, or may precede it. In (391) both readings are available, since John and the ball are separate and separable entities. By contrast, in (390) the non-simultaneous reading is not available, since it would require the ball to be in two places at once. The difference is illustrated in Figure 40 and Figure 41. Crucially for our purposes, however, under our analysis the specifier-head relationship entails that the specifier fully participates in the eventuality described by its head. It is the relationship between the heads that is ambiguous.

An important consequence of the specifier-head relationship between arguments and their eventuality is that where an eventuality does not have a specifier, as, for example, where the relevant argument position is suppressed, no nominal element is asserted by the predicate to participate in that event, even when ultimately an argument that must be assumed to participate in the event is accorded subject status to the predicate as a whole. We shall explore the implications of this for understanding the aspectual semantics of the resultative and perfect at 5.1.7 below.

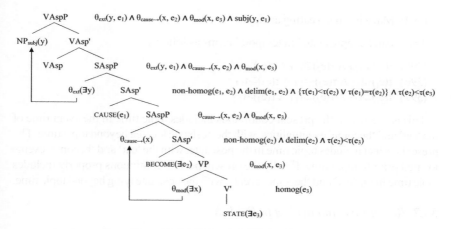

Figure 40: 'John rolled the ball down the hill'

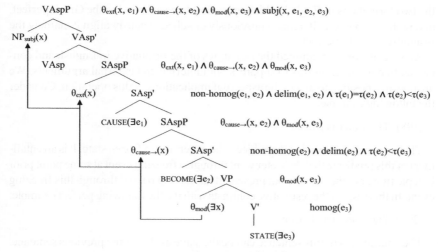

Figure 41: 'The ball rolled down the hill'

5.1.6 *Role of VAspP*

In contrast to the situation aspectual predicate, the role of VAsp is to relate the eventualities described by the predicate to topic time. To illustrate this, let us consider the sentence 'Mary eats an apple'. Here we can say that there is a durative eating event 'e' and a direct internal argument, 'an apple', that delimits the event 'e'. Now let us consider three aspectual versions of this sentence, with the present continuous, present perfect and present perfect continuous:

(392) Mary is eating an apple.

(393) Mary has eaten an apple.

(394) Mary has been eating an apple.

These can be represented in temporal terms as follows:

(395) $\tau(e_1) \supseteq t_{TT} \wedge \tau(e_2) \supseteq t_{TT} \wedge \tau(e_3) > t_{TT}$
(396) $\tau(e_1) < t_{TT} \wedge \tau(e_2) < t_{TT} \wedge \tau(e_3) \supseteq t_{TT}$
(397) $\tau(e_1) \supset t_{TT} \wedge \tau(e_2) \supset t_{TT} \wedge \tau(e_3) > t_{TT}$

This is to say that the present continuous includes topic time in the event time of the 'eat' and 'become' eventualities, with the poststate located beyond topic time. The present perfect includes topic time in the poststate, with the 'eat' and 'become' events located prior to topic time. Finally the present perfect continuous properly includes topic time in the 'eat' and 'become' events, with the poststate lying beyond topic time.

5.1.7 Resultative and perfect in English

Before we embark on assessing the aspect of Greek perfect predicates in the terms that we have been introducing, it is important that we first apply them in the case of the two formations in English which most closely correspond to the Greek perfect, and with which one will, either consciously or subconsciously align it, namely the resultative and the perfect.

At 3.5.2 above we examined the semantics of the resultative in English and concluded that its function was to suppress both internal and external arguments. We are now in a position to assess the aspectual implications of this operation. Consider the following example:

(398) The water is frozen.

This sentence denotes that the subject 'the water' is in a frozen state. It is an entailment of this predicate that the water went through a freezing event at some point prior to topic time, but the water is not presented has having passed through this freezing event. In this respect the resultative contrasts with the the following perfect example:

(399) The water has frozen.

The entailments of this sentence can be the same as that of the previous sentence, namely that the water is in a frozen state, and that there was a freezing event prior to topic time. However, there are two important differences with the resultative:

1. Whereas in the resultative example, the subject is not presented as having passed through the event described by the predicate, in the perfect predicate it is presented as having done so.
2. In the resultative example the water must be frozen at topic time, while in the perfect example there are two interpretations: either the water is now frozen, or (marginally) that the water did freeze in the past but is no longer frozen.

These differences can be seen to emerge from the argument structure. Figure 42 gives the structure of the resultative sentence, 'The water is frozen'. Since the resultative operates on the argument structure of the predicate, suppressing both internal and external arguments, there are no landing sites for the underlying (mod) argument before the subject position. As such, the water is not asserted to participate in the aspectual events become and cause. The resultative also has an aspectual value, however: it includes topic time in the temporal trace of the poststate described by the predicate. The prior become and cause subeventualities are left merely as entailments of the predicate without being explicitly related to topic time.

By contrast with the resultative, the perfect operates only on the VAspP, leaving the argument structure of the VP in tact, as represented in Figure 43. Accordingly, the underlying argument moves both to the internal and external positions before it reaches subject position. The perfect then relates all three eventualities to topic time.

Notice that in the English resultative the become subeventuality cannot be modified by an adjunct expression:

(400) #The water is frozen by the cold.

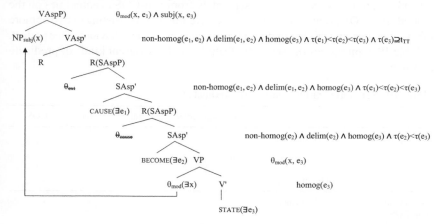

Figure 42: Resultative COS predicate

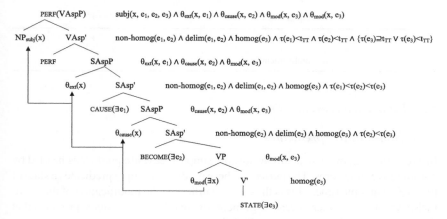

Figure 43: Perfect COS predicate

This suggests that there is a rule in English whereby in the resultative the become subeventuality cannot have a bar-level projection. By contrast, there is no such difficulty in the case of the English perfect:

(401) The water has been frozen by the cold.

5.1.8 *Outline of the present chapter*

The present chapter is divided into three sections, dealing with homogeneous eventualities, non-homogeneous non-COS eventualities and COS eventualities respectively. These are further subdivided according to the lexical aspectual semantic features identified in the chapter 2, namely durativity and terminativity, but extended to the syntactic level. At the syntactic level the corresponding features are durativity and telicity.

COS eventualities are dealt with separately from non-COS eventualities on the grounds that COS eventualities are complex eventualities consisting of two or more subeventualities, and this has important consequences for the behaviour of the perfect.

Table 19 summarises the semantic features of the different kinds of predicate examined.

Table 19. Semantic feature analysis of predicate types

		Homogeneous	Durative	Telic	COS
Homogeneous	Non-durative	+	-	-	-
	Durative Atelic	+	+	-	-
	Durative Telic	+	+	+	-
Non-homogeneous non-COS	Achievement	-	-	+	-
	Activity	-	+	-	-
	Accomplishment	-	+	+	-
COS	Achievement	-	-	+	+
	Accomplishment	-	+	+	+

5.2 *Homogeneous eventualities*

5.2.1 *Non-durative predicates*

In event and argument structure terms, the simplest case are predicates headed by non-durative state verbs. The perfect of these predicates simply predicates a state of the subject at topic time. This is the case regardless of the modification of the eventuality variable by either internal arguments or adverbial expressions, provided that these do not contribute any temporal attributes.

Consider the following examples of predicates consisting of unmodified perfects:

(402) = (108)

trépetai		dè	katà	stenōpòn
turn.PRES-IND-NON-ACT-I-3-SG	*PTCL*		*down*	*corridor.M-ACC-SG*

ēremēkóta...
be-quiet.*PERF-PTPL-ACT-M-ACC-SG*
'Instead he turned down a **quiet** narrow corridor...' (Jos. *AJ* 19.104)

(403) = (107)

... metatheînai	toùs	**ēgnoēkótas**
change.AOR-INF-ACT	*ART.M-ACC-PL*	*not-know.PERF-PTPL-ACT-M-ACC-PL*

holoskherōs astokhoûsin...
completely fail.PRES-IND-ACT-3-PL
'... [the Carthaginians] completely fail... to change **those who are ignorant**.'
(Plb. 1.67.5)

In both cases, the first involving the perfect *ēremēkóta*, from the state verb *ēreméō* 'be quiet', the second involving the perfect *ēgnoēkótas* from the state verb *agnoéō* 'not to know', the perfect performs no other function other than to include topic time in the state.[301]

The addition of an internal argument with no temporal properties does not change the temporal reference of the predicate. In the following example, the perfect of *ékhō* is construed with the abstract *elpís*:

(404) = (117)

hḗ	te	Mariámmē...			
ART.F-NOM-SG	*PTCL*	*Mariam.F-NOM-SG*			

ékhtheto...		tôi	mēd'	ei
be-annoyed.IMPF-IND-NON-ACT-I-3-SG	*ART.M-DAT-SG*	*NEG*	*if*	

páskhoi	ti deinòn	
suffer.pres-opt-act-3-sg	*INDEF-PRON.N-ACC-SG terrible.N-ACC-SG*	

ekeînos	elpída	toû
that.M-NOM-SG	*hope.F-ACC-SG*	*ART.M-GEN-SG*

biōsesthai	di'	autòn	**eskhēkénai**...
live.fut-inf-mid	*through*	*he.m-acc-sg*	**have.*PERF-INF-ACT***

'Mariam... was annoyed by the fact that she did not **have the hope** of living through [the king] if something should happen to him...' (Jos. *AJ* 15.204)

As before, the function of the perfect is simply to include topic time in the state.[302]

---

[301] i.e. $\exists x \exists e[\text{be-quiet}(e) \land \text{homog}(e) \land \theta_{ext}(x, e) \land \tau(e) \supseteq t_{TT}]$
$\exists x \exists e[\text{not-know}(e) \land \text{homog}(e) \land \theta_{ext}(x, e) \land \tau(e) \supseteq t_{TT}]$
[302] $\exists e \exists x \exists y[\text{have}(e, x) \land \text{homog}(e) \land \theta_{ext}(x, e) \land \theta_{mod}(y, e) \land \tau(e) \supseteq t_{TT}]$

Modification of the event variable is possible by both manner and deictic time adverbials. If the adverb is compatible with topic time interpretation, the temporal constitution of the event described by the predicate remains unchanged, and once again the perfect simply includes topic time in the state:[303]

(405) = (111), (180)

kaì	tò		mèn	phármakon	**euthùs**
and	ART.N-ACC-SG		PTCL	*poison*.N-ACC-SG	*immediately*
espoudakóti				zēteîn	oukh
be-eager.PERF-PTPL-ACT-M-DAT-SG		*look-for*.PRES-INF-ACT			NEG
heuréthē.					
find.AOR-IND-PAS-3-SG					

'And though he **immediately set about eagerly** to look for a poison, none was found.' (Jos. *AJ* 16.254)

From this evidence, it might be supposed that the fundamental function of the perfect is to predicate a Kimian state of the subject. Since state verbs denote state by their lexical semantics, the perfect need simply tie the relevant state to topic time. However, such a deduction is undermined by the fact that a number of manner adverbial expressions are compatible with non-durative perfects:

(406)

perì	pánta	**espoudákei**
about	*ll*.N-ACC-PL	*be-eager*.PLPF-IND-ACT-3-SG
tà	kataskeuásmata	**philotímōs**...
ART.N-ACC-PL	*weapon*.N-ACC-PL	*lavishly*

'[Philotimos] was **lavishly zealous** concerning all his weaponry...' (Callixenus *Frag.* 1.3)

(407)

dià	tò	**hrāithúmōs**	autoùs
on-account	ART.N-ACC-SG	*carelessly*	*they*.M-ACC-PL
eskhēkénai	katà	tò	
have.PERF-INF-ACT	*at*	ART.N-ACC-SG	
paròn		perì	tḕn	en
be-present.PRES-PTPL-ACT-N-ACC-SG	*about*	ART.F-ACC-SG	*in*
toîs	hóplois	gumnasían	
ART.N-DAT-PL	*weapon*.N-DAT-PL	*training*.F-ACC-SG	

'... because [the Athenians] **were rather lax** at that time about training for war.' (Plb. 4.7.6)

In this way the behaviour of state verbs in the perfect is exactly parallel to that of noise verbs:

---

[303] $\exists e \exists x [\text{be-eager}(e) \wedge \text{homog}(e) \wedge \theta_{\text{ext}}(e, x) \wedge \text{Immediately}(e) \wedge \tau(e) \supseteq t_{TT}]$

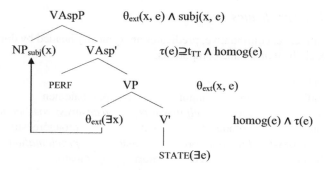

Figure 44: Perfect of a state

(408) = (160)

hai	gunaîkes	apantôsai
ART.F-NOM-PL	*woman.F-NOM-PL*	*meet.PRES-PTPL-ACT-F-NOM-PL*

metà xiphôn	kaì	pelékeōn
with sword.N-GEN-PL	*and*	*axe.M-GEN-PL*

deinòn **tetriguîai**
terribly *shriek.PERF-PTPL-ACT-F-NOM-PL*

ēmúnonto	toùs...
drive-back.IMPF-IND-NON-ACT-I-3-PL	*ART.M-ACC-PL*

pheúgontas
flee.PRES-PTPL-IND-M-ACC-PL

'... the women met [them], holding swords and axes, and **shrieking terribly** tried to drive back those who were fleeing...' (Plu. *Gaius Marius* 19.7)

In general terms, then, for non-durative predicates, the perfect simply includes topic time in the eventuality described by the predicate, without modification, and without any reference to any situation prior to topic time. This is presented in Figure 44.[304]

5.2.2 Durative predicates

The predicates discussed in the previous section carried no implication of any situation prior to topic time. Durative state predicates, by contrast, defined as they are by the presence of durativity, i.e. dur(e), are characterised by carrying entailments relating to time extending beyond topic time. The feature of durativity may be contributed either by the lexical verb, an internal argument or an adverbial expression. There are, furthermore, two kinds of homogeneous durative predicate, distinguished in terms of telicity. These properties are carried over into the predicates headed by a perfect.

---

[304] Where an object is present, the state eventuality would be seen to project a θ_{mod} argument, per Figure 17, p. 97 above.

5.2.2.1 *Atelic predicates*

Atelic durative, i.e. continuative, predicates are typically headed by durative state verbs, especially of *ménō* and compounds:

(409) = (121)

oud'	àn	autoì	parabaíēmen
NEG	*PTCL*	*self.M-NOM-PL*	*transgress.AOR-OPT-ACT-1-PL*
toû	nómou	tḕn	proagóreusin
ART.M-GEN-SG	*law.M-GEN-SG*	*ART.F-ACC-SG*	*proclamation.F-ACC-SG*
theoû…		eis	nûn	aparábatoi
God.M-GEN-SG		**to**	**now**	*untransgressing.M-NOM-PL*
memenēkótes				
remain.PERF-PTPL-ACT-NOM-PL				

'… nor would we transgress the proclamation of the law of God, since… we **have remained to this moment** guiltless of transgressing it…' (Jos. *AJ* 18.266)

In temporal terms these eventualities are like those found in non-durative predicates, except that their duration extends prior to topic time and they continue to hold at topic time.[305]

Durative state predicates may also arise by construction with internal arguments with temporal properties. In the following example, *ékhō* 'to have' is construed with *sunḗtheia*, 'habit', which carries an inherent notion of durativity. This in turn contributes the durative denotation of the predicate as a whole. As with other durative homogeneous eventualities, the perfect includes topic time in the situation time:[306]

(410)

toû	gàr	katakóptesthai	**sunḗtheian**
ART.N-GEN-SG	*PTCL*	*cut-down.PRES-INF-NON-ACT-I*	*custom.F-ACC-SG*
eskhēkótes		hupò	Galatôn
have.PERF-PTPL-ACT-NOM-PL		*by*	*Gaul.M-GEN-PL*
oudèn	édúnanto		deinóteron
nothing.N-ACC-SG	*be-able.IMPF-IND-ACT-3-PL*		*worse.N-ACC-SG*
ideîn			
see.AOR-INF-ACT			

'For since [the Romans] had **had the habit** of being defeated by the Gauls, they could not see anything worse [happening]…' (Plb. 2.20.8)

A deictic temporal adverbial may locate the eventuality prior to topic time. The following example involves the non-durative verb *kataphronéō* 'to despise':

---

[305] $\exists e \exists x [\text{Remain}(e, x) \wedge \text{homog}(e) \wedge \text{dur}(e) \wedge \theta_{ext}(x, e) \wedge \tau(e) \supset t_{TT} \wedge \text{From\_the\_previous\_winter}(\exists t_i \in \tau(e) \wedge t_i \prec t_{TTi})]$

[306] $\exists e \exists x \exists y [\text{Have}(e, y) \wedge \text{homog}(e) \wedge \theta_{ext}(y, e) \wedge \theta_{mod\text{-}dur}(x, e) \wedge \text{dur}(e) \wedge \tau(e) \supset t_{TT}]$

(411) = (112)

sunébaine...	Dēmétrion		
happen.IMPF-IND-ACT-3-SG	*Demetrius.M-ACC-SG*		
katapephronēkóta	dè	**próteron**...	
despise.PERF-PTPL-ACT-M-ACC-SG	*PTCL*	***previously***	
Rōmaíous...	portheîn...	tàs...	poleis
Romans.M-ACC-PL	*sack.PRES-INF-ACT*	*ART.F-ACC-PL*	*city.F-ACC-PL*
hupò	Rōmaíous	tattoménas...	
under	*Romans.M-ACC-PL*	*rule.PRES-PTPL-NON-ACT-I-M-ACC-PL*	

'For it happened... that Demetrius... **having previously despised**
Romans... **began sacking**... the cities... which were under Roman rule.'
(Plb. 3.16.2f.)

The adverb *próteron* changes the reading of the predicate from a non-durative state to a durative one. The perfect then treats the predicate as any other durative homogeneous predicate and includes topic time in the situation time.

Verbs which normally describe non-durative states may be used to describe a continued state if controlled by a predicate which carries this denotation. In the next example the perfect active participle *eskhēkótes* plays a complement role to the verb *diateléō* 'to continue' (also perfect), meaning 'to continue'. This parallels the canonical use of *diateléō*, whereby a complementary participle conveys the action which is being continued.[307]

(412) = (118), (127)

thaumáseie	d'	án	tis
wonder.AOR-OPT-ACT-3-SG	*PTCL*	*PTCL*	*INDEF-PRON.MF-NOM-SG*
tôn	anthrṓpōn	tḕn	pròs
ART.M-GEN-PL	*person.M-GEN-PL*	*ART.F-ACC-SG*	*to*
hēmâs	apékhtheian,	hḕn...	
we.ACC-PL	*hostility.F-ACC-SG*	*REL-PRON.F-ACC-SG*	

---

[307] In this example *eskhēkótes* is translated construed with a perfect in English, 'have continued'. But 'continue', being a control verb in English, cannot be construed with a perfect infinitive: #... which they have continued to have held. *eskhēkótes* appears, at least to an English speaker, therefore, to function as a present participle. *diateléō* appears to behave in a similar way in Greek. There are a total of 102 instances of the active form of *diateléō* attested in the original corpus. In 91 of these, the vast majority, the verb takes a participial complement, indicating the action which is being continued. In all but two cases where the verb takes a participial complement, it is the present participle which is used. This is the case regardless of the aspect of *diateléō* itself. The choice of the present participle is entirely to be expected given the semantics of *diateléō*: 'to continue' is semantically concerned with the ongoing nature of an activity, rather than its endpoints. The two examples where non-present participles are used are also instructive in this regard: *pepeisménoi* [*persuade.PERF-PTPL-NON-ACT-I-M-NOM-PL*] *diateloíēmen* [*continue.AOR-OPT-ACT-1-PL*] (Jos. *AJ* 8.108) and *hestòs* [*set-up.PERF-PTPL-ACT-M-NOM-SG*] *dietélei* [*continue.IMPF-IND-ACT-3-SG*] (Jos. *AJ* 6.2). Both of these involve perfect participles where there is a clearly defined resultant state, and, at least in the case of *hestós*, a verb whose perfect is well known to be able to lose any reference to an event occurring prior to topic time. In the light of these pieces of evidence, it seems likely that Josephus saw the functioning of *eskhēkótes* at (412) as in some way parallel to a present participle, i.e. without the implication of any event occurring prior to topic time, and with denotation of continued state.

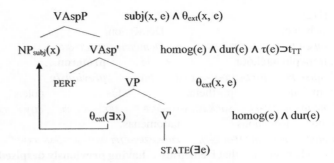

Figure 45: Perfect of a durative atelic state

diatetelékasin   eskhēkótes.
continue.PERF-IND-ACT-3-PL   *have.PERF-PTPL-ACT-M-NOM-PL*
'Someone might wonder at the hostility people show us, which... **they
have continued to hold.**' (Jos. *AJ* 3.179)

In sum, the perfect of durative atelic state predicates differs from that of pure state
predicates only in that the perfect properly includes, rather than simply including,
topic time in the runtime of the state eventuality, as represented in Figure 45.

5.2.2.2 *Telic predicates*

Telicity may be contributed either by the lexical verb, or by another element in the
event-argument structure modifying the eventuality variable. An important group
of telic durative predicates are telic because of the terminativity of the lexical verb,
i.e. terminative state verbs such as *stratēgéō*:

(413) = (124)
  Thouránios   dè   ou
  Thouranius.m-nom-sg *PTCL* *NEG*
  stratēgôn   mèn éti, all'
  be-general.pres-ptpl-act-m-nom-sg *PTCL* *still* *but*
  estratēgēkós...
  be-general.PERF-PTPL-ACT-M-NOM-SG
  'Thourianios, who was no longer praetor, but **had formerly served as
  such...**' (App. *BC* 4.4.18)

Here then, in contrast to other state predicates, topic time is not included in the
temporal trace of the eventuality, but is located prior to topic time, per Figure 46.[308]
  Durative predicates may be delimited by means of an adjunct. In the following
example, involving *hupoménō*, 'to withstand', the predicate is delimited by means
of a 'for α time' expression, *polloùs khrónous* 'for many years':

---

[308] $\exists x \exists e [\text{Be-praetor}(e, x) \land \text{homog}(e) \land \theta_{ext}(x, e) \land \text{dur}(e) \land \text{delim}(e) \land \tau(e){<}t_{TT}]$.

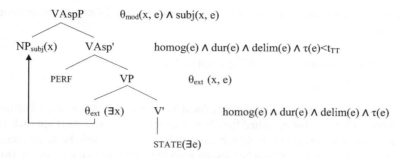

Figure 46: Perfect of a telic state

(414) = (123)

heîlon	dè	kaì		tò
take.AOR-IND-ACT-3-PL	*PTCL*	*PTCL*		*ART.N-ACC-SG*
Muttístraton,	**polloùs**			**khrónous**
Myttistratus.M-ACC-SG	***many.M-ACC-PL***			***year.M-ACC-PL***
hupomemenēkòs		tền		poliorkían...
withstand.PERF-PTPL-ACT-N-ACC-SG	*ART.F-ACC-SG*			*siege.F-ACC-SG*

'And they took Myttistratus, **which had withstood** the siege **for many years**...' (Plb. 1.24.11)

As is clear from the fact that Myttistratus was taken, the eventuality terminates prior to topic time, and an anterior reading of the perfect follows.[309]

5.2.3 *Conclusion*

In this section we have considered the semantics of homogeneous predicates headed by perfects. In general the properties of the tenseless predicate in terms of homogeneity, durativity and telicity are carried over into the predicate headed by the perfect. Thus in non-durative predicates, the perfect simply predicates the eventuality of the subject without change. Similarly in durative telic predicates both the durativitity and the telicity are carried over. Finally, in atelic durative predicates, the durativity of the tenseless predicate is in general carried over into the semantics of the predicate headed by the perfect. However, in this case examples were found where the perfect occurred in an artificially bounded predicate. Nevertheless, the fact that boundedness was not guaranteed in such predicates suggests that the semantics of the perfect do not in themselves entail boundedness, even if this is an implicature. Furthermore, the fact that the perfect inherits the temporal and aspectual properties of its predicate leaves open the question of what the semantics of the perfect actually denote. For this it will be important

---

[309] $\exists e \exists x \exists y[$Withstand$(e, x) \wedge$ homog$(e) \wedge \theta_{ext}(x, e) \wedge$ dur$(e) \wedge$ delim$(y, e) \wedge \tau(e) < t_{TT}]$, where 'x' is Mysistratus and 'y' is 'many years'.

to consider the other main class of eventualities, namely non-homogeneous eventualities.

5.3 Non-homogeneous non-COS eventualities

5.3.1 Introduction

Non-homogeneous eventualities consist of achievement, accomplishment and activity predicates. They are distinguished from homogeneous eventualities in their inability to be infinitely subdivided to yield sub-eventualities which match the denotation of the original eventuality. When headed by a perfect, we find that they differ from predicates describing homogeneous eventualities in that a bound is always imposed on the event they describe, regardless of the telicity of the tenseless predicate.

While COS eventualities are also by definition non-homogeneous, these are dealt with separately in the following section. This is because, consisting as they do of a substructure consisting of an event and poststate, the properties of these predicates headed by a perfect are different from other non-homogeneous predicates.

5.3.2 Activity predicates

Activity predicates, such as 'run', are atelic, and thus share with some states the property atelicity. Furthermore, they are divisible down to a certain granularity to yield sub-events of the same denotation as the original event. However, because this cannot be done to an infinite degree, they lack the property of homogeneity shared by all states, and, as I am arguing, noise events. Furthermore, because of this their events have a certain minimal duration, and activity predicates are therefore durative.

Activity predicates headed by a perfect are rare in the type of Greek investigated here. However, where they occur they are always bounded:

(415) = (136)

ho		d'	ouk	**orthôs**	autòn
ART.M-NOM-SG		*PTCL*	*NEG*	***properly***	*he.ACC-SG*
éphē		**pepoiēkénai**...			
say.PAST-IND-ACT-3-SG		***act.PERF-INF-ACT***			

'But he said that he had not **acted properly**...' (Jos. *AJ* 6.102)

There is no set terminal point in the event schema structure of this predicate. Yet the perfect in this example clearly refers to an event that has terminated at topic time. It must be inferred, therefore, that the perfect performs a bounding operation on the predicate, and locates the event prior to topic time, as represented in Figure 47. The means by which this bounding takes place is discussed in chapter 7.

Although the perfect is seen to place an arbitrary bound on activity predicates and locate the terminal point prior to topic time, location of the event prior to topic time may be explicitly denoted by means of deictic temporal adverbials, such as *mikròn émprosthen*:

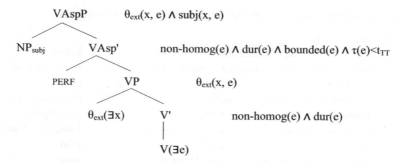

Figure 47: Perfect of an activity

(416) ... horôn   hoùs
     see.PRES-PTPL-ACT-M-NOM-SG   *rel-pron.M-ACC-PL*
     akēkóei   **mikròn**
     hear.PLPF-IND-ACT-3-SG   *a-little*
     émprosthen   apolōlótas...
     before   *destroy.PERF-PTPL-ACT-M-ACC-PL*
     '[Their father met them as they were wailing, upset] at seeing beyond hope
     those whom **he had but a little before heard** had been lost.' (Jos. *AJ* 7.179)

5.3.3 *Accomplishment predicates*

Accomplishment predicates share with activity predicates durativity and lack of
homogeneity. However, unlike activity predicates they are by definition telic. Durativity and telicity are two features shared with telic state predicates, whose perfects
we found to be past referring and anterior. It is therefore perhaps not surprising that
the perfect of accomplishment predicates are also past referring and anterior:

(417) ... eis   tḕn   mētrópolin   epalindrómoun...
     to   *ART.F-ACC-SG*   *mother-city.F-ACC-SG*   *run-back.IMPF-IND-ACT-3-PL*
     tôn   dè   Rōmaíōn   kaì
     ART.M-GEN-PL   *PTCL*   *Roman.M-GEN-PL*   *and*
     tôn   summákhōn
     ART.M-GEN-PL   *ally.M-GEN-PL*
     pezoùs   mèn   **pentakiskhilíous**   **kaì**
     infantry.M-ACC-PL *PTCL*   *fifteen-thousand.M-ACC-PL* *and*
     triakosíous   **anēirēkótes...**
     three-hundred.M-ACC-PL   *kill.PERF-PTPL-ACT-M-NOM-PL*
     '... they ran back to the mother city... but of the Romans and their allies
     they had killed fifteen thousand three hundred of the infantry...'
     (Jos. *BJ* 2.555)

The following example, involving the perfect of *poiéō* 'do' is parallel:

(418) = (23), (135)

hoi	dè	ánthrōpoi	tò	kréas
ART.M-NOM-PL	*PTCL*	*human.M-NOM-PL*	*ART.N-ACC-SG*	*meat.N-ACC-SG*
esthíousin,		tà	d'	ostâ
eat.PRES-IND-ACT-3-SG		*ART.N-ACC-PL*	*PTCL*	*bone.N-ACC-PL*
hríptousin,		hóper		ánthrōpos
throw.PRES-IND-ACT-3-PL		*REL-PRON.N-ACC-AG*		*human.M-NOM-SG*
ṑn		kagṑ		**nûn**
be.PRES-PTPL-M-NOM-SG		*and-I.NOM-SG*		*now*
pepoíēka.				
do.PERF-IND-ACT-1-SG				

'Men, however, eat the meat, but throw away the bones, which is exactly what I, who am also a man, **have now done.**' (Jos. *AJ* 12.213)

Note, however, that the derivation of this reading is different from that of telic state predicates. Adopting the analysis of accomplishment predicates proposed in 5.1.4, whereby accomplishments are composite eventualities consisting of a VP and two light verbs 'become' and 'state', we can say that the perfect includes topic time in the state eventuality, and locates the two prior eventualities prior to topic time.

Activity verbs, such as 'run' may head accomplishment predicates where construed with a quantised path argument delimiting the event. Consider the following example involving the perfect of *trékhō*:

(419) ... tôn   [khíl]ia   **dedramēkótōn**

ART.M-GEN-PL   *thousand.N-ACC-PL*   *run.PERF-PTPL-ACT-M-GEN-PL*

stádia...

stade.N-ACC-PL

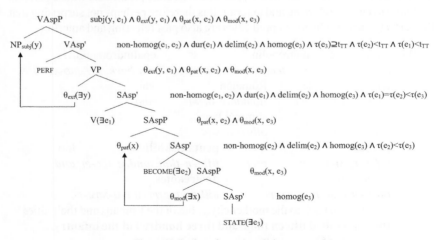

Figure 48: Perfect of an accomplishment

'... of those who **have run** a thousand stades...' (Philodemus *Perì orgês* [= *On Anger*] 182.8.35 – 40)

In this example, the event is bounded by a quantised internal argument, *khília stádia*, 'a thousand stades'. This argument turns an activity predicate to an accomplishment, and as in previous cases of the perfect heading accomplishment predicates, it adopts the set terminal point of the predicate, and locates the set terminal point prior to topic time so that topic time is not included in event time.

Although accomplishment predicates headed by a perfect always carry anterior readings, as with activity predicates the anteriority may be denoted explicitly by means of deictic temporal adverbs, such as *édē, próteron, émprothen* etc.:

(420) hoi dè toús te
ART.M-NOM-PL PTCL ART.M-ACC-PL PTCL
protérous **anēirékesan** édē...
former.M-ACC-PL **kill.PLPF-IND-ACT-3-PL** *already*
'The others **had already killed** the former men.' (App. *Hisp.* 3.16)

(421) ... keleúei dêsai
order.PRES-IND-ACT-3-SG *bind.AOR-INF-ACT*
tòn Agríppan
ART.M-ACC-SG *Agrippa.M-ACC-SG*
lelukòs **próteron** autòn...
release.PERF-PTPL-ACT-M-NOM-SG **previously** *he.ACC-SG*
'... he gave the order to bind Agrippa, though **he had previously released him**...' (Jos. *AJ* 18.233)

5.3.4 Conclusion

Non-homogeneous non-COS predicates headed by a perfect differ from homogeneous predicates in that they are always bounded. In the case of achievement and accomplishment predicates, the bounding is inherited from the tense-and aspect-less predicate. However, in the case of activity predicates the bounding is imposed by the perfect itself. Unlike homogeneous predicates, where the eventuality described holds in most cases at topic time, in non-homogeneous predicates the terminal point of the eventuality is always located prior to topic time. In accomplishment predicates the perfect includes topic time in the eventual state of the internal argument. However, this is not a possibility for activity predicates, an issue to which we will return in chapter 7.

5.4 COS accomplishment predicates

5.4.1 Introduction

COS events are more complex than both homogeneous and non-homogeneous eventualities. This is because they consist of a subevent leading to a poststate. A predicate of this kind headed by a perfect also demonstrates some special behaviour.

Specifically, while the poststate is always inherited by the perfect headed predicate, there is no requirement that the subevent be inherited in the same way. Accordingly, in many cases it is hard to detect any reference to an event taking place prior to topic time, and in a few cases the occurrence of such an event is specifically excluded.

All COS predicates share the property of telicity. Beyond this there exist both achievement COS predicates and accomplishment COS predicates. I will deal with each of these in turn.

5.4.2 *Unaccusative and anticausative predicates*

In the perfect of non-COS accomplishment predicates we saw that past reference and anteriority were obligatory. By contrast, perfect-headed accomplishment COS predicates may carry reference to a prior subevent, but apparently need not do so. Compare the use of *héstēka* in the first example with that of *héstēka* and *bébēka* in the second:

(422) exērtukòs   en   têi   nuktì
get-ready.PERF-PTPL-ACT-M-NOM-SG   *in*   *ART.F-DAT-SG*   *night.F-DAT-SG*
déka naûs   tàs   árista   pleoúsas,
ten   *ship.F-ACC-PL*   *ART.F-ACC-PL*   *best*   *sail.PRES-PTPL-ACT-F-ACC-PL*
autòs   mèn   epì   toû   liménos
self.M-NOM-SG   *PTCL*   *on*   *ART.M-GEN-SG*   *harbour.M-GEN-SG*
hestòs   etheórei
stand.PERF-PTPL-ACT-M-NOM-SG   *watch.IMPF-IND-ACT-3-SG*
tò   sumbaînon...
ART.N-ACC-SG   *happen.PRES-PTPL-ACT-N-ACC-SG*
'[The Roman Consul...] had prepared his ten fastest-sailing vessels during the night, and **having taken up a position** on the harbour, was watching what would happen...' (Plb. 1.46.8)

(423) = (147), (323)
en   dè   Delphoîs   Palládion
in   *PTCL*   *Delphi.M-DAT-PL*   *Palladium.N-NOM-SG*
héstēke   khrusoûn   epì
set-up.PERF-IND-ACT-3-SG   *golden.N-NOM-SG*   *on*
phoínikos   khalkoû
date-palm.M-GEN-SG   *bronze.M-GEN-SG*
bebēkós...
go.PERF-PTPL-ACT-N-NOM-SG
'And in Delphi there **stands** a statue of Pallas, **mounted** on a bronze date palm.' (Plu. *Nic.* 13.3)

In the first example the become event by which the final state is achieved is in view, namely an event of changing position on the part of the Roman general. In the second example, however, there seems little sign of the events leading to the poststates in question.

To establish what is happening, let us examine the second example, that in which reference to the subevent appears to have been removed, in neo-Davidsonian terms. The two tense-aspectless predicates involved here may be represented as follows:

(424) en Delphoîs Palládion **hista-**:
$\exists e_1 \exists e_2 \exists x \exists y [\text{BECOME}(e_1) \wedge \text{delim}(e_1) \wedge \text{non-homog}(e_1) \wedge \theta_{\text{cause\_int}}(e_1, x) \wedge$
$\text{STATE}(e_2) \wedge \text{homog}(e_2) \wedge \text{Up}(e_2, x) \wedge \theta_{\text{mod}}(e_2, x) \wedge \text{In}(e_2, y) \wedge \tau(e_1){<}\tau(e_2)]^{310}$

(425) epì phoínikos khalkoû **bain-**:
$\exists e_1 \exists e_2 \exists x \exists y [\text{BECOME}(e_1) \wedge \text{delim}(e_1) \wedge \text{non-homog}(e_1) \wedge \theta_{\text{cause}}(e_1, x) \wedge$
$\text{STATE}(e_2) \wedge \text{homog}(e_2) \wedge \theta_{\text{mod}}(e_2, x) \wedge \text{Upon}(e_2, y) \wedge \tau(e_1){<}\tau(e_2)]$

The statue of Pallas must at some point have undergone the events denoted by e_1. However, the predicates headed by the perfects do not appear reference to events directly, but only the target states, i.e.:

(426) en Delphoîs Palládion héstēke:
$\exists e_2 \exists x [\text{homog}(e_2) \wedge \theta_{\text{mod}}(e_2, x) \wedge \text{Up}(e_2, x) \wedge \text{In}(e_2, y) \wedge \tau(e_2){\supseteq}t_{\text{TT}}]$

(427) epì phoínikos khalkoû bebēkós:
$\exists e_2 \exists x [\text{homog}(e_2) \wedge \theta_{\text{mod}}(e_2, x) \wedge \text{Upon}(e_2, y) \wedge \tau(e_2){\supseteq}t_{\text{TT}}]$

Taking the case of the *bébēka* predicate first, it appears that the perfect performs a function on COS predicates so that it suppresses the become event leading to the poststate along with its arguments, and returns only the target state described by the predicate. Similarly in the case of the *héstēka* predicate, the perfect could be said to suppress both the become and cause subeventualities. On this basis whether or not a previous event is described by the predicate could be said to be on level of implicature, rather than an entailment of the use of the perfect with such predicates in itself.

Support for the view that the perfect can suppress become and cause subevents comes from various sets of circumstances where these eventualities are apparently not in view. One such is where a clause outside the predicate references only the poststate and not the subevent:

(428) epeì d' ho Kaîsar...
when PTCL ART.M-NOM-SG *Caesar.M-NOM-SG*
lambánei tòn
come-upon.PRES-IND-ACT-3-SG ART.M-ACC-SG
Agríppan **hestēkóta**...
Agrippa.M-ACC-SG **stand.PERF-PTPL-ACT-M-ACC-SG**
'When Caesar... **came upon Agrippa standing**...' (Jos. *AJ* 18.190)

Presumably Agrippa must have stood up at some point, but this is not at all in view. The reference is purely to the fact that Caesar found Agrippa in a standing position.

---

[310] For the purpose of comparison this predicate is taken for the time being as a simple COS rather than causative COS predicate.

Thus, it would seem that reference to the subevent is on the level of an implicature rather than as an entailment.

Direct reference to the cause/become subevents is also ruled out where the poststate is modified by an adverbial such as *éti*, 'still', which locates the point of reference at topic time, and blocks reference to any event that brought the situation:[311]

(429) = (149)

kaì... hē		thálassa...	toîs...	hósoi
and ART.F-NOM-SG		*sea.*f-nom-sg ART.M-DAT-PL		*as-many-as.*M-NOM-PL
tôn	neôn	**epebebḗkesan**		
ART.F-GEN-PL	*ship.*F-GEN-PL	**board.**PLPF-IND-ACT-3-PL		
éti...	ên	aporṓtéra		
still	*be.*PAST-IND-3-SG	*impassable.*N-NOM-SG		

'And... the sea... was impassable... for those **who were still on board**
the ships...' (App. *BC* 5.10.90)

Here, while logically those on the ships must have boarded at some point, the use of *éti* ensures that the assertion of the predicate is that they continue to be on board at topic time.

Finally, there are cases where the subject can in fact never have undergone the become eventuality described by the predicate:[312]

(430) = (6), (145)

hē	dè	Teúta...	polismátion...
ART.F-NOM-SG	PTCL	*Teuta.*F-NOM-SG	*small-town.*N-NOM-SG
anakekhōrēkòs		mèn	apò tês
withdraw.PERF-PTPL-ACT-N-NOM-SG		PTCL	*from* ART.F-GEN-SG
thaláttēs...			
*sea.*F-GEN-SG			

'Teuta... a small town... **withdrawn** from the sea...' (Plb. 2.11.16)

On the basis of the evidence provided so far, then, we could offer the provisional trees for unaccusative COS and anticausative COS perfect predicates given at Figures 49 and 50.

However, the analysis cannot be quite so straightforward, since there are circumstances under which a perfect COS predicate does directly reference the subevent prior to the poststate. This happens if the subevent variable is explicitly modified by an adverbial expression. Compare the following minimal pair of examples involving the perfect *pépēga*, perfect of *pḗgnumi* 'to fix':

---

[311] Parallels: *éti... sunestôsēs* (*establish.*PERF-PTPL-ACT-F-GEN-SG, App. *BC* 2.1.6), *éti periestôtas* (*encircle.*PERF-PTPL-ACT-M-ACC-PL, App. *Han.* 8.51).

[312] The viewpoint aspectless predicate may be represented as follows:

1. $\exists e_1 \exists e_2 \exists x [\text{BECOME}(e_1) \wedge \text{dur}(e_1) \wedge \text{delim}(e_1) \wedge \theta_{cause}(x, e_1) \wedge \text{STATE}(e_2) \wedge \text{homog}(e_2) \wedge \text{Away}(e_2, x) \wedge \theta_{mod}(e_2, x) \wedge \tau(e_1) < \tau(e_2)]$

The perfect then apparently reduces this to the poststate only, and includes TT in event time:

2. $\exists e_2 \exists x [\text{STATE}(e_2) \wedge \text{homog}(e_2) \wedge \theta_{mod}(e_2, x) \wedge \text{Away}(e_2, x) \wedge \tau(e_2) \supseteq t_{TT}]$

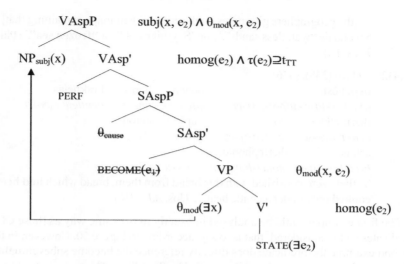

Figure 49: Perfect of an unaccusative COS sentence

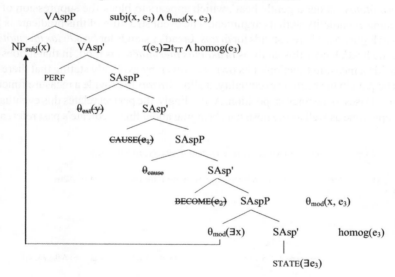

Figure 50: Perfect of an anticausative COS predicate

(431)   tà   d'   epékeina   thînes
      ART.N-NOM-PL   *PTCL*   *beyond.N-NOM-PL*   *sand.M-NOM-PL*
      ánudroi...   è̄   skuthikòn   krúon
      waterless.M-NOM-PL   *or*   *Scythian.N-NOM-SG* *cold.N-NOM-SG*
      è̄   **pélagos pepēgós**...
      or   **sea.N-NOM-SG**   **freeze.PERF-PTPL-ACT-N-NOM-SG**

'... [the geographers give notes on the edge of their maps explaining that] beyond lie "waterless sands"... or "Scythian cold" or **"frozen sea"**.' (Plu. *Thes.* 1.1)

(432) = (156) (248), (346)

pepēgósi		mónon	hupò	brakheías
fix.PERF-PTPL-ACT-M-DAT-PL		*only*	*under*	*gentle.F-GEN-SG*
thermótētos	toîs	ap'	autôn	
heat.F-GEN-SG	*ART.M-DAT-PL*	*from*	*they.GEN-PL*	
ártois	dietréphonto...			
bread.M-DAT-PL	*nourish.IMPF-IND-NON-ACT-I-3-PL*			

'... they were nourished with this bread from them, bread which **had been cooked** only under a gentle heat...' (Jos. *AJ* 2.316)

The first example could be analysed in exactly in the same way as those COS predicates so far considered, that is to say, according to Figure 50. However, in the second example the predicate does directly reference the become subeventuality. This has to be the case because it is modified by the adjunct phrase *hupò brakheías thermótētos* 'under a gentle heat', which appears to block the suppression of the become eventuality with its argument. The event structure of this predicate is laid out in Figure 51, where *x* stands for *ártois* 'bread', *y* stands for *brakheías thermótētos* 'gentle heat'. Under this analysis *brakheías thermótētos* is mod, in that it does not provide a measure function of its own. However, by explicitly stating that there is a participant in the become eventuality, it allows *artois* to provide a measure function when it rises to the internal position. Accordingly, the perfect relates this eventuality to topic time as well as the poststate, bringing about this predicate's past reference.

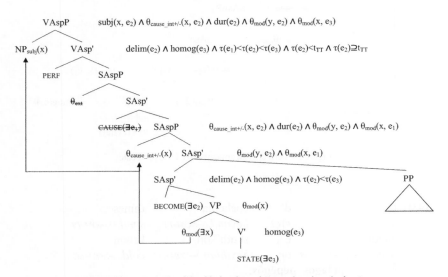

Figure 51: *pepēgósi hupò brakheías thermótētos toîs ap' autôn ártois*

A similar effect is produced where the become event variable is modified by the resultative adverbial *édē* 'already', 'before now'. This adverbial modifies both the poststate, asserting that it holds at topic time, and the prestate eventuality, asserting that it took place prior to topic time. Accordingly, the apparent suppression of the become eventuality is blocked:[313]

(433) = (325)

... potòn	aitḗsanti
drink.M-ACC-SG	*ask.AOR-PTPL-ACT-M-DAT-SG*
dídōsi	gala
give.PRES-IND-ACT-3-SG	*milk.N-ACC-SG*
diephthoròs	**édē.**
go-off.PERF-PTPL-ACT-N-ACC-SG	*already*

'... he gave a drink to him when asked for it, milk **which had gone off already**...' (Jos. *AJ* 5.207)

(434) = (144)

nûn dè...	lampróteron	ekkópsai	kaì
now PTCL	*noble.COMP-N-NOM-SG*	*fell.AOR-INF-ACT*	*and*
aneleîn	sunestôsan		édē
kill.AOR-INF-ACT	*establish.PERF-PTPL-ACT-F-ACC-SG*		*already*
kaì	**pephukuîan**		
and	**grow.PERF-PTPL-ACT-F-ACC-SG**		

'[he uttered the saying that]... in the present situation it was... a more noble task to fell and kill [the tyranny] now it was already established and was **full-grown**.' (Plu. *Sol.* 30.5)

Another means by which an accomplishment COS predicate headed by a perfect can retain reference to the prestate subevent is if the attribute gained as a result of the process inherently takes time to acquire, and thus contributes the semantic feature of durativity:

(435)

agōnieîsthai	tês	te	mákhēs
fight.FUT-INF-NON-ACT-I	*ART.F-GEN-SG*	*PTCL*	*battle.F-GEN-SG*
empeírous	**gegonótas...**		
experienced.M-ACC-PL	**become.M-ACC-PL**		

'[Pausanias brought word to Aristeides that it would be better] to fight **having gained experience** of battle...' (Plu. *Arist.* 16.1)

Gaining experience of a thing necessarily entails the passage of time. In this case, however, the durativity derives from the semantics of the poststate. It could

---

[313] $\exists e_1 \exists e_2 \exists x [\text{BECOME}(e_1) \land \text{delim}(e_1) \land \text{non-homog}(e_1) \land \theta_{\text{cause+/-}}(x, e_1) \land \text{STATE}(e_2) \land \text{Off}(x, e_2) \land \text{homog}(e_2) \land \theta_{\text{mod}}(x, e_2) \land \acute{e}d\bar{e}\{\tau(e_1) < t_{TT} \land \tau(e_2) \supseteq t_{TT}\}]$. *tetharsēkótes (have-courage.PERF-PTPL-ACT-M-NOM-PL) édē* ('already') (Jos. *AJ* 14.391), as a non-durative state predicate, should probably be viewed as asserting that the state started holding prior to topic time, as in NE 'I am already here'.

therefore be said to be a moot point whether or not there is direct reference to the prestate subevent.[314]

5.4.3 *Causative COS predicates*

While unaccusative verbs such as *anakhōréō*, 'I withdraw', always describe COS events, we saw in the previous chapter that certain verbs, notably those capable of labile transitivity, are indeterminate between COS and non-COS readings, and their perfects were concomitantly ambivalent between (result-)state and anterior readings. While in most cases, as for example in the case of *hístēmi* 'to set up', specialised stems are used to distinguish COS and non-COS senses, in the case of some verbs, notably *hupostéllō*, the distinction is entirely due to the argument projection of the verb. Specifically, if a cause and undergoer are supplied, these surface as subject and object respectively. By contrast, if only an undergoer is supplied, this surfaces as the subject:

(436) = (8), (158), (309)

heistḗkei		dè		katá		ti
set-up.PLPF-IND-ACT-3-SG		*PTCL*		*in*		*INDEF-PRON.N-ACC-SG*
prosbatòn	olígais		bathmîsi		khōríon	
accessible.N-ACC-SG	*few.F-DAT-PL*		*step.F-DAT-PL*		*space.N-ACC-SG*	
hupestalkòs			tôi			kat'
hide.PERF-PTPL-ACT-N-ACC-SG			*ART.DAT-M-SG*			*in*
autò	skótōi.					
it.N-SG-ACC	*darkness.M-DAT-SG*					

'[Claudius] had stood in a space, accessible by a few paces, **taking cover** in the darkness there.' (Jos. *AJ* 19.216)

(437) = (9), (159), (308)

ho		dè	Phílippos...		hupó
ART.M-NOM-SG		*PTCL*	*Philip.M-NOM-SG*		*under*
tina			lóphon		**hupestálkei**
INDEF-PRON.MF-ACC-SG			*hill.M-ACC-SG*		***hide.PLPF-IND-ACT-3-SG***
toùs		Illurioùs...			
ART.M-ACC-PL		*Illyrians.M-ACC-PL*			

'But Philip... **had sent** the Illyrians behind a hill...' (Plb. 5.13.5)

We need to account for the fact that in the first case a (result-)state is described, while in the second an anterior event is described. That is to say an event of hiding is explicit in the second example, but not the first. Analyses of the two examples are given in Figure 52 and Figure 53, respectively. The critical factor is the modification of the event variable. The important question is which eventuality is modified by the argument that ends up being the subject. In the case of *hupestálkei* the eventual subject specifies only the cause eventuality. It therefore follows that the internal argument

---

[314] The following is a possible analysis: $\exists e_1 \exists e_2 \exists x[\text{BECOME}(e_1) \wedge \text{delim}(e_1) \wedge \text{non-homog}(e_1) \wedge \theta_{\text{cause}}(x, e_1) \wedge \text{experienced}(e_2) \wedge \text{dur}(e_2) \wedge \text{homog}(e_2) \wedge \tau(e_1) < t_{TT} \wedge \tau(e_2) \supseteq t_{TT}]$

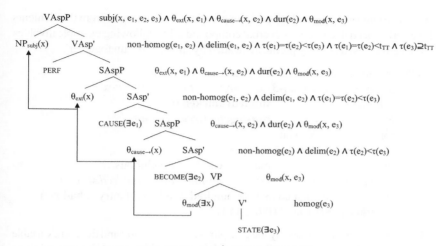

Figure 52: *hupestalkòs tôi kat' autò skótōi*

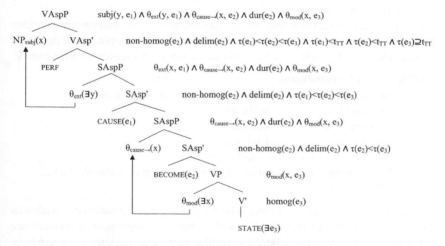

Figure 53: *hupó tina lóphon hupestálkei toùs Illurioùs*

is in a result state at topic time. Anteriority then arises from the fact that the cause event with which the subject is directly associated takes place prior to topic time. By contrast, in the case of *hupestalkós*, the eventual subject specifies all three eventualities, including the poststate. It follows, therefore, that the subject is in the result state at topic time, and a resultative reading follows from that.

5.4.4 *Unaccusativised activity predicates*

Not all unaccusative COS predicates show event variable suppression. In particular, unaccusativised activity predicates always carry reference to the become eventuality preceding the poststate. Blocking of event variable suppression by the perfect need not be restricted to appended adverbial expressions, but can come from the elements of the verbal head itself, as in preverbal compounds. The following example involves an unaccusativised activity predicate headed by *suntrékhō* 'run together'.

(438) epuntháneto   gàr   eis   tòn
     learn.AOR-IND-NON-ACT-3-SG   *PTCL*   *to*   *ART.M-ACC-SG*
     Stráton   **sundedramēkénai**
     Stratus.M-ACC-SG   **run-together.PERF-INF-ACT**
     tòn   Aitōlôn
     ART.M-GEN-PL   *Aetolian.M-GEN-PL*
     pezoùs   mèn   eis   triskhilíous…
     infantry.M-ACC-PL   *PTCL*   *up-to*   *three-hundred.M-ACC-PL*
     'For he learned that up to three hundred Aetolian infantry… **had run together to Stratus…**' (Plb. 5.14.1)

The event is unaccusativised by the goal phrase *eis tòn stráton* and the event variable is modified by the preverb *sun-*. Since the subevent variable cannot be removed since it is directly modified by *sun-*, the perfect simply includes topic time in the resulting state, and sets the event time prior to it.

However, the verb is in principle semantically ambiguous, and the preverb may either be taken to modify the event variable, as in the previous example, or the poststate. As such the preverb is able to unaccusativise the normally non-terminative *trékhō*:

(439) … **sundedramēkótos**   ókhlou
     run-together.PERF-PTPL-ACT-M-GEN-SG   *crowd.M-GEN-SG*
     surphetôdous,   takhéōs
     vulgar.M-GEN-SG   *quickly*
     parédosan   hautoús…
     give-up.AOR-IND-ACT-3-PL   *self.M-ACC-PL*
     '… when the mob **had gathered**, they quickly gave themselves up…'
     (Plb. 4.75.5)

Accordingly in this instance there is no modification of the subevent variable by means of an adverbial expression. The perfect, however, appears to retain reference to the subevent 'run'. This is because, unlike unaccusatives such as *anakhōréō*, which denote purely a change in location without any information being given regarding the manner of travel, verbs describing activities typically prescribe a means by which the motion takes place. Accordingly, the lexical verb itself may be said to provide adverbial modification enough to preserve reference to the event which brings the poststate about. The perfect then includes topic time in the target state, and preserves its denotation of the subevent 'run' as if the prestate subevent were modified by an adverb:

(440) $\exists e_1 \exists e_2 \exists e_3 \exists x[\text{run}(e_1) \land \text{non-homog}(e_1) \land \text{dur}(e_1) \land \theta_{\text{ext}}(x, e_1) \land \text{BECOME}(e_2)$
$\land \text{delim}(e_2) \land \text{non-homog}(e_2) \land \theta_{\text{cause}}(x, e_2) \land \text{STATE}(e_3) \land \text{homog}(e_3) \land$
$\text{Together}(e_3) \land \tau(e_1) = \tau(e_2) < \tau(e_3) \land \tau(e_1) < t_{TT} \land \tau(e_2) < t_{TT} \land \tau(e_3) \supseteq t_{TT}]$

5.4.5 Delimiting the poststate

In the examples of COS predicates so far considered, the poststate has not itself been bounded. However, the poststate can be bounded, either explicitly by means of a 'for α time' expression, or from the context more generally, whereby it becomes clear that the event is bounded. The following provides an example of bounding by a 'for α time' expression:

(441) ... hoi **tò** **próteron** **étos**
ART.M-NOM-PL *ART.N-ACC-SG* *previous.N-ACC-SG* *year.N-ACC-SG*
húpatoi **gegonótes**...
consul.M-NOM-PL **become.PERF-PTPL-ACT-M-NOM-PL**
'... [all fell, among whom were Marcus and Gnaeus] who **had been consuls for the preceding year**...' (Plb. 3.116.11)

The next example describes the acquisition of the consulship. Here, because we know that other people were consul in this year,[315] we also know that the poststate does not hold at topic time:

(442) = (133)
hôn heîs mèn ên
REL-PRON.M-GEN-PL *one.M-NOM-SG* *PTCL* *be.PAST-IND-3-SG*
Gáios Lutátios ho
Gaius.M-NOM-SG *Lutatius.M-NOM-SG* *ART.M-NOM-SG*
tèn húpaton arkhèn
ART.F-ACC-SG *consul.M-ACC-SG* *command.F-ACC-SG*
eilēphós...
take.PERF-PTPL-ACT-M-NOM-SG
'Of these one was C. Lutatius, **who had [previously] held** the consulship, the other two the praetorship.' (Plb. 3.40.9)

From the context, therefore, the reader is obliged to understand that C. Lutatius could not have been consul at topic time.

5.5 COS achievement predicates

5.5.1 COS predicates

COS predicates make up a large proportion of achievement predicates. These are mostly headed by achievement verbs and thus the telicity and non-durative temporal constitution are set by the lexical semantics of the verbal head. Since achievements are of non-durative, they are able to be included in topic time without any temporal implications for the period prior to topic time, as in the following example:[316]

---

[315] See n. 171.

[316] Parallels: *proskekhēkénai* (*gape-at.PERF-INF-ACT*), complement to *anagkazómetha* (*compel.PRES-SUBJ-NON-ACT-I-1-PL*) (Plb. 4.42.7) and *tethnánai* (*die.PERF-INF-ACT*), complement to *keleúsēi* (*order.AOR-SUBJ-ACT-3-SG*) (Jos. *AJ* 6.149).

(443) = (128)

hiketeúō,	páter,	éphē,
beseech.PRES-IND-ACT-1-SG	father.M-VOC-SG	say.PAST-3-SG
mēdén	mou	**prokategnōkénai…**
in-no-way	I.GEN-SG	**prejudge.**PERF-INF-ACT

"'**I beseech** you, father," he said, "in no way **to prejudge** (i.e. be in a state of prejudice regarding) me…"' (Jos. *BJ* 1.621)

The following example is similar and involves the perfect optative of the verb *thnḗskō* 'die', expressing a wish to die:

(444) **tethnaíēs,** eîpen, áner
die.PERF-OPT-ACT-2-SG say.AOR-IND-ACT-3-SG man.M-VOC-SG
'He said, "**I wish you were dead**, man…"' (Jos. *AJ* 2.55)

While in both of these examples the occurrence of a subeventuality taking place at topic time which gives rise to the poststate is a necessary inference, description of this event can may be made explicit by modification of the eventuality variable by means of the adverb *euthús* 'immediately':

(445) = (129)

ho	dè	Nikías	**euthùs**	autòs
ART.M-NOM-SG	PTCL	*Nikias.M-NOM-SG*	**immediately**	*self.M-NOM-SG*
kaì	parà	phúsin	hupò	tês
and	*beyond*	nature.F-ACC-SG	*by*	ART.F-GEN-SG
en	tôi	parónti	hrṓmēs	kaì
in	ART.F-DAT-SG	present.M-DAT-SG	strength.F-GEN-SG	*and*
túkhēs	**anatetharrēkṓs…**			
fortune.F-GEN-SG	**regain-courage.**PERF-PTPL-ACT-M-NOM-SG			

'But Nicias himself, immediately and unnaturally **encouraged** by his strength and good fortune in the present situation…' (Plu. *Nic.* 18.6)

The following is a parallel involving *gínomai* 'become', i.e. where the target state is denoted by means of an adjective:

(446) toûto **euthùs** eis elpídas toîs
this.N-NOM-SG **immediately** *to* help.F-ACC-PL ART.M-DAT-PL
Ioudaíois ou mikròn **egegónei.**
Jew.M-DAT-PL not small.N-NOM-SG **become.**PLPF-IND-ACT-3-SG
'This **immediately became** a not insignificant source of hope for the Judaeans.' (Jos. *AJ* 15.150)

However, it is not a requirement that the prestate and topic time overlap. This is explicitly the case where the temporal trace of the prestate may be located prior to topic time by means of an anterior adverbial:

(447) gnṓmēs te tês autês
opinion.F-GEN-SG *PTCL* *ART.F-GEN-SG* *same.F-GEN-SG*
koinōnoì kaì **próteron** ề
sharing.M-NOM-PL *even* **before** **than**
suneltheîn **gegónamen.**
meet.AOR-INF-ACT **become.PERF-IND-ACT-3-PL**
'... we came to be of the same mind **even before we met.**' (Jos. *AJ* 19.55)

In this example the point at which the two came to be of the same mind is expressly asserted to be prior to topic time by means of the adverb *próteron* 'formerly'. Thus the role of the anterior adverb is explicitly to locate event time prior to topic time.

However, there are instances where *próteron* is used and where the poststate no longer holds at topic time:

(448) hòs kaì desmṓtēi
REL-PRON.M-NOM-SG *even* *prisoner.M-DAT-SG*
moi genoménōi
I.DAT-SG *become.AOR-PTPL-NON-ACT-I-M-DAT-SG*
diakoneîsthai katháper **en tôi**
minister.PRES-INF-NON-ACT-I *just-as* **in** *ART.N-DAT-SG*
próteron kathestēkóti
previously establish.PERF-PTPL-ACT-N-DAT-SG
skhḗmati... ouk enélipes.
state.N-DAT-SG *NEG* *fail.AOR-IND-ACT-2-SG*
'... you who did not fail to minister to me when I was a prisoner, just as if I was in the state [of dignity] in which **I had formerly been established...**' (Jos. *AJ* 18.193)

In this example we know that the result of the 'establishing' event does not hold at topic time, since at topic time the individual whose state is referred to is in prison, and it is clearly his pre-prison state that he is describing. Note, however, that we know that the poststate is bounded from the context. That is to say that we know from the surrounding material what state the subject is in.

Similarly, where the event variable is modified by *pollákis* 'often', bounding of (several) instances of the event variable is entailed:

(449) hò dè kaì polloîs kaì
ART.M-NOM-SG *PTCL* *and* *many.M-DAT-PL* *and*
pollákis ḗdē **paraítion**
often *already* *cause.N-NOM-SG*
gégone tês apōleías.
become.PERF-IND-ACT-3-SG *ART.F-GEN-SG* *destruction.F-GEN-SG*
'This **has often been the cause** for many of their demise.' (Plb. 5.75.2)

5.5.2 *Causative COS predicates*

Achievement predicates are characterised by being non-durative, i.e. in being tied to a single (instantaneous) conceptual moment, and telic. Achievement predicates are not homogeneous in that, while they consist of a single conceptual moment, this conceptual moment cannot be subdivided to yield a set of sub-eventualities with the same denotation as the original eventuality.

Since achievement predicates consist of a single conceptual moment, it is possible to find them describing events that initialise and terminate at (the start of) topic time. In the following case, a causative change of state is described, i.e. where the internal argument changes state:

(450) Anníbas...   katesképteto   kaì
      Hannibal.M-NOM-SG   *spy-out.IMPF-IND-NON-ACT-I-3-SG*   *and*
      prounoeîto   perì   tês
      provide.IMPF-IND-NON-ACT-I-3-SG   *for*   *ART.F-GEN-SG*
      kheimasías...   **mégan**   **phóbon**
      winter.F-GEN-SG...   **great.M-ACC-SG**   **fear.M-ACC-SG**
      kaì   **pollḕn**   **aporían**
      and **much.F-ACC-SG** **difficulty.F-ACC-SG**
      parestakṑs   taîs   pólesi...
      present.PERF-PTPL-ACT-M-NOM-SG *ART.F-DAT-PL* *city.F-DAT-PL*

      'Hannibal... began spy out and prepare for a place to set up camp and making provision for the winter, **putting** the cities... **in a state of terror** and great difficulty.' (Plb. 3.94.7)

Since neither the poststate subeventuality nor the internal argument have durative denotation, both the event and poststate can be cotemporal with topic time.

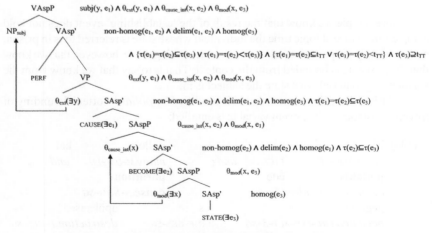

Figure 54: Perfect of a causative COS achievement

The following provides a parallel example with *parékhō*, construed with the equally non-durative abstract noun *khará*, 'joy':

(451) epanekhóroun phugêi **megálēn**
 retreat.IMPF-IND-ACT-3-PL flight.F-DAT-SG **great.F-ACC-SG**
 níkēs... **xaràn** Mithridátēi
 victory.F-GEN-SG **joy.F-ACC-SG** *Mithridates.M-DAT-SG*
 pareskhēkótes
 provide.PERF-PTPL-ACT-M-NOM-PL
 '[Anilaios and those who stood firm around him] **started fleeing** to a wood, thereby **giving great joy** of victory to Mithridates.' (Jos. *AJ* 18.366)

The joy provided to Mithridates is a consequence of Anilaios withdrawing. The temporal structure of this predicate is exactly parallel to that of the perfect in other achievement predicates.

However, while such predicates may not in themselves provide grounds for past reference to be conveyed in the perfect, elements outside of the predicate may play this role. Accordingly, where the grounds for a subsequent action is given, an achievement predicate headed by a perfect naturally yields an anterior reading:

(452) kakôs oûn ho Periklês
 badly PTCL *ART.M-NOM-SG Pericles.M-NOM-SG*
 akoúōn dià tàs
 hear.PRES-PTPL-ACT-M-NOM-SG on-account ART.F-ACC-PL
 déka taútas triéreis,
 tent his.F-ACC-PL trireme.F-ACC-PL
 hōs **mikràn** mèn **boḗtheian** toîs
 as **small.F-ACC-SG** PTCL **help.F-ACC-SG** *ART.M-DAT-PL*
 deētheîsi... **pareskhēkós...**
 need.M-DAT-PL *provide.PERF-PTPL-ACT-M-NOM-SG*
 'So Pericles, receiving criticism on account of the ten triremes, **as having provided meagre support** for those in need...' (Plu. *Per.* 29.3)

(453) allà kaì epì pleîon, háte kaì
 but PTCL *for more since* PTCL
 ekpephobēkótes **autoùs,**
 frighten.PERF-PTPL-ACT-M-NOM-PL **they.M-ACC-PL**
 ethrasúnonto.
 embolden.IMPF-IND-NON-ACT-I-3-PL
 '... but they were emboldened yet further, since they had now **thoroughly terrified them.**' (Cassius Dio 46.44.3)

In both examples perfect participles are introduced by causal particles, *hōs* and *háte* respectively, asserting, insofar as they assert cause, that the prestate events described by the predicate had occurred prior to topic time.

5.6 *Conclusion*

From the data presented in this chapter we may draw the following conclusions:

1. The perfect may include topic time in a state (i.e. homogeneous atelic) eventuality described by the predicate where the predicate describes such an eventuality, i.e. pure state, and accomplishment predicates.
2. The perfect may properly include topic time in a state where that state is durative, leading to obligatory past reference.
3. Where a non-causative set of eventualities precedes the state eventuality, these are also related to topic time, leading to past reference and anteriority.

In COS predicates, apart from in cases of adverbial modification of the become eventuality, the perfect appears to relate only the poststate variable to topic time. The common denominator in all this appears to be that the perfect includes topic time in a predicate's state eventuality, and all other temporal entailments follow from this. We may, therefore, hazard a preliminary definition of the semantics of the Greek perfect, namely:

The Greek perfect includes topic time in any state eventuality described by a predicate.

This definition productively accounts for the interaction of the perfect with many pure state, continuative state, COS and accomplishment predicates, since these all describe state subeventualities and the perfect may include topic time in these. However, it is clear that such a definition is not entirely sufficient for our needs. In particular, it cannot account for the perfects of telic state predicates, where the state terminates prior to topic time, nor activity predicates, where no state described by the predicate is described by the perfect as holding at topic time.

There is an additional issue to address, namely how one should account for the various interactions of the perfect with COS predicates, whereby not only participants but also cause and become eventualities may be suppressed. Should one regard all implication of such eventualities in the case of COS predicates as simply a matter of pragmatic inference, or is it possible to isolate the conditions under which this takes place?

These issues will be addressed in turn: chapter 6 analyses the behaviour of COS predicates taking into account the existence of extent predicates, i.e. predicates that do not describe eventualities as taking place in time. Chapter 7 then provides a framework for understanding the interaction of the perfect with telic state and activity predicates, whereby the perfect derives a non-durative atelic homogeneous eventuality from the predicate and predicates this of the subject at topic time. We will then be in a position in the conclusion to present a unified semantic for the perfect that takes account of all the data.

VI

6. The interaction of the perfect with COS predicates

6.1 *Introduction*

This chapter aims to address the second of the two problems highlighted in chapter 5, namely how to account for the interaction of the Greek perfect with COS predicates: unlike other accomplishments, very often the cause and/or become subeventualities that precede the poststate are often not in view, and in some cases, can never in fact have taken place in time. One solution proposed in chapter 5 is to suppose that the perfect suppresses these subeventualities where these are left unmodified. The present chapter revises this view, showing that by taking into account the behaviour of extent predicates, where there is no temporal trace, it is unnecessary to posit the suppression of subeventualities in this way.

6.2 *Extent predicates*

6.2.1 *COS and extent predicates*

Unlike either pure states or continued states, COS predicates are complex events consisting of a become subevent and a poststate. We observed in the previous chapter that in these predicates the perfect appears to delete the become variable where this is not overtly modified by an internal argument or adverb, leaving only the homogeneous non-durative variable. We illustrated this using the following example:

(454) = (147), (323), (423)

en dè   Delphoîs   Palládion
in PTCL *Delphi.M-DAT-PL* *Palladium.N-NOM-SG*
héstēke   khrusoûn   epì
set-up.PERF-IND-ACT-3-SG *golden.N-NOM-SG* *on*
phoínikos   khalkoû
date-palm.M-GEN-SG   *bronze.M-GEN-SG*
bebēkós...
go.PERF-PTPL-ACT-N-NOM-SG
'And in Delphi there **stands** a statue of Pallas, **mounted** on a bronze date palm.' (Plu. *Nic.* 13.3)

The perfect appears to perform two operations on the predicate: it suppresses the become subeventuality, after which, as with other state predicates, topic time is included in the temporal trace of the (now sole) eventuality variable. Compared with pure state predicates, then, the perfect is performing an additional operation, that of suppressing the become subeventuality.

This problem is not restricted to the Greek perfect. It is also a feature of derived stative predicates in English, as opposed to resultative predicates. First consider the following resultative examples:[317]

(455) The broken vase.
(456) The darkened photo.
(457) The cracked pavement.

All three of these resultative predicates presuppose complex COS events, whereby a prior subevent brings about the resultant state. Now compare these examples with the following derived stative examples:[318]

(458) He has no scars but there is a slightly darkened portion of skin on his right leg...
(459) Lower Knoll, is a sunken area of land that is located on the eastern side of the Avenues...
(460) Elementary school writing paper is manufactured with broken lines on it.

Each of these examples differ from the first set, in that there is no assertion of any event taking place prior to topic time. Thus no event of darkening took place on the skin in (458). In (459) there is no need for the piece of land 'Lower Knoll' to have ever undergone an event of sinking (although it may have done). Finally, in (460) the lines never undergo an event of breaking: they are simply formed that way.

In the literature two approaches have been taken to accounting for derived statives. One, taken by Dubinsky & Simango (1996) in their analysis of passive and stative in Chichewa, has been to posit deletion of the prior subeventuality leading to the derived state. As Koontz-Garboden (2011: 311) observes, a major difficulty with this kind of analysis is that the same morphological material is present in both the resultative and derived stative instances: there is nothing *a priori* to suggest that the prior sub-eventuality is supposed to be deleted in one verb and not another. One should also predict that morphologically simple adjectives and derived statives should yield the same semantics, yet this appears not to be the case (see Koontz-Garboden 2011: 311).

There is also a structural argument against deletion. Taking the case of example (454) above, the verb from which the perfect *héstēka* is derived, namely *hístēmi*, means 'cause/become to be up'. To the extent that the morphological material of the form does not change, the perfect still presupposes an event structure involving a path to a position 'up'. It is clearly more economical and desirable, therefore, to keep the prior subeventuality variable in both cases, and account for the lack of the entailment of a prior subevent in the derived stative cases by other means.[319]

---

[317] Examples from Koontz-Garboden (2011: 286).

[318] Examples from Koontz-Garboden (2011: 287).

[319] A related difficulty is that positing such an operation breaks the so-called Monotonicity Hypothesis (see Koontz-Garboden 2011: 286). For a detailed investigation of the Monotonicity Hypothesis, see Koontz-Garboden (2007).

Another approach, put forward by Koontz-Garboden (2011) building on the work of Gawron (2009), separates time from events, so that events may exist either temporally or spatially. He considers the following examples:[320]

(461) His skin darkens on his right leg near the femoral artery.
(462) The valley sinks even further five miles ahead.
(463) The line breaks right at the point where you're supposed to begin the sentence.

Koontz-Garboden appeals to Kennedy and Levin's notion (see Kennedy & Levin 2008) of a derived measure function, or difference function, defined as '… the difference between an object's projection on the scale and an arbitrary degree d (the comparative standard)' (see Kennedy & Levin 2008: 172). It is possible to see COS predicates as difference functions that project a scale of some quality measuring it in respect to a 'standard', the endpoint of the COS event, against which positions on the scale are measured. In the case of the verb 'darken', then, the COS predicate projects a scale measured with respect to the end of the scale 'being dark'. The key point is that progression along this scale need not be, and in the examples given above, is not, a function of time. Rather, in these cases change is a function of position in space.

For our purposes we can now reanalyse a predicate such as <x darken>, by generalising sets of times to sets of points either in time or space. Therefore, instead of the verb projecting a temporal trace $\tau(e_1)$, we can say that it projects a 'position trace', i.e. $\pi(e)$. $\pi(e)$ then maps the eventualities to locations in time or space. A precedence relation is asserted to hold between the two sets of positions so that the location of e_2 provides the comparative standard of darkness by which the darkness of e_1 is measured. The tenseless form of the sentence 'The photo darkens gradually' can therefore be represented as follows:

(464) $\exists e_1 \exists e_2 \exists x [\text{photo}(x) \wedge \text{BECOME}(e_1) \wedge \theta_{\text{cause}}(x, e_1) \wedge \text{gradually}(e_1) \wedge \text{plural}(e_1) \wedge$
       $\text{STATE}(e_2) \wedge \text{dark}(e_2, x) \wedge \text{homog}(e_2) \wedge \theta_{\text{mod}}(x, e_2) \wedge \pi(e_1) < \pi(e_2)]$

Notice that the feature durativity, i.e. $\text{dur}(e_1)$, is replaced in this representation by Ramchand's (1997: 127) feature plurality, i.e. $\text{plural}(e_1)$. The feature plurality is simply the more general concept to which durativity belongs, denoting that more than two conceptual points exist on the scale, whether temporal or spatial, over which the event is projected to occur. Importantly, the semantics of the verb 'darken' do not predetermine the kinds of positions, whether spatial or temporal, that are to be described by the predicate. This can only be established at the level of the predicate. Thus the addition of the adverbial expression 'with time' would make clear that the predicate is to be interpreted temporally and not spatially:

(465) The photo darkens gradually with time.
(466) $\exists e_1 \exists e_2 \exists x [\text{Photo}(x) \wedge \text{BECOME}(e_1) \wedge \theta_{\text{cause}}(x, e_1) \wedge \text{plural}(e_1) \wedge \text{non-homog}(e_1)$
       $\wedge \text{Gradually}(e_1) \wedge \text{With\_time}(e_1) \wedge \text{STATE}(e_2) \wedge \text{dark}(e_2, x) \wedge \text{homog}(e_2) \wedge$
       $\theta_{\text{mod}}(x, e_2) \wedge \tau(e_1) < \tau(e_2)]$

---

[320] Examples taken from Koontz-Garboden (2011: 289).

Conversely, the eventuality variable can be modified with an adverb that makes clear that it the predicate should be evaluated in terms of locations in space, not time:

(467)　The photo darkens towards the edge.

This sentence is identical to (465), except for the adverbial expression 'towards the edge' as opposed to 'with time'. Yet this change makes clear that the predicate is a function of locations rather than times. Example (467) can therefore be analysed as follows, with a spatial position trace function modifying the eventuality variable, i.e. σ(e):

(468)　$\exists e_1 \exists e_2 \exists x [Photo(x) \wedge \text{BECOME}(e_1) \wedge \theta_{cause}(x, e_1) \wedge plural(e_1) \wedge \text{non-homog}(e_1) \wedge$
　　　　$Gradually(e_1) \wedge Towards\_the\_edge(e_1) \wedge \text{STATE}(e_2) \wedge dark(e_2, x) \wedge homog(e_2)$
　　　　$\wedge \theta_{mod}(x, e_2) \wedge \sigma(e_1){<}\sigma(e_2)]$

Another way of putting this is to say that eventualities are in reality simply paths which can be traversed either in time or space. However, not all eventualities are free to be traversed in space only. Koontz-Garboden (2011: 299), citing Levin (1993: 243–244), observes that extent-only readings do not apply to all verbs. Thus the verb 'to cook' in English does not demonstrate the same behaviour:[321]

(469)　The side of beef is cooking between the rib and the joint.
(470)　#The side of beef cooks between the rib and the joint.

Example (469) is fine if understood as describing the spatial location of a cooking process taking place in time. However, it is not possible to use these predicates to describe different degrees of cookedness as a function of location in space. This is demonstrated by the infelicity of (470). In the case of the verb 'to cook', then, the semantics of the verb itself prescribe that the event be mapped to points in time rather than positions in space.

Similarly, passives of non-COS predicates cannot describe variation as a function of spatial location. Consider the following predicate:

(471)　Make a chair.

Like a COS predicate, this describes a path to an endpoint with respect to which the progress of the eventuality can be measured: in this case the chair represents the point with respect to which progress in the event may be measured. Accordingly, as with COS predicates, it is in principle possible to generalise the semantic structure in terms of a scale and a comparative standard by which progress can be measured. However, it is not possible to predicate different levels of completeness of the chair over different locations. Contrast the following:

---

[321] Examples from Koontz-Garboden (2011: 299). The approach developed here on the basis of Koontz-Garboden may appear to have superficial similarities with Campbell's spatial view of tense and aspect (Campbell 2007). However, there the point is that tense and viewpoint aspect are essentially spatial rather than temporal, whereas I argue that predicates (not tense and aspect) are paths in space-time.

(472) The chair is being made between the bed and the door.
(473) #The chair is made between the seat and the seat back, but not below the seat.

The first example is perfectly acceptable as a sentence describing where a chair is constructed over time. However, the second sentence is not felicitous if taken to assert that a chair is not constructed at a certain point in space. As with the verb 'to cook', then, the verb 'to make' prescribes that the event be mapped to times and not locations.

It is worth considering why predicates headed by these verbs should behave differently from those described at (461)-(463) above, and why their semantic compositions should prescribe a temporal trace rather than a spatial trace. Let us consider again the following examples:

(474) The photo darkens at the edge.
(475) #The side of beef cooks between the rib and the joint.

The key difference between these examples is that in the first case there is a path to increasing darkness which is not dependent on passing through the dimension of time: getting darker can be a function of location as much as it can be a function of time, since different locations can have different degress of darkness. By contrast, in the second case, although the beef is related spatially to the rib and the joint, it is not possible to pass to an area of a greater degree of cookedness, by means of cooking, by moving in space: cooking is fundamentally a result of the application of heat over time. Similarly, in the case of making a chair, there is no path to a complete chair without passing through time, since making fundamentally involves someone acting in time to produce a result.

Ultimately whether or not a predicate is to be assessed as an extent predicate or temporal predicate is a result of the predicate's interaction with its immediate context. Nevertheless, some verbs, such as 'cook' appear never to be able to head extent predicates. The property of being able to describe flexibility of avoiding the time dimension is a property of so-called extent verbs, like 'to darken' and is limited to them. Those verbs that do not share this property may be termed NON-EXTENT VERBS.[322]

This framework allows us to explain why the resultative of some COS predicates always implies a prior event, while others do not. Consider the following examples:

(476) The island is withdrawn from the sea.
(477) The offer was made but is now withdrawn.
(478) The beef is now cooked.

While the verb 'to withdraw' when used in the resultative may or may not carry the implication of a prior event, 'to cook' must carry the implication of a prior event.

---

[322] It should be said, however, that not all verbs that describe changes in position in space behave as an extent verb. Thus the verb 'open' cannot now be used as a function of locations. A Google search of the sentence 'The valley opens into a plain' returned approximately two independent sources, and involving only documents written in the nineteenth century, such as the following: "Some miles further on the valley opens into a plain of some extent..." (see Oreti April 21, 1892). By contrast, a search for 'The valley opens out into a plain' returned 65,300 results including many contemporary ones.

This is to say that there is no resultative predicate of 'to cook' that can be used without the implication of a prior event of cooking.

6.2.2 Achievements in a difference scale framework

In the previous section we have shown how the semantic description of COS predicates can be generalised so as to describe a scale in any dimension defined in terms of a comparative standard with respect to which the condition of the subject is measured. So far, however, we have only considered accomplishment COS predicates, where we generalised durativity to the feature of plurality. What may be said to be the difference between accomplishments and achievements in these terms?

Parallel to the situation in the time dimension, where the difference between accomplishments and achievements is the presence or absence, respectively, of the semantic feature of durativity, so in predicates of the more general positions, the difference between accomplishments and achievements is the presence or absence of plurality. Consider the following example:[323]

(479) The water from Barrancs and Escaleta ravines disappears into the ground at Forau de Aigualluts.

Here the achievement verb 'disappear' is used in an entirely spatial sense. The sentence can be analysed as follows:

(480) $\exists e_1 \exists e_2 \exists x [\text{The\_water}(x) \wedge \text{BECOME}(e_1) \wedge \text{non-homog}(e_1) \wedge \theta_{cause}(x, e_1) \wedge \text{plural}(e_1) \wedge \text{into\_the\_ground}(e_1) \wedge \text{at\_Forau\_de\_Aigualluts}(e_1) \wedge \text{STATE}(e_2) \wedge \text{invisible}(e_2) \wedge \text{homog}(e_2) \wedge \theta_{mod}(x, e_2) \wedge \sigma(e_1) < \sigma(e_2)]$

The difference between the analysis at (480) and that at (464) is the absence of the semantic feature of plurality. An accomplishment, such as 'to darken', has a scale including many points before reaching the goal of 'darkness'. By contrast, in an achievement, such as 'disappear', there are only two conceptual locations: 'not invisible' and 'invisible'.

6.2.3 Non-COS extent predicates

We have shown that some verbs lack the possibility of heading extent predicates. Indeed, from the foregoing discussion, one might suppose that extent predicates are restricted to change of state predicates. However, the set of verbs which are in themselves ambiguous as to whether they head temporal or spatial predicates is perhaps bigger than one might first think, since it appears that atelic verbs such as 'roll' may also head extent predicates.

Prototypically, the verb 'roll' subcategorises for a mobile underlying cause, as in the following example:

---

[323] 'Garonne', 2015. *Wikipedia*. Retrieved May 9, 2015, from http://en.wikipedia.org/wiki/Garonne

(481) The ball rolls.

(482) $\exists e_1 \exists e_2 \exists x [roll(e_1) \wedge dur(e_1) \wedge the\_ball(x) \wedge \theta_{cause}(x, e_1) \wedge \tau(e_1)]$

However, consider the following:

(483) ... they can see the mountains roll for miles and miles.[324]

It seems, then, that atelic non-COS verbs *per se* do not require an event to take place in the time dimension. This may at first seem surprising, since neither the verb nor the predicate as a whole project a 'difference scale' as we saw in the case of change of state predicates. However, in principle a scale need not describe a difference or change. Rather, it may simply denote a scale over which nothing changes, or over which a particular set of differences take place repeatedly, as in the case of 'rolling'. Again the crucial factor is whether the predicate describes a path for the traverser which does not pass through the time dimension.

6.2.4 *Disambiguation of extent and temporal readings*

We have seen that extent readings, if they are not already determined by the verb, must be determined on the basis of the predicate. However, it is important establish the basis on which the disambiguation take place. The criterial factor appears to be whether or not *all* the participants involved may be understood as fixed locations in space, loc(x). If so, then the predicate is to be read as an extent predicate. However, if one of the participants is not a fixed location, the predicate must be taken to be a predicate of times. Consider the following examples:

(484) a. Mount Everest rises to nearly nine thousand metres.
     b. The Sun rises in the East every morning.

(485) a. The mountains roll for miles and miles.
     b. The ball rolls.

In the first of the examples in (484), there are two participants, 'Everest', which is taken to be a fixed location, and 'nine thousand metres', which, by virtue of it being an absolute standard, may also be taken to be a fixed location. By contrast, the second example includes three participants: 'the Sun', 'the East' and 'every morning'. Only one of these, namely 'the East', may be said to be a fixed location, while 'the Sun' is (from the perspective of the Earth at least) mobile, and 'every morning' is a time. Similarly, in the second pair of examples the difference between the first (extent) and second (temporal) readings is that in the first neither entity is mobile or a time, while in the second 'the ball' is mobile.

Since whether a sentence is to be read as an extent or a temporal predicate is a function of the semantic characteristics of its participants, I propose that the temporality of a VP is established at the highest node within the VP. The difference between (485a)

---

[324] http://www.alpinemountainchalets.com/blog/4-reasons-to-plan-a-smoky-mountain-vacation-in-january/, accessed 16/05/2015.

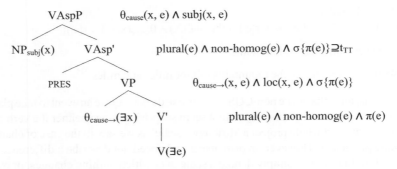

Figure 55: 'The mountains roll for miles and miles.'

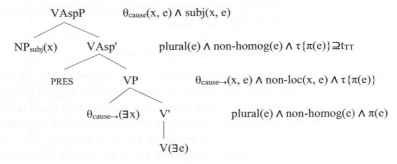

Figure 56: 'The ball rolls.'

and (485b) in these terms is represented in Figure 55 and Figure 56 respectively.[325] Of course, where the verbal head itself prevents an extent reading, as with the verb 'cook', temporality is specified at a lower level, for which see Figure 57. In this figure $\tau(e)\cdot\supset t_{TT}$ reads 't_{TT} is a non-final subset of $\tau(e)$' (see Bary 2009: 78). This differs from $\tau(e)\supseteq t_{TT}$ i.e. '$\tau(e)$ includes t_{TT}' in so far as the former specifies that the final point of $\tau(e)$ is not included in t_{TT}, and is therefore appropriate for explicitly imperfective statements.

6.2.5 *Viewpoint aspect and difference scales*

The analysis presented so far has not taken account of viewpoint aspect marking. What may be said to be the significance of aspect marking in a predicate over locations rather than times? Let us consider again the following example:

(486) The photo darkens towards the edge.

The sentence is in the present tense. Yet the role of the tense marker is not to relate the predicate to a set of times, but to a set of locations.

At 2.1.5 above we introduced the concepts of topic time and utterance time. The former we defined, following Klein (1992: 535), as 'the span of time to which the

---

[325] These sentences are of course potentially causative. However, for the sake of simplicity of representation of the issue of temporality I have represented them as non-causative.

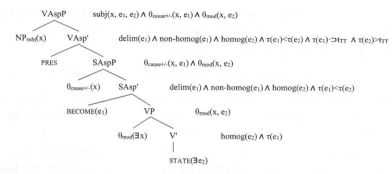

Figure 57: 'The beef is cooking.'

claim made on a given occasion is constrained'. Different aspects then mark various relationships that can exist between an eventuality's temporal trace and topic time. However, at (486) it is not a span of time about which a claim is being made, but rather a set of locations. In order to account for examples like (486), therefore, we need to have access to a more general concept that does not specify whether it is times or locations about which a claim is being made. Accordingly, I introduce the concept of a TOPIC POSITION (TP), which in this case is a TOPIC LOCATION (TL) rather than a topic time.

We may now provide the following analysis for (486) as follows, with the imperfective including the set of positions comprising topic position p_{TP}, in the set of spatial locations denoted by $\sigma(e_1)$:

(487) $\exists e_1 \exists e_2 \exists x[Photo(x) \wedge BECOME(e_1) \wedge non\text{-}homog(e_1) \wedge \theta_{cause}(x, e_1) \wedge plural(e_1)$
$\wedge STATE(e_2) \wedge Dark(e_2) \wedge \theta_{mod}(x, e_2) \wedge homog(e_2) \wedge towards\text{-}the\text{-}edge(e_2) \wedge$
$\pi(e_1) < \pi(e_2) \wedge \sigma\{\pi(e_1)\} \cdot \supset p_{TP}]$

6.2.6 Tense and extent predicates

Unlike aspect, which relates $\tau(e)$ to topic time, tense relates topic time to utterance time. Unlike topic time, therefore, utterance time has always to be a time, and can never be a spatial location. Accordingly the sentence 'The photo darkens at the edge' is a statement about a set of locations at utterance time, and can be represented as follows:

(488) $\exists e_1 \exists e_2 \exists x[Photo(x) \wedge become(e_1) \wedge non\text{-}homog(e_1) \wedge \theta_{cause}(x, e_1) \wedge plural(e_1)$
$\wedge state(e_2) \wedge Dark(e_2) \wedge \theta_{mod}(x, e_2) \wedge homog(e_2) \wedge towards\text{-}the\text{-}edge\{e_2\} \wedge$
$\pi(e_1) < \pi(e_2) \wedge \sigma\{\pi(e_1)\} \cdot \supset p_{TP} \wedge t_{TP} \supseteq t_{TU}\}]$

6.2.7 The resultative construction

It is now possible to revise our semantic description of the aspectual content of the resultative construction in such a way as to account for its non-temporal uses. The resultative construction, when presented with a COS predicate, may be said to return the comparative standard as a homogeneous atelic eventuality which includes the set of positions making up topic position in either time or space, p_{TP}. Let us consider the resultative of the sentence, 'The photo darkens towards the edge', namely:

(489) The photo is darkened towards the edge.

This can then be analysed as follows, where R denotes the resultative:

(490) $\exists e_1 \exists e_2 \exists x[\text{Photo}(x) \wedge \text{BECOME}(e_1) \wedge \text{non-homog}(e_1) \wedge \text{plural}(e_1) \wedge \theta_{cause}(x, e_1) \wedge \text{state}(e_2) \wedge \text{Dark}(e_2) \wedge \theta_{mod}(x, e_2) \wedge \text{homog}(e_2) \wedge \text{towards-the-edge}\{e_1\} \wedge \pi(e_1) < \pi(e_2) \wedge R\{\sigma\{(e_2)\} \supseteq p_{TP}\} \wedge t_{TP} \supseteq t_{TU}]$

Contrast this with a non-extent predicate, which, in the resultative must imply that the subject, at some point, has traversed the path described by the predicate in time.

(491) The beef is cooked now.

Since non-extent verbs prescribe a specifically temporal trace, there is no path to the result state that does not pass through time. Accordingly, the result state must entail that an event has occurred at some point in time prior to topic time:

(492) $\exists e_1 \exists e_2 \exists x[\text{Beef}(x) \wedge \text{cook}(e_1) \wedge \text{BECOME}(e_2) \wedge \text{non-homog}(e_2) \wedge \text{plural}(e_2) \wedge \theta_{cause+/-}(x, e_2) \wedge S(e_3) \wedge \theta_{mod}(x, e_3) \wedge \text{STATE}(e_3) \wedge \text{homog}(e_3) \wedge \tau(e_1) = \tau(e_2) < \tau(e_3) \wedge R\{\tau(e_3) \supseteq t_{TT}\} \wedge t_{TP} \supseteq t_{TU}\}]$

6.2.8 Extent predicates in Greek

Extent predicates exist in Greek as well as English. Consider the following example from Strabo, where mountains are said to 'enter', 'leave', 'withdraw', 'come' and 'bend':

(493) taûta   gàr   arxámena
       this.N-NOM-PL   PTCL   begin.AOR-PTPL-NON-ACT-I-NOM-PL
       apò   tês   Ligustikês   eis
       from   ART.F-GEN-SG   Ligurian.F-GEN-SG   to
       tền   Turrēnían
       ART.F-ACC-SG   Tyrrenia.F-ACC-SG
       embállei,   stenền   paralían
       enter.PRES-IND-ACT-3-SG   narrow.F-ACC-SG   shore.F-ACC-SG
       apoleíponta;   eît'
       leave.PRES-PTPL-ACT-N-NOM-PL   then
       anakhōroûnta   eis   tền
       withdraw.PRES-PTPL-ACT-N-NOM-PL   into   ART.F-ACC-SG
       mesógaian   kat'   olígon,   epeidàn
       interior.F-ACC-SG   by   little.N-ACC-SG   when
       génētai   katà   tền
       become.AOR-SUBJ-NON-ACT-I-3-SG   opposite   ART.F-ACC-SG
       Pisâtin,   **epistréphei**
       Pisan-territory.F-ACC-SG   return.PRES-IND-ACT-3-SG

pròs	héō	kaì	pròs
towards	*east.ACC-SG*	*and*	*towards*
tòn	Adrían…		
ART.M-ACC-SG	*Adriatic.M-ACC-SG*		

'… for these mountains, after beginning in Liguria, **enter** Tyrrhenia, **leaving** only a narrow seaboard, and then, **withdrawing** into the interior little by little, when they **come** to be opposite the territory of Pisa, **bend** towards the east and towards the Adriatic…' (Strabo 5.1.3, trans. Jones)

On the basis of the framework outlined in the previous sections, we can analyse the predicate e.g. *tà órē anakhōroûnta eis tền mesógaian kat' olígon* 'the mountains withdrawing into the interior little by little' as follows:

(494) $\exists e_1 \exists e_2 \exists x \exists z [\text{BECOME}(e_1, x) \wedge \text{non-homog}(e_1) \wedge \theta_{\text{cause}\rightarrow}(x, e_1) \wedge \text{state}(e_2) \wedge \text{withdrawn}(e_2, x) \wedge \text{homog}(e_2) \wedge \pi(e_1) < \pi(e_2) \wedge \text{mountains}(x) \wedge \text{loc}(x) \wedge \text{into}\{\text{goal}(z, e_1, e_2)\} \wedge \text{interior}(z) \wedge \text{loc}(z) \wedge \text{gradually}(e_1) \wedge \sigma\{\pi(e_1)\} \cdot \supset p_{TP} \wedge t_{TP} \supseteq t_{TU}]$

The verb *anakhōréō*, as an extent verb, projects a general 'position trace' for the two eventuality variables, i.e. $\pi(e_1)$ and $\pi(e_2)$. Since all the particpiants of the predicate may be regarded as fixed locations, this can read at the level of the predicate as a predicate of locations in space.

Some verbs are not found in extent uses, however. Thus *hístēmi, pḗgnumi* and *baínō* are, at least in Strabo, only found heading non-extent predicates. This is significant, since Strabo, including as he does so much geographical description, is a great source of extent predicates.[326]

6.2.9 Implications for the semantics of the perfect

Rather than positing that the perfect deletes reference to the prestate, as we did in chapter 5, a more economical hypothesis is that the perfect asserts that the subject exists at the end of a path, without implying that that path has been traversed in time. The assertion of whether or not the entity has traversed the path in time is then a function of whether or not the verb or predicate itself ascribes a specifically temporal trace to the events it describes.

Under this view, the Greek perfect is a kind of difference function, locating the subject at the end of a scale of difference derived from the semantics of the predicate in

---

[326] It is nevertheless still possible to find verbs which one would not necessarily consider as extent verbs, such as *poiéō* 'make, act', heading extent predicates, as at Strabo 2.4.8: *hḗ ge tôn Iapúgōn ákra… tền Italían dikóruphon poioûsa* (*make.PRES-PTPL-ACT-F-NOM-SG*) 'the promontory of the Iapyges… renders Italy bi-crested'. It is worth considering why the verb *poiéō* should be permitted to head an extent predicate when *hístēmi*, apparently, is not. The answer, I suggest, lies in the fact that *poiéō*, in contrast to *hístēmi*, readily construes with two nominals to generate a secondary resultative construction, as in this case. Where this resultative construction predicates a spatial location of an entity, the predicate is understood as one of extent and not of time.

question. The comparative standard of the scale is, in aspectual terms, homogeneous and atelic. The perfect *per se* only ascribes a temporal trace to this derived standard, and includes topic time in this, i.e. asserting that this derived standard holds at topic time. A perfect predicate which carries anterior denotation is then viewed as a special kind of difference function, where the scale of difference is a function of time. This is to say that these are predicates with a temporal trace, rather than the more general position trace. The temporality of the trace is established via an evaluation of the semantic components of the non-external elements of the predicate. In the present chapter, I will show how this approach accounts for the various interpretations available for the perfect of COS predicates.

6.3 *Temporal versus extent readings of perfect predicates*

6.3.1 *Introduction*

We can distinguish three kinds of perfect COS predicates:

1. Predicates that do not entail that any cause event takes place prior to topic time. This type is restricted to extent predicates.
2. Predicates entailing that a cause event takes place prior to topic time, but do not accord any duration to the event. These may be either extent or non-extent predicates.
3. Predicates entailing both that a cause event takes place prior to topic time, and that this event has duration. These may be either extent or non-extent predicates. However, they only occur where the prestate subevent is directly modified either by an argument or an adverbial expression.

6.3.2 *Prestate not logically present in time*

This type is restricted to extent COS predicates, i.e. predicates which do not ascribe a specifically temporal trace to their events, as in the following example:

(495) = (6), (145), (430)

hē	dè	Teúta…	polismátion…
ART.F-NOM-SG	*PTCL*	*Teuta.F-NOM-SG*	*small-town.N-NOM-SG*
anakekhōrēkòs		mèn	apò	tês
withdraw.PERF-PTPL-ACT-N-NOM-SG	*PTCL*	*from*	*ART.F-GEN-SG*
thaláttēs…			
sea.F-GEN-SG			

'Teuta… a small town… **withdrawn** from the sea…' (Plb. 2.11.16)

Here the perfect clearly describes the existence of the subject at the end of a path of 'withdrawing'. The extent reading is licenced on the basis of the semantics of the direct arguments. Specifically, where the direct arguments are fixed locations, a location reading is triggered. Example (495) is represented in Figure 58 accordingly.

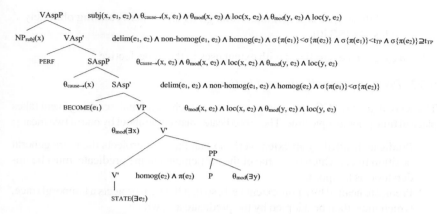

Figure 58: *polismátion (x) anakekhōrēkòs apò tês thaláttēs (y)*

The following parallel cases can all be analysed in the same way:

(496) = (150)

tò   dè   prò   autôn
ART.N-NOM-SG   *PTCL* *in-front* *they.GEN-PL*
apóbasis...   kúklōi
landing.F-NOM-SG   circle.M-DAT-SG
periestaphánōken   tòn   pánta
surround.PERF-IND-ACT-3-SG *ART.M-ACC-SG* *all.M-ACC-SG*
liména...
harbour.M-ACC-SG

'In front of them a... landing area **surrounds** the entire harbour round in a circle...' (Jos. *AJ* 15.337)

(497) = (337)

pétran   ouk   olígēn   têi
rock.F-ACC-SG   *NEG*   *small.F-ACC-SG*   *ART.F-DAT-SG*
periódōi...   pantakhóthen
circle.F-DAT-SG   from-all-sides
perierrṓgasi   batheîai
break-around.PERF-IND-ACT-3-PL   *deep.F-NOM-PL*
pháragges...
ravine.F-NOM-PL

'Deep ravines **break** (lit. are broken) **around** a not insignificant high rock from all sides in a circle...' (Jos. *BJ* 7.280)

(498) = (151)

toútōn...   mía   d'   egkarsía
this.F-GEN-PL   *one.F-NOM-SG*   *PTCL* *oblique.F-NOM-SG*
pásas   **hupézōken**
all.F-ACC-PL   **undergird.PERF-IND-ACT-3-SG**

'Of these [passages]... one **undergirds** all of them running obliquely...'
(Jos. *AJ* 15.340)

Each case can be paralleled with extent uses in the imperfective.[327]

6.3.3 *Prestate logically present in time*

The second group of COS predicates are those which entail that a causing event takes place in time prior to topic time. These predicates may come about by one of two means:

1. Predicate headed by an extent verb, so that the verb projects the more general position trace, which by virtue of the participants in the predicate, must be understood as temporal.
2. Predicate headed by a non-extent verb, so that the verb projects a temporal trace, which must then be adopted by the predicate as a whole.

I will address each of these cases in turn.

6.3.3.1 *Extent verbs*

In predicates headed by extent verbs, which do not project their own temporal trace, whether or not the predicate is accorded a temporal trace appears to be correlated with the possibility of movement or change on the part of the direct arguments. Where the direct arguments are not fixed locations but mobile entities, they are assessed to traverse the path in time on account of the mobile nature of their arguments:

(499) = (141)

ou	tharrḗsas		dè	toûto
NEG	*have-courage.AOR-PTPL-ACT-M-NOM-SG*		*PTCL*	*this.N-ACC-SG*
poieîn	**anakekhōrēkṑs**			
do.PRES-INF-ACT	**withdraw.PERF-PTPL-ACT-M-NOM-SG**			
estratopédeue		tês	Zakánthēs	en
encamp.IMPF-IND-ACT-3-SG	*ART.F-GEN-SG*		*Zakanthe.F-GEN-SG*	*in*
toîs	pròs	thálattan	méresin.	
ART.N-DAT-PL	*towards*	*sea.F-ACC-SG*	*part.N-DAT-PL*	

'Not having the courage to do this, **having withdrawn** [Bostar] encamped in the parts of Zakanthe that are near the sea.' (Plb. 3.98.5)

Bostar is human and therefore mobile, the path is naturally navigated in time rather than purely in space, per the analysis at Figure 59.

The following examples involving the same verbs as (496) and (497) may be considered parallel:

---

[327] e.g. *peristephanoúsēs* (Jos. *AJ* 6.108), *peristephanoûsa* (Galen *De usu partium* 3.477); *perirrēgnúmenon* (Plu. *Alexander* 60) and *hupozónnutai* (Athenaeus Mechanicus, *De machinis* [= *On Machines*] 24).

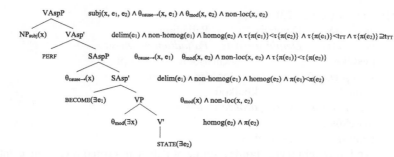

Figure 59: *Bostar (x) anakekhōrēkós*

(500) tinōn   pheúgein   epì
  INDEF-PRON.M-GEN-PL *flee.PRES-INF-ACT*   *to*
  tà   hópla   hōrmēkótōn
  ART.N-ACC-PL   *arms.N-ACC-PL*   *start.PERF-PTPL-ACT-M-GEN-PL*
  hoi   **periestephanōkótes**
  ART.M-NOM-PL   **surround.PERF-PTPL-ACT-M-NOM-PL**
  tòn   ókhlon...   anéskhon
  ART.M-ACC-SG   *crowd.M-ACC-SG*   *hold-up.AOR-IND-ACT-3-PL*
  tà   xíphē
  ART.N-ACC-PL   *sword.N-ACC-PL*

'... when some of them had rushed to arms, those **who had surrounded the multitude...** put up their swords.' (Dion. Hal. *Ant. Rom.* 3.30.2)

Although not from the Koine proper, the following example from Aristotle can be considered parallel:

(501) tà   mèn perì   tòn   thṓraka
  ART.N-ACC-PL   *PTCL* *around* *ART.M-ACC-SG*   *thorax.M-ACC-SG*
  malakà   ékhontes
  soft.N-ACC-PL   *have.PRES-PTPL- ACT-M-NOM-PL*
  dià   tò   **perierrōgénai**
  ON-ACCOUNT-OF   *ART.N-ACC-SG*   **break-around.PERF-INF-INTR-ACT**
  tò   óstrakon
  ART.N-ACC-SG   *shell.N-ACC-SG*

'[Before now crayfish have been caught] having soft parts around the thorax because the shell had (been) **broken around...**' (Aristotle *History of Animals* 601a)

6.3.3.2 Non-extent verbs

Where a predicate is headed by a verb which projects its own temporal trace, such as *histēmi* 'set up', *baínō* 'go' or *pḗgnumi* 'fix', however, the predicate always entails a prior event, even where the participants are fixed locations, as in the following examples:

(502) = (147), (323), (423), (454)

en   dè   Delphoîs   Palládion
in   PTCL   *Delphi.M-DAT-PL*   *Palladium.N-NOM-SG*
héstēke   khrusoûn   epì
set-up.PERF-IND-ACT-3-SG   *golden.N-NOM-SG*   *on*
phoínikos   khalkoû
date-palm.M-GEN-SG   *bronze.M-GEN-SG*
bebēkós...
go.PERF-PTPL-ACT-N-NOM-SG
'And in Delphi there **stands** a statue of Pallas, **mounted** on a bronze date
palm.' (Plu. *Nic.* 13.3)

(503) **pépēge**   d'   ho   ouranòs
fix.PERF-IND-INTR-ACT-3-SG PTCL ART.M-NOM-SG   *heaven.M-NOM-SG*
ék   te   tês   amerístou   phúseōs
from   PTCL   ART.F-GEN-SG   *undivided.F-GEN-SG* *nature.F-GEN-SG*
kaì   tês   meristês
and   ART.F-GEN-SG   *divided.F-GEN-SG*
'Heaven **has been established** both from indivisible and divisible substance.'
(Philo *On The Decalogue* 21.103)

The predicate headed by *hístēmi* in the first example can be analysed as follows:

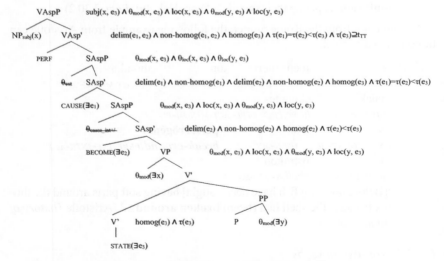

Figure 60: *en dè Delphoîs (y) Palládion (x) héstēke*[328]

---

[328] For the suppression of the internal and external arguments here see below 6.4 and 6.5.

It seems best to treat the following example of *huphístēmi* in the same way:

(504) = (250)

háteros	dè	ho
other.M-NOM-SG	*PTCL*	*ART.M-NOM-SG*

kaloúmenos	Ákra	kaì
call.PRES-PTPL-NON-ACT-I-NOM-SG	*Akra.F-NOM-SG*	*PTCL*

tḕn	**kátō**	**pólin**
ART.F-ACC-SG	*lower*	*city.F-ACC-SG*

huphestṑs	amphíkurtos.
place-under.PERF-PTPL-ACT-M-NOM-SG	*on-each-side.M-NOM-SG*

'The other [hill], called Akra, **supports the lower city** [of Jerusalem] on each side.' (Jos. *BJ* 5.137)

Although at first sight one might be tempted to treat this example as an extent predicate, the following considerations render this interpretation of the facts unlikely:

1. After an extensive search of TLG, no extent uses of *huphístēmi* outside the perfect could be found. The closest parallels all involved the participants being able to move.[329]
2. Example (504) differs from perfects covered in extent uses in the previous section, in that there the participants could not be projected as participating in any event in time by which the result state could be reached. In this example, however, it is possible to project such an event, if we compare it with an example such as the following:

(505) = (251)

thaumásas	d'	ho
wonder.AOR-PTPL-ACT-M-NOM-SG	*PTCL*	*ART.M-NOM-SG*

basileùs	toû	phutoû
king.m-nom-sg	art.gen-sg	*plant.N-GEN-SG*

tò	mégethos…
ART.N-ACC-SG	*size.N-ACC-SG*

kormòn	éreisma	têi	stégēi
trunk.M-ACC-SG	*support.N-ACC-SG*	*ART.F-DAT-SG*	*roof.F-DAT-SG*

hupéstēse.
place-under.AOR-IND-ACT-3-SG

'The king, in wonder at the size of the plant… **placed the trunk under** the roof as a support.' (Plu. *De Iside et Osiride* 357 a 8)

The picture here is not of the king building the roof of his house, and, after the fact, deciding to use the tree to support the roof. Far more likely, the king decided, as he was building his house, to use the tree as a pillar to support the roof. Accordingly, the use of *huphístēmi* in (504) is analogous to that in (505): while it is true that the city is built on top of Akra, rather than Akra being placed under it after the city was built, nevertheless Akra serves as a support for (lit. is established under) the lower city of Jerusalem by virtue of the lower city being built above it.

---

[329] e.g. *húdōr dè hopóson àn êi, aéri huphístatai* (Aristotle *De Caelo* 311a26).

6.3.4 *Metaphorical extension of extent predicates to non-distance scales*

In the case of at least one verb heading extent predicates, *apoleípō*, extent-type readings are applied to non-spatial scales, as in the following example involving population:

(506) epeì   plḗthei   ge   oudemiâs   àn
      since   *population.N-DAT-SG*   *PTCL*   *none.F-GEN-SG*   *PTCL*
      apoleípesthai   dóxeie
      fall-short.*PRES-INF-NON-ACT-I*   *seem.PRES-OPT-ACT-3-SG*
      tôn   exō   Hrṓmēs   póleōn;
      ART.F-GEN-PL   *outside-of*   *Rome.F-GEN-SG*   *city.F-GEN-PL*
      'Since in population at least [Gades] would not **fall short** of any of the cities outside of Rome.' (Strabo 3.15)

This kind of usage can be paralleled in the perfect, as in the following example, which concerns a quality scale:

(507) [hē   phúsis   tês   Khananaíōn
      ART.F-NOM-SG   *nature.F-NOM-SG*   *ART.F-GEN-SG*   *Canaanite.M-GEN-PL*
      gês...]   kállos   ouk
      land.F-GEN-SG   *beauty.N-ACC-SG*   *NEG*
      apoléloipen   hetérāi.
      fall-short.*PERF-IND-ACT-3-SG*   *other.F-DAT-SG*
      '[The nature of the land of Canaan] **is** not **inferior** to any other land in beauty.' (Jos. *AJ* 5.78)

6.4 *Suppression of the internal argument in non-causative COS predicates*

In chapter 5 we observed that where the become eventuality is not explicitly modified, the perfect has the appearance of suppressing that eventuality. This seemed particularly clear in cases like the following:

(508) = (149), (429)
      kaì...   hē   thálassa...   toîs...   hósoi
      and   *ART.F-NOM-SG*   *sea.F-NOM-SG*   *ART.M-DAT-PL*   *as-many-as.M-NOM-PL*
      tôn   neôn   **epebebḗkesan**
      ART.F-GEN-PL   *ship.F-GEN-PL*   **board.*PLPF-IND-ACT-3-PL***
      éti...   ên   aporōtéra
      still   *be.PAST-IND-3-SG*   *impassable.N-NOM-SG*
      'And... the sea... was impassable... for those **who were still on board** the ships...' (App. *BC* 5.10.90)

However, the framework we have introduced in the present chapter offers another way of interpreting this information. Indeed, at 6.3.3.2 we analysed *hístēmi* and *pḗgnumi* as non-extent verbs requiring a temporal reading of their predicate. This was on the basis of the fact that, unlike many other verbs, such as *anakhōréō*, extent predicates headed by these verbs are very difficult to find, suggesting that they may not exist.

If this is correct, it follows that (508) actually asserts that an event prior to topic time took place. Accordingly, to bring this out in English we should translate with resultative in English.

(509) 'And... the sea... was impassiable... for those who were still **embarked on** the ships...'

Under this analysis, the function of the perfect in these predicates would be, as with any other resultative, to suppress the *internal argument*, not the become eventuality that it specifies. As with the resultative in English, the function of the perfect is then to include topic time in the temporal trace of the poststate eventuality described by the predicate. An analysis of (509) is provided in these terms at Figure 61.

Notice that the entailments are identical to that of the English resultative, namely that there was a become event prior to the poststate, but no participants of the predicate are asserted to have traversed the path of this eventuality.

Where the Greek perfect differs from the English resultative, however, is in its capacity, optionally, for the become subeventuality to be modified by adjuncts and adverbial expressions. In these cases, the perfect does relate the become subeventuality to topic time, giving rise to non-resultative interpretation in English. Compare the following examples involving *pégnumi*:

(510) = (431)

tà	d'	epékeina	thînes
ART.N-NOM-PL	*PTCL*	*beyond.N-NOM-PL*	*sand.M-NOM-PL*
ánudroi...		è̄	skuthikòn	krúon
waterless.M-NOM-PL	*or*	*Scythian.N-NOM-SG*	*cold.N-NOM-SG*

è̄ **pélagos**   **pepēgós...**

or *sea.N-NOM-SG*   *freeze.PERF-PTPL-ACT-N-NOM-SG*

'... [the geographers give notes on the edge of their maps explaining that] beyond lie "waterless sands"... or "Scythian cold" or **"frozen sea"**.' (Plu. *Thes.* 1.1)

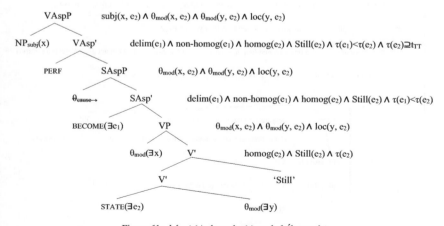

Figure 61: *hósoi (x) tôn neôn (y) epebebḗkesan éti*

(511) = (156), (248), (346), (432)

pepēgósi   mónon   hupò   brakheías
fix.PERF-PTPL-ACT-M-DAT-PL only   *under*   *gentle.F-GEN-SG*
thermótētos   toîs   ap'   autôn
heat.F-GEN-SG   ART.M-DAT-PL   from   they.GEN-PL
ártois   dietréphonto…
bread.M-DAT-PL   nourish.IMPF-IND-NON-ACT-I-3-PL
'… they were nourished with this bread from them, bread which **had been cooked** only under a gentle heat…' (Jos. *AJ* 2.316)

The first example is parallel to those cases of non-extent verbs considered in 6.3.3.2, where a prestate event described by the predicate must have occurred in time, but this event is not explicitly related to topic time, so that it is merely an entailment of the predicate. This contrasts with the second example where the prestate is explicitly related to topic time by virtue of its modification by the phrase *hupò brakheías thermótētos* 'under a gentle heat'. It is this difference that leads the perfect to relate the prestate to topic time explicitly in this example.

Achievement COS predicates behave in exactly the same way as accomplishment COS predicates in this respect. The only difference is that the become subeventuality can appear to be subsumed into topic time. This is because, unlike in the case of accomplishment COS predicates, where the temporal traces of the prestate and the poststate are related by the discrete precedence relation <, so that the temporal traces cannot overlap, in this case they may overlap with the start of the poststate. Thus when the perfect includes topic time in the poststate, the temporal trace of the prestate *can* be included in topic time if topic time and the poststate start simultaneously. As before, however, the prestate is only explicitly related to topic time where it is explicitly modified. Compare the following examples:

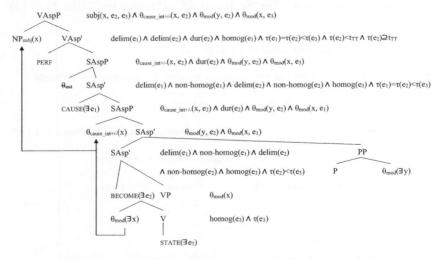

Figure 62: *pepēgósi hupò brakheías thermótētos (y) toîs ap' autôn ártois (x)*

(512) kaì   hólōs   epêrto   têi
and   entirely   lift-up.PLPF-IND-NON-ACT-I-3-SG   ART.F-DAT-SG
gnṓmēi,   kaì   toùs   stratiṓtas
spirit.F-DAT-SG   and   ART.M-ACC-PL   soldier.M-ACC-PL
anatetharrēkótas   hórôn
encourage.PERF-PTPL-ACT-M-ACC-PL   *see.PRES-PTPL-ACT-M-NOM-SG*
pareskeuázeto   diagōnísasthai...
prepare.IMPF-IND-NON-ACT-I-3-SG   fight.AOR-INF-NON-ACT-I
'And he was completely stirred up in his mind, and seeing that his soldiers
were **encouraged**, he prepared to fight...' (Plu. *Demetrius* 48.2)

(513) = (129)
ho   dè   Nikías   **euthùs**   autòs
*ART.M-NOM-SG   PTCL   Nikias.M-NOM-SG   **immediately**   self.M-NOM-SG*
kaì   parà   phúsin   hupò   tês
and   beyond   nature.F-ACC-SG   by   ART.F-GEN-SG
en   tôi   parónti   hrṓmēs   kaì
in   ART.N-DAT-SG   present.N-DAT-SG   strength.F-GEN-SG   and
túkhēs   **anatetharrēkṓs**...
*fortune.F-GEN-SG   **regain-courage.PERF-PTPL-ACT-M-NOM-SG***
'But Nicias himself, immediately and unnaturally **encouraged** by his strength
and good fortune in the present situation...' (Plu. *Nic.* 18.6)

These examples can be analysed as follows:

(514) $\exists e_1 \exists e_2 \exists x [\text{BECOME}(e_1) \land \text{delim}(e_1) \land \text{non-homog}(e_1) \land \theta_{\text{cause\_int+/-}}(e_1, x) \land \text{STATE}(e_2)$
$\land \text{encouraged}(e_2) \land \text{homog}(e_2) \land \theta_{\text{mod}}(e_2, x) \land \text{soldiers}(x) \land \tau(e_1) < \tau(e_2) \land$
$\tau(e_2) \supseteq t_{\text{TT}}]$

(515) $\exists e_1 \exists e_2 \exists x \exists y [\text{BECOME}(e_1) \land \text{delim}(e_1) \land \text{non-homog}(e_1) \land \theta_{\text{cause\_int+/-}}$
$(x, e_1) \land \text{STATE}(e_2) \land \text{encouraged}(e_2) \land \text{homog}(e_2) \land \theta_{\text{mod}}(e_2, x) \land$
$\text{immediately}\{\exists \tau(e_1)_i \in \tau(e_1) \land \exists t_i \in t_{\text{TT}} \land \tau(e_1)_i = t_i\} \land \theta_{\text{mod}}(e_2, x) \land \text{by\_means\_}$
$\text{of\_etc.}(y, e_1)\} \land \text{soldiers}(x) \land \tau(e_1) \subseteq \tau(e_2) \land \tau(e_2) \supseteq t_{\text{TT}}]$

Alternatively, an anterior adverbial may independently relate the prestate to topic
time, as with *pálai* 'long ago' in the next example:

(516) = (131)
hē   dè   boulḕ   **pálai**
*ART.F-NOM-SG   PTCL   Senate.F-NOM-SG   **long-ago***
diegnōkuîa   polemêsai...   hôde
decide.PERF-PTPL-ACT-F-NOM-SG   *go-to-war.AOR-INF-ACT*   thus
apekrínato...
reply.AOR-IND-ACT-3-SG
'... the Senate, **having decided long ago** to go to war... replied thus...'
(App. *Pun.* 11.74)

This can be analysed as follows:

(517) $\exists e_1 \exists e_2 \exists x [\text{BECOME}(e_1) \wedge \text{delim}(e_1) \wedge \text{non-homog}(e_1) \wedge \theta_{cause+/-}(x, e_1) \wedge \text{STATE}(e_2) \wedge$
$\text{decided}(e_2) \wedge \text{homog}(e_2) \wedge \theta_{mod}(x, e_2) \wedge \text{Senate}(x) \wedge \{\tau(e_1) < \tau(e_2) \vee \tau(e_1) \subseteq \tau(e_2)\}$
$\wedge \text{long\_ago}\{\tau(e_1) < t_{TT}\} \wedge \tau(e_2) \supseteq t_{TT}\}]$

In this case, inherent in the meaning of *pálai* 'long ago' is that the event takes place prior to topic time. There is no need for the perfect to relate the prestate's temporal trace to topic time, since the adverbial has already done this.

To sum up, there is no need to posit eventuality suppression on the part of the Greek perfect. Rather, in temporal predicates the perfect has the capacity to suppress the internal argument unless the become eventuality is explicitly modified. The key differences, therefore, between the Greek perfect and the English resultative, are:

a) that the Greek perfect, but not the English resultative, allows modification of the become subeventuality by adverbs or adjuncts;
b) when the become subeventuality is so modified, this blocks the suppression of the arguments of modified eventualities, so that, in terms of aspect, the Greek perfect explicitly relates any modified subeventuality to its participants and to topic time.

Otherwise the perfect behaves as an English resultative, as in the following example, where the perfect of *thnēískō* 'to die' is used in the optative expressing a wish for the future:

(518) = (444)

tethnaíēs,	eîpen,	áner
die.PERF-OPT-ACT-2-SG	*say.AOR-IND-ACT-3-SG*	*man.M-VOC-SG*

'He said, "**I wish you were dead**, man..."' (Jos. *AJ* 2.55)[330]

On the basis of this, therefore, it is possible to posit a principle, that the Greek perfect explicitly relates to topic time only eventualities which are specified by participants.

6.5 *Suppression of the external argument*

We have seen so far that the Greek perfect has the capacity to suppress the internal argument of an unmodified become subeventuality, and that this accounts for the fact that in many instances the Greek perfect, unlike the English perfect but like the English resultative, does not explicitly assert that the subject has traversed the path of the predicate or relate that eventuality. However, in the causative COS cases so far considered, notably in the case of *pépēga*, we have assumed that the perfect also suppresses the external argument. However, it is important to establish to what extent this is true. Certainly one way of explaining the presence of specialised anticausative

---

[330] i.e. $\exists e_1 \exists e_2 \exists x \exists y [\text{BECOME}(e_1) \wedge \text{delim}(e_1) \wedge \text{non-homog}(e_1) \wedge \text{STATE}(e_2) \wedge \text{dead}(e_2) \wedge \text{homog}(e_2) \wedge$
$\theta_{mod}(x, e_2) \wedge \{\tau(e_1) < \tau(e_2) \vee \tau(e_1) \subseteq \tau(e_2)\} \wedge \text{PERF}\{\text{subj}(x, e_2) \wedge \tau(e_2) \supseteq t_{TT}\}]$

stems would be to posit such a function. Could this also be true for the perfect per se, even in cases of lability, so that the perfect as a category could be regarded much as an English resultative (barring, of course, eventuality modification)?

However, to say this would leave unexplained how the perfect active of labile verbs could be used in an anticausative way, since as we argued previously, the lability of these verbs throughout the verb system, including the perfect, relies on the internal argument being able to be interpreted as both an internal and an external cause. If the perfect suppressed the external argument in such cases, we would have an account of the lability of the perfect stem that differed from the other stems. This, however, from the point of view of economy, seems undesirable.

It is better to preserve the external argument position in labile perfects. The external argument position may then be suppressed only by a specialised anticausative stem. Such a stem must be used where the internal argument cannot be construed as an external cause, i.e. in events, such as cooking or freezing, where the subject cannot spontaneously decide to engage in the action described by the predicate.[331]

If this is true, however, it follows that the anticausative use of labile perfects, unlike non-COS unaccusative and root perfect formations, should be incapable of resultative interpretation, since the presence of the external argument position stops the suppression of the internal argument, as represented in Figure 52 above. Accordingly, these should always be read as true perfects. If this is right, we should change our translation of *hupestalkṓs* in Jos. *AJ* 19.216. So far we have translated this as a present 'taking cover', assuming that it is the result state that is in view. However, if the foregoing argument is sound, we should in fact translate this as a perfect in English:

(519) = (8), (158), (309), (436)

heistḗkei		dè	katá	ti
set-up.PLPF-IND-ACT-3-SG		*PTCL*	*in*	*INDEF-PRON.N-ACC-SG*
prosbatòn		olígais	bathmîsi	khōríon
accessible.N-ACC-SG		*few.F-DAT-PL*	*step.F-DAT-PL*	*space.N-ACC-SG*
hupestalkṑs			tôi	kat'
hide.PERF-PTPL-ACT-N-ACC-SG		*ART.DAT-M-SG*	*in*	
autò	skótōi.			
it.N-SG-ACC	*darkness.M-DAT-SG*			

'[Claudius] had stood in a space, accessible by a few paces, **having taken cover** in the darkness there.' (Jos. *AJ* 19.216)

It also follows that other COS verbs with subjects serving as both underlying and external causes, such as possession COS verbs like *lambánō* 'take' and psych verbs such as *progignṓskō* 'to prejudge', should be analysed as asserting that the become eventuality is traversed and related to topic time, as in the following examples:

---

[331] For the unexpected behaviour of *hístēmi* in this regard see 4.2.5.

(520) = (152)

kálliston	ōiéthēsan	tòn
good.*SUPERL-M-ACC-SG*	*think.AOR-IND-ACT-3-PL*	*ART.M-ACC-SG*
kairòn	toû	pròs	ekeínēn
opportunity.M-ACC-SG	*ART.N-GEN-SG*	*towards*	*that.F-ACC-SG*
mísous	**eilēphénai**
hatred.N-GEN-SG	**take.*PERF-INF-ACT***

'[Perceiving that Herod was so disposed towards Mariamne his sister and mother] considered they **had the best opportunity** [to realise] their hatred towards her...' (Jos. *AJ* 15.213)

(521) = (128), (443)

hiketeúō,	páter,	éphē,
beseech.*PRES-IND-ACT-1-SG*	*father.M-VOC-SG*	*say.PAST-IND-ACT-3-SG*
mēdén	mou	**prokategnōkénai...**
in-no-way	*I.GEN-SG*	**prejudge.*PERF-INF-ACT***

'"**I beseech** you, father," he said, "in no way **to prejudge** me..."' (Jos. *BJ* 1.621)

This also offers us another explanation for the apparently obligatory relating of the become subeventuality to topic time in unaccusativised activity predicates discussed above at 5.4.4: such predicates must by virtue of their nature as activity predicates, have an external argument, and this argument cannot therefore be suppressed without removing a key element of the core semantics of the verb. Accordingly, the perfect cannot suppress the external argument, and it makes no sense for there to exist an explicitly detransitivising root formation to suppress the external argument, allowing for resultative interpretation.

Conversely, this framework gives us an explanation for why so often perfects without underlying arguments interpretable as external causes, like *peíthō* and *hístēmi*, often feel so much more stative than the perfects of verbs with cause arguments that can be interpreted as external causes, since the former, in contrast to the latter, need not assert that the internal argument has traversed the path of the predicate. It follows then that the apparently idiosyncratic behaviour of verbs like *peíthō* and *hístēmi* need not be seen as fossilised archaisms, but may rather be seen as a productive part of the verb system.

There is nevertheless an apparent inconsistency in the perfect's behaviour in the following two cases, which provides a potential challenge the foregoing analysis:

(522) = (149), (429), (508)

kaì...	hē	thálassa...	toîs...	hósoi
and	*ART.F-NOM-SG*	*sea.f-nom-sg*	*ART.M-DAT-PL*	*as-many-as.M-NOM-PL*
tôn	neôn	**epebebḗkesan**
ART.F-GEN-PL	*ship.F-GEN-PL*	**board.*PLPF-IND-ACT-3-PL***
éti...	ên	aporōtéra
still	*be.PAST-IND-3-SG*	*impassable.N-NOM-SG*

'And... the sea... was impassiable... for those **who were still on board** the ships...' (App. *BC* 5.10.90)

(523) = (141), (499)

ou	tharrḗsas		dè	toûto
NEG	*have-courage.AOR-PTPL-ACT-M-NOM-SG*		*PTCL*	*this.N-ACC-SG*
poieîn	**anakekhōrēkòs**			
do.PRES-INF-ACT	***withdraw.PERF-PTPL-ACT-M-NOM-SG***			
estratopédeue		tês	Zakánthēs	en
encamp.IMPF-IND-ACT-3-SG	*ART.F-GEN-SG*		*Zakanthe.F-GEN-SG*	*in*
toîs	pròs	thálattan	méresin.	
ART.N-DAT-PL	*towards*	*sea.F-ACC-SG*	*part.N-DAT-PL*	

'Not having the courage to do this, **having withdrawn** [Bostar] encamped in the parts of Zakanthe that are near the sea.' (Plb. 3.98.5)

In (522) the predicate's become eventuality is unmodified and the perfect suppresses it, yielding a resultative reading that is compatible with *éti* 'still', in keeping with what we have seen in other cases. However, in (523), it is hard to avoid the interpretation that Bostar is presented as participating in the become eventuality. That is to say, the predicate asserts that Bostar has moved.

One solution would be to suppose that the perfect operates differently according to the animacy of the internal argument: where the internal argument is capable of entirely spontaneous action, as in the case of a human, for example, then the internal argument is not suppressed, while in cases where the internal argument is inanimate, it is suppressed. However, while it is true that many of the resultative examples so far quoted involve inanimate internal arguments, this cannot account for the discrepancy here, since in both cases the internal argument position is filled by animate participants.

Another approach is to suppose that *epibaínō* projects an internal cause argument, as we have suggested in the case of *hístēmi*, while *anakhōréō* is in fact not an unaccusative, but projects an external argument and a cause argument in internal position, so that the mod argument projected by the poststate is able to move to external position. However, if this were the case, one would expect to find causative examples of *anakhōréō* parallel to *hupostéllō*, and a causative stem in the imperfective and perfect of *epibaínō*.

Instead, therefore, I suggest that the solution lies in the wider context: notice that in (523) the predicate immediately after the perfect predicate presupposes that the subject, Bostar, is in a different location from where he is at the end of the predicate immediately preceding the perfect predicate. This is to say that the surrounding predicates require the subject to be asserted to traverse the path of the perfect predicate. The result is akin to adverbial modification, whereby the change part of the predicate path is directly modified by the predicate, and the become eventuality therefore has to be related both to its participants and to topic time. This in turn suggests that the semantic evaluation of the perfect is not complete at the level of the sentence, but must also take into account of the surrounding predicates. Furthermore, it suggests that one predicate has the capacity to 'run' a participant along the path a preceding predicate in order to correct results. Indeed, the imperfect *estratopeúdeue* is superordinate to the perfect participle, providing the possible syntactic means for this evaluation to take place. In both respects this predicate contrasts with that in (522), where the pluperfect is indicative, and where the point in any case is to assert that there is no movement. I will leave the establishing of how this works in detail to future research.

6.6 A special case

The perfect of *phúō* 'to grow', *péphuka*, is a more complicated case, and as such deserves special treatment. It is associated with at least three different kinds of uses. First, it may describe a result state:

(524) = (144), (434)

nûn	dè...	lampróteron	ekkópsai	kaì
now	*PTCL*	*noble.COMP-N-NOM-SG*	*fell.AOR-INF-ACT*	*and*

aneleîn		sunestôsan		édē
kill.AOR-INF-ACT		*establish.PERF-PTPL-ACT-F-ACC-SG*		already

kaì	**pephukuîan**
and	**grow.PERF-PTPL-ACT-F-ACC-SG**

'[he uttered the saying that]... in the present situation it was... a more noble task to fell and kill [the tyranny] now it was already established and was **full-grown**.' (Plu. *Sol*. 30.5)

Secondly, it may describe a situation of things growing in a particular geographical area:

(525) = (1)

déndra	perì	autôi	**péphuke**
tree.N-NOM-PL	*around*	*it.MN-DAT-SG*	**grow.PERF-IND-ACT-3-SG**

kaì	stêlai	kúklōi	líthou
and	*slab.F-NOM-PL*	*circle.M-DAT-SG*	*stone.M-GEN-SG*

leukoû	pepégasin...
white.M-GEN-SG	*fix.PERF-IND-ACT-3-PL*

'Trees **grow** around [the temple to Artemis], and slabs of white stone are fixed in a circle...' (Plu. *Them*. 8.2)

Thirdly, it may describe a natural attribute or characteristic of something:

(526) = (146)

tôi	gàr	húdati	tền...
ART.N-DAT-SG	*PTCL*	*water.N-DAT-SG*	*ART.F-ACC-SG*

apophráttein	eísodon	hē
prevent.PRES-INF-ACT	*entry.F-ACC-SG*	*ART.F-NOM-SG*

ásphaltos	**péphuken**...
asphalt.F-NOM-SG	**grow.PERF-IND-ACT-3-SG**

'For asphalt **is by nature** able to prevent water entering through the wickerwork...' (Jos. *AJ* 2.221)

The first, resultative, use is easily explained within the framework we are proposing here: the participant, tyranny, is presented as a plant, which by virtue of being able to grow, is mobile. The second usage describes a situation of trees growing over a particular geographical area. As such, the usage approximates to an extent usage. In fact, parallel extent uses of other parts of the verb are also attested:

(527) hḗper   kaì   en   têi   gêi
     REL-PRON.F-NOM-SG *also* *in* *ART.F-DAT-SG* *land.F-DAT-SG*
     phúetai   pollḕ
     grow.PRES-IND-NON-ACT-I-3-SG *much.F-NOM-SG*
     katà   tḕn   Ibērían
     in   *ART.F-ACC-SG* *Iberia.F-ACC-SG*
     '... which [oak] also **grows** a lot on land, in Iberia.' (Strabo 3.2.7)

The third use, whereby *phúō* describes a natural attribute of an object, presents the greatest challenge. At first sight, this usage looks like it describes a pure state without any reference to a prestate of any kind. In other words, it appears to parallel the extent uses we have described. The difficulty here is that it is very difficult to find extent uses outside the perfect, other than that given at (527) and a parallel example at Strabo 15.1.18. The kind of usage we are looking for would presumably parallel the following examples like 'rise':

(528) The mountains rise to a height of several thousand metres.

In other words, one might expect examples of the following kind:

(529) #The mountains grow to a height of several thousand metres.

As shown by the '#' sign, this is infelicitous in English, and is presumably not felicitous in Greek either, given the lack of examples. Nor would it be able, in fact, to account for the behaviour of *péphuka* in (526), since this does not describe the result of any kind of process of 'growing'.

We should rather seek an explanation elsewhere. It should be noted that *phúō* not only means '(cause to) grow', but also 'cause to be', 'generate':

(530) pôs   d'   àn   heûren   ho
     how   *PTCL* *PTCL* *find.AOR-IND-TR-ACT-3-SG* *ART.M-NOM-SG*
     Zeùs   tòn   Hērakléa
     Zeus.M-NOM-SG *ART.M-ACC-SG* *Heracles.M-ACC-SG*
     phûsai...?
     phúō.AOR-INF-ACT
     'How would Zeus have found a way **to create** Heracles...?' (Plu. *De communibus notitiis adversus Stoicos* [= *Against the Stoics on Common Conceptions*] 1065c, trans. after Cherniss)

(531) toû   mèn   oûn   prṓtou
     ART.M-GEN-SG   *PTCL* *PTCL* *first.M-GEN-SG*
     phúntos   anthrṓpou   tò...
     phúō.AOR-PTPL-INTR-ACT-M-GEN-SG *person.M-GEN-SG* *ART.M-NOM-SG*

kállos
beauty.N-NOM-SG
'The beauty of the first-**created** person...' (Philo *De opificio mundi* [= *On the Account of the World's Creation Given by Moses*] 145)

As an extention of this, the intransitive uses of the verb can describe attributes which people naturally have, that is by virtue of their creation:

(532) = (300)

éphu		dè	kaì	tò
phúō.AOR-IND-ACT-3-SG		*PTCL*	*PTCL*	*ART.N-ACC-SG*
sôma	mégas			
body.N-ACC-SG	*tall.M-NOM-SG*			

'His body **was** tall [lit. he was tall as to his body]...' (App. *Pun.* 16.106)

Although I have not been able to find a parallel with an inanimate object as subject of *phúō* in this sense, it seems most reasonable to take the use of *péphuka* in (526) as referring to a created order, a view of the world that Josephus, as a Jew, is likely to have shared, where asphalt has certain properties by virtue of its creation. Analysed in this way, this use of *péphuka* behaves as a non-extent verb by entailing the occurrence of an event in time prior to topic time.

6.7 Conclusion

In this chapter we analysed the behaviour of the perfect of COS predicates. The following types were identified:

1. Predicates where there can be no prestate event prior to topic time;
2. Predicates where a prestate event prior to topic time is entailed by the predicate but not explicitly related to topic time;
3. Predicates where a prestate event prior to topic time is both entailed by the predicate and explicitly related to topic time.

The first type is restricted to extent predicates with exclusively fixed location arguments. The behaviour of these predicates are therefore accounted for by the fact that these predicates do not have a temporal trace.

The second two groups are distinguished by whether or not the become subeventuality described by the predicate is related to topic time or not. We observed a constraint on the function of the perfect, whereby it relates eventualities to topic time in terms of participation. If the become eventuality is unmodified, the perfect suppresses the internal argument position and the mod argument projected by the poststate rises straight to subject position. The become subeventuality is not related to topic time because it is not specified as having a participant. Accordingly in these cases the perfect appears to behave as an English resultative by predicating the poststate of the subject, entailing that this is preceded by a become eventuality, but without explicitly relating this eventuality to topic time. However, if the become eventuality is modified by an adjunct or adverb, this blocks the suppression of the internal argument. Accordingly, the mod argument projected by the poststate is allowed to move to internal position. The become eventuality is therefore specified by a participant, and the perfect relates the eventuality to topic time. The determining factor is whether or not the become eventuality is modified by an adjunct or adverbial.

We argued, however, that, unlike the English resultative, the Greek perfect cannot in itself suppress the external argument. Rather, a specialised anticausative stem must be used to achieve this. Indeed, we proposed that where a predicate projects an external argument, and a cause participant is interpretable as an external cause, such a perfect should always be read as relating all the events and participants of the predicate to topic time, and so resultative interpretation is impossible. By contrast, where the external argument is suppressed by means of a specialised stem, resultative readings are available. This, in turn, we argued, accounts for the intuition that the anticausative perfect stems are somehow more stative than other perfects.

On the basis of the evidence and arguments offered in this chapter, we can modify the definition of the function of the perfect to the following. The Greek perfect:

a) Includes topic time in any state eventuality described by a predicate;

b) Suppresses the internal argument of an unmodified become subeventuality;

c) Relates any remaining subeventuality or subeventualities described by the predicate to topic time via the event structure relations of the predicate.

VII

7 Deriving homogeneous atelic eventualities from states and non-states

7.1 *Introduction*

In chapter 5 we saw that in the case of pure and continued state predicates the perfect straightforwardly includes topic time in the temporal trace of a homogeneous non-durative and atelic eventuality variable already described by the predicate. We also saw that the perfect does this for accomplishment predicates. In chapter 6 we went on to see that it does the same for COS predicates. Accordingly, we provisionally proposed that the aspectual semantic contribution of the perfect is primarily to include topic time in the temporal trace of any state eventuality described by the predicate, with other aspectual phenomena following from interactions with the argument structure of the predicate.

Unfortunately, however, there are a number of cases where such a definition does not account for the semantics of the perfect. This is the case in particular where the perfect heads an activity or telic state predicate, i.e. when heading a predicate that does not itself describe any atelic state eventuality in which to include topic time. Furthermore, as we shall see in 7.7, there are cases where the perfect of COS and pure state predicates does not describe the poststate of the predicate at topic time, but rather a poststate that terminated prior to topic time.

In the present chapter I modify the definition of the semantics of the Greek perfect proposed previously to take account of these data, by proposing that the fundamental function of the perfect is to derive a homogeneous atelic eventuality from the predicate which it heads, and include topic time in this derived eventuality. Where the predicate already describes such an eventuality, i.e. in state predicates, in most cases it is this eventuality in which the perfect includes topic time. However, where the perfect heads a predicate that does not predicate a state of the eventual subject, the perfect derives a homogeneous atelic eventuality from it, and includes topic time in the temporal trace of this derived eventuality. In these cases, I argue that the process by which the perfect derives such an eventuality from the predicate is by negation.

This process is first described in 7.2, before I move on to show how this works out in connection with telic states (7.3), activities (7.4) non-COS accomplishments (7.5) and causative COS predicates (7.6), before going on to address state predicates (7.7). In 7.8 I offer an explanation for the obligatory anteriority of perfect predicates deriving a secondary eventuality. On the basis of the evidence put forward I go on to propse a semantic definition of the perfect in 7.9, before considering the inability of the perfect indicative to collocate with definite time adverbials in 7.10, concluding with a discussion of noise predicates in 7.11.

7.2 Deriving a homogeneous atelic eventuality by negation

The problem of how to interpret the semantics of the perfect heading predicates that do not describe a state for the eventual subject is not a new one. Indeed, this is a problem for the English perfect as much as it is for the Greek perfect. As noted at 1.2, Parsons proposes that after the termination of every event there is state that holds for all time, the resultant state, or R-state, contrasted with the target state, or T-state, the state described in predicates with a preset poststate. Haug (2004: 409–10) adopts this framework, in addition to the notion of EVENT REALISATION (see Bohnemeyer & Swift 2001) and proposes a formulation of the semantics of the Greek perfect in later periods:[332]

> ... the perfect of a predicate P at this point refers to the state resulting from the event denoted by P (in the perfective aspect) being realized. As we shall see, this is a bit vague concerning atelic predicates, since no such state can be clearly defined, but this vagueness was probably exactly what triggered the further semantic evolution.

There are, however, two difficulties with this approach as it stands. The first is terminological: it seems a little forced to refer to Parsons' R-states as states, since this has the effect of nullifying the significance of statehood, if every event eventuates in some kind of state. This is brought out in Haug's exegesis, as he notes the vagueness of the state that is to be associated with atelic eventualities.

The second problem is that under Haug's proposal, state predicates have to be realised in the perfective, and a state derived from them so that *sesígēka* (from *sigáō*, 'be silent') means 'the event of my falling silent was realized in the past and the result still holds'. However, as we have seen in our analysis of state predicates at 5.2 it is not clear that the perfect of state predicates, at least in literary Koine, carry any entailments regarding the prior existence of the state described. In order to resolve these problems, we need a clearer notion of what kind of eventualities could hold after the termination of an event.

In view of these difficulties, I have previously proposed that the perfect derives from a predicate a PARTICIPANT PROPERTY for the subject as a function of the subject existing at or beyond a terminal point of the event described by the predicate.[333] This goes some way to resolving the problems. However, there are still some inadequacies:

a) It is unclear how the notion of 'property' is to be assessed in event structure terms, and if it is to be regarded as an eventuality, what characteristics it is to have.

b) The means of deriving a terminal point from the predicate is not explained.

In what follows, therefore, I set out to define more precisely how the perfect derives this property, and how it might be assessed in terms of event structure.

---

[332] See now Bohnemeyer & Swift (2004).

[333] Crellin (2014: 14), cf. Crellin (2012a: 281). For the participant property notion in the case of the English perfect, see Smith (1997: 107). For application to the Greek perfect in earlier periods see Haug (2004: 396–7).

Up to this point we have argued that states are equivalent to homogeneous atelic eventualities. However, ontological states, such as 'knowing', 'standing', 'being frozen' etc. are not the only eventualities that match this description. Specifically, negative sentences have the aspectual characteristics of states (see de Swart 1996, 1999; see Verkuyl 1993: 163). Evidence for this comes from sentences such as the following (see de Swart 1996: 229):[334]

(533) John didn't know the answer to the problem. *This* lasted until the teacher did the solution on the board.

(534) What happened next was that the consulate didn't give us our visa.

In the first example, the demonstrative 'this' refers anaphorically to the negative of a stative eventuality, namely John not knowing the answer. In the second example it is stated that the negative accomplishment 'the consulate not giving a visa' is something that 'happened'. Since these sentences are true at all points in time at which the sentence holds without change, without any implications for their truth value outside of those parameters, they may be said to be homogeneous, atelic and non-durative.[335] This means that applying the negative operator to a sentence will always result in a homogeneous non-durative atelic eventuality. Accordingly, we could say that the perfect, when heading a predicate that does not describe an atelic state for the eventual subject, derives a homogeneous atelic eventuality from the predicate by negation and predicates this of the subject. Note that I do not say that it derives a state. For the purposes of the present study, the term 'state' is used solely for Parsons' target states. Derived eventualities of the kind described here I refer to by their event-aspectual properties.

However, the proposal that the negative of a predicate always returns a homogeneous atelic predicate may appear to be disproved by examples such as:

(535) I am not rolling this ball slowly.

Modification of 'rolling' by the adverb 'slowly' appears to indicate non-homogeneous interpretation. However, here we need to consider the scope of the negation. In event structure terms there are two readings of the sentence at (535):

(536) $\exists x \exists y \exists e[\theta_{ext}(x, e) \wedge roll(e) \wedge \theta_{cause}(y, e) \wedge \neg Slowly(e)]$

(537) $\exists x \exists y \exists e_1 \exists e_2[\theta_{ext}(x, e_1, e_2) \wedge \neg\{roll(e_1) \wedge \theta_{mod}(y, e_1) \wedge Slowly(e_1)\}(e_2) \wedge homog(e_2)]$

In the first reading, the sentence asserts that the external argument is rolling the ball 'not slowly', but that there is still an event of rolling taking place. The second reading, by contrast, asserts that there is a homogeneous eventuality

---

[334] Kamp & Reyle (1993: 555) argue against this proposal. However, for further arguments in favour see de Swart (1996: 229f.).

[335] See de Swart (1996: 229) who points out that 'negative sentences are true at all instants of the interval for which the sentence hold, which is the defining property of states according to Dowty (1979).'

of 'not rolling the ball slowly'. It is our claim that applying the negative operator to an entire predicate, in the manner of the second, not the first, reading, always returns a homogeneous, non-durative and atelic eventuality.

If the perfect in these cases derives the negative of a predicate, how can it be said to differ in principle from the negative itself? This is to say, why is it that the perfect of a telic or non-homogeneous predicate asserts something about the past, while the simple negative does not? The simple statement 'I am not a praetor' simply asserts that the subject is not a praetor at topic time. There are however, two ways for this to be true: the subject never was a praetor, or the subject was a praetor and has now ceased to be a praetor. Here, with Haug, we adopt Bohnemeyer & Swift's notion of event realisation, so that, unlike the negative operator, the perfect first instantiates the predicate in time, or 'realises' it. This is to say that, in order to derive the state for the subject run the event, to a terminal point, i.e. to a negation point, a point at which it can ascribe a derived homogeneous atelic predicate derived from the original predicate to the subject. We can say, then, that there is a constraint on the perfect which is not present in the case of the negative operator, namely that the predicate as a whole must be able to be said to hold for the subject at some point in time, or simply that the event described by the predicate must be realised.[336] However, it is clear from the behaviour of the perfect with state predicates that the perfect need not realise the event to termination if the predicate already describes a homogeneous atelic eventuality. Accordingly, the perfect only realises the predicate as part of the derivation process. In this way we can account for the perfect's different behaviour with state and non-state predicates.

However, if the perfect can, if necessary, derive a homogeneous atelic eventuality from any predicate, in predicates which describe a state for the eventual subject there must in fact be two interpretations available:

1. The perfect derives the positive version of the state described by the predicate;
2. The perfect derives the negative version of the state described by the predicate, but as a function of the predicate having taken place in time.

Haug (2004: 410) notes this issue, but proposes that the ambiguity is lexically resolved. Thus while *sesígēka* asserts that the state of being silent holds at topic time, in the case of *akḗkoa*, the perfect of *akoúō* 'hear', asserts that the hearing event terminates prior to topic time. However, as we will see at 7.7, at least in literary Koine Greek, the ambiguity appears to be resolved not lexically but by context.[337]

---

[336] Note that this constraint on the perfect is compatible with the interaction of the perfect with extent predicates, as discussed in chapter 6. The requirement is simply that the path described by the predicate exists in time. It is not a requirement that any of the participants of the predicate traverse the path in time.

[337] In any case, it is not necessary to analyse *akoúō* as a state verb. While the subject may not be engaged in any dynamic process, by definition the source of hearing must be engaged in a kind of dynamic process. Accordingly, the event seen as a whole can be construed as dynamic. This is contrasted with the event of 'seeing': one may see a homogeneous situation perfectly well, without any requirement for dynamicity on the part of the source.

7.3 Telic state predicates

We saw at 5.2.2.2 that the perfect of telic state predicates, such as *hupateúō* 'be consul' and *stratēgéō* 'be praetor', always denotes that the state described by the predicate has terminated by topic time, but that the subject participated in the eventuality described by the predicate prior to topic time, as in the following example:

(538) = (124), (413)

Thouránios	dè3	ou			
Thouranius.m-nom-sg	PTCL	NEG			
stratēgôn			mèn	éti,	all'
be-general.pres-ptpl-act-m-nom-sg		PTCL		*still*	*but*

estratēgēkôs...
be-general.PERF-PTPL-ACT-M-NOM-SG

'Thourianios, who was no longer praetor, but **had formerly served as such**...'
(App. *BC* 4.4.18)

Examples like this are problematic for the proposal, made at the end of the last chapter, that the semantic contribution of the perfect is to include topic time in any state described by the predicate. Clearly, the perfect does not respond to telic states in the same way as it does to atelic states. It appears that the state in which the perfect includes topic time must be atelic. The only way to do this in the case of telic states is to derive the negative of the telic state, which must be an atelic state. In example (538), this equates to asserting that Thouranios was a general prior to topic time, but is no longer at topic time. The viewpoint aspect-less predicate may be represented as follows:

(539) $\exists e \exists x [\text{be-praetor}(e, x) \wedge \text{homog}(e) \wedge \text{dur}(e) \wedge \text{delim}(e) \wedge \theta_{ext}(x, e) \wedge \text{Thouranius}(x, e)]$

The perfect predicate, including the derived state, then looks as follows:

(540) $\exists x \exists e_1 \exists e_2 [\text{be-praetor}(e_1, x) \wedge \text{homog}(e_1) \wedge \text{dur}(e_1) \wedge \text{delim}(e_1) \wedge \theta \text{ext}(x, e_1) \wedge$
$\text{PERF}\{\neg e_1(e_2) \wedge \text{homog}(e_2) \wedge \text{subj}(x, e_1, e_2) \wedge \tau(e_1){<}\tau(e_2) \wedge \tau(e_1){<}\text{tTT} \wedge \tau(e_2){\supseteq}t_{TT}\}]$

Notice that this predicate is both non-durative and atelic, unlike its positive counterpart. The meaning is therefore that, 'there is a subject, *x*, who was praetor for a period prior to topic time but is at topic time no longer a praetor.'

7.4 Activity predicates

Activities share with telic state predicates the attribute that they do not describe a final homogeneous atelic eventuality (state) for the subject. Here, however, the problem is not telicity but homogeneity: the perfect, we propose, can only include topic time in a *homogeneous* and atelic eventuality. Accordingly, when heading an activity predicate the perfect has to derive such an eventuality from it. The perfect can do this in exactly the same way as it does for telic states, by instantiating the event in time and deriving the negative inverse of the eventuality described by it. This is because, as we argued in 7.2, the negative of any eventuality returns an atelic state.

Let us consider the following example of the perfect of *poieō* in an atelic predicate:

(541) = (136), (415)

ho	d'	ouk	**orthôs**	autòn
ART.M-NOM-SG	*PTCL*	*NEG*	***properly***	*he.ACC-SG*
éphē		**pepoiēkénai**...		
say.PAST-IND-ACT-3-SG		***act.PERF-INF-ACT***		

'But he said that he had not **acted properly**...' (Jos. *AJ* 6.102)

The viewpoint aspect-less predicate may be represented as follows:

(542) $\exists e \exists x[act(e) \wedge \theta_{ext}(x,e) \wedge dur(e) \wedge non\text{-}homog(e) \wedge \neg properly(e)]$

This predicate is made slightly more complicated by the fact that it already contains a negative, namely *ouk orthôs* 'not properly'. However, the negative used in the derivation of the atelic state that it needs has scope over the entire predicate, not simply a part of it. Accordingly the perfect would assert that the subject is not acting improperly at topic time, but that he did prior to topic time:

(543) $\exists e \exists x[act(e_1) \wedge \theta ext(x, e_1) \wedge dur(e) \wedge non\text{-}homog(e) \wedge \neg properly(e_1) \wedge \text{PERF}\{\neg e_1(e_2) \wedge homog(e_2) \wedge subj(x, e_1, e_2) \wedge \tau(e_1) < \tau(e_2) \wedge \tau(e_1) < t_{TT} \wedge \tau(e_2) \supseteq t_{TT}\}]$

7.5 Non-COS accomplishment predicates

At 5.3.3 above we analysed accomplishment predicates as describing a poststate for the internal argument, or direct object, and the perfect of these predicates asserting that this poststate holds at topic time. Unlike for telic state and activity predicate, this is consistent with the perfect including topic time in the poststate described by the predicate, and relating other eventualities to topic time accordingly. However, there are reasons for thinking that even here the perfect primarily derives a state not for the direct object, but for the subject, and only as a corollary of this also derives a state for the object. It has frequently been observed that the force of the perfect of accomplishment predicates is to characterise the subject and not the object.[338] Examples like the following tend to support such a claim:

(544)

gunaîkas	dè	plēsíon	
woman.F-ACC-PL	*PTCL*	*nearby*	
Deinoménēs			Iò
Deinomenes.M-NOM-SG			*Io.F-ACC-SG*
tḕn	Inákhou...	**pepoíēken**	
ART.F-ACC-SG	*Inachus.M-GEN-SG*	***make.PERF-IND-ACT-3-SG***	

'Deinomenes **is/was the maker of** the [statues of] women nearby, Io the daughter of Inachus and Kallisto the daughter of Lycaon.' (Pausanias 1.25.1)

The point here is not so much that there are statues made, but rather that Deineomenes made them. Of course, such assessments are quite subjective. However, there

---

[338] e.g. McKay (1965: 8–9).

are predicates where the internal argument does not enter into a very well defined state, as where the internal argument consists of an anaphoric reference to another eventuality described by a separate clause:

(545) = (23), (135), (418)

hoi	dè	ánthrōpoi	tò	kréas
ART.M-NOM-PL	*PTCL*	*human.M-NOM-PL*	*ART.N-ACC-SG*	*meat.N-ACC-SG*
esthíousin,		tà	d'	ostâ
eat.PRES-IND-ACT-3-SG		*ART.N-ACC-PL*	*PTCL*	*bone.N-ACC-PL*
hríptousin,		hóper		ánthrōpos
throw.PRES-IND-ACT-3-PL		*REL-PRON.N-ACC-AG*		*human.M-NOM-SG*
ȍn		kagȍ		**nûn**
be.PRES-PTPL-M-NOM-SG		*and-I.NOM-SG*		*now*

pepoíēka.

do.PERF-IND-ACT-1-SG

'Men, however, eat the meat, but throw away the bones, which is exactly what I, who am also a man, **have now done**.' (Jos. *AJ* 12.213)

The predicate *hóper nûn pepoíēka* consists of a verb in the perfect, *pepoíēka*, 'I have done', an adverb *nûn* meaning 'now', and a direct object argument *hóper*, which is in fact an event argument relating back to the previous predicates *tò kréas esthíousin, tà d' ostâ hríptousin*. Accordingly, it is just as easy in such cases to say that the perfect derives a state for the external as for the internal argument. One could therefore analyse the perfect of such accomplishments as given in Figure 63.

Importantly, the negative eventuality derived for the subject is the negative of the eventuality in which the eventual subject participant participates, i.e. the cause subeventuality. The analysis asserts that the poststate for the both the subject and object holds at topic time. The simultaneity of the state of the object and the derived state of the subject arises from the fact that the eventualities that give rise to their respective poststates are simultaneous, since in accomplishments the become and cause events take place over the same spans of time.

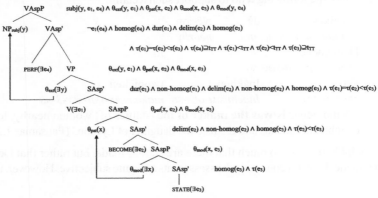

Figure 63 – Perfect of an accomplishment

The state derived for the subject can have no endpoint, since one cannot change the past. However, it is an open question whether the object's poststate must hold at topic time in order for the perfect to be used, or whether in fact the perfect can be used to describe an eventuality where the poststate for the object no longer holds at topic time, something that is certainly possible in English. I leave this for future research to discover.

7.6 Causative COS predicates

The perfect of causative COS predicates can be analysed in a similar way to that of accomplishments. Let us consider again the following example from Polybius involving the pluperfect of *hupostéllō* 'to hide':

(546) = (9), (159), (308), (437)

ho	dè	Phílippos...	hupó
ART.M-NOM-SG	*PTCL*	*Philip.M-NOM-SG*	*under*
tina		lóphon	**hupestálkei**
INDEF-PRON.MF-ACC-SG		*hill.M-ACC-SG*	*hide.PLPF-IND-ACT-3-SG*
toùs		Illurioùs...	
ART.M-ACC-PL		*Illyrians.M-ACC-PL*	

'But Philip... **had sent** the Illyrians behind a hill...'   (Plb. 5.13.5)

Here the viewpoint aspect-less predicate can be analysed as follows:

(547) $\exists x \exists e_1 \exists e_2 \exists e_3[\text{cause}(e_1) \wedge \text{delim}(e_1) \wedge \text{non-homog}(e_1) \wedge \theta\text{ext}(y, e_1) \wedge \text{become}(e_2) \wedge \text{delim}(e_2) \wedge \text{non-homog}(e_2) \wedge \theta_{\text{cause}} \rightarrow (x, e_2) \wedge \text{state}(e_2) \wedge \text{hidden}(e_3) \wedge \text{homog}(e_3) \wedge \theta_{\text{mod}}(x, e_3) \wedge \text{the\_Illyrians}(x) \wedge \text{Philip}(y) \wedge \tau(e_1) \overline{<} \tau(e_2) < \tau(e_3)]$

As in the case of the accomplishment predicates described in the previous section, the perfect derives the negative of the eventuality participated in by the eventual subject, Philip:

(548) $\exists x \exists e_1 \exists e_2 \exists e_3 \exists e_4[\text{CAUSE}(e_1) \wedge \text{delim}(e_1) \wedge \text{non-homog}(e_1) \wedge \theta_{\text{ext}}(y, e_1) \wedge \text{BECOME}(e_2) \wedge \text{delim}(e_2) \wedge \text{non-homog}(e_2) \wedge \theta_{\text{cause}}\rightarrow(x, e_2) \wedge \text{STATE}(e_3) \wedge \text{hidden}(e_3) \wedge \text{homog}(e_3) \wedge \theta_{\text{mod}}(x, e_3) \wedge \text{the\_Illyrians}(x) \wedge \text{Philip}(y) \wedge \tau(e_1) \overline{<} \tau(e_2) < \tau(e_3) \wedge \text{PERF}\{\neg e_1(e_4) \wedge \text{homog}(e_4) \wedge \text{subj}(y, e_1, e_4) \wedge \tau(e_2) < \tau(e_4) \wedge \tau(e_1) < t_{TT} \wedge \tau(e_2) < t_{TT} \wedge \tau(e_3) \supseteq t_{TT} \wedge \tau(e_4) \supseteq t_{TT}\}]$

7.7 Deriving states from states: the perfect of atelic state predicates

7.7.1 Introduction

In the predicates discussed so far, the perfect can be said unambiguously to derive a poststate for the subject from its predicate. Indeed, in the case of activity and telic state predicates, this is the only possible way of deriving a state from the predicate. However, if the perfect can in principle derive a homogeneous atelic eventuality from any predicate, then the perfect of predicates which already describe a state in which the subject participates will be ambiguous, since it may derive either the (post)state described by the predicate itself, or the negative of this state which is will also be atelic and homogeneous. In this section I show how this ambiguity does indeed show itself in the way in which the Greek perfect is used, and how the ambiguity is resolved.

7.7.2 Pure state predicates

In the majority of cases the perfect of pure state predicates describe situations where the temporal trace of the eventuality described by the original predicate includes topic time, as we saw at 5.2.1 above. However, the perfect is also, optionally, able to derive a secondary homogeneous atelic eventuality from such predicates by the mechanism of negation, as we have been seeing in this chapter. Because the perfect must first realise the state eventuality described by the predicate before it derives from it the negative of the state described, the state described by the original predicate is located prior to topic time, giving rise to anterior denotation. Consider the following example:

(549) éti   dè   Phregéllai...   nûn   mèn
      still   *PTCL*   *Phregellai...*   *now*   *PTCL*
      kốmē,   pólis   dé   pote
      village.F-NOM-SG   *city.F-NOM-SG*   *PTCL*   *once*
      gegonuîa   axiólogos   kaì
      become.PERF-PTPL-ACT-F-NOM-SG   *important.F-NOM-SG*   *and*
      tàs   pollàs   tôn   árti
      ART.F-ACC-PL   *many.F-ACC-PL*   *ART.F-GEN-PL*   *recently*
      lekhtheîsōn   perioikídas
      mention.AOR-PTPL-PAS-F-GEN-PL   *dependent-town.F-ACC-PL*
      próteron   **eskhḗkuîa**
      previously   **have.PERF-PTPL-ACT-F-NOM-SG**

'In addition to these Phregellai... which is now a village, but was once an important city and previously **had** many of the places just mentioned as dependent towns.' (Strabo 5.3.10)

The core predicate alone (i.e. without the adverb *próteron* 'previously') could be interpreted as describing a situation at topic time or prior to topic time:

(550) $\exists e \exists x \exists y [\text{Have}\{\text{have}(e) \land \tau(e) \land \text{homog}(e) \land \theta_{ext}(x, e) \land \theta_{mod}(y, e) \land \text{Phregellai}(x) \land \text{Places}(y) \land \text{PERF}\{\tau(e) \supseteq t_{TT} \land \text{subj}(x, e)\}]$

(551) $\exists e \exists x \exists y [\text{Have}\{\text{have}(e_1) \land \tau(e_1) \land \text{homog}(e_1) \land \theta_{ext}(x, e_1) \land \theta_{mod}(y, e_1) \land \text{Phregellai}(x) \land \text{Places}(y) \land \text{PERF}\{\neg e_1(e_2) \land \text{homog}(e_2) \land \tau(e_1) < \tau(e_2) \land \tau(e_2) \supseteq t_{TT} \land \tau(e_1) < t_{TT} \land \text{subj}(x, e_1, e_2)\}]$

However, the presence of the adverb *próteron*, i.e. $\tau(e) < t_{TT}$ makes clear that the state of affairs described by the predicate pertains only prior to topic time, and that only the second analysis can be applied in this case. The following is a parallel example:

(552) toûton dè... exapésteile...
this.M-ACC-SG *PTCL* *send.AOR-IND-ACT-3-SG*
parakalôn... labeîn
urge.PTPL-PRES-ACT-M-NOM-SG *receive.AOR-INF-ACT*
dōreàs pollaplasíous hôn
gift.F-ACC-PL *many.F-ACC-PL* *REL-PRON.F-GEN-PL*
próteron ên **eskhēkṓs.**
previously *be.IMPF-IND-ACT-3-SG* **have.PERF-PTPL-ACT-M-NOM-SG**
'He sent him away... urging him receive many more gifts than that **which he had had previously.**' (Diod. Sic. 18.50.4)

Here the predicate *hôn próteron ên eskhēkṓs* 'which he had had previously' describes a situation holding only for a period of time prior to topic time. At topic time a different situation holds, namely having 'more gifts'.

In these two examples an anterior adverb has made clear which reading should be adopted. However, this is not always the case. In the examples we will discuss in the case of continued state and COS predicates, sometimes broader contextual information has to be taken into account in order to disambiguate the readings.

7.7.3 Continued state predicates

In our previous analysis of continued states at 5.2.2.1, we considered only cases where the state described holds at topic time, such as the following:

(553) = (7), (19), (120)

epì gàr tền proüpárkhousan
on *PTCL* *ART.F-ACC-SG* *exist-before.PRES-PTPL-ACT-F-ACC-SG*
khíona kaì **diamemenēkuîan** **ek**
snow.F-ACC-SG and **remain.PERF-PTPL-ACT-F-ACC-SG** **from**
toû **próteron** **kheimônos** árti
ART.M-GEN-SG **earlier** **winter.M-GEN-SG** *recently*
tês ep' étous peptōkuías...
ART.F-GEN-SG *present-year* *fall.PERF-PTPL-ACT-F-GEN-SG*
'For on top of the snow which **had remained from the previous winter**, that from the present year had just fallen...' (Plb. 3.55.1)

However, as with pure states there are also cases where the perfect describes a continued state that ceases before topic time:

(554) = (123), (414)

heîlon dè kaì tò
take.AOR-IND-ACT-3-PL *PTCL* *PTCL* *ART.N-ACC-SG*
Muttístraton, **polloùs** **khrónous**
Myttistratus.M-ACC-SG **many.M-ACC-PL** **year.M-ACC-PL**

hupomemenēkòs   tḕn   poliorkían...
withstand.PERF-PTPL-ACT-N-ACC-SG   *ART.F-ACC-SG*   *siege.F-ACC-SG*
'And they took Myttistratus, which **had withstood** the siege **for many years**...'
(Plb. 1.24.11)

In (553) the temporal trace of the continued state eventuality includes topic time, while in (554) it precedes it. Accordingly, the perfect per se is felicitous with either reading, and in the first simply includes topic time in the temporal trace of the continued state, while in the second the perfect instantiates the predicate in time, derives the negative corollary of the original predicate and includes topic time in this derived eventuality.

Notice that in these cases it is the surrounding context that enables the reader to disambiguate the readings. Anterior interpretation is obligatory in (554) on account of the previous sentence, which asserts that Myttistratus was taken at topic time. This topic time is inherited by the predicate headed by the perfect. Accordingly, the two sentences taken together do not allow the interpretation that Myttistratus is still standing at topic time. By contrast, the continued state interpretation is obligatory in (553) since the new snow is explicitly asserted to fall on the old snow, which must therefore still be in evidence at topic time.

7.7.4 COS predicates

As we have seen, the majority of COS predicates headed by perfects describe situations that hold at topic time. However, it is possible for the perfect to describe a situation which has terminated prior to this point.

(555) = (448)
          hòs   kaì   desmṓtēi
          REL-PRON.M-NOM-SG   *even*   *prisoner.M-DAT-SG*
          moì   genoménōi
          I.DAT-SG   *become.AOR-PTPL-NON-ACT-I-M-DAT-SG*
          diakoneîsthai   katháper   **en**   **tôi**
          minister.PRES-INF-NON-ACT-I   *just-as*   **in**   *ART.N-DAT-SG*
          próteron   **kathestēkóti**
          previously   *establish.PERF-PTPL-ACT-N-DAT-SG*
          skhḗmati...   ouk   enélipes.
          state.N-DAT-SG   *NEG*   *fail.AOR-IND-ACT-2-SG*
          '... you who did not fail to minister to me when I was a prisoner, just as if
          I was in the state [of dignity] in which **I had formerly been established**...'
          (Jos. *AJ* 18.193)

Taking the predicate in isolation from its context, the state to which Agrippa refers may either hold at topic time or prior to topic time. The perfect of the first reading would therefore tie the poststate to topic time. By contrast, the perfect of the second reading would have to derive a negative of the poststate in order to hold at topic time, since if the poststate held prior to topic time, it would not hold at topic time, according to the following analyses:[339]

(556) $\exists e_1 \exists e_2 \exists e_3 \exists x \exists y[\text{CAUSE}(e_1) \wedge \text{non-homog}(e_1) \wedge \text{delim}(e_1) \wedge \text{BECOME}(e_2) \wedge \text{non-homog}(e_2) \wedge \text{delim}(e_2) \wedge \theta_{\text{cause\_int}+/-}(x, e_2) \wedge \text{STATE}(e_3) \wedge \text{Established}(x, e_3) \wedge \text{homog}(e_3) \wedge \tau(e_1) = \tau(e_2) < \tau(e_3) \wedge \theta_{\text{mod}}(x, e_3) \wedge \text{Agrippa}(x) \wedge \text{loc}(x, y, e_3) \wedge \text{state\_of\_dignity}(y) \wedge \text{Previously}\{\tau(e_2) < t_{TT}\} \wedge \text{PERF}\{\tau(e_3) \supseteq t_{TT} \wedge \tau(e_2) < t_{TT} \wedge \text{subj}(x, e_2, e_3) \wedge \theta_{\text{ext}}\}]$

(557) $\exists e_1 \exists e_2 \exists e_3 \exists e_4 \exists x \exists y[\text{CAUSE}(e_1) \wedge \text{non-homog}(e_1) \wedge \text{delim}(e_1) \wedge \text{BECOME}(e_2) \wedge \text{non-homog}(e_2) \wedge \text{delim}(e_2) \wedge \text{STATE}(e_3) \wedge \text{established}(x, e_3) \wedge \text{homog}(e_3) \wedge \tau(e_1) = \tau(e_2) < \tau(e_3) \wedge \theta_{\text{mod}}(x, e_3) \wedge \text{Agrippa}(x) \wedge \text{loc}(x, y, e_3) \wedge \text{state\_of\_dignity}(y) \wedge \text{Previously}\{\tau(e_3) < t_{TT}\} \wedge \text{PERF}\{\neg e_1(e_4) \wedge \text{homog}(e_4) \wedge \tau(e_3) < t_{TT} \wedge \tau(e_4) \supseteq t_{TT} \wedge \text{subj}(x, e_3, e_4) \wedge \theta_{\text{ext}} \wedge \theta_{\text{cause\_int}+/-}\}]$

The context then enables the reader select which of these readings is correct: Agrippa is in prison at topic time, and so only the second reading is possible.

In the previous example it was possible to establish which reading of the perfect is appropriate on the basis of the context. However, this is not always the case. Sometimes it is only with access to real world knowledge that it is possible to resolve which interpretation is correct:

(558) = (133), (442)

hôn	heîs	mèn	ên
REL-PRON.M-GEN-PL	*one.M-NOM-SG*	*PTCL*	*be.PAST-IND-3-SG*
Gáios	Lutátios		ho
Gaius.M-NOM-SG	*Lutatius.M-NOM-SG*		*ART.M-NOM-SG*
tền	húpaton		arkhền
ART.F-ACC-SG	*consul.M-ACC-SG*		*command.F-ACC-SG*
eilēphós...			
***take.*PERF-PTPL-ACT-M-NOM-SG**			

'Of these one was C. Lutatius, who **had** [previously] **held** the consulship, the other two the praetorship.' (Plb. 3.40.9)

Again two readings are available for this predicate: either C. Lutatius has taken the consulship and still has it at topic time, or he has taken the consulship, held it, but no longer has it at topic time. We establish the correct interpretation from real-world knowledge: the consuls in the year described here, 218 B.C., were Publius Cornelius Scipio and Tiberius Sempronius Longus, not C. Lutatius:[340] C. Lutatius could not have been consul at topic time.[341]

---

[339] Notice that, according to the principles laid out in 6.4 and 6.5, in the first of these analyses the perfect suppresses the external argument but leaves the internal argument in tact, since its eventuality, e_2, is modified by *próteron*. In the second, however, *próteron* modifies e_3. Accordingly, the internal argument is no longer protected by the adverb and is also suppressed.

[340] See Shuckburgh (1889) ad Plb. 3.39.

[341] See n. 171.

7.8 *Obligatory anteriority in derived states*

It was noted at 2.4.2 that the perfects of non-COS verbs, i.e. those heading accomplishment and activity predicates, always carry anterior denotation. The same observation was made at 2.2.4 in the case of terminative state verbs. The framework introduced in the present chapter now offers us an explanation for why this should be the case in these predicates but not in predicates which already describe a state in which the subject can participate: since the perfect includes topic time in an atelic state predicated of the subject, the only way for a state to be derived from predicates headed by such verbs is to instantiate the predicate in time prior to topic time and predicate a secondary, i.e. derived, homogeneous atelic eventuality for the subject. Since this predicate is instantiated prior to topic time, anterior interpretation must follow.

Another way of stating this is that, since the external argument must be distinct in the active of such predicates, so must the eventuality which it specifies. The perfect cannot suppress the internal argument, since, as these predicates do not participate in the causative alternation, an external argument must be distinctly identified, leaving the internal argument inaccessible to the perfect to suppress it. Nor do there exist for these verbs specialised anticausative perfect forms. In accordance with the principle introduced at 6.4, whereby the perfect must relate to topic time any eventuality which is specified by a participant, the perfect must therefore relate the eventuality specified by the external argument to topic time. Since this eventuality is necessarily prior to the derived poststate, anterior interpretation is obligatory. In fact, on the basis of the discussion in 7.7, we can make the broader assertion, that any perfect predicate with a derived homogeneous atelic eventuality must carry anterior denotation, since in such cases the subject must always participate in an eventuality which terminates prior to topic time, and the perfect must relate this eventuality to topic time because it is must be specified by the eventual subject participant.

7.9 *Semantic contribution of the Greek perfect*

We can summarise the implications of the foregoing sections for the semantics of the Greek perfect in the following definition of its semantics:

a) The Greek perfect derives from the predicate a homogeneous atelic eventuality for the subject participant and includes topic time in this eventuality;
b) Where the predicate already describes such an eventuality, the perfect may include topic time in this eventuality directly;
c) Where the predicate does not describe such an eventuality, and optionally where it does, the perfect may secondarily derive an eventuality of the required type via event realisation and negation.

7.10 *Tense and the time adverbial problem*

So far in this study we have been almost exlusively concerned with the aspect of the perfect, that is to say, of the way in which the perfect relates an eventuality's temporal trace to topic time. However, in the indicative the perfect, unlike the participle and non-indicative forms of the perfect, also relates topic time to utterance time by including utterance time in topic time. However, this also gives rise to the time adverbial problem, as with the English perfect.

The definite perfect time adverbial problem is that the perfect indicative may not be modified by an adverb or adverbial phrase which locates a particular point in time relative to utterance time. By contrast, both the pluperfect and the perfect participle can be modified by adverbials which relate eventualities described by the predicate to specific

(559) = (18)

Sēmâs	kaì	Iaphthâs	kaì	Khamâs	étesin
Shem	*and*	*Japheth*	*and*	*Ham*	*year.N-DAT-PL*
hékatòn	émprosthen	tês			epombrías
one-hundred	*before*	*ART.F-GEN-SG*			*flood.F-GEN-SG*

gegonótes...
become.PERF-PTPL-ACT-M-NOM-PL
'... Shem, Japheth and Ham, **having been born** one hundred years before the flood...' (Jos. *AJ* 1.109)

(560) **egegónei**   dé   tis   kaì
become.PLPF-IND-ACT-3-SG   *PTCL*   *INDEF-PRON.3-SG-NOM*   *PTCL*

palaià	prórrēsis	étesí	pou	prósthen
old.F-NOM-SG	*prophesy.F-NOM-SG*	*year.N-DAT-PL*	*PTCL*	*previously*

hexakosíois
six-hundred.N-DAT-PL
'An old prophesy **had been given** six hundred years previously.'
(Jos. *BJ* 7.432)

This is not to say that the perfect indicative cannot be modified by temporal adverbials. However, the adverbials which are able to modify the perfect indicative may only locate an eventuality's temporal trace with respect to topic time. Chief among these are anterior adverbials such as *próteron* and *émprosthen*. A frequent formula is the following:

(561) hōs   kaì   próteron   **dedélōka**
       as   *also*   *earlier*   **explain.PERF-IND-ACT-1-SG**
'as I have also **explained** previously.' (Jos. *AJ* 4.311)

This can be given the following analysis, where PERF contributes the aspectual component and PRES contributes the tense component:

(562) $\exists x \exists e_1 \exists e_2 [\text{relate}(e_1) \wedge \text{non-homog}(e_1) \wedge \text{dur}(e_1) \wedge \theta_{ext}(x, e_1) \wedge \text{Previously}\{\tau(e_1){<}t_{TT}\}$
$\wedge \text{PERF}\{\neg e_1(e_2) \wedge \text{homog}(e_2) \wedge \text{subj}(x, e_1, e_2) \wedge \tau(e_1){<}\tau(e_2) \wedge \tau(e_2){\supseteq}t_{TT}\} \wedge$
$\text{PRES}\{t_{TU}{\supseteq}t_{TT}\}]$

Klein (1992: 544f.) presents a solution to the time adverbial problem by:

1. Positing a particular semantic description of the perfect;

2. Positing a general pragmatic constraint, termed the P-DEFINITENESS CONSTRAINT.

After summarising Klein's proposals, I will show that Klein's solution can be applied equally successfully to the semantic description of the perfect advocated here.

For Klein (1992: 538) the semantic description shared by all tenses of the perfect is, 'TT in posttime of TSit', where POSTTIME describes the time after the set of times in which an eventuality (or for us potentially set of eventualities) takes place, which he calls SITUATION TIME, or TSit. This is regardless of the event structural characteristics of that eventuality. In other words, the perfect simply denotes that topic time is in the time period after an eventuality or set of eventualities described by a predicate has/have taken place. Furthermore, the semantics of the perfect are indefinite with respect both to the time period elapsed between the set of times in which the eventuality is said to occur and topic time, as well as the frequency of occurrence of the eventuality described by the predicate.

Klein (1992: 546) then posits a pragmatic rule, the p-definiteness constraint. In his expression of this rule, Klein (1992: 544) first posits the existence of a property of expressions, namely P-DEFINITENESS:

> [A]n expression whose lexical content explicitly specifies the position of a time span in relation to TU is 'p-definite'.

Thus the predicate 'be in London yesterday' is p-definite, since the expression of the predicate specifies a particular time with respect to TU. By contrast, 'be in London previously' is not p-definite, since, although the span of time of being in London is marked as being prior to TU, no particular span of time in relation to TU is specified. The p-definiteness constraint then runs as follows:

> In an utterance, the expression of TT and the expression of TSit cannot both be independently p-definite.

In other words, it is not possible in a given utterance for both topic time and an eventuality's temporal trace to have their relationship with utterance time be explicitly and independently specified. An English example involving the pluperfect makes this clear:

(563) At 10am today, Isabella had visited London yesterday.

The problem with this sentence is not its truth: at topic time, which is specified as being 10am today, Isabella had visited London yesterday. The problem is a pragmatic one: why specify that Isabella had visited London yesterday at 10am today, when this is true of all time points after yesterday, since inherent in the semantics of perfect forms is the notion that topic time is in the posttime of TSit? As soon as the eventuality/eventualities described by the predicate are terminated, all subsequent time points are in its posttime, including 10am today.

This allows us to explain the problem with the present perfect and definite time adverbials, in sentences such as the following:

(564) I have walked to the park yesterday.

The problem with this sentence is that both topic time and situation time are p-definite, thus breaking the p-definiteness constraint. The predicate is p-definite, because in the tenseless predicate 'walk to the park yesterday' the event of walking is located at a particular point in time with respect to utterance time. In addition topic time is also p-definite, because, unlike the other tenses of the perfect, the present perfect ties topic time to a particular time with respect to utterance time, by including utterance time in topic time. In other words, this example is problematic because it asserts that the statement 'I have walked to the park yesterday' is true *at the time of speaking*. However, because of the aspectual semantics of the perfect, it is true of every point in time after yesterday, and there is no pragmatic value in asserting its truth for the moment of speaking.

For Klein the perfect includes topic time in the posttime of situation time. As we have shown, such a definition is not adequate for the Greek perfect, since it is unable to account for those instances where *inter alia* a single eventuality described by a predicate includes topic time, as in state predicates . However, the time adverbial problem is not relevant in such cases, since only one eventuality includes topic time, and the perfect indicative includes topic time in utterance time. To assert, therefore, that the eventuality took place prior to utterance time would entail a straight contradiction in such cases.

The time adverbial problem in Greek is therefore only relevant where a perfect predicate describes more than one subeventuality. Since tense in Greek, as in English, relates topic time to utterance time, we predict that it should not be possible for the temporal trace of any eventuality described by a predicate headed by the perfect indicative to be independently p-definite, beyond the subeventuality which includes topic time. We should therefore not expect, and indeed do not find, cases where the temporal trace of any prior subeventuality is also related directly to utterance time via adverbial modification, such as *dedélōka ekhthés* 'I have explained yesterday'. By contrast the pluperfect indicative and the perfect participle, should be compatible with definite adverbial modification, since these are not p-definite. There should be no problem, however, where the temporal trace of an eventuality other than that which includes topic time is located with respect to topic time by means of an anterior adverbial, since anterior adveribials are not p-definite. This accounts for uses such as that found at (560).

pálai provides an interesting test case for Klein's (and our) proposal. This adverb is usually translated 'long ago', an adverbial expression which in English relates an eventuality directly to utterance time. Accordingly, this adverb is not felicitous with the present perfect:

(565) ?I have seen you long ago.

In any case we would not expect any problem with perfect forms outside of the present perfect indicative:

(566) = (131), (516)

hē	dè	boulè	**pálai**
ART.F-NOM-SG	PTCL	Senate.F-NOM-SG	*long-ago*
diegnōkuîa		polemêsai...	hôde
decide.PERF-PTPL-ACT-F-NOM-SG		*go-to-war.AOR-INF-ACT*	thus

apekrínato...
reply.AOR-IND-ACT-3-SG
'... the Senate, **having decided long ago** to go to war... replied thus...'
(App. *Pun.* 11.74)

i.e.:

(567) $\exists x \exists e_1 \exists e_2 [\text{BECOME}(e_1) \wedge \text{delim}(e_1) \wedge \theta_{\text{cause}+/-}(x, e_1) \wedge \text{STATE}(e_2) \wedge$
$\text{decided}(x, e_2) \wedge \theta_{\text{mod}}(x, e_2) \wedge \text{homog}(e_2) \wedge \{\tau(e_1) < \tau(e_2) \vee \tau(e_1) \subseteq \tau(e_2)\} \wedge$
$\text{Long-ago}\{\tau(e_1) < t_{\text{TU}} \wedge \text{pdef}\{\tau(e_1)\}\} \wedge \text{PERF}\{\tau(e_2) \supseteq t_{\text{TT}}\}]$

More surprisingly, however, *pálai* also appears to have no problem collocating with the present perfect indicative in Greek:

(568)

tèn	mèn	andreían
ART.F-ACC-SG	*PTCL*	*courage.F-ACC-SG*
sou	kaì	pístin
you.GEN-SG	*and*	*faith.F-ACC-SG*
akēkóamen		**pálai**...
hear.PERF-IND-ACT-1-PL		*long-ago*

'**We have heard** of your courage and faith **long ago**.' (Jos. *AJ* 13.45)

To be felicitous in English, instances of the perfect such as this have to be rendered with the simple past:

(569) We heard of your bravery and faith long ago...

This could lead to the (erroneous) conclusion that the perfect in literary Koine Greek is not in fact a perfect any longer. However, the issue in this case is rather with the adverb *pálai*. For, unlike English, this adverb is not restricted to specifying the temporal trace of an eventuality with respect to utterance time, but may be used to specify the relationship between an eventuality's temporal trace and topic time:

(570)

Messénēn...	**pálai**	ophthalmiôntes...
Messene.F-ACC-SG	***long-previously***	*eye.PRES-PTPL-ACT-M-NOM-SG*
euthùs	**epekheírēsan**	
immediately	***attempt.AOR-IND-ACT-3-PL***	
paraspondeîn		
break-faith.PRES-INF-ACT		

'[some Campanian mercenaries of Agathocles,] having **for some time** had Messene in their sights... immediately **set about** breaking faith.'
(Plb.1.7, trans. after Shuckburgh)

In this example *pálai* describes a time point 'long ago' with respect that the event described by *epekheírēsan* 'they attempted'. This is to say that it relates the temporal trace of the eventuality not to utterance time, but rather to topic time. In most cases where *pálai* would be used, topic time and utterance time would in fact be indistinguishable, and so translation in English with 'long ago' would be perfectly acceptable. The difference only manifests itself in cases where topic time does not include utterance time, or, as in the case of the present case, where the p-definiteness constraint is at risk of being contravened. For our purposes here, however, the above example demonstrates that, since *pálai* does not inherently specify the relationship between situation time and utterance time, its use with the present perfect indicative does not break the p-definiteness constraint.

7.11 Noise predicates

As noted at 2.5, a long-standing problem for the Greek perfect has been its behaviour with noise predicates. There we suggested that noise eventualities need not be interpreted as straightforward activity predicates as one might at first suppose. A significant part of the problem with analysing the perfect of noise predicates has been the apparent incongruity of analysing noises as states, which they are self-evidently not on any intuitive understanding of the notion of statehood. However, in this chapter we have decoupled the notion of statehood *per se* from the Greek perfect, making the weaker assertion that the perfect derives a homogeneous atelic eventuality from the predicate which it heads. If we are right to analyse noise eventualities as (at least potentially) homogeneous and atelic, it follows directly that that the perfect should be able to derive this eventuality directly from the predicate and include topic time in it. In these terms, one could further infer that the difference between the present and the perfect is between a noise eventuality conceived of as ongoing and unchanging versus one lacking the feature of homogeneity. Such an interpretation is at least plausible in examples like the following:

(571) = (160), (408)

hai	gunaîkes	apantôsai
ART.F-NOM-PL	*woman.F-NOM-PL*	*meet.PRES-PTPL-ACT-F-NOM-PL*
metà xiphôn	kaì	pelékeōn
with sword.N-GEN-PL	*and*	*axe.M-GEN-PL*
deinòn	**tetriguîai**	
terribly	**shriek.PERF-PTPL-ACT-F-NOM-PL**	
ēmúnonto		toùs ...
drive-back.IMPF-IND-NON-ACT-I-3-PL		*ART.M-ACC-PL*
pheúgontas		
flee.PRES-PTPL-IND-M-ACC-PL		

'... the women met [them], holding swords and axes, and **shrieking** terribly tried to drive back those who were fleeing...' (Plu. *Gaius Marius* 19.7)

(572)

ho	d'	apopēdḗsas	
ART.M-NOM-SG	*PTCL*	*leap-back.AOR-PTPL-ACT-M-NOM-SG*	
steinês	épheuge		deilòs
narrow.F-GEN-SG	*flee.IMPF-IND-ACT-3-SG*		*cowardly.M-NOM-SG*
es mukhòn	tróglēs,	ásēma	
into corner.M-ACC-SG	*hole.F-GEN-SG*	*inarticulately*	

trízōn   tón

squeak.PRES-PTPL-ACT-M-NOM-SG   ART.M-ACC-SG

te   próxenon   thlíbōn.

PTCL patron.M-ACC-SG   *strike.PRES-PTPL-ACT-M-NOM-SG*

'... but he leapt away and fled in fear into the innermost nook of the narrow hole, **squeaking** unintelligibly and squeezing his host.' (Babrius, *Fables*, 108.21-3: *The Town Mouse and the Country Mouse*)

According to this understanding, Plutarch's point in using the perfect in (571) is to assert the monotonicity and homogeneity of the shriek, while in the second case, the squeaking of the mouse is understood as a dynamic noise event.

However, it is less clear that such a distinction can be made in the case of *kékraga* from *krázō*. The examples given at (161) and (162), given at 2.5 above, involve intelligible speech, which cannot be understood as homogeneous. Accordingly, we must suppose that the use of *kékraga*, at least, is partly the result of lexicalisation, perhaps from an original distinction along the lines we have suggested.

7.12 *Conclusion*

In this chapter we have modified the provisional account of the semantics of the Greek perfect given in chapter 5. There we proposed that the perfect includes topic time in any state eventuality described by the predicate, and relates any subeventualities described by the predicate to topic time via this state eventuality. In chapter 6 we added the condition that the perfect only relates to topic time eventualities which are explicitly specified by a participant, thus accounting for the resultative-like behaviour of perfect predicates where the become eventuality is unmodified. However, the definition still leaves unexplained those cases where the perfect heads a predicate where no state eventuality is described, or where the state in question has a set expiry. Accordingly, in this chapter we proposed that the Greek perfect derives a homogeneous atelic eventuality for the subject from the predicate which it heads. Where the predicate already describes such an eventuality, the perfect will in most cases include topic time in this eventuality, thus accounting for its behaviour with pure state, continued state and COS predicates. However, where the predicate does not describe such an eventuality, the perfect will derive an eventuality of the required event structure by first realising the predicate and then deriving the negative corollary of the eventuality, which is always homogeneous and atelic. The perfect then includes topic time in this eventuality. Furthermore, the perfect may optionally derive such an eventuality from state predicates which already describe homogeneous atelic eventualities for the eventual subject. I ended by accounting for the obligatory anteriority of such derived predicates in terms of event realisation and event participation. Moving on from this, I adapted Klein's explanation for the time-adverbial problem in the English perfect to Greek, and showed that the p-definiteness constraint appears to hold here too. Finally, I offered a partial explanation for the behaviour of the perfect of noise predicates in these terms, suggesting that the perfect asserts that the noise event described by the predicate is homogeneous, in contrast to the present where such an interpretation is not necessary.

VIII

8 CONCLUSION: THE SEMANTICS OF THE GREEK PERFECT

This investigation has sought to provide a semantic explanation for the various phenomena with which the Greek perfect is associated. The two basic issues presented by the Greek perfect active are the temporal problem and transitivity problem:

1. The temporal problem: the Greek perfect can describe a situation that terminates prior to topic time.

(573) = (2), (134)

hền	gàr	ho	tês
REL-PRON.F-ACC-SG	*PTCL*	*ART.M-NOM-SG*	*ART.F-GEN-SG*
Thēseḯdos	poiētḕs		Amazónōn
Theseid.F-GEN-SG	*author.M-NOM-SG*		*Amazon.F-GEN-PL*
epanástasin	**gégraphe**		
uprising.F-ACC-SG	**write.PERF-IND-ACT-3-SG**		

'For the author of the Theseid **wrote** "The insurrection of the Amazons".'
(Plu. *Thes.* 28.1)

However, there is often little apparent reference to any prior event that brought about the situation described at topic time, even if such an event must have taken place at some point:

(574) = (3)

hoi	dè	perì	tòn
ART.M-NOM-PL	*PTCL*	*around*	*ART.M-ACC-SG*
Khárēta…		kaíper	**katapeplēgótas**
Khares.M-ACC-SG		*although*	**terrify.PERF-PTPL-ACT-M-ACC-PL**
toùs		hoplítas	táttousin…
ART.M-ACC-PL		*soldiers.M-ACC-PL*	*command.PRES-IND-ACT-3-PL*

'But Chares'… band… commanded the soldiers, even though **they were terrified**…' (Jos. *BJ* 4.18)

In a few cases no such event can have taken place:

(575) = (6), (145), (430), (495)

hē	dè	Teúta…	polismátion…
ART.F-NOM-SG	*PTCL*	*Teuta.F-NOM-SG*	*small-town.N-NOM-SG*

anakekhōrēkòs   mèn   apò   tês
withdraw.PERF-PTPL-ACT-N-NOM-SG   *PTCL*   *from*   *ART.F-GEN-SG*
thaláttēs...
sea.F-GEN-SG
'Teuta... a small town... **withdrawn** from the sea...' (Plb. 2.11.16)

2. The transitivity problem: the perfect active of many verbs appears to detransitivise, removing the external argument, in a similar way to the passive in English. Thus (573) describes an affected subject. Indeed, transitive and intransitive senses may appear in a single stem:

(576) = (8), (158), (309), (436), (519)
heistḗkei   dè   katá   ti
set-up.PLPF-IND-ACT-3-SG   *PTCL*   *in*   *INDEF-PRON.N-ACC-SG*
prosbatòn   olígais   bathmîsi   khōríon
accessible.N-ACC-SG   *few.F-DAT-PL*   *step.F-DAT-PL*   *space.N-ACC-SG*
hupestalkṑs   tôi   kat'
hide.PERF-PTPL-ACT-N-ACC-SG   *ART.DAT-M-SG*   *in*
autò   skótōi.
it.N-SG-ACC   *darkness.M-DAT-SG*
'[Claudius] had stood in a space, accessible by a few paces, **taking cover** in the darkness there.' (Jos. *AJ* 19.216)

(577) = (9), (159), (308), (437), (546)
ho   dè   Phílippos...   hupó
ART.M-NOM-SG   *PTCL*   *Philip.M-NOM-SG*   *under*
tina   lóphon   **hupestálkei**
INDEF-PRON.MF-ACC-SG   *hill.M-ACC-SG*   *hide.PLPF-IND-ACT-3-SG*
toùs   Illurioùs...
ART.M-ACC-PL   *Illyrians.M-ACC-PL*
'But Philip... **had sent** the Illyrians behind a hill...'(Plb. 5.13.5)

3. The continuity problem: the temporal trace of a perfect predicate may start prior to topic time and continue up to and including topic time:

(578) = (7), (120), (553)
epì   gàr   tḕn   proüpárkhousan
on   *PTCL*   *ART.F-ACC-SG*   *exist-before.PRES-PTPL-ACT-F-ACC-SG*
khíona kaì   **diamemenēkuîan**   **ek**
snow.F-ACC-SG and   *remain.PERF-PTPL-ACT-F-ACC-SG*   *from*
toû   **próteron**   **kheimônos**   árti
ART.M-GEN-SG   *earlier*   *winter.M-GEN-SG*   *recently*
tês   ep' étous   peptōkuías...
ART.F-GEN-SG   *present-year*   *fall.PERF-PTPL-ACT-F-GEN-SG*

'For on top of the snow which **had remained from the previous winter**, that from the present year had just fallen...' (Plb. 3.55.1)

By contrast, in the case of other atelic predicates, the event in question is assumed to have terminated prior to topic time, even where no explicit endpoint is provided by the predicate.

(579) = (136), (415), (541)

ho	d'	ouk	**orthôs**	autòn
ART.M-NOM-SG	PTCL	NEG	*properly*	he.ACC-SG
éphē		**pepoiēkénai**...		
say.PAST-IND-ACT-3-SG		*act.PERF-INF-ACT*		

'But he said that he had not **acted properly**...' (Jos. AJ 6.102)

Thus in Greek the equivalent of 'I have lived in Paris for three years (and still live there' is possible, but not 'I have been making cakes (and am still making them)'.

Finally, the Greek perfect suffers from the time adverbial problem, as does the English perfect:

4. The time adverbial problem: The present perfect appears to resist definite time adverbial modification, and it is thus possible to find definite time adverbials modifying the pluperfect and the participle, but not the indicative form, at least in the literary Koine.[342]

In chapter 2 we introduced a lexical aspectual framework to take account of the pheneomena described, making use of the three features of homogeneity, durativity and terminativity. Past reference in the perfect was found to be guaranteed by the presence of the feature of durativity, while anteriority in the perfect was certain where terminativity and durativity were present, or where the verb was durative and non-homogeneous. The principal exception to this was found to be COS verbs: despite potentially encoding both durativity and terminativity in their lexical semantics, past reference was found not to be obligatory. Accordingly, while lexical aspectual semantics clearly have an important role in determining the temporal and aspectual characteristics of perfect predicates, it was clearly necessary to take syntactic factors into account, and assess the perfect's semantics at the level of the predicate.

In chapter 3 we introduced two syntactic-semantic frameworks to be used in the remainder of the study, namely neo-Davidsonian event semantics and Government-Binding theory. In order to maintain a clear distinction between different argument structures, we proposed a form of analysis that combined the two.

Chapter 4 set out to take account of the syntactic phenomena associated with the Greek perfect, for the time being leaving aside the tense and aspect questions. We found that the kind of detransitivisation observed in the Greek perfect was not in fact unique to it, but is a feature of the Greek verb system more generally in predicates describing causative change of state. There are two kinds of detransitivisation in which Greek verbs were in general found to participate:

---

[342] See n. 26 above for an example from the New Testament which breaks this requirement.

(a) Full labile transitivity, where any active stem may optionally be used to describe a subject which undergoes the event described by the predicate rather than being its external cause.

(b) Verbs with specialised causative and anticausative stems.

Furthermore, the distinction is semantically based. Thus verbs describing events where the undergoer could entirely spontaneously undergo the event, as particularly in the case in change of location verbs, were found to belong to the fully labile group, while verbs describing events where some external cause is always necessary, as typically in the case of change of nature verbs, were found to belong to the group with specialised stems. We saw that in general the perfect adheres to the pattern seen elsewhere in the system, albeit without a one-hundred percent matching of items in the second group.

Chapter 5 moved on to incorporate an analysis of the aspectual value of the perfect within the syntactic framework developed thus far. Here we found that where a predicate describes any kind of poststate, the perfect includes topic time in the temporal trace of this eventuality. Other subeventualities described by the predicate are then located prior to topic time accordingly. Furthermore, where the predicate describes a continued state, the perfect properly includes topic time in this state. Again the exception was found to be COS predicates, where in many cases it appears that only the poststate described by the predicate is related to topic time (again by inclusion). On the basis of these findings, we proposed a provisional definition of the semantic contribution of the Greek perfect:

> The Greek perfect includes topic time in any state eventuality described by a predicate.

However, it was clear that this definition as it stands is not entirely adequate. This is most obviously the case for telic state and activity predicates, where the predicate does not describe a poststate, and yet the perfect is still able to head predicates of these types. There is the further problem of how to explain the behaviour of COS predicates, where only the poststate is regularly related to topic time. Indeed, in some cases the prestate subeventualities can never have taken place in time.

Chapters 6 and 7 set out to take account of these phenomena. Thus chapter 6 addressed the behaviour of COS predicates. We found three types:

(a) Perfect predicates where the predicate's become subeventuality can never have occurred in time.

(b) Perfect predicates where the become subeventuality must have occurred in time, but is not explicitly related to topic time.

(c) Perfect predicates where the become subeventuality both occurs in time and is explicitly related to topic time.

The first group were found to be predicates of extent. This is to say that their verbs, optionally, may head predicates which are not functions of time, but are rather simply paths in space. The perfect of such predicates simply denotes that the subject exists at the end of a particular path. The second and third groups are by contrast both temporal. Here the critical factor is whether or not the become subeventuality is explicitly modified or not. If not, we argued that the perfect suppresses, not the become subeventuality, but rather the internal argument which, via the Aspectual Interface Hypothesis, provides the measure function for the event. Furthermore, we proposed that the perfect only relates to topic time those subeventualities which are overtly specified, or participated in, by an argument. Accordingly, the perfect does not relate the become subeventuality in such predicates to topic time, since it has no overt specifier or participant. In these cases the reading of the perfect is, in English terms, resultative. However, where the become subeventuality is modified, either by an adverb or an adjunct, the internal argument position remains unsuppressed. Accordingly, the mod argument projected by the poststate is free to move to internal position. The become eventuality therefore has an overt specifier/participant, and the perfect relates the subeventuality to topic time, giving rise to a(n English) perfect-like interpretation.

It was found that the Greek perfect, unlike the English resultative, does not itself have the capacity to suppress the external argument. For this to happen a special anticausative stem should be used whose role is to suppress the external argument. In such cases, the semantic derivation of the perfect follows normally thereafter.

On the basis of the arguments made in chapter 6, we modified the definition of the function of the perfect offered previously, so that the Greek perfect:

(a) Includes topic time in any state eventuality described by a predicate
(b) Suppresses the internal argument of an unmodified become subeventuality;
(c) Relates to topic time any subeventuality or subeventualities with specified participants in keeping with the situation aspectual relationship that these eventualities bear to the state eventuality which already includes topic time.

Chapter 7 then addressed the issue of predicates that do not describe a poststate, notably telic states and activities. Here it was found that the perfect derives a secondary homogeneous atelic eventuality from the realised predicate. This secondary eventuality is derived via negation, since the negative of any predicate yields a homogeneous atelic eventuality. However, the capacity of the perfect to derive such an eventuality opens up the possibility of ambiguity in predicates that already describe a poststate with the required eventstructural characteristics. Indeed, this turns out to be the case: while in most cases the perfect of such predicates derives the state eventuality described by the predicate itself, in some cases it was found to derive a secondary homogeneous atelic eventuality by the same means. The ambiguity was found ultimately to be resolved only by an evaluation of the context.

We may therefore summarise the syntactic-semantic derivation of the perfect, as a series of consecutive operations, as follows:

(a) The internal argument of an unmodified become subeventuality is suppressed;
(b) The Greek perfect derives from the predicate a homogeneous atelic eventuality for the subject participant and includes topic time in this eventuality:

  (i) Where the predicate already describes such an eventuality, the perfect may derive this eventuality directly;

  (ii) Where the predicate does not describe such an eventuality, and optionally where it does, the perfect may secondarily derive an eventuality of the required type via event realisation and negation;

(c) Any subeventuality or subeventualities with specified participants is related to topic time in keeping with the situation aspectual relationship that these eventualities bear to the state eventuality which already includes topic time.

It can be readily seen from this definition that both aspect, i.e. deriving a homogeneous atelic eventuality from the predicate, and argument structure relations, i.e. suppressing the internal argument where the become event is unmodified, are integral to the perfect's semantics. Furthermore, the fact that the perfect only relates eventualities to topic time which are overtly specified as having a participant shows that the perfect is fundamentally participant-focused, and relates the aspect of an eventuality to topic time via the participation of arguments. In this the perfect may be said to differ from the imperfective and perfective, which are event-focused, relating a predicate's eventualities to topic time regardless of participation.

AUTHOR CONTACT INFORMATION

Robert Samuel David Crellin
Bathway House
144 London Road West Bath,
BA1 7DD
United Kingdom
robertcrellin@cantab.net

TEXTUAL SOURCES

Acts of Paul and Thecla, in R.A. Lipsius (ed.), *Acta apostolorum apocrypha*, Vol. 1, Leipzig: Mendelssohn, 1891 (repr. Hildesheim: Olms, 1972): 235–271.

Gospel of Peter, in M.G. Mara (ed.), *Évangile de Pierre*, [Sources chrétiennes 201. Paris: Éditions du Cerf, 1973]: 40–66.

Homeric Hymns, T.W. Allen, W.R. Halliday, and E.E. Sikes (eds.), *The Homeric hymns*, 2nd edn., Oxford: Clarendon Press, 1936.

Life of Adam and Eve, in D. Bertrand (ed.), *La Vie grecque d' Adam et d' Eve*, Paris: Librairie Adrien Maisonneuve, 1987: 68–106.

Nestle-Aland. *Novum Testamentum Graece [=NA28]*, Nestle, E. et al. (eds.), 28th rev. edition, Stuttgart: Deutsche Bibelgesellschaft.

Perseus Digital Library. G. R. Crane (ed.) Tufts University. http://www.perseus.tufts.edu

Septuaginta [= LXX], A. Rahlfs (ed.), 9th ed., Stuttgart: Württemberg Bible Society, 1935 (repr. 1971).

Shepherd of Hermas, in M. Whittaker (ed.), *Die apostolischen Väter I. Der Hirt des Hermas*, [Die griechischen christlichen Schriftsteller 48, 2nd edn. Berlin: Akademie Verlag, 1967]: 1–98.

Thesaurus Linguae Graecae® Digital Library [= TLG]. M. C. Pantelia (ed.) University of California, Irvine. http://www.tlg.uci.edu

Aelian, *Tactics*, in H. Köchly and W. Rüstow (eds.), *Asclepiodotos' Taktik. Aelianos' Theorie der Taktik* [Griechische Kriegsschriftsteller vol. 2.1. Leipzig: Engelmann, 1855]: 218–470.

Aelius Herodianus, *Perì hrēmátōn*, in A. Lentz, *Grammatici Graeci, vol. 3.2*, Leipzig: Teubner, 1870 (repr. Hildesheim: Olms, 1965): 787–824.

Aeschylus, *Prometheus Bound*, in Denys Page (ed.), *Aeschyli Tragoediae*, Oxford: Clarendon, 1972: 287–329.

Appian of Alexandria, *The Civil Wars*, in L. Mendelssohn (ed.), *Appiani Historia Romana*, Leipzig: Teubner, 1879.

Appian of Alexandria, *The Foreign Wars*, in L. Mendelssohn (ed.), *Appiani Historia Romana*, Leipzig: Teubner, 1879.

Aristonicus of Alexandria, *De signis Iliadis*, in L. Friedlander (ed.) *Aristonici Perì sēmeíōn Iliádos reliquiae emendatiores*, Göttingen: Dieterich, 1853 (repr. Amsterdam: Hakkert, 1965): 39–350.

Aristophanes, *Birds*, in N. G. Wilson (ed.), *Aristophanis fabulae*, Vol. 1, Oxford: OUP, 2007: 339–427.

Aristotle, *De caelo*, in P. Moraux (ed.), *Aristote. Du ciel*, Paris: Les Belles Lettres, 1965: 1–154 (268a1-313b22).

Aristotle, *History of Animals, Volume III: Books 7-10*, D. M. Balme (ed. and trans.), Cambridge Mass.: Harvard University Press, 1991.

ASCLEPIODOTUS, *Tactics*, in C.H. Oldfather and W.A. Oldfather (eds.), *Aeneas Tacticus, Asclepiodotus, Onasander*, Cambridge, Mass.: Harvard University Press, 1923 (repr. 1962): 244–332.

ATHENAEUS MECHANICUS, *De machinis*, in R. Schneider (ed.), *Griechische Poliorketiker*, Vol. 1 [Abhandlungen der königlichen Gesellschaft der Wissenschaften zu Göttingen, Philol.-hist. Kl. N.F. 12, no. 5. Berlin: Weidmann, 1912]: 8-36.

BABRIUS, *The Country Mouse and the Town Mouse*, IN *Babrius and Phaedrus: Fables*, with an English translation by Ben E. Perry, Cambridge Mass.: Harvard University Press, 1965.

CALLIXENUS, *Fragmenta*, in K. Müller (ed.), *Fragmenta historicorum Graecorum* (FHG) 3, Paris: DIDOT, 1841-1870: 55-66.

CASSIUS DIO, *Histories*, in U.P. Boissevain (ed.), *Cassii Dionis Cocceiani historiarum Romanarum quae supersunt*, 3 vols., Berlin: Weidmann, 1:1895; 2:1898; 3:1901 (repr. 1955).

CERCIDAS, *Fragmenta*, in J. U. Powell (ed.), *Collectanea Alexandrina*, Oxford: Clarendon, 1925 (repr. 1970): 202–218.

DINARCHUS, N. C. Conomis (ed.), *Dinarchi orationes cum fragmentis*, Leipzig: Teubner, 1975.

DIO CHRYSOSTOM, *Orations*, in J. von Arnim (ed.), *Dionis Prusaensis quem vocant Chrysostomum quae exstant omnia, vols. 1-2*, 2nd edn., Berlin: Weidmann, 1:1893; 2:1896 (repr. 1962): 1:1-338; 2:1–306.

DIODORUS SICULUS, *Bibliotheca historica*, in K.T. Fischer (post I. Bekker & L. Dindorf) and F. Vogel (eds.), *Diodori bibliotheca historica*, 5 vols., 3rd edn., Leipzig: Teubner, 1:1888; 2:1890; 3:1893; 4-5:1906 (repr. 1964).

DIONYSIUS OF HALICARNASSUS, *Anitiquitates Romanae*, in K. Jacoby (ed.), *Dionysii Halicarnasei antiquitatum Romanarum quae supersunt*, 4 vols., Leipzig: Teubner, 1:1885; 2:1888; 3:1891; 4:1905 (repr. 1967).

DIONYSIUS THRAX, *Ars Grammatica*, in G. Uhlig, *Grammatici Graeci*, Vol. 1.1, Leipzig: Teubner, 1883 (repr. Hildesheim: Olms, 1965): 5–100.

EPICTETUS, *Dissertationes*, H. Schenkl (ed.), *Epicteti dissertationes ab Arriano digestae*, Leipzig: Teubner, 1916.

GALEN, CLAUDIUS, *De compositione medicamentorum secundum locos libri x*, in C.G. Kühn (ed.), *Claudii Galeni opera omnia, vols. 12-13*, Leipzig: Knobloch, 12:1826; 13:1827 (repr. Hildesheim: Olms, 1965): 12:378-1007; 13:1–361.

GALEN, CLAUDIUS, *De usu partium*, G. Helmreich (ed.), *Galeni de usu partium libri xvii*, Leipzig: Teubner, 1:1907; 2:1909 (repr. Amsterdam: Hakkert, 1968): 1:1-496; 2:1–451.

HERODIAN, *Ab excessu divi Marci libri octo*, K. Stavenhagen (ed.), Leipzig: Teubner, 1922 (repr. 1967).

HIPPOCRATES, *De corde [= On the Heart]*, in É. Littré (ed.), *Oeuvres complètes d'Hippocrate*, Vol. 9, Paris: Baillière, 1861 (repr. Amsterdam: Hakkert, 1962): 80-92.

HOMER, *The Iliad*, in T. W. Allen and D. B. Monro (eds.), *Homeri opera*, 5 vols. Oxford: OUP, 1920.

HOMER, *The Odyssey*, with an English translation by A. T. Murray, London: Heinemann, 1919.

JOSEPHUS, FLAVIUS, *The Works of Flavius Josephus*, W. Whiston (trans.), Auburn and Buffalo, NY, John E. Beardsley, 1895.

JOSEPHUS, FLAVIUS, *Flavii Josephi opera*, B. Niese (ed.), 7 vols., Berlin: Weidmann, 1887–95.

LUCIAN, *Soloecista*, in M.D. Macleod (ed.), *Lucian*, Vol. 8, Cambridge, Mass.: Harvard University Press, 1967: 4-44.

MENANDER, *Fragments*, in T. Kock (ed.), *Comicorum Atticorum fragmenta*, Vol. 3, Leipzig: Teubner, 1888: 3–152, 155–164, 166–241, 246–271.

PAUSANIAS, *Description of Greece*, F. Spiro (ed.), *Pausaniae Graeciae descriptio*, 3 vols., Leipzig: Teubner, 1903.

PHILO OF ALEXANDRIA, *De opificio mundi*, in L. Cohn (ed.), *Philonis Alexandrini opera quae supersunt*, Vol. 5, 1906 (repr. Berlin: De Gruyter, 1962): 1-60.

PHILO OF ALEXANDRIA, *De virtutibus*, in L. Cohn (ed.), *Philonis Alexandrini opera quae supersunt*, Vol. 5, 1906 (repr. Berlin: De Gruyter, 1962): 266–335.

PHILO OF ALEXANDRIA, *On the Decalogue. On the Special Laws*, books 1-3, with English translation by F. H. Colson, Cambridge Mass.: Harvard University Press, 1937.

PHILODEMUS, *Perì orgês*, in G. Indelli, Filodemo, *L'ira* [La scuola di Epicuro 5. Naples: Bibliopolis, 1988]: 106–108.

PHRYNICHUS, *Eclogae*, E. Fischer (ed.), *Die Ekloge des Phrynichos, Sammlung griechischer und lateinischer Grammatiker (SGLG) 1*, Berlin: De Gruyter, 1974.

PHRYNICHUS, *Praeparatio Sophistica*, J. de Borries (ed.), *Phrynichi sophistae praeparatio sophistica*, Leipzig: Teubner, 1911.

PLUTARCH, *De communibus notitiis adversus Stoicos*, in R. Westman (post M. Pohlenz), *Plutarchi Moralia*, Vol. 6.2, 2nd edn., Leipzig: Teubner, 1959: 62–122.

PLUTARCH, *De Iside et Osiride [= On Isis and Osiris]*, in W. Sieveking (ed.), *Plutarchi Moralia*, Vol. 2.3, Leipzig: Teubner, 1935 (repr. 1971): 1-80.

PLUTARCH, *De sera numinis vindicta*, in M. Pohlenz, *Plutarchi moralia*, Vol. 3, Leipzig: Teubner, 1929 (repr. 1972): 394-444.

PLUTARCH, *Lives, Volume I: Theseus and Romulus. Lycurgus and Numa. Solon and Publicola*, with an English translation by Bernadotte Perrin, Cambridge Mass.: Harvard University Press, 1914.

PLUTARCH, *Lives, Volume II: Themistocles and Camillus. Aristides and Cato Major. Cimon and Lucullus*, with an English translation by Bernadotte Perrin, Cambridge Mass: Harvard University Press, 1914.

PLUTARCH, *Lives, Volume III: Pericles and Fabius Maximus. Nicias and Crassus,* with an English translation by Bernadotte Perrin, Cambridge Mass: Harvard University Press, 1916.

PLUTARCH, *Lives, Volume IV: Alcibiades and Coriolanus. Lysander and Sulla,* with an English translation by Bernadotte Perrin, Cambridge Mass.: Harvard University Press, 1916.

PLUTARCH, *Lives, Volume V: Agesilaus and Pompey. Pelopidas and Marcellus,* with an English translation by Bernadotte Perrin, Cambridge Mass.: Harvard University Press, 1917.

PLUTARCH, *Lives, Volume VI: Dion and Brutus. Timoleon and Aemilius Paulus,* with an English translation by Bernadotte Perrin, Cambridge Mass.: Harvard University Press, 1918.

PLUTARCH, *Lives, Volume VII: Demosthenes and Cicero. Alexander and Caesar,* with an English translation by Bernadotte Perrin, Cambridge Mass.: Harvard University Press, 1919.

PLUTARCH, *Lives, Volume IX: Demetrius and Antony. Pyrrhus and Gaius Marius,* with an English translation by Bernadotte Perrin, Cambridge Mass. Harvard University Press, 1920.

PLUTARCH, *Lives, Volume X: Agis and Cleomenes. Tiberius and Gaius Gracchus. Philopoemen and Flamininus,* with an English translation by Bernadotte Perrin, Cambridge Mass: Harvard University Press, 1921.

PLUTARCH, *Moralia vol. I: The Education of Children. How the Young Man Should Study Poetry. On Listening to Lectures. How to Tell a Flatterer from a Friend. How a Man May Become Aware of His Progress in Virtue,* with an English Translation by Frank Cole Babbit, Harvard University Press, 1927.

PLUTARCH, *Moralia vol. V: Isis and Osiris. The E at Delphi. The Oracles at Delphi No Longer Given in Verse. The Obsolescence of Oracles,* with an English Translation by Frank Cole Babbit, Harvard University Press, 1927.

PLUTARCH, *Moralia vol. XII: Concerning the Face which appears in the Orb of the Moon. On the Principle of Cold. Whether Fire or Water is more useful. Whether Land or Sea Animals are cleverer. Beasts are rational. On the eating of Flesh,* with an English Translation by Harold Cherniss, Harvard University Press, 1957.

PLUTARCH, *Moralia vol. XIII: Part 2,* with an English Translation by Harold Cherniss, Harvard University Press, 1976.

POLYBIUS, *Histories,* E. S. Shuckburgh (trans.), New York: Macmillan, 1889.

POLYBIUS, *Histories,* in T. Büttner-Wobst (ed.), *Polybii historiae,* Vols. 1-4, Leipzig: Teubner, 1893–1905.

POSIDONIUS, *Fragments,* in W. Theiler (ed.), *Posidonios. Die Fragmente,* Vol. 1, Berlin: De Gruyter, 1982.

SOPHOCLES, *Electra,* in H. Lloyd-Jones and N. G. Wilson (ed.), *Sophoclis Fabulae,* Oxford: Clarendon, 1990: 59–118.

STRABO, *Geography, Volume I: Books 1-2*, with an English translation by Horace L. Jones, Cambridge Mass.: Harvard University Press, 1917.

STRABO, *Geography, Volume II: Books 3-5*, with an English translation by Horace L. Jones, Cambridge Mass.: Harvard University Press, 1923.

THEODOSIUS, *Canones isagogici de flexione verborum*, in A. HILGARD, *Grammatici Graeci*, Vol. 4.1, Leipzig: Teubner, 1894 (repr. Hildesheim: Olms, 1965): 43-99.

THEOGNETUS, *Fragments*, in T. Kock (ed.), *Comicorum Atticorum fragmenta*, Vol. 3, Leipzig: Teubner, 1888, 364-365.

Thucydides, Histories, H.S. Jones and J.E. Powell (eds.), *Thucydidis historiae*, 2 vols., Oxford: Clarendon Press, 1942.

XENOPHON, *Anabasis*, with an English translation by Carleton L. Brownson, revised by John Dillery, Cambridge Mass.: Harvard University Press, 1998.

REFERENCES

GARONNE, *Wikipedia: The Free Encyclopedia*, Wikimedia Foundation, Inc. 22 July 2004, accessed 09/05/2015.

ALEXIADOU, A., & SCHÄFER, F., 2006. 'Instrument Subjects Are Agents or Causers', *Proceedings of the 25th West Coast Conference on Formal Linguistics*: 40–48.

ALLAN, R. J., 2002. *The Middle Voice in Ancient Greek. A Study in Polysemy*. Ph.D. dissertation, University of Amsterdam.

ANDERSEN, P. K., 1993. 'Zur Diathese', *Historische Sprachforschung/ Historical Linguistics 106*(2): 177–231.

ANDERSEN, P. K., 1994. *Empirical Studies in Diathesis*. Münster: Nodus Publikationen.

BACH, E., 1981. 'On Time, Tense and Aspect: an Essay in English Metaphysics', in: P. Cole (ed.), *Radical Pragmatics*. Academic Press, 63–81.

BACH, E., 1986. 'The algebra of events', *Linguistics and Philosophy*: 5–16.

BAKER, M., 1989. 'Object sharing and projection in serial verb constructions', *Linguistic Inquiry 20*, 513–553.

BAKER, M., 1996. 'On the structural positions of themes and goals', in J. Rooryck & L. Zaring (eds.), *Phrase Structure and the Lexicon*. Dordrecht: Springer.

BARY, C., 2009. *Aspect in Ancient Greek: a semantic analysis of the aorist and imperfective*. Ph.D. dissertation, Radboud Universiteit Nijmegen.

BENTEIN, K., 2012. 'The periphrastic perfect in Ancient Greek: a diachronic mental space analysis', *Transactions of the Philological Society 110*(2): 171–211.

BICKFORD, J. A., 1998. *Tools for analyzing the World's Languages: Morphology and Syntax*. Dallas: Summer Institute of Linguistics.

BOHNEMEYER, J., & SWIFT, M., 2001. *Default aspect: the semantic interaction of aspectual viewpoint and telicity*. Paper presented at the Perspectives on Aspect conference, Utrecht 2001.

BOHNEMEYER, J., & SWIFT, M., 2004. 'Event realization and default aspect', *Linguistics and Philosophy 27*: 263–296.

BUTT, M., & RAMCHAND, G. C., 2005. 'Complex aspectual structure in Hindi/ Urdu', in *The Syntax of Aspect: deriving thematic and aspectual Interpretation*. Oxford: OUP.

BYBEE, J. L., PERKINS, R. D., & PAGLIUCA, W., 1994. *The Evolution of Grammar*. Chicago: University of Chicago Press.

CAMPBELL, C., 2007. *Verbal Aspect, the Indicative Mood, and Narrative*. New York: Peter Lang.

CAMPBELL, C., 2008. *Verbal Aspect and non-Indicative Verbs: further Soundings in the Greek of the New Testament.* New York: Peter Lang.

CARNIE, A., 2013. *Syntax: A generative Introduction,* 3rd ed. Wiley-Blackwell.

CARRIER-DUNCAN, J., 1985. 'Linking of thematic roles in derivational word formation', *Linguistic Inquiry 16*: 1–34.

CASTAÑEDA, H.-N., 1967. 'Comments on D. Davidson's "The Logical Form of Action Sentences"', in N. Rescher (ed.), *The Logic of Decision and Action,* Vol. The Logic. Pittsburgh: Pittsburgh University Press, 104–112.

CHANTRAINE, P., 1927. *Histoire du parfait grec.* Paris: Société de linguistique de Paris.

CHANTRAINE, P., 1967. 'Le parfait mycénien', *Studi Micenei ed Egeo-Anatolici 3*: 19–27.

CHIERCHIA, G., 1995. 'Individual-level predicates as inherent generics', in *The Generic Book.* Chicago, London: University of Chicago Press, 176–223.

CHOMSKY, N., 1965. *Aspects of the Theory of Syntax.* Cambridge Mass.: M.I.T. Press.

CHOMSKY, N., 1970. 'Deep Structure, Surface Structure, and Semantic Interpretation', in Roman Jakobsen & Shigeo Kawamoto (eds.), *Studies in General and Oriental Linguistics presented to Shiro Hattori on the Occasion of his sixtieth Birthday.* Tokyo: TEC Corporation.

CHOMSKY, N., 1977. *Essays on Form and Interpretation.* North-Holland.

CHOMSKY, N., 1981. *Lectures on Government and Binding.* Dordrecht: Foris.

CHOMSKY, N., 1991. 'Some notes on economy of derivation and representation', in R. Frieden (ed.), *Principles and Parameters in Comparative Grammar.* Cambridge: MIT Press.

CHOMSKY, N., 1992. *A Minimalist Program for Linguistic Theory.* MIT Occasional Papers in Linguistics, Distributed by MIT Working Papers in Linguistics.

CHOMSKY, N., 1993. *Lectures on Government and Binding: the Pisa Lectures,* 7th ed., Berlin: Mouton de Gruyter.

CLACKSON, J., 2007. *Indo-European Linguistics: an Introduction.* Cambridge: CUP.

COMRIE, B., 1976. *Aspect.* Cambridge: CUP.

CRELLIN, R., 2012a. 'Basics of verbal aspect', *Journal for the Study of the New Testament 35*(2): 196–202.

CRELLIN, R., 2012b. *The Greek Perfect Active System: 200 BC - AD 150.* Ph.D. dissertation, University of Cambridge.

CRELLIN, R., 2014. 'The Greek perfect through Gothic eyes: evidence for the existence of a unitary semantic for the Greek perfect in New Testament Greek', *Journal of Greek Linguistics 14*(1).

CUTRER, M., 1994. *Time and Tense in Narratives and everyday Language.* Ph.D. dissertation, University of California at San Diego.

DAHL, Ö., & HEDIN, E., 2000. 'Current relevance and event reference', in Ö. Dahl (ed.), *Tense and Aspect in the Languages of Europe*. Berlin & New York: Mouton de Gruyter, 385–401.

DAVIDSON, D., 1967a. 'The logical form of action sentences', in N. Rescher (ed.), *The Logic of Decision and Action*. Pittsburgh: University of Pittsburgh Press, 37–71.

DAVIDSON, D., 1967b. 'Reply to comments', in N. Rescher (ed.), *The Logic of Decision and Action*. University of Pittsburgh Press, 115–120.

DE FOUCAULT, J.-A., 1972. *Recherches sur la langue et le style de Polybe*. Paris: Les Belles Lettres.

DE SWART, H. D. E., 1996. 'Meaning and Use of not ... until', *Journal of Semantics 13*: 221–263.

DE SWART, H. D. E., 1999. 'Negation and the Temporal Structure of Narrative Discourse', *Journal of Semantics 16*(1): 1–42. doi:10.1093/jos/16.1.1

DECKER, R. J., 2001. *Temporal Deixis of the Greek Verb in the Gospel of Mark with Reference to Verbal Aspect*. New York: Peter Lang.

DONALDSON, J. W., 1859. *A complete Grammar for the Use of Students*. Cambridge: Deighton, Bell & Co.

DORON, E., 2005. 'The aspect of agency', in *The Syntax of Aspect: deriving thematic and aspectual Interpretation*. Oxford: OUP, 154–173.

DOWTY, D., 1979. *Word Meaning and Montague Grammar*. Dordrecht: Kluwer.

DOWTY, D., 1991. 'Thematic Proto-Roles and Argument Selection', *Language 67*(3): 547–619.

DUBINSKY, S., & SIMANGO, S. R., 1996. 'Passive and stative in Chechewa: Evidence for modular distinctions in grammar' *72*(4): 749–781.

DUHOUX, Y., 2000. *Le verbe grec ancien: éléments de morphologie et de syntaxe historiques: deuxième édition, revue et augmentée*. Louvain-la-neuve: Peeters.

ENDERTON, H. B., 1977. *Elements of Set Theory*. Elsevier.

EVANS, T. V, 2001. *Verbal Syntax in the Greek Pentateuch*. Oxford: OUP.

FANNING, B., 1990. *Verbal Aspect in New Testament Greek*. Oxford: OUP.

FAUCONNIER, G., 1985. *Mental Spaces*. Cambridge: MIT Press.

FAUCONNIER, G., 1997. *Mappings in Thought and Language*. Cambridge: Cambridge University Press.

FOLEY, W., & VAN VALIN, R., 1984. *Functional Syntax and Universal Grammar*. Cambridge: Cambridge University Press.

GAWRON, M., 2009. *The Lexical Semantics of Extent Verbs*. Ph.D. dissertation, San Diego State University.

GEORGE, C. H., 2005. *Expressions of Agency in Ancient Greek*. Cambridge: Cambridge University Press.

GERÖ, E.-C., & VON STECHOW, A., 2003. 'Tense in time: the Greek Perfect', in *Words in Time: Diachronic Semantics from Different Points of View*, 251–294. Berlin: de Gruyter.

GILDERSLEEVE, B. L., 1900. *Syntax of Classical Greek. From Homer to Demosthenes*. New York.

GOOD, R., 2010. *The Septuagint's Translation of the Hebrew Verbal System in Chronicles*. Leiden; Boston: Brill.

GOODWIN, W. W., 1894. *A Greek Grammar*. Basingstoke and London: Macmillan.

GRICE, H. P., 1975. 'Logic and Conversation', in P. Cole & J. Morgan (eds.), *Syntax and Semantics*, Vol. 3. New York: Academic Press.

GRIMSHAW, J., 1990. *Argument Structure*. Cambridge, MA: MIT Press.

GRUBER, J. S., 1965. *Studies in Lexical Relations*. Ph.D. dissertation, MIT. Retrieved from http://dspace.mit.edu/handle/1721.1/13010, accessed 22/09/2014.

GVOZDANOVIĆ, J., 2012. 'Perfective and Imperfective Aspect', in R. I. Binnick (ed.), *The Oxford Handbook of Tense and Aspect*. Oxford University Press. doi:10.1093/oxfordhb/9780195381979.013.0027

HALE, K., & KEYSER, S., 1993. 'On argument structure and the lexical expression of syntactic relations', in K. Hale & S. Keyser (eds.), *The View from Building 20: Essays in Linguistics in Honor of Sylvain Bromberger*. Cambridge Mass.: MIT Press.

HARDER, P., 1996. *Functional Semantics: A Theory of Meaning, Structure and Tense in English*. Berlin, New York: Mouton de Gruyter.

HASPELMATH, M., 1992. 'From resultative to perfect in Ancient Greek', *Función 11-12*: 187–224.

HASPELMATH, M., 2001. *Language Typology and Language Universals: an international Handbook*, Vol. 1. Berlin: Walter de Gruyter.

HAUG, D. T. T., 2004. 'Aristotle's kinesis / energeia-test and the semantics of the Greek perfect', *Linguistics 42*(2): 387–418.

HAUG, D. T. T., 2008. 'From resultatives to anteriors in Ancient Greek: on the role of paradigmaticity in semantic change', in T. Eythorsson (ed.), *Grammatical Change and Linguistic Theory: the Rosendal Papers*. Amsterdam; Philadelphia: John Benjamins Publishing Company, 285–305.

HIGGINBOTHAM, J., 1985. 'On semantics', *Linguistic Inquiry 16*: 547–593.

HIGGINBOTHAM, J., 2000. 'On Events in Linguistic Semantics', in J. Higginbotham, F. Pianesi & A. Varzi (Eds.), *Speaking of Events*. Oxford: OUP, 49–79.

HOPPER, P. J., & THOMPSON, S. A., 1980. 'Transitivity in Grammar and Discourse', *Language 56*(2): 251–299.

HORNBLOWER, S., SPAWFORTH, A. & EIDINOW, E. (eds.), 2012. *The Oxford Classical Dictionary*. 4th rev. ed., Oxford: OUP.

HORROCKS, G., 2010. *Greek: A History of the Language and its Speakers*, 2nd ed. Wiley-Blackwell.

HORROCKS, G., & STAVROU, M., 2007. 'Grammaticalized aspect and spatio-temporal culmination', *Lingua 117*(4): 605–644.

HUMBERT, J., 1945. *Syntaxe grecque*. Paris: C. Klincksieck.

JACKENDOFF, R., 1972. 'Semantic Interpretation in Generative Grammar', *Linguistic Inquiry 18*: 369–412.

JANNARIS, A., 1897. *An historical Greek Grammar: chiefly of the Attic Dialect as written and spoken from classical Antiquity down to the present Time, founded upon the ancient Texts, Inscriptions, Papyri and present popular Greek*. London: Macmillan.

JASANOFF, J. H., 2003. *Hittite and the Indo-European Verb*. Oxford: OUP.

KAMP, H., 1979a. 'Events, instants and temporal reference', in R. Bauerle, U. Egli & A. von Stechow (eds.), *Semantics from different Points of View*. Berlin: Springer.

KAMP, H., 1979b. 'Some remarks on the logic of change', in C. Rohrer (ed.), *Time, Tense and Quantifiers*. Tübingen: Niemeyer.

KAMP, H., & REYLE, U., 1993. *From Discourse to Logic*. Dordrecht: Kluwer Academic Publishers.

KATZ, G., 2000. 'Anti neo-Davidsonianism', in *Events as Grammatical Objects: the converging Perspectives of Lexical Semantics and Syntax*. Center for the Study of Language and Information.

KATZ, G., 2003. 'Event arguments, adverb selection, and the stative adverb gap', in E. Lang, C. Maienborn & Cathrine Fabricius-Hansen (eds.), *Modifying Adjuncts*. Berlin: Walter de Gruyter, 455–474.

KEMMER, S., 1993. *The Middle Voice*. Amsterdam: John Benjamins.

KENNEDY, C., & LEVIN, B., 2008. 'Measure of change: The adjectival core of degree achievements.', in L. McNally & C. Kennedy (eds.), *Adjectives and adverbs: Syntax, semantics, and discourse*. Oxford: Oxford University Press, 156–182.

KENNY, A., 1963. *Action, Emotion and Will*. London: Routledge and Keagan Paul.

KIPARSKY, P., 1987. *Morphology and Grammatical Relations*. Ph.D. dissertation, Stanford University.

KIPARSKY, P., 2002. 'Event structure and the perfect', in B. Z. C. David I. Beaver, Luis D. Casillas Martinez & S. Kaufmann (eds.), *The Construction of Meaning*. CSLI Publications.

KLAIMAN, M. H., 1991. *Grammatical Voice*. Cambridge, UK; New York: CUP.

KLEIN, W., 1992. 'The present perfect puzzle', *Language 68*(3): 525–552.

KLEIN, W., 1994. *Time in Language*. London: Routledge.

KNAPP, C., 1928. 'The Testudo', *The Classical Weekly 12*(8): 57f.

KOHLMANN, R., 1881. *Über das Verhältnis der Tempora des lateinischen Verbums zu denen des Griechishen*. Eisleben.

KOONTZ-GARBODEN, A., 2007. *States, Changes of State, and the Monotonicity Hypothesis*. PhD thesis, Stanford University.

KOONTZ-GARBODEN, A., 2011. 'The lexical semantics of derived statives', *Linguistics and Philosophy 33*: 285–324.

KRATZER, A., 1996. 'Severing the external argument from its verb', in J. Rooryck & L. Zaring (eds.), *Phrase Structure and the Lexicon*, Vol. 33. Springer, 109–137.

KRIFKA, M., 1989. 'Nominal Reference, temporal constitution and quantification in event semantics', in B. R. J. V. Benthem & P. V. E. Boas (eds.), *Semantics and Contextual Expressions*. Dordrecht: Foris.

KRIFKA, M., 1992. 'Thematic relations as links between nominal reference and temporal constitution', in *Lexical Matters*. Stanford: Center for the Study of Language and Information, 30–53.

KRIFKA, M., 1998. 'The Origins of Telicity', in *Studies in Linguistics and Philosophy Volume 70*. Springer, 197–335.

KROEGER, P. R., 2004. *Analysing Syntax: A Lexical Functional Approach*. Cambridge: CUP.

KROEGER, P. R., 2005. *Analysing Grammar: An Introduction*. Cambridge: CUP.

KÜHNER, R., & GERTH, B., 1898. *Ausführliche Grammatik der griechischen Sprache: Teil 2 Satzlehre*. Hannover & Leipzig: Hahnsche Buchhandlung.

KULIKOV, L., 1999. 'Split causativity: remarks on correlations between transitivity, aspect and tense', in W. Abraham & L. Kulikov (eds.), *Tense-aspect, Transitivity and Causativity: Essays in Honour of Vladimir Nedjalkov*. Amsterdam; Philadelphia: John Benjamins.

KULIKOV, L., 2003. 'The labile syntactic type in a diachronic perspective: the case of Vedic', *SKY Journal of Linguistics* (16): 93–112.

LABIDAS, N., 2009. *Transitivity Alternations in Diachrony: Changes in Argument Structure and Voice Morphology*. Newcastle upon Tyne: Cambridge Scholars Publishing.

LARSON, R., 1988. 'On the Double Object Construction', *Linguistic Inquiry 19*(3): 335–391. doi:10.2307/25164901

LARSON, R., 1990. 'Double objects revisited: reply to Jackendoff', *Linguistic Inquiry 21*(4): 589–632.

LEVIN, B., 1983. *On the Nature of Ergativity*. Ph.D. dissertation, MIT, Cambridge, Mass. Retrieved from http://dspace.mit.edu/bitstream/handle/1721.1/15663/10708440-MIT.pdf, accessed 13/05/2015

LEVIN, B., 1993. *English Verb Classes and Alternations: A preliminary Investigation*. Chicago, IL: University of Chicago Press.

LEVIN, B., & RAPPAPORT HOVAV, M., 1995. *Unaccusativity*. Cambridge, MA: MIT Press.

LEVIN, B., & RAPPAPORT HOVAV, M., 2005. *Argument Realization*. Cambridge: CUP.

LIDDELL, H. G., SCOTT, R., & JONES, H. S., 1925. *A Greek-English Lexicon*. 9th rev. ed. Oxford: Clarendon.

LI, Y., 1990. 'On V-V compounds in Chinese', *Natural Language and Linguistic Theory 8*: 177–208.

MACHOBANE, 'MANILLO, 1989. *Some Restrictions on the Sesotho Transitivising Morphemes*. Ph.D. dissertation, McGill University.

MAIENBORN, C., 2008. 'On Davidsonian and Kimian States', in I. Comorovski & K. von Heusinger (eds.), *Existence: Semantics and Syntax*. Kluwer Academic Publishers, 107–30.

MALDEN, H., 1865. 'On perfect tenses in Greek, and especially the first perfect active', *Transactions of the Philological Society 10*(1): 168–180.

MANDILARAS, B. G., 1973. *The Verb in the Greek non-literary Papyri*. Athens: Hellenic Ministry of Culture and Sciences.

MANNEY, L. J., 2000. *Middle Voice in Modern Greek*. Amsterdam: John Benjamins.

MARANTZ, A., 1981. *On the Nature of Grammatical Relations*. Ph.D. dissertation, MIT.

MARANTZ, A., 1984. *On the Nature of Grammatical Relations*. Cambridge, MA: MIT Press.

MAYSER, E., 1926. *Grammatik der griechishen Papyri aus der Ptolemärzeit*, Vol. 2: Satzlehre. Berlin & Leipzig: Walter de Gruyter.

McCOARD, R. W., 1978. *The English Perfect: Tense Choice and Pragmatic Inferences*. Amsterdam: North-Holland.

McKAY, K. L., 1965. 'The use of the ancient Greek perfect down to the end of the second century AD', *Bulletin of the Institute of Classical Studies 12*: 1–21.

McKAY, K. L., 1980. 'On the perfect and other aspects in the Greek non-literary papyri', *Bulletin of the Institute of Classical Studies 27*(1): 23–49.

McKAY, K. L., 1981. 'On the perfect and other aspects in New Testament Greek', *Novum Testamentum 23*(4): 289–329.

MOORHOUSE, A. C., 1982. *The Syntax of Sophocles*. Leiden.

MOSER, A., 1988. *The History of the Perfect Periphrases in Greek*. Ph.D. disssertation, University of Cambridge.

MOSER, A., 2008. 'The changing relationship of tense and aspect in the history of Greek', *Sprachtypologie Und Universalienforshung*: 1–18.

MOURELATOS, A. P. D., 1978. 'Events, processes and states', *Linguistics and Philosophy*(2): 415–434.

MURASUGI, K., 1992. *Crossing and Nested Paths: NP Movement in Accusative and Ergative Languages*. Ph.D. dissertation, MIT.

OLSEN, M. B., 1997. *A Semantic and Pragmatic Model of Lexical and Grammatical Aspect*. New York & London: Garland Publishing.

ORETI, April 21, 1892. 'A tour round the "Takis"', *Southland Times*. Retrieved from http://paperspast.natlib.govt.nz/cgi-bin/paperspast?a = d&d = ST18920421.2.13, accessed 02/03/2016.

ORRIENS, S., 2009. 'Involving the past in the present. The Classical Greek perfect as a situating cohesion device', in S. Bakker & G. Wakker (eds.), *Discourse Cohesion in Ancient Greek*. Leiden: Brill, 221–239.

PARSONS, T., 1990. *Events in the Semantics of English*. Cambridge, MA: MIT Press.

PARSONS, T., 2000. 'Underlying states and time travel', in A. Varzi, J. Higginbotham & F. Pianesi (eds.), *Speaking of Events*. Oxford: OUP.

PARTEE, B. H., 1999. 'Nominal and temporal semantic structure: aspect and quantification', in *Prague Linguistic Circle Papers*, Vol. 3. Amsterdam: John Benjamins, 91–105.

PASLAWSKA, A., & VON STECHOW, A., 2003. 'Perfect readings in Russian', in A. Alexiadou, M. Rathert & A. von Stechow (eds.), *Perfect Explorations*. Berlin: Mouton de Gruyter, 307–362.

PEREL'MUTER, I. A., 1988. 'The stative, resultative, passive and perfect in ancient Greek (Homeric Greek)', in V. P. Nedjalkov (ed.), B. Comrie (ed. and trans.), *Typology of Resultative Constructions*, 277–287. Amsterdam; Philadelphia: John Benjamins.

PERLMUTTER, D., 1978. 'Impersonal passives and the unaccusative hypothesis', in *Proceedings of the Fourth Annual Meeting of the Berkeley Linguistics Society*, Berkeley Linguistics Society, University of California, Berkeley, 157–89.

POLLOCK, J.-Y., 1989. 'Verb movement, Universal Grammar, and the structure of IP', *Linguistic Inquiry* 20(3): 365–424. doi:10.2307/4178634

PORTER, S. E., 1989. *Verbal Aspect in the Greek of the New Testament*. New York: Peter Lang.

PORTER, S. E., 2011. 'Greek linguistics and lexicography', in A. J. Kostenberger & R. W. Yarbrough (eds.), *Understanding the Times*. Nottingham: Apollos (Inter-Varsity Press), 19–61.

PORTNER, P., 2003. 'The (temporal) semantics and (modal) pragmatics of the perfect', *Linguistics and Philosophy* 26: 459–510.

POTTS, C., 2005. *The Logic of Conventional Implicatures*. Oxford: OUP.

QUINE, 1960. *Word and Object*. Cambridge Mass.: MIT Press.

RAMCHAND, G. C., 1997. *Aspect and Predication: the Semantics of Argument Structure*. Oxford: Clarendon Press.

RAPPAPORT HOVAV, M., DORON, E., & SICHEL, I., 2010. *Lexical Semantics, Syntax, and Event Structure*. Oxford: OUP.

RAPPAPORT HOVAV, M., & LEVIN, B., 1998. 'Building verb meanings', in M. Butt & R. Geuder (eds.), *The Projection of Arguments: Lexical and Syntactic Constraints*. Stanford, CA: CSLI.

RAPPAPORT HOVAV, M., & LEVIN, B., 2005. 'Change-of-state verbs: implications for theories of argument projection', in *The Syntax of Aspect: deriving thematic and aspectual Interpretation*. Oxford: OUP, 274–286.

REICHENBACH, H., 1947. *Elements of Symbolic Logic*. MacMillan.

RIJKSBARON, A., 2002. *Syntax and Semantics of the Verb in Classical Greek: an Introduction*, 3rd ed. Amsterdam: J. C. Gieben.

RITZ, M.-E., 2012. 'Perfect Tense and Aspect', in *The Oxford Handbook of Tense and Aspect*. Oxford University Press, 881–907. doi:10.1093/oxfordhb/9780195381979.013.0031

ROBERTSON, A. T., 1919. *A Grammar of the Greek New Testament in the Light of historical Research*, 3rd ed. New York: Hodder & Stoughton.

ROTHSTEIN, S., 2004. *Structuring Events: a Study in the Semantics of Lexical Aspect*. Blackwell.

ROTHSTEIN, S., 2008. 'Introduction', in S. Rothstein (ed.) *Theoretical and Crosslinguistic Approaches to the Semantics of Aspect*, Amsterdam: John Benjamins.

RUIPÉREZ, M. S., 1954. *Estructura del Sistema de Aspectos y Tiempos del Verbo Griego antiguo: Análisis funcional sincrónico*. Salamanca.

RUIPÉREZ, M. S., 1982. *Structure du système des aspects et des temps du verbe en Grec ancien: analyse fonctionnelle synchronique*. Paris: Belles Lettres.

SÆBØ, K. J., 2001. *An Analysis of the Anticausative Alternation*. Retrieved from http://folk.uio.no/kjelljs/AAAoz.dvi.pdf, accessed 02/03/2016.

SHUCKBURGH, E. S. (trans.), 1889. *The Histories of Polybius*. New York: Macmillan.

SICKING, C. M. J., & STORK, P., 1996. 'The synthetic perfect in Classical Greek', in *Two Studies in the Semantics of the Verb in Classical Greek*. Leiden: E. J. Brill, 121–245.

SIHLER, A. L., 1995. *New Comparative Grammar of Greek and Latin*. Oxford: OUP.

SMITH, C. S., 1991. *The Parameter of Aspect*, 1st ed. Dordrecht: Kluwer.

SMITH, C. S., 1997. *The Parameter of Aspect*, 2nd ed. Dordrecht: Kluwer.

SMITH, C. S., 1999. 'Activities: states or events?', *Linguistics and Philosophy* 22(5): 479–508.

SMITH, C. S. & RAPPAPORT, G. C., 1997. 'The aspectual system of Russian', in C. Smith, *The Parameter of Aspect*, 2nd ed. Dordrecht: Kluwer, 227–261.

SMYTH, H. W., 1920. *A Greek Grammar for Colleges*. Cambridge, MA: Harvard University Press.

STAHL, J. M., 1907. *Kritisch-historische Syntax des Griechischen Verbums der klassischen Zeit*. Heidelburg.

STROIK, T., 2006. 'Arguments in middles', in *Demoting the Agent: Passive, Middle and other Voice Phenomena*. Amsterdam: John Benjamins, 301–326.

TAYLOR, B., 1977. 'Tense and continuity', *Linguistics and Philosophy* 1(2): 199–220.

TENNY, C., 1987. *Grammaticalizing Aspect and Affectedness*. Ph.D. dissertation, MIT.

TENNY, C., 1992. 'The aspectual interface hypothesis', in I. Sag & A. Szabolsci (eds.), *Lexical Matters*. Stanford: Center for the Study of Language and Information.

TENNY, C., 1994. *Aspectual Roles and the Syntax-Semantics Interface*. Dordrecht: Kluwer Academic Publishers.

TENNY, C., & PUSTEJOVSKY, J., 2000. 'A history of events in linguistic theory', in C. Tenny, & J. Pustejovsky (eds.), *Events as Grammatical Objects: the converging Perspectives of Lexcial Semantics and Syntax*. Center for the Study of Language and Information.

TURNER, N., 1963. *A Grammar of New Testament Greek: Syntax*, Vol. 3. Edinburgh: T. & T. Clark.

VAN VALIN, R. D., 2004. 'Semantic Macroroles in Role and Reference Grammar', in *Semantische Rollen*. Gunter Narr Verlag, 62–82.

VÁZQUEZ, R. M., 1993. 'Una interpretación estructural del perfecto griego antiguo', *Revista Española de Lingüística*: 87–94.

VENDLER, Z., 1957. 'Verbs and Times', *The Philosophical Review* 66(2): 143–160.

VERKUYL, H., 1972. *On the Compositional Nature of Aspects*. Dordrecht: Reidel.

VERKUYL, H., 1993. *A Theory of Aspectuality: the Interaction between Temporal and Atemporal Structure*. Cambridge: CUP.

WACKERNAGEL, J., 1904. *Studien zum griechischen Perfektum*. Göttingen: W.F. Kaestner.

WILLI, A., 2003. *The Languages of Aristophanes*. Oxford: OUP.

WILLIAMS, E., 1981. 'Argument structure and morphology', *Linguistic Review 1*: 81–114.

INDEX

Printed and bound by CPI Group (UK) Ltd, Croydon, CR0 4YY

13/04/2025

14656563-0003